CENSORED

CENSORED 2003

The Top 25 Censored Stories

PETER PHILLIPS & PROJECT CENSORED

INTRODUCTION BY ROBERT W. McCHESNEY
CARTOONS BY TOM TOMORROW

SEVEN STORIES PRESS
New York / London / Sydney / Toronto

Seven Stories Press
140 Watts Street
New York, NY 10013
http://www.sevenstories.com

In Canada: Hushion House, 36 Northline Road, Toronto, Ontario M4B 3E2

In the U.K.: Turnaround Publisher Services Ltd., Unit 3, Olympia Trading Estate,
Coburg Road, Wood Green, London N22 6TZ

In Australia: Tower Books, 2/17 Rodborough Road, Frenchs Forest NSW 2086

College professors may order examination copies of Seven Stories Press titles
for a free six-month trial period. To order, visit www.sevenstories.com/textbook,
or fax on school letterhead to (212) 226-1411.

ISSN 1074-5998

9 8 7 6 5 4 3 2 1

Book design by Cindy LaBreacht

Cover photo © Jordan Silverman. IMC activists in Los Angeles filming as LAPD entered
a hotel to disrupt a banner hang by the Rainforest Action Network. In the end, only half
the banner was hung.

Printed in the U.S.A.

CENSORED 2003 IS DEDICATED TO THE

GLOBAL INDYMEDIA ACTIVISTS www.indymedia.org

PACIFIC Adelaide, Aotearoa, Jakarta, Melbourne, Sydney

AFRICA Nigeria, South Africa

EUROPE Austria, Athens, Barcelona, Belgium,Bristol, Euskal, Herria, Finland, France, Germany, Ireland, Italy, Madrid, Netherland, Norway, Portugal, Russia, Sweden, Switzerland, Thessaloniki, United Kingdom

CANADA Alberta, Hamilton, Maritimes, Montreal, Ontario, Ottawa, Quebec, Thunder Bay, Vancouver, Victoria, Windsor

LATIN AMERICA Argentina, Bolivia, Brasil, Chiapas, Colombia, Mexico, Qollasuyu, Uruguay, Tijuana

SOUTHERN ASIA India

WESTERN ASIA Israel, Jerusalem

UNITED STATES Arizona; Atlanta; Austin; Baltimore; Boston; Buffalo; Central Florida; Chicago; Danbury, Conn.; Washington, D.C.; Eugene; Hawaii; Houston; Ithaca; Los Angeles; Madison; Maine; Michigan; Milwaukee; Minneapolis/St. Paul; New Jersey; New Mexico; North Carolina; New York City; New York Capitol; Philadelphia; Portland; Richmond; Rocky Mountain; Rochester; San Diego; San Francisco Bay Area; Santa Cruz; Seattle; St. Louis; Urbana-Champaign; Utah; Vermont; Western Mass.

THIS MODERN WORLD

by TOM TOMORROW

Contents

Preface

Freedom of information is in crisis in the United States. Big media no longer values news as vital to the democratic process. Instead the media giants release news as guileful information designed to build governmental-protective dependency and consumptive behaviors (see Chapter 6, "The Big Ten Media Giants"). Corporate media in the U.S.—interlocked with capitalism's core—spews top-down propaganda interwoven with titillation, gossip, and emotion (see Chapter 4, "Junk Food News and News Abuse"). The "experts," who dominate the news and speak from credentialed hier-archies, diminish our capacities for understanding (see Chapter 8, "Power Sources"). Real news stories that challenge the powerful are repressed or spun to fit the dominant ideological frame (see Chapter 7 by Norman Solomon).

News stories that speak to collective social concerns of the *demos* find little space in the bylines of the dailies or the timelines of the broadcast domains (see Chapters 1 & 3). Investigative reporting has died on the vine. The media stenographers no longer ask the hard questions—no longer pur-sue the truth. They no longer stimulate our minds or answer our questions (see Chapters 2 & 9).

Instead of precipitating a reevaluation of our media, 9-11 accelerated the loss of truth. Post-September Justice Department repression has mushroomed, but it found deep roots in the fungal soil of bureaucratic dysfunction. Weapons profits soared as the bombs dropped. Oily slime surrounded the policymakers. Some watched with revenge in their hearts.

Nevertheless, not all the news is bad. Other places are emerging for truth and discovery—places where activists dream of shared power, places where decisions form from within. We can share and tell our stories. We can find our own news and report our victories (see Chapter 5, "Rebuild Democracy with Grassroots Community News").

Peter Phillips
June 20, 2002

THIS MODERN WORLD

by TOM TOMORROW

Acknowledgments

Project Censored is managed through the Department of Sociology in the School of Social Sciences at Sonoma State University. We are an investigative sociology and media analysis project dedicated to the freedom of information throughout the United States.

More than 200 people were directly involved in the production of CENSORED 2003. University and program staff, students, faculty, community experts, research interns, funders, and our distinguished national judges all contributed time, energy, and money to make this year's book an important resource for the promotion of freedom of information in the United States.

I want to personally thank those close friends and intimates who have counseled and supported me through another year of Project Censored. Most important, my wife Mary Lia-Phillips, who as my lover, friend, and partner provides daily consultative support to Project Censored. The men in the Green Oaks breakfast group, Noel Byrne, Bob Butler, Rick Williams, Colin Godwin, and Bill Simon, are personal advisors and confidants who help with difficult decisions. Thanks go also to Carl Jensen, founder of Project Censored, and director for 20 years. His continued advice and support are very important to the Project. Trish Boreta, Project Censored coordinator is an important daily associate administrator of the Project. Her dedication and enthusiasm are greatly appreciated. Katie Sims, our story coordinator, deserves a special thank-you; she supervised the processing of more than 900 story nominations for this year's book.

A big thanks goes to the people at Seven Stories Press. They are more than a publishing house, but rather have become close friends, who help edit our annual book in record time, and serve as advisors in the annual release process of the most *Censored* stories. Publisher Dan Simon is a dedicated freedom of information activist, who deserves full credit for assembling an excellent support crew including: production director Jon Gilbert; managing editor M. Astella Saw; editors Mikola De Roo and Greg Ruggiero; academic marketing director Tara Parmiter; publicists Lars Reilly and Ruth Weiner; and book designer Cindy LaBreacht.

Thanks also to the great sales staff at Publishers Group West, who see to it that every independent bookstore, chain store, and wholesaler in the U.S. is aware of *Censored* each year. Thanks to H؛shion House, our distributors in Canada, as well as Turnaround Publishers Services Ltd. in Great Britain and Tower Books in Australia.

Thank you to Robert W. McChesney, who wrote the introduction to Censored 2003. Dr. McChesney is a national media scholar and a has been Project Censored judge for several years.

Thanks also to the authors of the most *Censored* stories for 2003, for without their often unsupported efforts as investigative news reporters and writers, the stories presented in *Censored* would not be possible.

Our guest writers this year are Norman Solomon, Robert Hackett, Mark Crispin Miller, Ina Howard, Marc Herold, Karen Talbot, and Jeanne Heifetz. They each wrote an original article on an important contemporary media or censorship issue.

This year's book again features the cartoons of Tom Tomorrow. "This Modern World" appears in more than 90 newspapers across the country. We are extremely pleased to use Tom Tomorrow's wit and humor throughout the book.

Our national judges, some of whom have been involved with the Project for 25 years, are among the top experts in the country concerned with First Amendment freedoms and media. We are honored to have them as the final voice in ranking the top 25 most *Censored* stories.

An important thanks goes to our major donors and funders, including Anita Roddick and The Body Shop International, Sonoma State University Instructionally Related Activity Fund, the School of Social Sciences at Sonoma State University, and thousands of financial supporters from throughout the United States. Without their core financial support, Project Censored simply could not continue.

This year we had 92 faculty/community evaluators assisting with our story assessment process. These expert volunteers read and rated the nominated stories for national importance, accuracy, and credibility. In March, they participated with the students in selecting the final top 25 *Censored* stories for 2003.

Most of all, we need to recognize the Sonoma State University students in the Spring 2002 Media Censorship class and the Fall 2001 Sociology of Media class, who worked long hours nominating and researching some 900 under-published news stories. Each student has become an expert in library database research. Student education is the most important aspect of Project Censored, and we could not do this work without their dedication and effort.

Ron Liskey is our webmaster. Under his supervision, the Project Censored Web site, www.projectcensored.org, has blossomed.

Lastly, I want to thank our readers and supporters from all over the United States and the world. Hundreds of you nominated stories for consideration as the most *Censored* news story of the year. Thank you very much!

PROJECT CENSORED STAFF

Peter Phillips, Ph.D.	Director
Carl Jensen, Ph.D.	Director Emeritus and Project Advisor
Tricia Boreta	Coordinator/Editor
Katie Sims	Story Management Team Leader
Beverly Krystosek	Bookkeeping
Ron Liskey	Webmaster
Crystal Edney	Administrative Support
Diana Galvan	Administrative Support
Monica Galvan	Administrative Support
Kerry Ly	Administrative Support
Julieta Mancilla	Administrative Support
Victoria Pellinen	Administrative Support
Odilia Pablo	Administrative Support
Damian Uriarte	*Censored* Class Teacher's Assistant

SPRING AND FALL 2001 INTERNS AND COMMUNITY VOLUNTEERS

Matt Babb, Pascal Baboulin, Dana Balicki, Kerry Beck, Amy Bonczewski, Andrew Cochrane, Ambrosia Crumley, Sabina Domenici, Grace Farasey, Bonnie Faulkner, Molly Garrison, Sharone Goldman, Allan Hope, Todd Howard, Naomi Igra, David Immel, Muamba Kabongo, Patrick Kelleher, Sandi LaRoche, Michael McMurtrey, Jean McNally, Gabrielle Mitchell, Emily Oberg, Michael Oliva, Cassandra Pojda, Sarah Potts, Lisa Randall, Dora Ruhs, Chris Salvano, Dean Schneider, Marcia Simmons, Dana Small,

Lyric Smith, Paul Stutrud, Pat Thurston, Scott Underwood, Mitzi Valdes, Jeff Vandevoir, Lillian Vaughn, Jaleah Winn, Juliet Wong, Jonnett Woods, and Meika Zilberberg.

SPRING 2002 INTERNS AND COMMUNITY VOLUNTEERS

Krista Arata, Kerry Beck, Dan Bluthart, Adam Cimino, Kevin Cody, Henry Colbert, Ambrosia Crumley, Stephen Dietrich, Grace Farasey, Eric Garrison, Terrie Girdner, Alea Giles, Sharone Goldman, Laura Huntington, David Immel, Kristen Jacobs, Sean Kelson, Brooke Krystosek, Kaitlin, Jean McNally, Justin Myers, Kathleen O'Rourke-Christopher, Jessica Peterson, Luanna Peterson, Sarah Potts, Lisa Randall, Michael Runas, May Saelee, Chris Salvano, Paul Saran, Marcia Simmons, Jason Spencer, Kara Stout, Jennifer Swift, Joshua Travers, Scott Underwood, Lillian Vaughn, Natalie Villalobos, Melanie Westbrook, Leah Whyte, and Clayton Woodhull.

STUDENT RESEARCHERS IN SOCIOLOGY OF MEDIA CLASS, FALL 2001

Pascal Baboulin, Yecenia Castro, James Docker, Grace Farasey, Tiana Kammer, Tyler Kerlin, Meghan Lewis, Jean McNally, Jesse Navaez, Chris Salvano, Marcia Simmons, Terry Thabiti, Damian Uriarte, and Hervey Williams.

STUDENT RESEARCHERS IN MEDIA CENSORSHIP CLASS, SPRING 2002

Arinze Anoruo, Krista Arata, Eduardo Barragan, Adam Cimino, Adria Cooper, Derek Fieldsoe, Alessandra Diana, Lauren Fox, Kelly Hand, Caroline Hubbard, Laura Huntington, David Immel, Catherine Jensen, Tiana Kammer, Erich Lehmann, Connie Lytle, Grabrielle Mitchell, Michelle Oliva, Sarah Potts, Lauren Renison, Chris Salvano, Kara Stout, Anthony Sult, Joshua Travers, Erik Wagle, Donald Yoon, and Danielle Yount.

PROJECT CENSORED 2003 NATIONAL JUDGES

ROBIN ANDERSEN, associate professor and chair, Department of Communication and Media Studies, Fordham University

RICHARD BARNET, author of 15 books and numerous articles for *The New York Times Magazine; The Nation;* and *The Progressive*

LIANE CLORFENE-CASTEN, president of Chicago Media Watch

LENORE FOERSTEL, Women for Mutual Security, facilitator of the Progressive International Media Exchange (PRIME)

DR. GEORGE GERBNER, dean emeritus, Annenberg School of Communications, University of Pennsylvania; founder of the Cultural Environment Movement; author of *Invisible Crises: What Conglomerate Media Control Means for America and the World* and *Triumph and the Image: The Media's War in the Persian Gulf*

ROBERT HACKETT, professor, School of Communications, Simon Fraser University, Director of NewsWatch Canada

DR. CARL JENSEN, founder and former director of Project Censored; author, *Censored: The News That Didn't Make the News and Why, 1990 to 1996,* and *20 Years of Censored News* (1997)

SUT JHALLY, professor of communications and executive director of the Media Education Foundation, University of Massachusetts

NICHOLAS JOHNSON,* professor, College of Law, University of Iowa; former FCC Commissioner (1966–1973); author of *How To Talk Back To Your Television Set*

RHODA H. KARPATKIN, president of Consumers Union, non-profit publisher of *Consumer Reports*

CHARLES L. KLOTZER, editor and publisher emeritus, *St. Louis Journalism Review*

NANCY KRANICH, associate dean of the New York Unversity Libraries and past-president of the American Library Association

JUDITH KRUG, director of the Office for Intellectual Freedom, American Library Association; editor, *Newsletter on Intellectual Freedom; Freedom to Read Foundation News;* and *Intellectual Freedom Action News*

WILLIAM LUTZ, professor of English, Rutgers University; former editor of *The Quarterly Review of Doublespeak;* author of *The New Doublespeak: Why No One Knows What Anyone's Saying Anymore* (1966)

JULIANNE MALVEAUX, PH.D., economist and columnist, King Features and Pacifica radio talk show host

ROBERT W. MCCHESNEY, research associate professor in the Institute of Communications Research and the Graduate School of Library and Information Science at the University of Illinois, Urbana-Champaign; author of numerous books on media including *Rich Media, Poor Democracy* and *Telecommunications, Mass Media, and Democracy: The Battle for the Control of U.S. Broadcasting 1928–35*

JACK L. NELSON,* professor, Graduate School of Education, Rutgers University; author of 16 books and more than 150 articles, including *Critical Issues in Education* (1996)

MICHAEL PARENTI, political analyst, lecturer, and author of several books including *Inventing Reality; The Politics of News Media; Make Believe Media; The Politics of Entertainment,* and numerous other works

DAN PERKINS, political cartoonist, pen name Tom Tomorrow, creator of "This Modern World"

BARBARA SEAMAN, lecturer; author of *The Doctors' Case Against the Pill; Free and Female; Women and the Crisis in Sex Hormones;* and others; co-founder of the National Women's Health Network

ERNA SMITH, professor of journalism, San Francisco State University; author of several studies on mainstream news coverage on people of color

SHEILA RABB WEIDENFELD,* president of D.C. Productions, Ltd.; former press secretary to Betty Ford

HOWARD ZINN, professor Emeritus of Political Science at Boston University; author of *A People's History of the United States*

*Indicates having been a Project Censored judge since its founding in 1976

PROJECT CENSORED 2000 FACULTY, STAFF, AND COMMUNITY EVALUATORS

Julia Allen, Ph.D.	English
Melinda Barnard, Ph.D.	Communications
Philip Beard, Ph.D.	Modern Languages
Jim Berkland, Ph.D.	Community Expert, Geology
Barbara Bloom, Ph.D.	Criminal Justice Admin
Andrew Botterell, Ph.D.	Philosophy
Maureen Buckley, Ph.D.	Counseling
Elizabeth Burch, Ph.D.	Communications Studies
Noel Byrne, Ph.D.	Sociology

James R. Carr, Ph.D.	University of Nevada, Geology
Ray Castro, Ph.D.	Chicano & Latino Studies
Liz Close, Ph.D.	Nursing
Lynn Cominsky, Ph.D.	Physics & Astronomy
Steven Coombs, Ph.D.	Education
Bill Crowley, Ph.D.	Geography
Victor Daniels, Ph.D.	Psychology
Laurie Dawson	Labor, Education
Randall Dodgen, Ph.D.	History
Peter Duffy, J.D.	Community Expert, Politics & Law
Fred Fletcher	Community Expert, Labor Issues
Dorothy (Dolly) Friedel, Ph.D.	Geography
Susan Garfin, Ph.D.	Sociology
Elaine Leeder, Ph.D.	Sociology
Patricia Leigh Gibbs, Ph.D.	Sociology, Foothill College
Michael Lesch, Ph.D.	Education
Robert Girling, Ph.D.	Business, Economics
Mary Gomes, Ph.D.	Psychology
Myrna Goodman, Ph.D.	Sociology/Women's Studies
Scott Gordon, Ph.D.	Computer Science
Diana Grant, Ph.D.	Criminal Justice Administration
Velma Guillory-Taylor, Ed.D.	Sociology, Women's Gender Studies
Daniel Haytin, Ph.D.	Sociology
Laurel Holmstrom, M.A.	Academic Programs
Sally Hurtado, M.S.	Education
Pat Jackson, Ph.D.	Criminal Justice Administration
Tom Jacobson, J.D.	Environmental Studies & Planning
Sherril Jaffe, M.A.	English
Paul Jess	Community Expert, Environmental Law
Mary King, M.D.	Community Expert, Health & Medicine
Jeanette Koshar, Ph.D.	Nursing
John Kramer, Ph.D.	Political Science
Heidi LaMoreaux, Ph.D.	Hutchins School
Virginia Lea, Ph.D.	Education
Benet Leigh, M.A.	Communication Studies
Wingham Liddell, Ph.D.	Business Administration
Tom Lough, Ph.D.	Sociology
John Lund	Community Expert, Politics, Stock Market
Rick Luttmann, Ph.D./CFP	Mathematics

Robert Manning	Community Expert, Peace & Justice
Ken Marcus, Ph.D.	Criminal Justice
Perry Marker, Ph.D.	Education
Daniel Markwyn, Ph.D.	History
Doug Martin, Ph.D.	Chemistry
Elizabeth Martinez, Ph.D.	Modern Languages
Phil McGough, Ph.D.	Business Administration
Eric McGuckin, Ph.D.	Hutchins School, Anthropology
Robert McNamara, Ph.D.	Political Science
Andy Merrifield, Ph.D.	Political Science, Public Administration
Catherine Nelson, Ph.D.	Political Science
Leilani Nishime, Ph.D.	American Multicultural Studies
Linda Nowak, Ph.D.	Business, Marketing
Tim Ogburn	Community Expert, International Trade
Tom Ormond, Ph.D.	Kinesiology
Wendy Ostroff, Ph.D.	Hutchins School
Ervand M. Peterson, Ph.D.	Environmental Studies & Planning
Keith Pike	Community Expert, Native American Issues
Jorge E. Porras, Ph.D.	Modern Languages
Arturo Ramirez, Ph.D.	Chicano & Latino Studies
Jeffrey T. Reeder, Ph.D.	Modern Languages
David Reichard, Ph.D.	Hutchins School
Rabbi Michael Robinson	Community Expert, Social Justice
R. Thomas Rosin, Ph.D.	Anthropology
Gardner Rust, Ph.D.	Music
Richard Senghas, Ph.D.	Anthropology, Linguistics
Rashmi Singh, Ph.D.	American Multicultural Studies
Cindy Stearns, Ph.D.	Women & Gender Studies
John Steiner, Ph.D.	Sociology
Meri Storino, Ph.D.	Counseling
Elaine Sundberg, M.A.	Academic Programs
Bob Tellander, M.A.	Sociology, Political Science
Laxmi G. Tewari, Ph.D.	Ethnomusicology
Suzanne Toczyski, Ph.D.	Modern Languages and Literature
Carol Tremmel	Extended Education
Charlene Tung, Ph.D.	Women & Gender Studies
David Van Nuys, Ph.D.	Psychology
Francisco H. Vazquez, Ph.D.	Hutchins School
Greta Vollmer, Ph.D.	English

Alexandra Von Meier, Ph.D.	Environmental Studies & Planning
Albert Wahrhaftig, Ph.D.	Anthropology
Sandra Walton, MLIS	Library, Archival Management
Tim Wandling, Ph.D.	English
Tony White, Ph.D.	History
Rick Williams, Ph.D.	Community Expert, Politics & Law
Richard Zimmer, Ph.D.	Hutchins School

SONOMA STATE UNVERSITY SUPPORTING STAFF AND OFFICES

Bernard Goldstein: Chief Academic Officer and staff

Elaine Leeder: Dean of School of Social Sciences and staff

William Babula: Dean of School of Arts and Humanities

Barbara Butler and the SSU Library staff

Paula Hammett: Social Sciences Library Resources

Jonah Raskin and Faculty in Communications Studies

Susan Kashack and staff in SSU Public Relations Office

Colleagues in the Sociology Department: Noel Byrne, Kathy Charmaz, Susan Garfin, Dan Haytin, Robert Tellander, Myrna Goodman, and Department Secretary Bev Krystosek

The Project Censored crew (SSU Faculty, students, and PC staff).

THIS MODERN WORLD
BY TOM TOMORROW

INTRODUCTION

The Media Crisis of Our Times

BY ROBERT W. McCHESNEY
University of Illinois, Urbana-Champaign

Way back in the early months of 1999, in what already seems like ancient history, David Halberstam commented that the preceding year, 1998, "has been, I think, the worst year for American journalism since I entered the profession 44 years ago." Halberstam was referring to the trivialization of political journalism exemplified by the Lewinsky scandal, as well as the procession of inconsequential stories ranging from JonBenet Ramsey and Joey Buttafuoco to Tonya Harding and John Wayne Bobbitt, that found ample space in the journalism of the mid- and late 1990s. Throughout those years, Project Censored published annual volumes highlighting the important stories overlooked to make way for this gibberish, stories often concentrating on crucial environmental and public health issues, or unexamined misuse of corporate and governmental power.

Who would have ever thought that just a few years later these would look like the good old days, a veritable Golden Age?

Over the past two years, three stories of extraordinary importance—by everyone's accounts—have faced the U.S. news media. And in each of the three cases, the news media have flubbed the story thoroughly, with disastrous implications for world democratic governance, social justice, and world peace. This isn't like the good old days when we could giggle about the media's obsession with Kato Kaelin or Princess Di. It is sobering, depressing, and enlightening to consider how those stories have been covered.

Let's start with the War on Terrorism. Going to war is arguably the single most important decision any society can make. The track record of the U.S. news media in the twentieth century is that they often went along with fraudulent efforts to get the nation into one war or another by the administration in power, ranging from World War I and World War II to Korea, Vietnam, and the Gulf War. In each case, the administration in power believed that if it told the American people the truth, there would not be sufficient support to launch a war. So they lied. The Pentagon Papers reveal this process in the 1960s in shocking detail. These are considered the dark moments in U.S. journalism history. What is most striking in the U.S. news coverage following the September 11 attacks of 2001 is how it followed this lamentable pattern; the very debate over whether to go to war, or how best to respond, did not even *exist*. Tough questions were ignored. Why should we believe that a militarized approach will be effective? Moving beyond the 9-11 attacks, why should the United States be entitled to determine—as judge, jury, and executioner—who is a terrorist or a terrorist sympathizer in this global war? What about international law?

Most conspicuous was the complete absence of comment on one of the most striking features of the war campaign, something that any credible journalist would be quick to observe: the events taking place in Russia or China or Pakistan. There are very powerful interests in the United States who greatly benefit politically and economically by the establishment of an unchecked war on terrorism. This consortium of interests can be called, to use President Eisenhower's term, the military-industrial complex. It blossomed during the Cold War when the fear of Soviet imperialism—real or alleged—justified its creation and expansion. A nation with a historically small military now had a permanent war economy, and powerful special interests benefited by its existence.

For journalists to raise issues like these did not presuppose that they opposed government policies, merely that the policies needed to be justified and explained, so the support would be substantive, not ephemeral, the result of deliberation, not manipulation. Such has not been the case. Much of mainstream U.S. journalism has been, to be frank, propagandistic. In this climate it should be no surprise that most Americans support the war, though they knew next to nothing about the region we were fighting in and its history, or the U.S. role in the world.

Now let's be clear about why the coverage has been so deplorable. It is not due directly to concentrated corporate media ownership or meddling CEOs, although the very firms that are now saluting "America's New War" are also going before the Bush Administration asking for ownership deregulation that will make all of them much larger and more profitable. The main reason for this distorted coverage is due to the weaknesses of professional journalism as it has been practiced in the United States. Professional journalism itself arose in the United States in large part as a response to concentrated newspaper markets, so monopoly newspaper owners could offer a credible "nonpartisan" journalism to prevent their business enterprises from being undermined. To avoid the taint of partisanship, and to keep costs lower, professionalism makes official or credentialed sources the basis for news stories. Reporters report what people in power say, and what they debate. This tends to give the news an establishment bias. When a journalist reports what official sources are saying, or debating, she is professional. When she steps outside this range of official debate to provide alternative perspectives or to raise issues those in power prefer not to discuss, she is no longer being professional.

In matters of international politics, "official sources" are almost interchangeable with the term "elites," as foreign policy is mostly a preserve of the wealthy and powerful few, C. Wright Mills' classic power elite. At its worst, in a case like the current war on terrorism, where the elites and official sources are unified on the core issues, the nature of our press coverage is uncomfortably close to that found in authoritarian societies with limited formal press freedom. Have you noticed, for example, that coverage of the anthrax scare dried up almost overnight after it came out that the anthrax almost certainly came from U.S. government laboratories. No conspiracy, the sources simply dried up. There was nothing to be gained politically by pushing the story along.

Many working journalists would recoil at that statement. Their response would be that professional reliance on official sources is justifiable as "democratic" because the official sources are elected or accountable to people who are elected by the citizenry. The problem with this rationale for stenography is that it forgets a critical assumption of free press theory: even leaders determined by election need a rigorous monitoring, the range of which cannot be determined solely by their elected opposition. Otherwise the citizenry has no way out of the status quo, no capacity to criticize the political culture as a whole. If such a watchdog function grows lax, corruption invariably grows, and the electoral system decays. If journalism that goes outside the range of elite opinion is dismissed as unprofessional or partisan, and therefore justifiably ignored, the media merely lock in a corrupt status quo and can offer no way out. If journalists require having official sources on their side to pursue a story, it gives people in power a massive veto power over the exercise of democracy.

This problem becomes acute in a political environment like the United States, where electoral laws and campaign costs have made politics a fiefdom for the superwealthy and those who represent the superwealthy. Over 90 percent of the "hard money" contributions to congressional and presidential campaigns come from the wealthiest one percent of Americans. By relying on official sources, our journalism does not pose a democratic challenge to plutocracy, but rather cements it in. One need only think of the coverage Ralph Nader received, especially in *The New York Times*, in the 2000 presidential race. Andrei Sakharov's treatment by *Pravda* in the 1970s could not have been much worse.

There is no better example of this than the Enron scandal, which unfolded in late 2001 and throughout 2002. This was a shocking story because, although evidence of Enron's shady operations had been cropping up since at least the mid-1990s, the rah-rah corporate journalism of our era was falling all over itself praising Enron as the exemplar of the New Economy. Only when the company approached bankruptcy did it rate as a news story. And now that it is clear that the Enron affair is a stunning example of supreme political corruption, the coverage increasingly concentrates upon the business collapse of Enron, and the chicanery of Arthur Andersen, rather than the sleazy way in which it worked, legally as well as illegally, using the political system to make billions of dollars ripping off consumers, taxpayers, and workers. Indeed, what is most striking about the Enron scandal is how much of their dubious activity was fully legal, and similar to what is being engaged in by firms in scores of industries. The corruption of our political-economic system is palpable.

Nevertheless, this will not turn into a political crisis that will end careers and lead to major political reform; the opposition Democrats are in no hurry to push the story to its logical political conclusion, because many of them will be implicated as well. They are implicated not only with Enron, but with all the other firms that engage in similar behavior. So professional journalism is restricted to the range of what those in power pursue, and the balance of the population has no one representing *its* interests. What about those who simply want the whole truth to come out, and the system changed so this sort of corruption is less likely to ever occur in the future? They are out of luck. This is very bad for liberal democracy. If the press system cannot lead to peaceful and credible reform of corruption, it only means the problems will get worse, much worse, and the costs of an eventual resolution significantly greater.

Moreover, the corporate media have special incentive not to push the Enron story too far. Were discussion of Enron and energy policies to lead to any sustained examination of the way media and telecommunication policies are produced behind closed doors in Washington—arguably the most off-limits story in U.S. journalism in our times—it would find a thick stench that would rival anything Enron has done.

And finally, consider the manner in which the press reported President Bush's "victory" in the 2000 election. It is now clear that the majority of the people in Florida who went to vote for president in November 2000 intended to vote for Al Gore. The semiofficial recount conducted by the major news media in 2001 showed that by every conceivable way the votes might be counted, Al Gore won Florida. But Al Gore isn't president. Why is that? Or, to put it another way, why didn't the press coverage assure that the true winner would assume office? After all, if the free press cannot guarantee the integrity of elections, what good is it? The primary reason is due to sourcing: throughout November and early December of 2000, the news media were being told by all Republicans that the Republicans had won the election and Al Gore was trying to steal it. The Democrats, on the other hand, were far less antagonistic and showed much less enthusiasm to fight for what they had won. Hence the news coverage, reflecting what their sources were telling them, tended to reflect the idea that the Republicans had won and the Democrats were grasping for straws. When Greg Palast broke the story in Britain in November 2000 that the Florida Republicans had systematically and illegally excluded tens of thousands of poor Floridians from voting—in itself, certainly enough to cost Gore the state—no U.S. mainstream news medium dared pick it up, even though the story was true. Why? Most likely because journalists would have been out on their own, because the Democrats had elected not to fight on this issue. Once the Supreme Court made its final decision, the media were elated to announce that our national nightmare was over. The media had helped anoint a president. The only losers were the irrelevant and powerless souls who clung to the belief that whoever gets the most votes should win the election, and that the press should tell the whole truth and let the chips fall where they may.

The willingness of the mainstream U.S. news media to suspend criticism of President Bush almost *in toto* after September 11 should be considered in this light. (Suddenly the moronic child of privilege became another Lincoln, albeit one who preferred lifting weights to reading books.) When the recount report indicating that Gore won Florida was released two months after September 11, what was striking was how almost all the press reported that the results were mixed or that Bush had won. The reason for the press making this judgment was it only looked at the recount in the few counties where Al Gore had requested it; who actually won the actual election in Florida seemed not to interest the press one whit. In a manner of thinking, the press had no choice but to provide this interpretation. If the media conceded that Gore, in fact, had won the race in Florida, it would have made people logically ask, "why didn't the media determine this when it mattered?" Moreover, a concession that the United States had an unelected president would make the laudatory coverage of President Bush after September 11 look increasingly like the sort of paeans to "maximum leaders" expected from the news media in tinhorn dictatorships. As soon as the leaders are not the product of free and fair elections, the professional reliance on official sources—which is wobbly by democratic standards to begin with—collapses.

So we are in the midst of a profound crisis of media, a cornerstone of the entire rotten edifice of our decaying and corrupt political system. But, as the saying goes, the Chinese character for crisis is made up of two other characters, those for danger and for opportunity. The historical dangers of the times are self-evident: we have a government that is barely accountable to the electorate in service to the highest bidder, with most of their activities being unreported or misreported in the press, and this government is leading a long-term war against "evil-doers," to be defined in secret by the government. The cost is high in civil liberties, tax dollars, and lives, but keep those opinions to yourself unless you want to get paid a visit by the *federales*.

The opportunity arises because the severe limitations of the media system have helped to generate a significant wave of opposition. Demonstrations now take place when the National Association of Broadcasters meet, and at the FCC. Media activism is bubbling over at independent media centers, in local media watch groups, and in campaigns to limit advertising in schools and to get liquor billboards out of working-class and minority neighborhoods. The jig is up for these guys. People are wising up to the game of three-card monte the corporate media and their spoon-fed stooges in Washington have been playing with the American people. The corporate media system is not the natural embodiment of God's will, or that of the Founding Fathers for that matter. Our media system is the direct result of government laws and policies that *established* it. It is a distinctly *political* issue, though one the powers-that-be have kept hidden for decades. In the case of radio, television, cable, and satellite TV, this is obvious. The government grants monopoly rights to frequencies and/or franchises and gives them to private firms at no charge. Whoever gets these licenses is almost guaranteed a profit. The government does more than set the terms of the competition; it picks the winners of the competition. The value of this corporate welfare, over the past 70 years, is mind-boggling. It is certainly in the hundreds of billions, if not *trillions*, of dollars. Nearly all of our huge media giants today are built on the backs of this corporate welfare, though you would never know it to listen to their rhetoric.

Even films, music, traditional print media, and now the Internet depend upon government regulation for their existence. Copyright, for example, which is a government sanctioned and enforced monopoly, is the foundation for most of these industries. Without this clear government intervention into the market to *prevent* competition, these industries would look radically different. Tax codes that explicitly permit advertising to be written off as a legitimate business expense spur commercialism in media and society. The government is also a major purchaser of media content, and a major advertiser. In short, there is nothing natural about our media industries.

So the issue isn't one of private media versus government regulation, because the private media system is the direct result of aggressive regulation and massive subsidies made by the government. The issue is what sort of regulation the government will provide, and whose interests and what values will those regulations serve? The problem in the United States is that these policies have been and are being made in the public's name, but they are not being made with the public's informed consent.

There are no simple solutions to the problem of media. It will require study and debate and political organizing if we are to get the sort of media system befitting a self-governing people. There will never be perfect solutions either. This much is true. It will be impossible to live in a humane and peaceful world, not to mention a democratic society, when the media system is the province of a handful of massive profit-seeking firms, answerable only to their bottom lines. Democratizing media debates and reforming media systems are not the most important issues in the world today, but they are on any short list of necessary areas for democratic renewal. If the media system remains as is, it puts distinct barriers on the range and nature of political activity.

THIS MODERN WORLD

by TOM TOMORROW

How Project Censored Stories Are Selected

Sonoma State University Project Censored students and staff screen several thousand stories each year. About 700 of these are selected for evaluation by faculty and community evaluators. Our 89 faculty/community evaluators are experts in their individual fields and they rate the stories for credibility and national importance. Often more than one of our evaluators will examine and rate the same story. The top ranked 200 stories are then researched for national mainstream coverage by our upper division students in the annual Media Censorship class. The class examines the corporate media's coverage of the story and takes a second look at the credibility and accuracy of the story in relationship to other news articles on the topic. About 125 stories each year make the final voting level. A collective vote of all students, staff, and faculty narrows the stories down to 60 in early November. A second vote is taken a week later, after a short 300-word summary of each of the top 60 stories is prepared, and sent out with a voting sheet to all faculty/community evaluators, students, staff, and self-selected national judges. This Project-wide vote by some 150-plus people establishes which 25 stories will be listed in our annual book. The final ranking of stories is decided by our national judges, who receive a synopsis and full text copy of the top 25 stories.

While selection of these stories each year is a long, subjective process, we have grown to trust this collective effort as the best possible means of fairly selecting these important news stories. This process, we believe, gives us an annual summary list of the most important undercovered news stories in the United States.

PROJECT CENSORED MISSION STATEMENT Project Censored, founded in 1976, is a nonprofit project within the Sonoma State University Foundation, a 501(c)3 organization. Our principle objective is the advocacy for, and protection of, First Amendment rights and freedom of information in the United States. Through a faculty/student/community partnership, Project Censored serves as a national media ombudsman by identifying and researching important news stories that are underreported, ignored, misrepresented, or censored in the United States. We also encourage and support journalist, faculty, and student investigations into First Amendment and freedom of information issues. We are actively encouraging the development of a national interconnected, community-based media news service that will offer a diversity of news and information sources via print, radio, television, and internet to local mainstream audiences.

HOW TO INVEST IN FREEDOM OF INFORMATION Project Censored is a nonprofit tax-exempt organization. Funds for the Project are derived from sales of this book, and donations from hundreds of individuals. You can send a support gift to us through our website at www.projectcensored.org, or by mail to:

> Project Censored
> Sonoma State University
> 1810 East Cotati Avenue
> Rohnert Park, CA 94931

CHAPTER 1

The Top Censored Stories of 2001 and 2002

BY PETER PHILLIPS AND PROJECT CENSORED

Are Americans becoming heartless? Are we less sensitive to others? Is our society really becoming corrupt and degraded?

As we follow American corporate media today we can only answer yes to each of these questions. Washington sex scandals, celebrity exposés, gruesome murders, schoolyard attacks, gangs, crime, corruption, and conspicuous consumption fill the airwaves and newspapers. Media representatives say they need to protect their bottomline, and that these types of news stories increase ratings. Corporate media seem to have abdicated their First Amendment responsibility to keep the public informed. The traditional journalistic values of supporting democracy by maintaining an educated electorate now take second place to profits and ratings. When questioned about the appropriateness of sensationalized news coverage and heartless human episodes, corporate media responds by saying, "we are just giving the public what it wants." Media shift the responsibility for sensationalized coverage to a prurient citizenry's market demands for more blood, gore, and opulence.

Is the public really crying for more blood and gore or does the corporate media use highly emotional stories to create shock-addicting adrenaline rushes to maximize public viewing?

Within the consolidated corporate media world, nonsexy or unemotional stories seldom meet the entertainment standards of the industry. Hundreds of important stories fail to receive the news attention they deserve. Censorship today is a subtle system of information suppression in the name of corporate profit and self-interest.

It is also safe to say that major media in the United States effectively represent the interests of corporate America. The corporate media elites are the watchdogs of acceptable ideological messages. They establish the parameters of news and information and decide on the general use of the massive media resources. News and information in American society have become a top-down entertainment system with capsulized parrotings of government/corporate ideological messages.

One of the longest-lasting censored news stories is corporate media's failure to cover their own turf as evident by our number-one story for 2003. The top 25 "most censored" stories for 2003 are the news that the corporate media failed or refused to cover adequately. A number of these stories will appear in the corporate media sometime in the next few years. The mainstream news rarely acknowledges Project Censored. We do, however, shame them into covering these stories—often acting as if they discovered them themselves.

Project Censored has moved to a new cycle for the release of our annual censored stories. The *Censored* book will now come out in August of each year. By moving the process forward six months, *Censored 2003* has had a one-time 18-month review cycle.

Sonoma State University Project Censored students and staff screened several thousand stories during the last 18 months. Nine hundred stories were selected for evaluation by faculty and community evaluators. Our 90 Faculty/Community evaluators are experts in their individual fields and they rate the stories for credibility and national importance. Some 150 stories this year made it to the final voting level. Project-wide voting by more than 150 people established the 25 most important stories for *Censored 2003*. The top 25 stories were then ranked by our national judges including Michael Parenti, Robin Andersen, Carl Jensen, Lenore Foerstel, and some 20 other national journalists, scholars, and writers.

FCC Moves To Privatize Airwaves

Sources:
THE GUARDIAN (London), April 28, 2001 and
MEDIAFILE, Autumn 2001, Vol. 20, No. 4
Title: "Global Media Giants Lobby to Privatize Entire Broadcast System"
Author: Jeremy Rifkin

MOTHER JONES, September/October 2001
Title: "Losing Signal"
Author: Brendan L. Koerner

MEDIAFILE, May/June 2001
Title: "Legal Project to Challenge Media Monopoly"
Author: Dorothy Kidd

Faculty Evaluator:
Scott Gordon. Student Researcher: Laura Huntington and Lauren Fox

For almost 70 years, the Federal Communications Commission (FCC) has administered and regulated the broadcast spectrum as an electronic "commons" on behalf of the American people. For a fee, the FCC issues licenses to broadcasters that allow them to use, but not own, one or more specific radio or TV frequencies. Thus, the public has retained the ability to regulate, as well as influence, access to broadcast communications.

Several years ago, the Progress and Freedom Foundation, in their report "The Telecom Revolution: An American Opportunity," recommended a complete privatization of the radio frequencies, whereby broadcasters with existing licenses would eventually gain complete ownership of their respective frequencies. They could thereafter develop them in markets of their choosing, or sell and trade them to other companies. The few nonallocated bands of the radio frequency spectrum would be sold off, as electronic real estate, to the highest bidders. With nothing then to regulate, the FCC would eventually be abolished. The reasoning behind this radical plan was that government control of the airwaves has led to inefficiencies. In private hands, the frequencies would be exchanged in the marketplace, and the forces of free-market supply and demand would foster the most creative (and, of course, most profitable) use of these electronic "properties."

This privatization proposal was considered too ambitious by the Clinton Administration. However, in February 2001, mere months after a more "pro-business" president took office, 37 leading U.S. economists requested, in a joint letter, that the FCC allow broadcasters to lease, in secondary markets, the frequencies they currently use under their FCC license. Their thinking was that with this groundwork laid, full national privatization would follow, and eventually nations would be encouraged to sell off their frequencies to global media enterprises.

Michael K. Powell, FCC Chairman, and son of Secretary of State Colin Powell, in a recent speech compared the FCC to the Grinch, a kind of regulatory spoilsport that could impede what he termed a historic transformation akin to the opening of the West. "The oppressor here is regulation," he declared. In April 2001, Powell dismissed the FCC's historic mandate to evaluate corporate actions based on the public interest. That standard, he said, "is about as empty a vessel as you can accord a regulatory agency." In other comments, Powell has signaled what kind of philosophy he prefers to the outdated concept of public interest. During his first visit to Capitol Hill as chairman, Powell referred to corporations simply as "our clients."

Challenges to this proposed privatization of airways have emerged from a number of sources. One group, the Democratic Media Legal Project (DMLP) in San Francisco, argues that even the existing commercial media system, aided by the Telecommunications Act of 1996, is unconstitutional because it limits diversity of viewpoints, omits or misrepresents most social, political, and cultural segments, and is unaccountable to the public. Therefore, explains DMLP, advertising-based media and the 1996 Act, which encourages mergers and cross-ownership of media outlets to the exclusion of the vast majority of people, have deprived the people of their right to self-governance—as self-governance can occur only when we have the unimpeded and uncensored flow of opinion and reporting that are requisite for an informed democracy.

The course of wireless broadcasting is approaching an unprecedented and critical crossroads. The path taken by the United States, and by the other industrialized nations that may follow our lead, will profoundly influence the ability of the citizenry of each country to democratically control the media.

COMMENTS BY SCOTT GORDON, ASSOCIATE PROFESSOR OF COMPUTER SCIENCE, SONOMA STATE UNIVERSITY: During my six or seven years of involvement with Project Censored, I have reviewed several dozen stories. Most of the stories sent to me have related to computers, communications, or other technical topics, presumably because of my Computer Science background. Often I find that such studies contain technical misinterpretation, confusion, or are simply old news to me. This was the first one to strike me as clearly deserving of consideration as a top *Censored* story.

It is frustrating to watch an expanding technology deliver hundreds of additional channels to our homes, promising diversity and expanded access, yet somehow result in a greater homogeneity than ever before. Our nation faces a virtual crisis of information flow, where corporate mergers reduce our popular voice to but a handful of media goliaths. Now more than ever, we need a strong FCC to ensure that one of our most core American values, freedom of the press, is maintained.

I had not heard of this scary proposal until I read about it for the Project. Hopefully, more people will see it for the fundamentally un-American idea that it is.

UPDATE BY AUTHOR BRENDAN KOERNER: As part of the mind-numbing alphabet soup of Beltway agencies, the FCC rarely receives much attention from the mainstream press. To Joe Q. Public, the FCC is still best known for harassing George Carlin over his infamous "Seven Dirty Words" routine. Beyond that, the commission is pretty much a mystery.

But the Information Age has converted the once-moribund FCC into a bureaucratic powerhouse. The commission oversees an infrastructure of airwaves, telephone lines, and cable conduits that are the backbone of a $950 billion-a-year industry. As the financial stakes have risen, the private-sector lobbyists have become increasingly adept at peddling their pro-business agenda to the FCC. And the Bush-appointed commission, led by Beltway scion Michael K. Powell, is eager to acquiesce—a sad trend chronicled in "Losing Signal."

Since the article's publication last summer, the FCC has proven itself adept at demolishing regulations intended to insure diversity and fairness. The commission's willingness to approve long-distance applications from the "Baby Bell" phone companies, for instance, virtually guarantees the return of regional telco monopolies.

Yet the mainstream press has raised few warnings about the FCC's squashing of the public interest. Quite the opposite, in fact—business sections cheer the consolidation as a sign of robust economic health, and pooh-pooh concerns over diversity as alarmist.

There are few communications activists, at least compared to the legions of lawyers and lobbyists retained by big media and big telco. The most prominent muckrakers are Jeff Chester at the Center for Digital Democracy <www.democratic media.org>, the folks at the Media Access Project <www.mediaaccess.org>, and the Project on Media Ownership <www.promo.org>. But without more public support, they're bound to have a tough time taking on the FCC.

UPDATE BY AUTHOR DOROTHY KIDD: Since my story was written, things have just gotten worse for the U.S. public with regard to media democracy. Mergers are up and the number of dominant players controlling media production and distribution has shrunk to a handful. At the same time, almost all the federal government regulations that had limited monopoly, or had ensured a small measure of public service programming, have been abolished.

There are now few checks and balances to a corporate media system that is run solely for profit, permits very little diversity of programming, and considers important news of public concern just one more commercial-driven form of entertainment. As a result, the media system has curbed the rights of citizens to receive and produce the information and communication necessary for free debate in a democratic society.

The Democratic Media Legal Project, established to challenge the corporate media system, is now securing the funding and organization necessary to launch a protracted struggle in the courts, through the legislatures and among the public.

The mainstream media covered some of the economic and political aspects of these two trends. However, there was little or no mainstream coverage of any organized public response, very little discussion of the public implications, and no coverage of the DMLP.

The story of the DMLP is important because it represents a significant contribution to the growing media democracy movement. It calls the government and media corporations to task, arguing that the commercial media system is in violation of the First Amendment as it hinders the free exchange of a diversity of information and dialogue necessary to a democratic society.

You can get more information about the Legal Project from the Democratic Media Legal Project Web site, <www.geocities.com/figu12345/> or by e-mailing <dmlp@igc.org>.

2 New Trade Treaty Seeks to Privatize Global Social Services

Source:
THE ECOLOGIST, February 2001
Title: "The Last Frontier"
Author: Maude Barlow

Faculty Evaluator: John Kramer.
Student Researchers: Chris Salvano & Adria Cooper

Extensive international corporate media coverage including:
TORONTO STAR, March 3, 2002; THE HERALD (Glasgow), February 27, 2002; THE HINDU, November 11, 2001; THE WEEKEND AUSTRALIAN, August 25, 2001; THE GAZETTE (Montreal), June 15, 2001; and
THE FINANCIAL TIMES (London), October 19, 2000

A global trade agreement now being negotiated will seek to privatize nearly every government-provided public service and allow transnational corporations to run them for profit.

The General Agreement on Trade in Services (GATS) is a proposed free-trade agreement that will attempt to liberalize/dismantle barriers that protect government-provided social services. These are social services bestowed by the government in the name of public welfare. The GATS was established in 1994, at the conclusion of the "Uruguay Round" of the General Agreement on Tariffs and Trade (GATT). In 1995, the GATS agreement was adopted by the newly created World Trade Organization (WTO).

Corporations plan to use the GATS agreement to profit from the privatization of educational systems, health care systems, child care, energy and municipal water services, postal services, libraries, museums, and public transportation. If the GATS agreement is finalized, it will lock in a privatized, for-profit model for the global economy. GATS/WTO would make it illegal for a government with privatized services to ever return to a publicly owned, non-profit model. Any government that disobeys these WTO rulings will face sanctions. What used to be areas of common heritage like seed banks, air and water supplies, health care, and education will be commodified, privatized, and sold to the highest bidder on the open market. People who cannot afford these privatized services will be left out.

Services are the fastest growing sector of international trade. If GATS is implemented, corporations will reap windfall profits. Health care, education, and water services are the most potentially lucrative. Global expenditures on water services exceed $1 trillion each year, on education they exceed $2 trillion, and on health care they are over $3.5 trillion.

The WTO has hired a private company called the Global Division for Transnational Education to document policies that "discriminate against foreign education providers." The results of this 'study' will be used to pressure countries with public education systems to relinquish them to the global privatized marketplace.

The futures of accountability for public services and of sovereign law are at stake with the GATS decision. Foreign corporations will have the right to establish themselves in any GATS/WTO–controlled country and compete against non-profit or government institutions, such as schools and hospitals, for public funds.

The current round of GATS negotiations has identified three main priorities for future free-trade principles. First, GATS officials are pushing for "National Treatment" to be applied across the board. "National Treatment" would forbid governments from favoring their domestic companies over foreign-based companies. This idea already applies to certain services, but GATS will enforce it to include all services. This will create an expansion of megacorporate access to domestic markets and further diminish democratic accountability. The economically dominant Western countries would like to make it illegal for "developing" countries to reverse this exclusive access to their markets.

Second, GATS officials are seeking to place restrictions on domestic regulations. This would limit a government's ability to enact environmental, health, and other regulations and laws that hinder "free trade." The government would be required to demonstrate that its laws and regulations were necessary to achieve a WTO-sanctioned objective, and that no other commercially friendly alternative was available.

Third, negotiators are attempting to develop the expansion of "Commercial Presence" rules. These rules allow an investor in one GATS-controlled country to establish a presence in any other GATS country. The investor will not only be allowed to compete against private suppliers for business, but will also be allowed to compete against publicly funded institutions and services for public funds.

This potential expansion of GATS/WTO authority into the day-to-day business of governments will make it nearly impossible for citizens to exercise democratic control over the future of traditionally public services. One American trade official summed up the GATS/WTO process by saying, "Basically, it won't stop until foreigners finally start to think like Americans, act like Americans, and most of all shop like Americans."

UPDATE BY AUTHOR MAUDE BARLOW: The General Agreement on Trade in Services is the most far-reaching negotiation ever undertaken on the trade in services and will effect the lives of every human being on the planet. Yet very few people know that it is taking place. If the governments of the WTO are successful in coming to a substantive agreement, by 2005, services such as health care, water, culture and education, among many others, will be subject to the rules and disciplines of the WTO, and launched on an irreversible path to private control.

Since my original story was printed, negotiations in Geneva have intensified. By June 30, 2002, every country is to have submitted to every other country its wish list of services that it wants included in negotiations, and by March 31, 2003, each country is to submit its responses. All of this is being done behind closed doors, so that citizens are left to guess what services their governments are trading away. However, civil society groups did secure a leaked copy of the country demands of the European Commission, and they are shocking. The EC's demands include all aspects of culture, including print and broadcasting, postal services, energy services, water, hydroelectricity, telecommunications, and pension funds, among others. In addition, at the December 2001, WTO Ministerial meeting in Doha, Qatar, a new provision was added that commits countries to take down "tariff and non-tariff barriers" to environmental services—including water.

The mainstream press has all but ignored this story. It is difficult to grasp and complicated to explain. In the aftermath of the September 11 attacks on New York and Washington, and the ensuing war, it is even easier for governments, corporate lobby groups, and global institutions like the WTO to meet in total privacy, with very few enquiring journalists to deal with.

There is, however, excellent material on the GATS available. Public Citizen, Alliance for Democracy, Friends of the Earth International, and Public Services International all have information available. Information can also be found at The Council of Canadians, <www.canadians.org>, Polaris Institute <www.polaris institute.org>, and the Canadian Centre for Policy Alternatives <www.policy alternatives.ca>. <www.gatswatch.org>

3 United States' Policies in Colombia Support Mass Murder

Sources:
COUNTERPUNCH, July 1-15, 2001
Title: "Blueprints for the Colombian War"
Authors: Alexander Cockburn & Jeffrey St. Clair

ASHEVILLE GLOBAL REPORT, October 4, 2001
Title: "Colombian Army and Police Still Working With Paramilitaries"
Author: Jim Lobe

STEELABOR, May/June 2001
Title: "Colombian Trade Unionists Need U.S. Help"
Authors: Dan Kovalik & Gerald Dickey

RACHEL'S ENVIRONMENT & HEALTH NEWS, December 7, 2000
Title: "Echoes of Vietnam"
Author: Rachel Massey

Portions of this story were covered by the following mainstream U.S. sources:
ABC's 20/20; *The Los Angeles Times*, *The New York Times*, *The San Diego Union-Tribune*, *The Washington Post*, *U.S. News & World Report*

Faculty Evaluators: Jorge Porras & Fred Fletcher.
Student Researchers: Lauren Renison, Adam Cimino,
Erik Wagle, & Gabrielle Mitchell.

Over the past two years, Colombia has been Washington's third largest recipient of foreign aid, behind only Israel and Egypt. In July of 2000, the U.S. Congress approved a $1.3 billion war package for Colombia to support President Pastrana's "Plan Colombia." Plan Colombia is a $7.5 billion counternarcotics initiative. In addition to this financial support, the U.S. also trains the Colombian military.

Colombia's annual murder rate is 30,000. It is reported that around 19,000 of these murders are linked to illegal right-wing paramilitary forces. Many leaders of these paramilitary groups were once officers in the Colombian military, trained at the U.S.–sponsored School of the Americas (SOA).

According to the Human Rights Watch Report, a 120-page report titled "The 'Sixth Division': Military-Paramilitary Ties and U.S. Policy in Colombia," Colombian armed forces and police continue to work closely with right-wing paramilitary groups. The government of President Pastrana and the U.S. administration have played down evidence of this cooperation. Author Jim Lobe says that Human Rights Watch holds the Pastrana Administration responsible for the current, violent situation because of its dramatic and costly failure to take prompt, effective control of security forces, break their persistent ties to paramilitary groups, and ensure respect for human rights.

Authors Alexander Cockburn and Jeffrey St. Clair contend that the war in Colombia isn't about drugs. It's about the annihilation of popular uprisings by Indian peasants fending off the ravages of oil companies, cattle barons, and mining firms. It is a counterinsurgency war, designed to clear the way for American corporations to set up shop in Colombia.

Cockburn and St. Clair examined two Defense Department commissioned reports, the RAND Report and a paper written by Gabriel Marcella, titled "Plan Colombia: The Strategic and Operational Imperatives." Both reports recommend that the U.S. step up its military involvement in Colombia. In addition, the reports make several admissions about the paramilitaries and their links to the drug trade, the human rights abuses by the U.S.–trained Colombian military, and the irrationality of crop fumigation.

Throughout these past two years, Colombian citizens have been the victims of human rights atrocities committed by the U.S.–trained Colombian military and linked paramilitaries. Trade unionists and human rights activists face murder, torture, and harassment. It is reported that Latin America remains the most dangerous place in the world for trade unionists. Since 1986, some 4,000 trade unionists have been murdered in Colombia. In 2000 alone, more trade unionists were killed in Colombia than in the whole world in 1999.

Another problem resulting from the Colombian "drug war" has been the health consequences of the U.S.–sponsored aerial fumigation. Since January 2001,

Colombian aircraft have been spraying toxic herbicides over Colombian fields in order to kill opium poppy and coca plants. These sprayings are killing food crops that indigenous Colombians depend on for survival, as well as harming their health. The sprayings have killed fish, livestock, and have contaminated water supplies.

U.S. military aid is not improving conditions for the people of Colombia, but rather supporting a war against its citizens and those who are fighting for social justice. According to an American member of the international steelworker delegation, Jesse Isbell, who recently visited Columbia, "The U.S. says one thing to the American public when in reality it is [doing] something totally different. Our government portrays this as a drug war against cocaine, but all we are doing is keeping an ineffective government in power."

COMMENTS BY TONY WHITE, PROFESSOR OF HISTORY, SONOMA STATE UNIVERSITY:
Truth is often the first casualty of war and the "war on drugs" is no exception. Clinton's endorsement of Plan Colombia and George W.'s expansion of U.S. support for the incompetent and corrupt government of Colombia has very little to do with the supply of cocaine, but has a lot to do with protecting American mining, oil, and logging interests in the region. Our support of Plan Colombia also involves us in a decades-long civil war between the haves and have-nots. Our allies include the paramilitary groups which have committed numerous atrocities. The resort to aerial spraying threatens other crops and the health of Colombian peasants and may increase the number of guerrillas. Given the nature of the conflict and the terrain, this policy risks another Vietnam.

UPDATE BY AUTHOR DAN KOVALIK: The story of trade union assassination portrayed in the article has played an important role in the attempt to expose U.S. military aid to Colombia for what it is—the support for right-wing counterinsurgents who are committing 80 percent of the human rights abuses in Colombia. These forces, the paramilitaries, are targeting mostly unarmed activists, such as trade unionists, peace activists, and human rights workers who are challenging the unjust social order in Colombia. This story of the anti-union violence in particular has helped to create unprecedented links between trade unionists and peace activists who are now working together to oppose U.S. military aid to Colombia.

Following this story, the USWA, along with the International Labor Rights Fund (ILRF), brought lawsuits against both Coca-Cola and Drummond Company for their role in human rights abuses in Colombia. In particular, the USWA and ILRF brought claims against Drummond for the murder of the trade unionists, which happened while, as described in the story, the USWA delegation was in Colombia.

Sadly, however, the trade union assassinations have continued unabated, and have in fact increased in Colombia, with over 160 trade unionists being killed there last year. In addition, the U.S. military aid has continued despite these assassinations and our attempts to publicize them. Indeed, the U.S. Congress is presently debating whether to explicitly expand the role of the U.S. in Colombia by, for the first time, expressly earmarking aid for (1) counterinsurgency efforts; and (2) to protect oil pipelines in Colombia, like those of Occidental Oil, for example.

The USWA is attempting to ameliorate the effects of the military buildup and the violence through its Colombia Solidarity Fund, which has and continues to provide support for trade unionists under threat to relocate, sometimes within Colombia, sometimes out of the country, to find safe havens. Those wishing to support this effort can write to: Colombia Solidarity Fund, c/o Solidarity Center, 1925 K Street NW, Suite 300, Washington, DC 20006-1105.

While the mainstream press did not respond to the story as such, the media has presented some coverage of the two lawsuits mentioned above. In covering these lawsuits, the media has mentioned the anti-union violence described in the story. However, the media has been reluctant to give much credence to the allegations of the Colombian plaintiffs. For its part, *Time* magazine did a wonderful job of reporting the Coca-Cola lawsuit, filed in the U.S. by U.S. institutions and lawyers, and about the anti-union violence in Colombia. Curiously, however, *Time* chose to print this story in every edition in the world *except the United States*. I had to obtain a copy of the article from a friend in Canada where it was published.

You can obtain more information about this story, and about what actions you can take to help, from the *Steelabor* Web site, as well as <www.cokewatch.org>, <www.ilrf.org> and the web sites of Witness for Peace and Human Rights Watch.

UPDATE BY AUTHOR RACHEL MASSEY: The Bush Administration's requests for renewed funds to support the war in Colombia have led to significant debate in Congress, but simple questions about the spray campaigns still have not been answered. For example, the State Department has not clarified what formulations of glyphosate herbicides have been or will be used in the spray campaigns. Toxicity characteristics vary among formulations, so this is crucial information. The State Department also continues to keep secret the ingredients of other chemicals, such as surfactants and anti-foaming agents, that are added to the mix before application in Colombia.

In the Foreign Appropriations Bill for 2002, Congress established three criteria that must be met in order for the spray campaigns to continue. The bill requires the secretary of state to consult with the U.S. Environmental Protection Agency (EPA), the U.S. Department of Agriculture, and the Centers for Disease Control

(CDC) to determine that spray procedures in Colombia are consistent with U.S. label requirements for herbicide application, do not violate Colombian laws, and do not "pose unreasonable risks or adverse effects to humans or the environment." The State Department must also certify that procedures exist for compensating harm to human health or agricultural crops. As of mid-June 2002, the State Department's consultations with EPA are still in progress. Meanwhile, the U.S. Embassy in Bogotá has informed representatives of U.S. nongovernmental organizations that a new round of spray campaigns is expected to begin in early July.

The State Department has continued to produce and disseminate misleading information about the effects of the spray campaigns. For example, in December 2000, an investigative report published in the Dutch newspaper *NRC Handelsblad* reported an outbreak of severe skin problems among small children in the Colombian community of Aponte, Department of Nariño, in the aftermath of spraying. Responding to this article, the U.S. Embassy in Bogotá commissioned a report on health patterns in the Department of Nariño. The report claims to find no evidence of adverse effects from the spray campaigns. The report is clearly designed to achieve the desired answers; it includes no explanation of study methodology, and considers only 23 case reports, presenting these as the totality of data available for a period of about eight months. In addition, the report suggests that the doctor who originally treated the affected children was intimidated into silence. According to the report, after an initial telephone conversation with the report's authors, the doctor left his place of work permanently, leaving no forwarding contact information. This story illustrates some of the difficulties that Colombian citizens face when they speak publicly about the health effects of the "war on drugs."

Several U.S. and European organizations are working to stop the spray campaigns. Information and updates are available from Amazon Alliance , Tel: (202) 785-3334, <www.amazonalliance.org>; Center for International Policy. Tel: (202) 232-3317, <www.ciponline.org>; Earthjustice, Tel: (510) 550-6700, <www.earthjustice.org>; Institute for Science and Interdisciplinary Studies, Tel: (413) 559-5582, <http://isis.hampshire.edu>; Latin America Working Group, Tel: (202) 546-7010, <www.lawg.org>; and Transnational Institute, <www.tni.org/drugs/>. For listings of new documents on the spray campaigns, see the U.S. Fumigation Information Web site <www.usfumigation.org>. To join a delegation to Colombia and interact with Colombian citizens who are working for peace there, contact: Witness for Peace, Tel: (202) 588-1471, <www.witnessforpeace.org>.

4 Bush Administration Hampered FBI Investigation into Bin Laden Family Before 9-11

Sources:
PULSE OF THE TWIN CITIES, January 16, 2002
Title: "French Book Indicts Bush Administration"
Author: Amanda Luker

TIMES OF INDIA, November 8, 2001
Title: "Bush Took FBI Agents Off bin Laden Family Trail"
Author: Rashmee Z. Ahmed

THE GUARDIAN (London), November 7, 2001
Title: "FBI and U.S. Spy Agents Say Bush Spiked bin Laden Probes Before 11 September"
Authors: Greg Palast and David Pallister

Faculty Evaluator: Catherine Nelson
Student Researchers: Donald Yoon & David Immel

Corporate media coverage: LOS ANGELES TIMES, January 13, 2002

A French book *Bin Laden, la verite interdite* (*Bin Laden, The Forbidden Truth*) claims that the Bush Administration halted investigations into terrorist activities related to the bin Laden family and began planning for a war against Afghanistan before 9-11.

The authors, Jean-Charles Brisard and Guillaume Dasquie, are French intelligence analysts. Dasquie, an investigative reporter, publishes *Intelligence Online*, a respected newsletter on economics and diplomacy. Brisard worked for French secret services and in 1997 wrote a report on the Al Qaeda network.

In 1996, high-placed intelligence sources in Washington told *The Guardian*, "There were always constraints on investigating the Saudis." The authors allege that under the influence of U.S. oil companies, George W. Bush and his administration initially halted investigations into terrorism, while bargaining with the Taliban to deliver Osama bin Laden in exchange for economic aid and political recognition. The book goes on to reveal that former FBI deputy director John O'Neill resigned in July of 2001 in protest over the obstruction of terrorist investigations. According to O'Neill, "The main obstacles to investigating Islamic terrorism were U.S. oil corporate interests and the role played by Saudi Arabia in it." The restrictions were said to have worsened after the Bush Administration took over. Intelligence agencies were told to "back off" from investigations involving other members of the bin Laden family, the Saudi royals, and possible Saudi links to the acquisition of nuclear weapons by Pakistan. John O'Neill died on 9-11 in the World Trade Center.

An FBI file coded 199, which means a case involving national security, records that Abdullah bin Laden, who lived in Washington, originally had a file opened on him "because of his relationship with the Saudi-funded World Assembly of Muslim Youth—a suspected terrorist organization." The BBC reiterated a well-known claim, made by one of George W. Bush's former business partners, that Bush made his first million dollars 20 years ago from a company financed by Osama's elder brother, Salem. It has also been revealed that both the Bushs and the bin Ladens had lucrative stakes in the Carlyle Group, a private investment firm that has grown to be one of the largest investors in U.S. defense and communications contracts.

Brisard and Dasquie contend that the government's main objective in Afghanistan was to unite the Taliban regime in order to gain access to the oil and gas reserves in Central Asia. They report that the Bush Administration began negotiations with the Taliban directly after coming into power and representatives met several times in Washington, Islamabad, and Berlin.

There were also claims that the last meeting between the United States and Taliban representatives took place only five weeks before the attacks in New York and Washington.

Long before the 9-11 attacks, the United States had decided to invade Afghanistan in the interest of oil. In February of 1998, at the hearing before a subgroup of the Committee on International Relations, Congress discussed ways to deal with Afghanistan to make way for an oil pipeline. *Jane's Defense Newsletter* reported in March 2001 that an invasion of Afghanistan was being planned.

Times of India reported that in June of 2001, the U.S. government told India that there would be an invasion of Afghanistan in October of that year. By July of 2001, George Arney, with the BBC, also reported the planned invasion.

UPDATE BY AUTHOR AMANDA LUKER: Paula Zahn was right. If *Bin Laden: la verite interdite* is correct, it is huge. But, the national media will never give it a second glance.

The release of this book not only corroborates other investigations placing U.S. big oil interests in Central Asia negotiating a pipeline in the 1990s, but also exposes oil interests in the Bush Administration, including Vice President Dick Cheney, National Security Advisor Condoleeza Rice, and Bush, both senior and junior. With this book, Guillaume Dasquie and Jean-Charles Brisard question America's wartime intentions: Is the United States protecting "enduring freedom" or are the bombings really a means of securing a pliant regime in Afghanistan so the United States can gain control over future oil veins pumping across the Middle East? The mainstream coverage was dismissive. Dr. Daniel Goure, member of the conservative think tank The Lexington Institute, casually dismissed it on Minnesota Public Radio as a conspiracy theory, "debunked right, left, and center," even comparing it to the theory that Americans never went to the moon, that "it was all done in a studio in Hollywood." He neglects to mention the book was not written by conspiracy nuts but by two esteemed French intelligence experts. And who debunked it? He doesn't say.

At this moment [June 2002], the media is just beginning to skewer Bush for not increasing national security while knowing Taliban threats before September 11. Some are beginning to ask, "If he knew this, what else did he know?" Just a few months ago, the notion that Bush knew pre-September 11 was also dismissed as a conspiracy theory.

Americans should be given tools to questions those in power. Not every theory will be correct, but I, for one, am desperately curious what two European intelligence experts would have to say about U.S. foreign policy.

Dasquie and Brisard's book is still only available in French. On the Web site Intelligence Online (which Dasquie edits), the first chapter can be viewed in French: <www.intelligenceonline.com>, e-mail: <redaction@indigo-net.com>. For more information, the following resources may be useful: Consortium News' Bush Family "Oiligarchy" series <http://www.consortiumnews.com/2000/081400a1.html>; Z Net <www.zmag.org>; *Fortunate Son: George W. Bush and the Making of an American President* by J. H. Hatfield and Mark Crispin Miller; and *Unholy Wars: Afghanistan, America and International Terrorism* by John K. Cooley.

UPDATE BY THE GUARDIAN FOR AUTHOR GREG PALAST: Within two months of the attack on the World Trade Center, *The Guardian* investigative team and BBC Television's *Newsnight* obtained documents, evidence, and insider interviews exposing the Bush Administration's pre-September 11 directives to intelligence agencies blocking inquiries into the bin Laden family and Saudi Arabian financing of terror networks. Driving this policy of deliberate blindness, we have further reported, were the ill combination of petroleum politics and financial conflicts of interest: the Bush family and allies deep ties to Saudi Arabian royals, banks and arms dealers.

The story should be understood as one of our continuing series on Bush family finances by the Guardian Group (*The Guardian* and *The Observer*) and BBC *Newsnight*. The first of these in November 2000 exposed the purge of black voters from Florida's voter rolls that the U.S. Civil Rights Commission called "the first hard evidence of deliberate violations of civil rights."

The team's reports have been virtually blacked-out in the USA—though widely reported and lauded worldwide; in the case of the bin Laden report, from the *Times of India* across to Latin America's top publications. American journalist Palast had to relocate to Europe to write and broadcast this series.

Not all responses are kind. The story (and a follow-up report by BBC) drew threats of lawsuit from a Saudi "charity." This is serious stuff in a land lacking a First Amendment. A mining corporation that hired the senior Bush as a consultant did sue *The Guardian* over one of the reports; the successful defense bled our thin finances.

Despite the cost (admittedly with some of our network and newspaper executives biting their nails) we have soldiered on with the investigations. Our general theme—Bush family finances and oil—led us to break the story this month (again, not covered in the USA), that Hugo Chavez survived an attempted coup d'etat because of warnings to him in advance by the secretary-general of OPEC.

On the intelligence story, we are debriefing an arms dealer and other sources about a 1996 meeting between Al Qaeda's financial representative, gun merchants, and Saudi royals. Most important to us are U.S. agencies' knowledge of the meeting and their follow-up (or lack thereof). The print report also notes "Saudi links to the acquisition of nuclear weapons by Pakistan." The creation of the "Islamic" bomb is another target of our research.

Dan Rather, a guest on our BBC program last week, admitted the U.S. press coverage of bin Laden and war has been twisted into an unquestioning outlet of official PR. As a result, American public debate has been reduced to shouting between conspiracy theorists and the willfully ignorant "patriots." Our reports, that economic interests blinded official America to security threats, is not part of the dialogue.us

Recognition in the U.S. by Project Censored would encourage BBC and *The Guardian*'s risk-taking work.

Note: These stories are the result of a large team effort. Therefore, we would appreciate your recognizing the work of BBC *Newsnight* producer Meirion Jones and *Guardian* chief of investigations, David Leigh.

In addition, it is important to include with *The Guardian* story, the transcripts of the companion November 7, 2001 BBC *Newsnight* (see information below)—especially as *Newsnight* put up all the cash for this particularly costly segment of the investigation.

BBC: *Did Bush Turn a Blind Eye to Terrorism?*:
<http://www.gregpalast.com/detail.cfm?artid=104˘=1>.

UPDATE BY AUTHOR DAVID PALLISTER: I endorse Greg Palast's update response. I would add that this was a significant story in exposing the ultrasensitive relationship that exists between the U.S. and Saudi (because of oil, obviously), which tends to preclude any recognition of the fact that Saudi has provided the money, the cadres, and the ideology that had driven Al Qaeda. *The Guardian* has investigated in depth the connections between Saudi-sponsored charities and terrorism since 9-11, as well as exposing the appalling human rights record of the Saudi regime in terms on torturing citizens of Britain, Belgium, and Canada to make forced and false confessions of involvement in terrorist bombing.

5 U.S. Intentionally Destroyed Iraq's Water System

Source:
THE PROGRESSIVE, <www.progressive.org>, September 2001
Title: "The Secret Behind the Sanctions:
How the U.S. Intentionally Destroyed Iraq's Water Supply"
Author: Thomas J. Nagy
www.progressive.org

Faculty Evaluator: Rick Luttmann
Student Researchers: Adria Cooper, Erik Wagle, Adam Cimino & Chris Salvano

During the Gulf War, the United States deliberately bombed Iraq's water system. After the war, the U.S. pushed sanctions to prevent importation of necessary supplies for water purification. These actions resulted in the deaths of thousands of innocent Iraqi civilians many of whom were young children. Documents have been obtained from the Defense Intelligence Agency (DIA), which prove that the Pentagon was fully aware of the mortal impacts on civilians in Iraq and was actually monitoring the degradation of Iraq's water supply. The destruction of civilian infrastructures necessary for health and welfare is a direct violation of the Geneva Convention.

After the Gulf War, the United Nations applied sanctions against Iraq, which denied the importation of specialized equipment and chemicals, such as chlorine for purification of water. There are six documents that have been partially declassified and can be found on the Pentagon's Web site at <www.gulflink.osd.mil>. These documents include information that prove that the United States was fully aware of the costs to civilians, especially children, by upholding the sanctions against purification of Iraq's water supply.

The primary document is dated January 22, 1991, and is titled, "Iraq Water Treatment Vulnerabilities." This document predicts what will take place when Iraq can no longer import the vital commodities to cleanse their water supply. It states that epidemics and disease outbreaks may occur because of pollutants and bacteria that exist in unpurified water. The document acknowledges the fact that without purified drinking water, the manufacturing of food and medicine will also be affected. The possibilities of Iraqis obtaining clean water, despite sanctions, along with a timetable describing the degradation of Iraq's water supply was also addressed.

The remaining five documents from the DIA confirm the Pentagon's monitoring of the situation in Iraq. In more than one document, discussion of the likely outbreaks of diseases and how they affect civilians, "particularly children," is discussed in great detail. The final document titled, "Iraq: Assessment of Current Health Threats and Capabilities," is dated November 15, 1991, and discusses the development of a counter-propaganda strategy that would blame Saddam Hussein for the lack of safe water in Iraq.

The United States' insistence on using this type of sanction against Iraq is in direct violation of the Geneva Convention. The Geneva Convention was created in 1979 to protect the victims of international armed conflict. It states, "It is prohibited to attack, destroy, remove or render useless, objects indispensable to the survival of the civilian population such as foodstuffs, crops, livestock, drinking water installation and supplies, and irrigation works, for the specific purpose of denying them for their sustenance value to the civilian population or to the adverse Party, whatever the motive, whether in order to starve out civilians, to cause them to move away, or for any other motive."

Although two Democratic Representatives, Cynthia McKinney from Georgia and Tony Hall from Ohio, have spoken out about the degradation of Iraq's water supply and its civilian targets, no acknowledgment of violations has been made. The U.S. policy of destroying the water treatment system of Iraq and preventing its re-establishment has been pursued for more than a decade. The United Nations estimates that more than 500,000 Iraqi children have died as a result of sanctions and that unclean water is a major contributor to these deaths.

UPDATE BY THOMAS NAGY: "The Secret Behind the Sanctions" gives Americans an ax to break out of the cocoon of denial enveloping the genocidal intent and effects of nearly 12 years of economic sanctions against the people of Iraq. Tragically and criminally, these CIA documents were actively hidden from the American people till 1995 by which time a compliant mainstream media had driven the fatal lies of genocide denial deep into the American psyche.

Since the publication of the story, several anti-sanctions groups have reported that *The Progressive* article ranks among the most powerful in persuading the public of the evil of the sanctions. The article opened a new front against sanctions with the publication of David Duncan's "A Prayer for Children and Water" and Ned Breslin's "Water as a Weapon of War." Now the environmental community and water engineering community are alerted to the updated horror of the U.S. tactic of poisoning wells. The article has now been translated into Spanish, Danish, and Swedish with summaries available in French and German and stories on the content of the article appearing in newspapers as geographically removed as Katmandu, Nepal; Cork, Ireland; and Moscow, Russia. In the U.S., the mainstream media has ducked and covered with the exception of the *Orlando Sentinel*, the *Madison Capital Times,* and the *National Catholic Reporter*. In contrast, U.S. alternative media has acted honorably, including *Democracy Now* and *CounterSpin*. Until recently the only venue in Washington, D.C. to discuss the content of the article was at the Department of Defense ethics conference, JSCOPE. Recently I was able to reach audiences in the belly of the beast at a teach-in at American University, then at the World Congress of the International Physicians for the Prevention of Nuclear War–Physicians for Social Responsibility.

My advice to people working in this area is to look for editors, reporters, and advocates of the integrity of Matt Rothschild, Felicity Arbuthnot, and Sam Husseini and allies in the peace movement abroad (e.g., McMaster University and University College, Cork).

Tom Nagy is an ex-refugee, ex-public health postdoctoral fellow, pacifist, parent, and professor at George Washington University in Washington, D.C.

6 U.S. Government Pushing Nuclear Revival

Source:
BULLETIN OF THE ATOMIC SCIENTISTS, July/August 2001
Title: "The New-Nuke Chorus Tunes Up"
Author: Stephen I. Schwartz

Faculty Evaluator: Sasha Von Meier
Student Researcher: Erik Wagle

Corporate media coverage:
LOS ANGELES TIMES, March 17, 2002
and USA TODAY, March 18, 2002

The U.S. government is blazing a trail of nuclear weapon revival leading to global nuclear dominance. A nuke-revival group, supported by people like Stephen Younger, Associate Director for Nuclear Weapons at Los Alamos, proposes a "mini-nuke" capable of burrowing into underground weapon supplies and unleashing a small, but contained nuclear explosion. This weapons advocacy group is comprised of nuclear scientists, Department of Energy (DOE) officials, right-wing analysts, former government officials, and a congressionally appointed oversight panel. The group wants to ensure that the U.S. continues to develop nuclear capacity into the next half-century.

Achieving this goal of nuclear dominance will take far more than just refurbishing existing weapons and developing new ones. A decade-long effort that would cost in the $8 billion range would be needed just to bring old production sites up to standard. Billions more would be needed to produce and maintain a new generation of nuclear weapons. This plan has not been presented to the public for their consideration or approval.

The recent interest in the building of "mini-nukes" is based on two premises: 1) the belief that only nuclear weapons can destroy these underground networks of weapons and command centers, so the "mini-nuke" would deter other countries from using these underground systems and 2) that these new bombs would give government the option to launch a nuclear strike to take out a small target while delivering minimal civilian casualties. It is believed that these bombs could specifically target underground headquarters or weapon stockpiles in Korea, Iraq, or Iran.

Princeton theoretical physicist Robert W. Nelson has studied the question for the Federation of American Scientists. Nelson concluded, "No earth-burrowing missile can penetrate deep enough into the earth to contain an explosion with a nuclear yield even as small as 1 percent of the 15-kiloton Hiroshima weapon. The explosion simply blows out a massive crater of radioactive dirt, which rains down on the local region with an especially intense and deadly fallout." Nelson used data from the Plowshares program of the 1960s and from the 828 underground nuclear tests conducted in Nevada. The two sources show that full containment of a 5-kiloton explosion is only possible at 650 feet or more, while a 1-kiloton explosion must take place at least 450 feet into the earth. These figures are taken at optimum conditions, where weapons are placed in a specially sealed shaft in a well understood geological environment. The "mini-nukes" will be expected to penetrate into deeply hardened targets in unyielding conditions. Nelson also concludes that a 10-foot missile could only be expected to penetrate 100 feet into concrete and steel, a depth far too shallow to contain even a very small explosion.

The Panel to Assess the Reliability, Safety, and Security of the United States Nuclear Stockpile has recommended spending $4 billion to $6 billion over the next decade to restore the production capabilities of plutonium pit plants in the U.S.

The DOE is currently spending $147 million on pit production at Los Alamos this year and is requesting $218 million for 2002. A renovated Los Alamos will be capable of producing up to 20 pits a year by 2007. Last year the DOE received $2 million to design a new pit plant capable of producing 450 cores of plutonium a year. This would generate approximately half the amount of plutonium produced during the latter period of the Cold War. The facilities at some of these nuclear production plants are in drastic states of disrepair.

Only 26 percent of the weapons complex buildings are in excellent or good condition. One laboratory building at Los Alamos wraps pipes carrying radioactive waste in plastic bags to prevent leakage. The roofs at other facilities are allowing rainwater to seep into the rooms where nuclear weapons are inspected and repaired.

UPDATE BY AUTHOR STEPHEN I. SCHWARTZ: Since the article was published, there have been many new developments. The congressionally mandated study on destroying hardened targets, never formally released but obtained by an anti-nuclear organization and posted on the Internet in December 2001, did not explicitly call for new nuclear weapons, but noted that such weapons were the only way to defeat certain types of targets. The Bush Administration's Nuclear Posture Review, the details of which were leaked to the *Los Angeles Times* and *The New York Times* in early March 2002, alarmed many observers by broadening the circumstances under which U.S. nuclear weapons might be used. It also called for modifying nuclear weapons to destroy underground targets, for developing "nuclear weapons better suited to the nation's needs," and for reducing the amount of time required to resume nuclear testing. The *Washington Post* subsequently reported that Secretary of Defense Donald Rumsfeld wanted to explore the use of nuclear weapons in a missile defense system, a move hearkening back to the Safeguard system of the late 1960s and early 1970s when, coincidentally or not, Rumsfeld served as defense secretary under President Gerald Ford. In addition, the Foster Panel issued its third report in mid-March, once again raising questions about the long-term viability of the stockpile stewardship program and supporting a reduction in the amount of time necessary to resume nuclear testing.

On May 9, 2002, the House of Representatives refused, by a 243 to 171 vote, to eliminate all funding for earth-penetrating nuclear weapons from the fiscal 2003 defense authorization bill. That same day, however, the Senate Armed Services Committee eliminated funding for such weapons and further required the DOE to "clearly and specifically identify any funds requested in the future for new or modified nuclear weapons" and report on the requirements for any such weapons. The different versions of the defense bill will have to be reconciled by a conference committee later this summer.

There was no response to this story in the mainstream press during 2001. But since the disclosure of the Nuclear Posture Review in March 2002, I have spoken with numerous print and broadcast journalists and elements of the story have appeared in, among others, the *Cleveland Plain Dealer*, *Kansas City Star*, the *Christian Science Monitor*, *The Guardian* (London), as well as a report on NPR's *All Things Considered*. In addition, *Popular Mechanics* is preparing an article on bunker-busting nuclear weapons and *60 Minutes* is exploring a possible segment on the nuclear revival.

Readers interested in further information are advised to read the *Bulletin of the Atomic Scientists*, which will be publishing periodic updates as warranted (one appeared in the May/June 2002 issue). Visit the *Bulletin*'s Web site at <www.thebulletin.org>.

7 Corporations Promote HMO Model for School Districts

Sources:

MULTI-NATIONAL MONITOR, January/February 2002
Title: "Business Goes to School: The For-Profit Corporate Drive to Run Public Schools"
Author: Barbara Miner

THE PROGRESSIVE POPULIST, November 15, 2000
Title: "Dunces of Public Education Reform"
Author: Frosty Troy

NORTH COAST XPRESS, Winter 2000
Title: "Corporate-Sponsored Tests Aim to Standardize Our Kids"
Author: Dennis Fox

IN THESE TIMES, June 2001
Title: "Testing, Testing: The Miseducation of George W. Bush"
Author: Linda Lutton

Faculty Evaluators: Perry Marker, Tom Ormond, & Elaine Sundberg
Student Researchers: Lauren Fox, Derek Fieldsoe, & Joshua Travers

For decades, public schools have purchased innumerable products and services from private companies—from textbooks to bus transportation. Within the last decade, however, privatization has taken on a whole new meaning. Proponents of privatized education are now interested in taking over entire school districts. "Education today, like health care 30 years ago, is a vast, highly localized industry ripe for change," says Mary Tanner, managing director of Lehman Brothers, "The emergence of HMOs and hospital management companies created enormous opportunities for investors. We believe the same pattern will occur in education." So while the aptly named Educational Management Organizations (EMOs) are being promoted as the new answer to impoverished school districts and dilapidated classrooms, the real emphasis is on investment returns rather than student welfare and educational development.

According to some analysts, Bush's proposal for national standardized testing is helping to pave the way for these EMOs. Bush wants yearly standardized testing in reading and math for every student in the country between the third and eighth grades. "School districts and states that do well will be rewarded," Bush states in his education agenda, No Child Left Behind. "Failure will be sanctioned." The effect of Bush's testing plan will be nothing less than a total reconstruction of curriculum and instruction across the country. Perversely, schools with already limited resources, serving poor and minority communities, will be those under the greatest pressure to boost scores or face loss of funding.

Additionally, standardized testing funnels public dollars directly to non-public schools, including religious schools, through taxpayer-supported vouchers. School vouchers, proposed by Bush in his education plan to increase federal education spending, will reward schools that do well on annual standardized tests. Vouchers shunt kids out of the public schools system and into private for-profit institutions. Since only public school students take the standardized tests, kids whose parents can afford private schools don't have to agonize year after year about potential failure.

Standardized testing hits immigrant students especially hard. Bush wants to freeze funding in 2002, despite surging enrollment of students speaking limited English. Angelo Amador, a national policy analyst for the Mexican American Legal Defense and Education Fund, says, "With the pulling of bilingual education funding, states with high-stakes testing are pushing low-performing Latino students into special education classes or out of school altogether in an effort to keep their test scores high."

Critics charge that standardization's real goal is not to improve public education but to disparage it while building support for privatized, union-free alternatives. Proponents of corporate-run education claim that, by cutting the "fat" out of the system, they can improve student achievement with the same amount of money, and still turn a profit (ignoring the fact that the U.S. is ranked ninth globally in terms of money spent on education). The reality is that, though most EMOs have yet to show investors a profit, they generally cut teacher salaries, eliminate remedial, special, and bilingual education programs (mandated for public schools), and consistently perform at or below the level of surrounding schools in test scores.

Privatization opponents say that public education should serve and be run by the public, especially teachers and parents, as opposed to shareholders who run the for-profit companies.

UPDATE BY AUTHOR BARBARA MINER: There is no "silver bullet" to improving low-income public schools. Yet the business community, backed by powerful political interests, has tended to seize on the quick fix of treating public schools as little more than another business venture needing market discipline. The epitome of this approach has found expression in "for-profit" education management companies such as Edison Schools, who seek to make profits for their shareholders by operating public schools and squeezing dollars out of already under-funded budgets.

Across the country, underperforming districts have been under intense pressure to succumb to for-profit management, taking needed time and attention from more promising—but less lucrative—solutions such as smaller classes, improved teacher training, and adequate school funding.

The Wall Street investment community, prone to simplistic stereotypes of bloated bureaucracies running our urban schools, saw a chance to make profits off our public schools. Yet those involved in the daily life of public education know there is only one sure way to make money from public education: either reduce the salaries of teachers and staff, or reduce the services offered. There is little "fat" in urban public school budgets.

When Edison claimed it could provide more services, offer a longer school year and still make a profit, educators were understandably dubious. The investment community, willing to look the other way at questionable business promises, touted Edison's potential for years.

And then the bubble burst. In the months following the Enron debacle, weary investors decided to take a hard look at Edison's finances and broken promises. They were forced to acknowledge that Edison had never made a dime of profit and was unlikely to do so at any point in the foreseeable future. Edison's stock, which had stood at around $20 a share at the year's beginning, tumbled by late May to $1.30 a share.

As is often the case with pack journalism, the media suddenly "discovered" Edison's many problems—although educators and alternative publications had been sounding warnings for years. The mainstream media was forced to play catch-up and print information long available through the alternative media.

As a publicly traded company, many of Edison's finances are available to the public. As a start, do a search through the Web for Edison Schools. Yahoo's finance section is one of many places to start (search under EDSN). And there are a number of education activists with background on Edison, ranging from Rethinking Schools <www.rethinkingschools.org>, to Philadelphia Public School Notebook (E-mail: <psnotebook@aol.com>), to Parents Advocating School Accountability <www.pasasf.org>.

UPDATE BY AUTHOR FROSTY TROY: I am saddened to report that since "Dunces of Public Education Reform" first appeared, public education's critics have been goaded to even more extreme criticism by the Bush victory, especially on talk radio and the editorial pages of America's mostly conservative newspapers. (I search in vain for a so-called liberal press.)

I fear for the future of my country in which a third of the public school buildings are unsafe (GAO report), where a third of the math teachers and 40 percent of history teachers have neither a major nor minor in the subject they are teaching.

Popular radio evangelist James Dobson has called for closing California public schools. "Doctor" Laura seconded the motion on her radio show but said it should include the entire public school system.

Bush Education Secretary Rod Paige calls for vouchers despite their utter failure to address children of poverty. Consider the scandal in St. Petersburg, Florida, where *The New York Times* reports six voucher schools are havens of abuse and corruption, and kids have faced as many as seven teachers in seven months—paid as little at $10.50 an hour.

The president's "No Child Left Behind" program leaves thousands behind—eliminating after-school programs and the teacher education program—and fails by $9 billion to fully fund special education.

I won't stop writing on this subject and speaking out across the nation despite the gloomy outlook. I am galvanized by the certain knowledge that all America is or ever hopes to be can be found in her public school classrooms.

UPDATE BY AUTHOR DENNIS FOX: How we choose to educate our children is always important, so it's not surprising high-stakes tests attract significant attention. Downplaying profit motive as well as research exposing testing's technical flaws, the corporate-owned media generally echo the corporate-initiated call for education reform using corporate-designed standards and tests. Despite occasional criticisms of implementation details, the media pay minimal attention to whether testing obscures rather than remedies underlying economic disparities between high- and low-achieving school districts, or whether the corporate interest lies not in expanding children's skills and horizons but in channeling them into vacant spots in the future workforce's lower realms.

President Bush's No Child Left Behind Act, which passed overwhelmingly with the help of liberal Democrats, mandates annual testing for every public school child in the nation from third through eighth grade. The Bush plan has generated increased alternative press coverage of state and federal testing issues, including some proponents' financial interests in testing companies and/or private schools, Bush's close family ties to the major testing company McGraw-Hill, and the role of organizations like the Business Roundtable. Similar reports sometimes appear in mainstream media, though there the connections between corporate elites and state decision makers are often ignored or dismissed as evidence of business's pro-education savvy.

Despite increased coverage, it's important to remember that the bipartisan corporate-directed testing boom began long before Bush. If there's an underlying plot, it's corporate, not Republican or conservative. Too many liberals still believe testing is merely part of a well-intentioned plan gone wrong.

Encouragingly, test opponents from both left and right have scored scattered victories in a number of states, delaying test consequences through strategies ranging from lobbying to boycotting. It remains to be seen if this movement withstands the new federal mandate.

A related issue, just beginning to surface, is President Bush's second education plan: requiring states to beef up civics education. This return-to-the-Fifties effort will attract corporate support as well as that of mainstream media pundits who bemoan the dropping voter rolls even as they dismiss calls for significant electoral reform that might provide some reason to show up at the polls.

There was no mainstream media response to my story, though I used an earlier version as one of my regular columns in the weekly *Brookline TAB*. A handful of alternative media outlets ran it.

RESOURCES: Dennis Fox <http://people.uis.edu/dfox1>. My Web site includes coverage of Massachusetts test opposition and corporate issues, as well as links to groups and resources.

FairTest <http://fairtest.org/>, a primary national anti-testing organization.

MassRefusal <http://massrefusal.org>, a Massachusetts teacher boycott and analysis of corporate connections.

Commercialism in Education Research Unit <http://www.asu.edu/educ/epsl/ceru.htm>.

"Education, Inc: Turning Learning into a Business," Alfie Kohn & Pat Shannon <http://www.alfiekohn.org>.

"What Happened to Recess and Why are our Children Struggling in Kindergarten?" Susan Ohanian <http://susanohanian.org>.

Standardized Minds: The High Price of America's Testing Culture and What We Can Do to Change It, Peter Sacks

School Reform and the Attack on Public Education, Dave Stratman, <http://new democracyworld.org/edspeech.htm>

"Reading Between the Lines," Stephen Metcalf, *The Nation*, January 28, 2002 <http://www.thenation.com/doc.mhtml?i=20020128&c=1&s=Metcalf>.

"Goals 2000: What's in a Name?," Susan Ohanian <http://www.pdkintl.org/kappan/koha0001.htm>.

8 NAFTA Destroys Farming Communities in U.S. and Abroad

Sources:
FELLOWSHIP MAGAZINE, December 2000/January 2001
Title: "NAFTA's Devastating Effects are Clear in Mexico, Haiti"
Author: Anita Martin

THE HIGHTOWER LOWDOWN, September 2001
Title: "NAFTA Gives the Shafta to North America's Farmers"
Author: Jim Hightower

Faculty Evaluators: Tony White & Al Wahrhaftig
Student Researchers: Adam Cimino, Erik Wagle & Alessandra Diana

The North American Free Trade Agreement (NAFTA) and the International Monetary Fund (IMF) are responsible for the impoverishment of and loss of many small farms in Mexico and Haiti. NAFTA is also causing the economic destruction of rural farming communities in the United States and Canada. The resulting loss of rural employment has created a landslide of socioeconomic and environmental consequences that are worsening with the continued dismantling and deregulation of trade barriers.

When NAFTA came before Congress in 1993, U.S. farmers were told that the agreement would open the borders of Mexico and Canada, enabling them to sell their superior products and achieve previously unknown prosperity. Corporations who operate throughout the Americas, such as Tyson and Cargill, have since used the farming surplus to drive down costs, pitting farmers against each other and prohibiting countries from taking protective actions. These same corporations have entered into massive farming ventures outside the U.S. and use NAFTA to import cheaper agricultural products back into this country, further undermining the small farmers in the U.S. Since the enactment of NAFTA, 80 percent of foodstuffs coming into the U.S. are products that displace crops raised here at home. NAFTA has allowed multinational megacorporations to increase production in Mexico, where they can profit from much cheaper labor, as well as freely use chemicals and pesticides banned in the U.S..

In both Mexico and Haiti, NAFTA policies have caused an exodus from rural areas forcing people to live in urban slums and accept low paid sweatshop labor. Farmers in Mexico, unable to compete with the large-scale importation and chemical-intensive mass production of U.S. agricultural corporations, are swimming in a corn surplus that has swelled approximately 450 percent since NAFTA's implementation. Haiti's deregulation of trade with the U.S. has destroyed the island's rice industry in a similar manner. Urban slums, engorged with rural economic refugees, are contributing to the breakdown of cultural traditions and public authority, making the growing masses increasingly ungovernable.

The Mexican government clashes violently with any organized protest of NAFTA. Dissent in Chiapas and in Central Mexico has lead to the reported arrests, injuries, and deaths of dozens of activists. Community leaders like Minister Lucius Walker, executive of the Interreligious Foundation for Community Organization, state that, "The biggest challenge facing all of us in this new millennium is to build a citizens' movement to counter the corporate captivity of the Americas."

The 1993 NAFTA agreement desolated small farming communities in the U.S. and in Mexico and Haiti. With the scheduled 2009 lift on tariffs and import restrictions, as well as Bush's proposed Free Trade Area of the Americas (FTAA) adding 31 more countries to the NAFTA agreement, many additional farming communities are in danger.

UPDATE BY AUTHOR JIM HIGHTOWER: The story created such traction among lowdown readers because of its ability to dispel many of the mistruths, half-truths, distortions, and outright lies purported by NAFTA proponents and the Bush Administration. By holding the NAFTA rhetoric up for comparison with the hard, statistical data, citizens can make objective judgments about the effectiveness (or, in this case, failure) of this policy.

Careful consideration of NAFTA's record is central to discussions of Fast Track and the FTAA legislation now awaiting a vote by the U.S. House of Representatives in June. The proposed NAFTA expansion, formally called the Free Trade Area of the Americas (FTAA), would spread NAFTA's rules to an additional 31 Latin American and Caribbean nations by 2005. The publicized goal of the FTAA proposal is to facilitate trade and deepen economic integration by expanding the NAFTA provisions that eliminate tariff and non-tariff barriers to trade and investment throughout the hemisphere.

Compounding the situation, the recently passed 2002 Farm Bill expands Federal subsidies for program crops and adds new commodities, causing farmers to be more dependent on the federal government. If it were merely an act of largesse by a benevolent government, it might be looked upon more favorably. But in light of the impending Congressional elections in key farming regions where races are expected to be hotly contested, the move is merely Bush-Rove "strategy" designed to give the GOP control of both houses of Congress.

A person can get more information on this issue by contacting the public's number one trade-scheme watchdog, Global Trade Watch <www.tradewatch.org/>, 215 Pennsylvania Avenue SE, Washington, DC 20003; Tel: (202) 546-4611, or Mobilization for Global Justice <www.globalizethis.org/>, Tel: (202) 265-7714.

What's next? The World Bank and IMF meet in late September and early October in Washington, DC. Come to DC this summer to participate in protest planning.

9 U.S. Faces National Housing Crisis

Source:
IN THESE TIMES, November 2000
Title: "There's No Place Like Home"
Author: Randy Shaw

Faculty Evaluator: Susan Garfin
Student Researchers: Eduardo Barragan & Catherine Jensen

Corporate media coverage:
U.S. NEWSWIRE, January 18, 2002; other corporate coverage mostly limited to local and regional housing issues.

The national housing crisis affects nearly 6 million American families and is growing worse. Over 1.5 million low-cost housing units have recently been lost, and millions of children are growing up in housing that is substandard, unaffordable, and dangerous.

A new crisis in affordable housing is spreading across America. What was once a problem relegated to low-income families along the East and West Coasts, is now affecting the middle class all across the country. Middle-class working Americans are having just as much trouble finding affordable housing as low-income families did 10 years ago.

In San Francisco, the Department of Housing and Urban Development (HUD) is subsidizing housing for public school teachers. California business groups complain that the state's housing shortage hinders their ability to attract skilled workers, and chambers of commerce link the lack of affordable housing to a resultant slowdown in economic growth.

Julie Daniels earns $28,000 a year working full time as a certified nursing assistant for Stamford, Connecticut. A member of local 1199, Daniels and her three children have been unable to obtain affordable housing within traveling distance of her job. The family's only available housing option has been a homeless shelter, and the prospects that Daniels will obtain safe and affordable housing are unlikely.

Still, politicians refuse to add federal-funded housing to the U.S. budget. Low-cost housing programs are slowly being drained of funding. More than 100,000 federally subsidized units have been converted to market-rate housing in the past three years. While the $5 billion Federal Housing Administration surplus is tied up in Washington, neither major political party seems responsive to the current housing crisis. Neither party is addressing issues of living wage, adequate health care, or affordable housing.

Homelessness has become the result for many families across the nation. The economic slowdown, the welfare reform of 1996, and the events of September 11 are pushing hard-working Americans into the street. In New York alone it is estimated that 30,000 people are living in shelters, and many thousands more live on the street.

In Chicago, more than 20,000 units of public housing have been removed from service and some 50,000 people now reside in the streets.

In an era when there is only one apartment for every six potential renters in this country, Congress has taken no action to address this problem. Corporate media has only covered this issue locally and few corporate media reports have recognized this as a national crisis.

UPDATE BY AUTHOR RANDY SHAW: My article, "There's No Place Like Home," highlighted the lack of public debate about the nation's affordable housing shortage during the 2000 presidential race. Although millions of Americans lack safe and affordable housing, the federal government's role in creating our national housing crisis was not discussed. The mainstream media often mentions the impact of the affordable housing shortage in stories about crime, education, welfare policy, or the plight of the working poor, but no congressmember, senator, or president is ever held responsible for perpetuating the problem.

Since Bush took office, mainstream media coverage of the federal government's capacity to end the nation's housing and homelessness crisis has become a subject non grata. The Bush Administration only talks about housing in the context of increasing home ownership. With no government reports or speeches about the rental housing crisis to cover, the mainstream media has felt free to ignore the issue. It has been difficult for all domestic issues to get coverage since 9-11, but housing has particularly fallen out of sight.

Fortunately, rising public clamor about the housing crisis has resulted in significant media coverage at the state and local level. Newspapers from New Hampshire to Seattle are describing increased homelessness among the working poor, and this trend has been covered in such national outlets as the *Washington Post* and *The New York Times*. But the housing crisis remains a local, regional, and state story, with mayors, county supervisors, and governors targeted to address the problem. Cash-strapped local and state governments lack the funds to build the millions of housing units required to meet the nation's need, but local officials who try to shift the blame to the federal government are unaccustomed of passing the buck. The mainstream media coverage of the housing shortage thus contributes to the public sense that housing and homelessness are local problems, as the media steadfastly ignores the federal government's historic responsibility for ensuring decent and affordable housing for all Americans.

The chief national agenda for ending America's housing crisis is through enactment of a National Affordable Housing Trust Fund, which will ensure that 1.5 million new units are built in the next decade. Sponsored by Representative Bernie Sanders in the House and John Kerry in the Senate, the Trust Fund legislation is increasingly seen as the only means for building all of the units America needs. Those interested in learning more can contact the author at <thc@igc.org> or check the campaign Web site <www.nhtf.org/>.

10 CIA Double Deals In Macedonia

Sources:

<WWW.GLOBALRESEARCH.CA>, June 14, 2001
Title: "America at War in Macedonia"
Author: Michel Chossudovsky

<WWW.GLOBALRESEARCH.CA>, July 26, 2001
Title: "NATO Invades Macedonia"
Author: Michel Chossudovsky

Faculty Evaluators: Elizabeth Burch, Phil Beard & John Lund
Student Researchers: Alessandra Diana & David V. Immel

The CIA destabilized the political balance in Macedonia to allow easier access for a U.S.–British owned oil pipeline, and to prevent Macedonia from entering the European union (EU), thereby strengthing the U.S. dollar in a German deutschmark dominated region.

Without Macedonia in the EU, British and U.S. oil companies have an advantage over European counterparts in building oil pipelines. Actions toward destabilization intend to impose economic control over national currencies, and protect British–U.S. oil companies, such as BP-Amoco-ARCO, Chevron, and Texaco against Europe's TotalFinaElf. The British-U.S. consortium controls the AMBO Trans-Balkans pipeline project linking the Bulgarian port of Burgas to Vlore on the Albanian-Adriatic coastline. The power game is designed to increase British–U.S. domination in the region by distancing Bulgaria, Macedonia, and Albania from the influence of EU countries such as Germany, Italy, France, and Belgium. It's an effort supported by Wall Street's financial establishment, to destabilize and discredit the deutschmark and the Euro, with hopes of imposing the U.S. dollar as the sole currency for the region.

The Kosovo Liberation Army (KLA) and the National Liberation Army (NLA) were trained in Macedonia by British Special Forces and equipped by the CIA. British military sources confirm that Gezim Ostremi, NLA Commander, was sponsored by the U.N. and trained by British Special Forces to head the Kosovo Protection Corps (KPC). When Ostremi left his job as a United Nations Officer to join the NLA, the commander remained on the U.N. payroll. Attacks within Macedonia by the NLA/KLA last year, coincided chronologically with the process of EU enlargement and the signing of the historic Stabilization and Association Agreement (SAA) between the EU and Macedonia. These attacks paved the way for further U.S. military and political presence in the region.

In a strange twist the CIA, NATO, and British Special Forces provided weapons and training to the NLA/KLA terrorists, while at the same time, Germany provided Macedonia's security forces with all-terrain vehicles, advanced weapons, and equipment to protect themselves from NLA/KLA attacks. U.S. military advisers, on assignment to the NLA/KLA through private mercenary companies, remained in contact with NATO and U.S. military and intelligence planners. It was Washington and London who decided on the broad direction of NLA/KLA military operations in Macedonia.

Following the August 2001 Framework Peace Agreement, 3,500 armed NATO troops entered Macedonia with the intent of disarming Albanian rebels. Washington's humanitarian efforts for the NLA/KLA suggested its intent to protect the terrorists rather then disarm them. Vice President Dick Cheney's former firm, Halliburton Energy, is directly linked to the AMBO's Trans-Balkans Oil Pipeline.

Last year's conflict in Macedonia is a small part of a growing rift between the Anglo-American and European interests in the Balkans. In the wake of the war in Yugoslavia, Britain has allied itself with the U.S. and severed many of its ties with Germany, France, and Italy. Washington's design is to ensure the dominance of the U.S. military-industrial complex, in alliance with Britain's major defense contractors, and British–U.S. oil. These developments establish significant control over strategic pipelines, transportation, and communication corridors in the Balkans, Eastern Europe, and the former Soviet Union.

UPDATE BY AUTHOR MICHEL CHOSSUDOVSKY: While the CIA admits that Osama bin Laden was an "intelligence asset" during the Cold War, the relationship is said to go way back.

The fact that Al Qaeda continues to support KLA terrorist operations in Macedonia, with the full support of NATO and the U.S. government, has been carefully overlooked. With the complicity of NATO and the U.S. State Department, mujahideen mercenaries from the Middle East and Central Asia were first recruited to fight in the ranks of the Kosovo Liberation Army (KLA) in 1998-99, largely supporting NATO's war effort.

Bin Laden had visited Albania himself. His was one of several fundamentalist groups that had sent units to fight in Kosovo. He is believed to have established an operation in Albania in 1994. Albanian sources say Sali Berisha, who was then president, had links with some groups that later proved to be extreme fundamentalists. (*Sunday Times*, London, November 29, 1998)

Among the foreign mercenaries now fighting in Macedonia, in the ranks of self-proclaimed National Liberation Army (NLA), are mujahideen from the Middle East and the Central Asian republics of the former Soviet Union. Also within the KLA's proxy force in Macedonia are senior U.S. military advisers from a private mercenary outfit on contract to the Pentagon (*Scotland on Sunday*, Glasgow, June 15, 2001). Extensively documented by the Macedonian press and statements of the Macedonian authorities, the U.S. government and the "Islamic Militant Network" are working hand in glove in supporting and financing the self-proclaimed National Liberation Army (NLA), involved in the terrorist attacks in Macedonia. The NLA is a proxy of the Kosovo Liberation Army (KLA). In turn the KLA and the U.N.-sponsored Kosovo Protection Corps (KPC) are identical institutions with the same commanders and military personnel. KPC commanders on U.N. salaries are fighting in the NLA together with the Mujahideen. In a bitter twist, while supported and financed by Osama bin Laden's Al Qaeda, the NLA/KLA is also supported by NATO and the United Nations Mission to Kosovo (UNMIK).

The NLA/KLA terrorists are funded by U.S. military aid, the United Nations peace-keeping budget, as well as by several Islamic organizations including Osama bin Laden's Al Qaeda. Meanwhile, drug money is being used to finance the terrorists with the complicity of the U.S. government. U.S. military advisers mingle with mujahideen within the same paramilitary force, and western mercenaries from NATO countries fight alongside mujahideen recruited in the Middle East and Central Asia.

The Bush Administration has stated that it has proof that Osama bin Laden is behind the attacks on the WTC and the Pentagon. A major war, supposedly "against international terrorism," has been launched by the Bush Administration. In Macedonia, however, the evidence amply confirms that the Bush Administration (together with NATO) is directly supporting terrorist organizations that have links to Al Qaeda. In other words, the Bush Administration is harboring international terrorism as part of its foreign policy agenda. The main justification for waging the so-called war on terrorism has been a total fabrication. The American people have been deliberately and consciously misled by their government into supporting a major military adventure that affects our collective future.

11 Bush Appoints Former Criminals to Key Government Roles

Sources:
THE NATION, May 7, 2001
Title: "Bush's Contra Buddies"
Author: Peter Kornbluh

IN THESE TIMES, August 6, 2001
Title: "Public Serpent; Iran-Contra Villain Elliott Abrams is Back in Action"
Author: Terry Allen

EXTRA, September/October 2001
Title: "Scandal? What Scandal?"
Author: Terry Allen

THE GUARDIAN, February 8, 2002
Title: "Friends of Terrorism"
Author: Duncan Campbell

THE GUARDIAN, February 18, 2002
"No More Mr. Scrupulous Guy"
Author: John Sutherland

WASHINGTONIAN, April 2002
Title: "True or False: Iran-Contra's John Poindexter is Back at the Pentagon"
Author: Michael Zuckerman

Corporate media coverage: THE NEW YORK TIMES, August 1, 2001
LOS ANGELES TIMES, January 12, 2002 and September 30, 2001
and BALTIMORE SUN, September 7, 2001.

NOTE: While a number of corporate media newspapers mentioned the story in short briefs or on single individuals, a full look at the issue was ignored by most of the U.S. press.

Faculty Evaluator: Francisco Vazquez
Student Researchers: David Immel, Joshua Travers & Chris Salvano

Since becoming president, George Bush has brought back into government service men who were discredited by criminal involvement in the Iran-Contra affair, lying to Congress, and other felonies while working for his father George Bush, Senior, and Ronald Reagan.

In February 2001, John Poindexter was appointed to head the new Information Awareness Office (IAO), an offshoot of the Pentagon-based Defense Advanced Research Projects Agency (DARPA). After serving as Reagan's National Security Advisor, John Poindexter was charged and found guilty of conspiracy, obstruction of justice, and the destruction of evidence as he played a central role in the Iran-Contra affair. Costa Rica has officially declared Poindexter to be a drug trafficker, and has barred him from entering the country.

Poindexter's new job at IAO will supply federal agents with "instant" analysis of private e-mail and telephone conversations. As the vice president of Syntek Technologies, Poindexter helped develop the Orwellian "Project Genoa" for the IAO. Genoa will gather information about electronic conversations, financial transactions, passport tracking, airline ticket sales, phone records, and satellite surveillance into a matrix from which "useful information" will be made available to federal authorities.

Elliot Abrams was recently appointed to the National Security Council (NSC) as director of its Office for Democracy, Human Rights, and International Relations. In 1991, Abrams plead guilty to withholding evidence from Congress regarding his role in the Iran-Contra affair. As Reagan's Assistant Secretary of State for Human Rights and Humanitarian Affairs, he used to oversee U.S. foreign policy in Latin America, and was active in covering up some of the worst atrocities committed by the U.S.–sponsored Contras. According to congressional records, under Abram's watch, the Contras "raped, tortured, and killed unarmed civilians, including children," and "groups of civilians, including women and children, were burned, dismembered, blinded and beheaded." George Bush, Senior, subsequently pardoned him.

John Negroponte, the new ambassador to the U.N., served under Reagan as ambassador to Honduras from 1981-1985. He is known for his role in the coverup of human rights abuses by CIA trained paramilitaries throughout the region. Coincidentally, Honduran exiles associated with the paramilitary forces that had been living in the U.S., were exported to Canada prior to Negroponte's Senate confirmation hearing, thus rendering their testimony unavailable.

Otto Reich has been appointed as Assistant Secretary of State for Western Hemisphere Affairs (which includes Latin America). The Bush Administration used a "recess appointment" during January 2002 to side step the Senate confirmation hearing otherwise required of the appointment. Democrat opposition to Reich's nomination had been predicted.

In the eighties, Reich was head of the office for Public Diplomacy, which was censured by Congress for "prohibited covert propaganda activities" after influencing the media to favorably cover the Reagan Administration's position. That office is now defunct. He also helped terrorist Orlando Bosch gain entry into the U.S. after being imprisoned in Venezuela for bombing a Cuban airliner, killing its 73 passengers. Bosch spent time in a U.S. prison for attacking a Polish merchant vessel bound for Cuba. Thirty countries have refused Bosch asylum because of his criminality.

UPDATE BY AUTHOR TERRY ALLEN: It seemed like a good news story to me and my editors, Joel Bleifuss and Jim Naureckas: No sooner did Bush take office than he breathed new life into the corpse of the us-versus-them, good-versus-evil world view that had thrived during the Cold War. The resurrection was embodied in three Reagan-era retreads. These veterans of the U.S. "dirty" war against Central America were complicit in crimes against humanity, democracy, or both. It also seemed like news that Congress was rolling over and bleating weak objections, while most of the media regurgitated snippets of old news.

Bush nominees Otto Reich and Elliot Abrams had been convicted by Congress for relatively trivial aspects of policies that killed thousands and devastated the civil and political life of Central America; John Negroponte had lied about U.S. knowledge and sponsorship of grave human rights abuses in Honduras, and gotten away with it. In writing the story, I relied on extensive LexisNexis research, interviews, and my experience covering the Iran-Contra scandals and reporting from Central America during the wars. I cited all my sources in the pieces.

The articles, tucked away in small-circulation, independent outlets did not a wit of good in preventing Reich's appointment as the State Department's leader on Latin America, Abrams' appointment as a National Security Council director, or Negroponte's assumption of the post of U.S. ambassador to the U.N.

Nor did the stories prevent Bush II from taking up where Bush I and Reagan left off. The coup in Venezuela against Hugo Chavez sports the sticky fingerprints of all three men and the modus operandi of a long line of U.S.–led Cold War interventions.

THIS MODERN WORLD
by TOM TOMORROW

But if these covert ops were tragedy, the Chavez plot was farce. The rapid unraveling of the coup suggested that the Venezuelan plotters would have done better seeking advice from Supreme Court Justice Rehnquist rather than from Reich. It soon became public that Bush officials maintained a web of connections with the conspirators and appeared to have foreknowledge of the plot. using the same conduit Reagan used to fund the Contras, the National Endowment for Democracy, the administration had funneled money to Venezuelan opposition.

According to British media, Abrams gave a nod to the plotters; Otto Reich, a former ambassador to Venezuela, met repeatedly with Pedro Carmona and other coup leaders. The day Carmona seized the presidency, Reich summoned ambassadors from Latin America and the Caribbean to his office and endorsed the new government.

Meanwhile, Negroponte was hard at work at the U.N. enforcing the U.S. unilateralist ultimata. He attempted to undermine the treaty establishing the International Criminal Court to try people accused of genocide and war crimes. Given his history, it's easy to understand his squeamishness at the thought of accountability. Soon after the U.S. "unsigned" the ICC treaty, Negroponte threatened Security Council members with pulling U.S. observers and police from the U.N.'s peace-keeping operations in East Timor—unless U.N. (and therefore, U.S.) personnel were excluded from possible prosecution. The move failed.

Otto Reich is also back to his old tricks and cozying up to hard-right Latin American leaders. In an unsual move for such a high-ranking State Department official, he met with Alvaro Uribe less than a week after his election as president of Colombia. The hardliner and the U.S. are in sync in supporting a military solution to that nation's long-standing counterinsurgency.

An anti-Castro ideologue, Reich was quick to accuse Cuba of developing a biological warfare capacity. Before you could ask "Where's the evidence?" his own State Department published a sweeping 177-page report on global terrorism. The

Miami Herald wrote that Reich "appeared initially confused when asked why the report made no mention of Cuba's bio-weapons research."

"Is it an oversight?" asked Senator Byron Dorgan (D-ND).

"I do not know who publishes that particular document," said Reich.

"It's your department that publishes it," said Dorgan. "This is a State Department publication."

It's déjà vu all over again, and while the plot and dialogue are farce, the toll in lost liberties and lives is tragic. Again.

UPDATE BY AUTHOR DUNCAN CAMPBELL: There have been a number of interesting developments since this story appeared. In April, there was a military coup in Venezuela that resulted in the removal from office of President Hugo Chavez, albeit only for two days. What was interesting about the coup was that it was immediately condemned by the Organization of American States and, very forcefully, by President Fox of Mexico. In contrast, the initial U.S. response was ambiguous. There was no outright condemnation of the removal of a democratically-elected president. In fact, the impression given was that the removal of Chavez, who is a close ally of Fidel Castro, was to be welcomed. It was only after the OAS's condemnation of the coup and the return of Chavez that the U.S. stated its opposition to removing elected leaders by force. The person responsible at the State Department was Otto Reich, whose appointment as assistant secretary we had suggested sent an unfortunate and dangerous message to Latin America. We did not realize that his inability to see beyond his very narrow political agenda would have such damaging consequences so soon.

12 NAFTA's Chapter 11 Overrides Public Protection Laws of Countries

Sources:
THE NATION, October 15, 2001
Title: "The Right and U.S. Trade Law: Invalidating the 20th Century"
Author: William Greider

TERRAIN, Fall 2001
Title: "Seven Years of NAFTA"
Author: David Huffman

Faculty Evaluator: Elizabeth Martinez
Student Researchers: Sarah Potts & Chris Salvano

Mainstream coverage: Bill Moyers, PBS Documentary; *Trading Democracy*, February 5, 2002; and WASHINGTON TIMES, February 4, 2002.

Certain investor protections in NAFTA (North American Free Trade Agreement) are giving business investors new power over sovereign nations and providing an expansive new definition of property rights.

Chapter 11 of NAFTA, which allows a corporation to sue a government, contains a particularly disturbing "regulatory takings" clause. under this "takings" clause, intangible property, such as a corporation's potential future profits, is considered private property. Any law or regulation that is imposed to protect the public interest is considered "taking" that company's potential to make a profit. Therefore, the government should be required to compensate the owners for lost property/profit. This expanded definition of private property goes beyond established terms in U.S. jurisprudence and supercedes domestic law. NAFTA's investor protections and the "regulatory takings" idea mimic a radical revision of constitutional law that the right wing has been pushing for years.

Richard Epstein galvanized the idea of "regulatory takings" in the 1980s with his book *Takings: Private Property and the Power of Eminent Domain*. Regulations, Epstein argues, should be properly understood as "takings" under the Fifth Amendment. This would require governments to pay corporations whose property, tangible or intangible, is in some way diminished by public actions. Since any regulation will have some economic impact on private assets, the "takings" doctrine is therefore a vehicle for shrinking the reach of government and crippling its regulatory procedures. This has the potential to undermine long-established social welfare and environmental regulatory protections. "Takings" protections will also have a chilling effect on a government's future laws and regulatory procedures as they realize that any new legislation may leave them vulnerable to corporate lawsuits. A government may be confronted with enormous financial penalties simply for enacting or upholding regulations that protect the basic health and human rights of its citizens.

The *Methanex v. United States* case illustrates the type of lawsuit made possible by Chapter 11. Methanex is a Canadian company that manufactures the gasoline additive MTBE. Although MTBE was intended to mitigate the air pollution caused by gasoline use, in the mid-nineties it was identified as a hazard to California's water supplies. Even small amounts of MTBE leaking from pipelines or storage tanks caused water to become unfit to drink. After testing the chemical was also found to be carcinogenic.

In 1999, California governor Gray Davis issued an executive order to begin the phase out of MTBE. Four months later, Methanex Co. filed a lawsuit against the

U.S. government, asserting that California's new regulations damaged their future profits, and requested $970 million in compensation. But Methanex did not pursue its case in U.S. federal court, where the legitimacy of "potential profits" might have been publicly questioned. NAFTA provides for a three-judge arbitration tribunal, an offshore venue where suits can be resolved in secrecy. Although matters vital to public welfare are being decided in the unelected tribunals, the public is given no notice of the proceedings unless both parties agree to disclose the case.

The *Methanex v. United States* case is pending, but other companies have already triumphed in their quest to acquire financial compensation for the loss of potential profits. In 2000, the Metaclad Corporation won a suit against the Mexican government. The outcome of the case means that $16.7 million of Mexican taxpayers' money will go to Metaclad in compensation for profits lost because the government stopped it from building a toxic waste dump.

"Regulatory takings" laws have not yet been adopted into U.S. domestic law. The Supreme Court has so far declined to accept this redefinition of the Constitution. However, NAFTA's precedent has opened the door for the "takings" premise to become a standard facet of international law, and corporations are working to realize that goal.

In April 2001, a collection of 29 major U.S. multinational corporations and industry organizations (including GE, Ford, GM, International Paper, Motorola, Dow, DuPont, Chevron, Procter & Gamble, and 3M) wrote to U.S. Trade Representative Robert Zoellick, urging him to push for a Chapter 11–type provision in upcoming FTAA negotiations. The letter applauded NAFTA's regulatory takings clause, saying it provides "protection from regulations that diminish the value of investors' assets." Although FTAA negotiations are not yet complete, at present the draft of the agreement includes a provision nearly identical to Chapter 11 that allows for "investor-to-state" lawsuits.

If the potential profit laws succeed to the degree that some companies hope they will, such basic government regulations as minimum wage and OSHA standards may become null and void in favor of corporate profit. As Epstein writes in his *Takings* book, "It will be said that my position invalidates much of the twentieth-century legislation, and so it does."

COMMENTS BY R. RICHARD WILLIAMS, ATTORNEY AT LAW: A relatively small cadre of people have used the recent international treaty known as NAFTA to bring into law a radical definition of "governmental taking" that will, if honored by the signatory countries, destroy governmental regulatory programs in the United States, Canada, and Mexico. Totaling probably fewer then 1,000 people, this group includes international businessmen, lawyers, and government professionals, with little or no loyalty to the United States, or any other country, or to the laws of the U.S. enacted during the twentieth century as social welfare and environmental protection law.

Led by men such as Daniel Price and Richard Epstein, such law firms as Powell, Goldstein, Frazer & Murphy and Sullivan & Cromwell, the Federalist Society, and such large business enterprises as Methanex (Canada) and Ethyl Corporation (U.S.), the engineering of Chapter 11 of NAFTA places the fate of all laws being attacked in the hands of private arbitration/adjudication tribunals chosen by the parties and outside the reach of review or appeal by any Canadian, U.S., or Mexican courts. If allowed to prevail, Chapter 11 will revolutionize the law in such a way as to force "the international community to provide protection for property rights" (Edwin Williamson, Sullivan & Cromwell), defined as any expectation of profit, to an extent unimaginable since the 1940s. They even hope to destroy such laws as wages and hours laws.

This is really important stuff that will impact all three countries and communities all over the Western Hemisphere without any legislative input from any of us.

UPDATE BY AUTHOR WILL GREIDER: The story of NAFTA's Chapter 11 and its stark implications for American democracy is finally getting a little attention in the major media (*Wall Street Journal*, April 30, 2002, most recently), but mainly because the critics have succeeded in rallying opposition in Congress and especially among state local officials who recognize that this irregular, private court for capital subverts their sovereign right to enact laws to protect public health and the environment. My account in *The Nation* may have helped in educating at least elite public. I hope so.

This issue is central to the globalization debate because, despite the usual bromides about free trade, the international agreements are now mainly about setting rules for investment in countries where capital goes. The debate and development of these rules remains a closed and undemocratic exercise and for good reason. Multinational business and finance shapes the terms, write the new rules, and seeks to throttle the ability of individual nations and governments to resist. The big media has been, on the whole, quite reluctant to look at this dimension of globalization. It is simpler and less contentious to describe the new rules as "free trade" agreements when, in fact, they are designed to encircle the public's right to set rules for society.

The challenge to reform the global system is a long, difficult struggle and won't be won by one issue or one crisis. But I am actually fairly optimistic. The truth is getting through to people generally, despite the barriers of propaganda and the media's general inclination to play cheerleader rather than serious reporter.

UPDATE BY AUTHOR DAVID HUFFMAN: Since the writing of "Seven Years of NAFTA," Philip Morris has joined the ranks of corporations threatening to sue under the investor "protection" provisions of NAFTA's Chapter 11. Philip Morris' threat illustrates the new vulnerability of public health and environmental regulations. Philip Morris has been subject to government restrictions on cigarette advertising for years, but now NAFTA offers a way to block such restrictions. In response to a proposal by the Canadian government to ban the words "mild" and "light" from cigarette packaging, Philip Morris has warned that it may sue for damages. The Canadian and the U.S. governments have both been considering such a ban, because of evidence that mild and light cigarette brands confuse or mislead consumers into believing that these are safer than other types of cigarettes. Although Philip Morris has not yet filed a suit, the threat alone may be enough to discourage implementation of the ban.

How did democracy come to such a pass? It may seem astonishing that the NAFTA member governments so seriously compromised their ability to regulate in the public interest, on matters of vital importance like health and safety. In the case of the U.S., part of the explanation certainly lies in the process through which Congress approved NAFTA. Congress severely limited its ability to deliberate on the contents of NAFTA when it gave approval in 1993, by first agreeing to fast track legislation. Fast track is a mechanism created during the Nixon Administration that allows the executive branch to push international trade agreements through the legislature quickly, by allowing a maximum of only 20 hours of debate. In the whirlwind of fast track, Congress accepted the rationale that strong investor protections were needed to prevent expropriation of U.S. companies by the Mexican government, apparently without fully appreciating the ramifications for the U.S. In his October 15th article in *The Nation*, "The Right and U.S. Trade Law: Invalidating the 20th Century," William Greider explores, in depth, the story behind the adoption of NAFTA. Greider finds evidence that the corporate interests involved in the drafting of NAFTA were fully aware of the wider implications of Chapter 11, and pushed for the agreement's radical redefinition of property rights in order to force all three member governments, not just Mexico, to be more hesitant when it comes to regulations that interfere with corporate profits.

What can be done? The Canadian government has become sufficiently alarmed to propose an amendment to NAFTA that limits the extent of investor protections in Chapter 11. The U.S. federal government has yet to respond in kind, but state governments in the U.S. are mobilizing in response to the threat to state sovereignty highlighted by cases like *Methanex v. U.S.*, in which the Canadian company Methanex is suing for $970 million over California's ban on the toxic gasoline additive MTBE.

Beyond the obvious need to fix NAFTA, there is the need to prevent the same mistake being made on a larger scale with the FTAA, which will extend NAFTA to the entire Western Hemisphere. The mainstream media should recognize this impulse in its coverage of protests against the FTAA. President George W. Bush has been pushing for fast track for the FTAA. This fall, fast track will be in the House for a second time, and there is a good chance that it can be defeated with sufficient public opposition. To find out more about NAFTA, the FTAA, and the specifics on how you can help stop fast track, check out the following sources: Public Citizen <www.publiccitizen.org>, Tel: (202) 588-1000 and Global Exchange <www.globalexchange.org>, Tel: (415) 255-7296.

13 Henry Kissinger and Gerald Ford Lied to the American Public about East Timor

Source:
ASHEVILLE GLOBAL REPORT, December 13, 2001
Title: "Documents Show U.S. Sanctioned Invasion of East Timor"
Author: Jim Lobe (IPS)

Faculty Evaluator: Phillip Beard
Student Researcher: Connie Lytle

Corporate media coverage: SAN DIEGO UNION, December 12, 2001

The release of previously classified documents makes it clear that former President Gerald Ford and Secretary of State Henry Kissinger, in a face-to-face meeting in Jakarta, gave then-President Suharto a green light for the 1975 invasion of East Timor.

According to documents released by the National Security Archive (NSA), in December of 2001(the twenty-sixth anniversary of Indonesia's invasion of East Timor) Suharto told Ford during their talks on December 6, 1975 that, "We want your understanding if it was deemed necessary to take rapid or drastic action [in East Timor]." In a previously secret memorandum, Ford replied, "We will understand and not press you on the issue. We understand the problem and the intentions you have." Kissinger similarly agreed, with reservations about the use of U.S.–made arms in the invasion. Kissinger went on to say regarding the use of U.S. arms, " It depends on how we construe it, whether it is self-defense or is a foreign operation," suggesting the invasion might be framed in a way acceptable to U.S. law. Kissinger added, "It is important that whatever you do succeed quickly...the

U.S. Administration would be able to influence the reaction in America if whatever happens after we return [to the U.S.]. If you have made plans, we will do our best to keep everyone quiet until the President returns home."

For years Henry Kissinger has denied that any discussion of East Timor took place in Jakarta. The newly released dialogue between the three adds significantly to what is known about the role the U.S. played in condoning the Indonesian invasion. The dialogue was part of a batch of documents on U.S. policy effecting East Timor obtained through the National Security Archive.

Indonesia invaded East Timor the day after Ford and Kissinger left. As many as 230,000 East Timorese died as a result of Indonesia's invasion and the 23-year occupation of the country. As much as one-third of the population died as a result of starvation, disease, caused by counterinsurgency operations carried out by the Indonesian army from 1976 to 1999. According to Amnesty International, East Timor represents one of the worst cases of genocides in the twentieth century.

Under international pressure, Indonesia allowed a plebiscite in 1999, in which East Timorese overwhelmingly voted for independence. After the vote, Jakarta-backed militias rampaged the territory, burning and looting the country. The U.N. Security Council authorized an Australian-led international force to restore order. East Timor is now an independent country.

14 New Laws Restrict Access to Abortions in U.S.

Source:
MOTHER JONES, September/October 2001
Title: "The Quiet War on Abortion"
Author: Barry Yeoman

Faculty Evaluator: Greta Vollmer
Student Researcher: Kara Stout

A quiet war against abortion rights is being conducted by many local governments in the United States. Cities and counties are placing repressive legal restrictions on abortion providers under the guise of women's health laws. These restrictions can include: width of hallways, jet and angle type of drinking fountains, the heights of ceilings, and how long one must wait between initially seeing the doctor and when the procedure can be performed.

These legal ordinances are known as TRAP laws. TRAP stands for Targeted Regulation of Abortion Providers. These laws attempt to restrict all aspects of the physical environment related to an abortion. While deemed women's health laws, they are seldom applied to any medical facility other than abortion clinics. The goal of TRAP laws is to discourage a woman's legal right to choose abortion. In the words of one right-to-life leader, the idea is to create an environment "where abortion may indeed be perfectly legal, but no one can get one."

TRAP laws have been passed in several states, including Utah, Connecticut, Louisiana, South Carolina, Wisconsin, Alabama, Colorado, Mississippi, New Mexico, Oklahoma, Kentucky, Illinois, Nebraska, and Texas. Complying with TRAP laws can be very expensive. Remodeling modifications such as hallway width, angle and jet types for drinking fountains, ceiling height, doorway width, counseling room dimensions, air-circulation rates, outdoor weed-control practices, and separate changing rooms for men have resulted in the closing of cash-poor abortion clinics. Sometimes the clinics are closed only temporarily, but often the repairs are simply too expensive and the clinic is forced to cease operating altogether.

In 1992, when the *Planned Parenthood v. Casey* ruling established continued support for the 1973 *Roe v. Wade* decision, a new stealthier strategy was shaped by pro-life campaigners. Right-to-life advocates began thinking about other ways to attack abortion rights that were not so overtly challenging to the *Roe v. Wade* decision. By claiming that abortions take place in dirty facilities and cause such illnesses as depression and breast cancer, right-to-lifers have subtly moved away from the moral and legal debate and into a nebulous realm of "women's health."

Dorinda Bordlee, a right-to-life advocate and staff counsel for Americans united for Life, says, "What's good for the child is good for the mother. So now we're advocating legislation that is good for women." With this reasoning, anti-abortionist make laws sound plausible and even necessary. However, the dimensions of a counseling room will clearly not guarantee a safe and correct abortion. Counseling room size does not protect a woman's health, but it does restrict the availability of abortions.

Louisiana's newest anti-abortion law, known as the civil-liability law, would allow any woman who has had the procedure to sue the doctor for up to 10 years—not just for her own injuries, but also for "damages occasioned by the unborn child." While still being challenged in court, this civil-liability law threatens the viability of clinics in the entire state of Louisiana.

The Supreme Court has repeatedly supported a woman's right to abortion, but these laws are quietly taking that right away. If these laws remain unchallenged it may mean the end of legal abortions in the United States.

COMMENTS BY GRETA VOLLMER, PROFESSOR OF ENGLISH, SONOMA STATE UNIVERSITY:
The Supreme Court is only one vote away from overturning *Roe v. Wade*. This fact alone is disturbing. Yet in the meantime, abortion rights currently guaranteed by this critically important court case are being chipped away by restrictions and statutes implemented at the state and local levels. It is essential that the press continue to highlight all attempts to limit and constrain this fundamental right. The right to an abortion is moot if in fact a woman cannot find providers or services are targeted to such an extent by harassment through ordinance, such as the TRAP laws described in this article.

UPDATE BY AUTHOR BARRY YEOMAN: "The Quiet War on Abortion" was the first national magazine article detailing the myriad ways that pro-choice legislators and grassroots activists use legislation and lawsuits to chip away at women's reproductive rights. It informed readers about a stealthy strategy that previously had flourished underground.

Few mainstream media outlets picked up the story. However, the article won *Washington Monthly*'s December 2001 Journalism Award. It was also highlighted by the Henry J. Kaiser Foundation's Daily Reproductive Health Report. Pro-choice organizations like the Center for Reproductive Law and Policy and the National Abortion Federation have used it as part of their public awareness campaigns. And various pro-choice groups, including Planned Parenthood of Mar Monte and the Westchester Coalition for Legal Abortion, feature it on their Web sites. At California's Humboldt State College, historian Gayle Olson-Raymer uses the article as part of the syllabus for her terrorism class.

Across the country, there have been recent court hearings on these abortion restrictions, but no new decisions. Several bills were introduced this year in statehouses across the country, but so far nothing has passed. Two harassment lawsuits against clinics, one in North Dakota and the other in California, concluded unfavorably for the pro-life activists, though appeals are still possible.

Readers wanting additional information can go to the Web sites of Center for Reproductive Law and Policy <www.reproductiverights.org/crt_trap.html> or the National Abortion Federation <www.prochoice.org>.

15 Bush's Energy Plan Threatens Environment and Public Health

Sources:
ENVIRONMENT NEWS SERVICE, July 2001
Title: "Bush Energy Plan Could Increase Pollution"
Author: Cat Lazaroff
<WWW.TOMPAINE.COM> Alternet <www.alternet.org >
February 15, 2002
Title: "The Loyal Opposition: Bush's Global-warming Smog"
Author: David Corn

THE PROGRESSIVE POPULIST
March 15, 2002
Title: "Smog Screen"
Author: David Corn

Faculty Evaluator: Dorothy Friedel
Student Researcher: Derek Fieldsoe

The Bush Administration's energy plan will actually increase air pollution in the United States. The plan calls for increased fossil fuel consumption, and for decreased funding for research into renewable, clean energy development. The plan also lowers upgrade requirements on 30- to 60-year-old power plants that often emit 4 to 10 times as much sulfur dioxide, nitrogen oxide, carbon dioxide, and mercury as newer power plants. The administration stands behind this plan despite higher smog levels, increased respiratory related hospital visits, and record high asthma cases on the East Coast last year.

Although Bush conceded earlier in his presidency that global warming is underway and that steps must be taken to reduce emissions, the U.S. is still responsible for 25 percent of the world's emissions.

The Bush plan puts into jeopardy the New Source Review (NSR) provision, which is a vital part of the Clean Air Act. The NSR requires facilities to offset pollution increases with reductions elsewhere in the facility or demonstrate that the facility is using the best available pollution control. Major power, coal, and oil companies who own power plants that were built between 1940 and 1970, have sought to ease the restrictions of the NSR claiming that the law hurts their business due to high costs to upgrade to the best available pollution control technology. The EPA and several states have successfully sued a number of large utilities for violation of this NSR provision. These legal victories have led to millions of dollars in penalties.

Power plant air pollutants in some regions are known to cause as much damage to human lungs as smoking a pack of cigarettes a day. According to Carl Pope, executive director of the Sierra Club, "President Bush's invitation to weaken these pollution controls is an invitation to increase asthma and other health problems triggered by power plant smog."

While record smog levels on the East Coast have resulted in 6 million asthma attacks and 212,000 hospital visits due to respiratory problems last summer, George Bush claims his energy plan will be good for the environment and the economy. After rejecting the 1997 Kyoto accord (which was supported by every other industrialized nation in the world), Bush declared that, "Our immediate goal is to reduce America's greenhouse gas emissions relative to the size of our economy." While this sounds like a positive statement, it should be known that what the Bush energy plan actually means is that the rate of emission production will stay below the rate of economic growth but is likely to result in increasing pollution by 14 percent over the coming decade. So the plan calls for no immediate reduction, only slower increases. Emissio-producing businesses would only have to monitor and report their emissions to receive pollution credits, which could then be sold to other companies to increase their emissions.

Additionally, the Bush plan calls for a slashing of funding in research for renewable, clean forms of energy such as wind and solar power, which can provide very effective amounts of energy for U.S. consumption. The slashing of funding for research into clean renewable energy and increased dependence on fossil fuels will speed up the effects of global warming and have a detrimental effect on our health and environment.

UPDATE BY AUTHOR CAT LAZAROFF: Since July 2001, the Bush energy plan has been challenged and debated in Congress, the courts, and in newspapers across the nation. The collapse of energy giant Enron has led to new questions about the role that the fossil fuel industries played in crafting the White House energy plan and in steering it away from cleaner power sources and energy conserving strategies.

Major energy legislation (HR 4) has been passed by both the U.S. House of Representatives and the Senate. Both versions of the bill, now headed for a conference committee showdown, would enact key portions of the Bush energy plan, including increased subsidies for nuclear power, clean coal, and other fossil fuel sectors, while boosting tax incentives for energy efficiency and alternative energy sources such as wind, solar and fuel cells.

The bills both fail to tackle some prominent sources of air pollution, including vehicle emissions, which could be slashed if Congress approved higher fuel efficiency standards for passenger vehicles. However, the Senate version would triple the amount of ethanol added to gasoline across the nation by 2012, a step that could help states meet clean air standards without using water polluting MTBE.

President George W. Bush moved to reduce power plant emissions of three major pollutants—sulfur dioxide, nitrogen oxides, and mercury—through his Clear Skies initiative, unveiled in February 2002. Critics say the largely voluntary program, which would set nationwide emissions caps that companies could meet by trading pollution credits and other market based mechanisms, could actually increase the real emissions of these pollutants.

The Clear Skies initiative also aims to cut the nation's so-called carbon intensity, a measure of carbon emissions tied to U.S. economic activity. The proposal has been widely criticized both at home and abroad as an inferior tool for combatting global climate change, when compared to the international Kyoto Protocol that President Bush has rejected.

A number of states have passed or are reviewing legislation to curb carbon emissions from fossil fueled power plants, a trend that could eventually prompt calls by the energy industry for uniform nationwide standards.

Legal challenges to the New Source Review (NSR) provisions of the Clean Air Act continue, with hearings on a landmark case brought by the federally operated Tennessee Valley Authority beginning in May. Senior administration officials have said repeatedly that the NSR rule should be overhauled, and the EPA is still reviewing the provision, having missed several self-imposed deadlines for announcing any planned revisions.

In January 2002, the Justice Department announced that enforcement actions taken under NSR are legal and consistent with the Clean Air Act and the Administrative Procedure Act. EPA Administrator Christie Whitman has reportedly advised regional EPA offices to continue to seek new cases that can be prosecuted under NSR, while at the same time counseling utilities cited under NSR to avoid settling their cases until the Tennessee Valley Authority's case is decided.

Meanwhile, evidence continues to mount regarding the link between air pollution and human health problems. In April 2002, for example, a report released by a consulting firm and a former enforcement officer from the EPA charged that almost 6,000 premature deaths can be blamed each year on pollution from 80 power plants in the Midwest and Southeast.

More information on the White House Clear Skies initiative is available at <www.whitehouse.gov/news/releases/2002/02/20020214-5.html>.

The EPA's new source review materials are available at <www.epa.gov/ ttn/nsr/>.

An analysis of the energy efficiency provisions of the House and Senate energy bills, by the Alliance to Save Energy, is available at <www.ase.org/policy/energybillcomp.pdf>.

An analysis by the Natural Resources Defense Council of the role that the energy industry played in crafting the Bush energy plan is available at <www.nrdc.org/air/energy/aplayers.asp>.

Physicians for Social Responsibility has a briefer on the potential health effects of the Bush energy plan at <www.psr.org/energy2001/planpreview.html>.

A history of the development of the new source review is available at <www.clean airtrust.org/newsourcereview.html>.

UPDATE BY AUTHOR DAVID CORN: One trouble with the mainstream media is that, generally, its reporters and editors feel uncomfortable pointing an accusing finger at a subject—the President, for example—and say, "You're lying," or "That's ridiculous." When President George W. Bush finally released a plan to "address" global warming, the story—to the extent it was covered—was that he was issuing a proposal, not that he was being disingenuousness. A reporter did not have to look too closely to see Bush's proposal would allow the amount of greenhouse gases in the atmosphere to increase. Yet the people who run most media outlets do not believe they can publish a headline saying, "President Offers Misleading Global Warming Scheme." Perhaps consequently, Bush has continued to play games with global warming. In the end of May 2002, his EPA released a report confirming global warming was under way and caused by the burning of fossil fuels. He tried to distance himself from the report—while his administration used it to justify opposing emissions reductions (for the report also said global warming had progressed so far that emissions reductions might not remedy the situation). But, at the same time, the White House continued to claim Bush cared about the matter and used the occasion to promote his global warming plan. So he and his aides were dismissing the report and embracing its too-late-to-do-anything conclusion but still maintaining their do-little plan would make a difference. It was a hurricane of spin—and one that few reporters bothered to deconstruct or report.

16 CIA Kidnaps Suspects for Overseas Torture and Execution

Sources:
WEEKEND AUSTRALIAN, February, 23, 2002
Title: "Love Letter Tracks Terrorist's Footsteps"
Author: Don Greenlees

WORLD SOCIALIST Web site <www.wsws.org/articles/2002/mar2002/
cia-m20_ prn.shtml>, March 20, 2002
Title: "U.S. Oversees Abduction, Torture, Execution of Alleged Terrorists"
Author: Barry Grey

WASHINGTON POST, March 11, 2002, pg. A01
Title: "U.S. Behind Secret Transfer of Terror Suspects"
Authors: Rajiv Chandrasekaran and Peter Finn
Faculty Evaluator: Noel Byrne
Student Researcher: Sarah Potts

Corporate media coverage: PITTSBURGH POST-GAZETTE, March 17, 2002

U.S. agents are involved in abducting people they suspect of terrorist activities and sending them to countries where torture during interrogation is legal, according to U.S. diplomatic sources. Suspects are shipped to allied countries where they are denied legal assistance and imprisoned without any specific charges made against them. The prisoners have been taken to countries such as Egypt and Jordan (whose intelligence agencies have close ties to the CIA), where they can be subjected to interrogation tactics, including torture and threats to family, which are illegal in the United States.

One of the abductees, Muhammad Saad Iqbal Madni was believed by the CIA to be an Al Qaeda member with possible links to Richard Reid, the American Airlines shoe bomber. In January 2002, the CIA provided Indonesian intelligence officials with information that lead to Iqbal's arrest. A few days later, the Egyptian government requested that Iqbal—who had carried a passport for Egypt as well as Pakistan—be extradited in connection with terrorism, although they did not specify the crime. Indonesian agents quickly took him into custody, and two days later, without legal hearing or access to a lawyer, Iqbal was put on board an unmarked, U.S.-registered Gulfstream V jet, arranged by the CIA, and flown from Jakarta to Egypt.

Indonesian government officials told local media that Iqbal had been sent to Egypt because of visa violations. However, a senior Indonesian government official told reporters that revealing the U.S. role in Iqbal's case would have prompted criticism from Muslim-oriented political parties in the region. "We can't be seen as cooperating too closely with the United States," he said. Nevertheless, the official confirmed that, "This was a U.S. deal all along. Egypt just provided the formalities."

According to one U.S. diplomat, "After September 11, these sorts of movements have been occurring. It allows us to get information from terrorists in a way we can't do on U.S. soil."

Although such "movements" have intensified since 9-11, the U.S. has long been involved in this practice of kidnapping. These abductions, known to those in the business as "rendition," violate local and international extradition laws as well as internationally recognized human rights standards. According to the *Washington Post*'s sources, from 1993 to 1999, suspects were rendered to the U.S. from a variety of countries, including South Africa, Nigeria, Kenya, and the Philippines. U.S. officials have acknowledged some of these operations, but the *Post*'s sources say that dozens of other covert renditions occurred, the details of which remain cloaked in secrecy.

Some documented cases include reports of suspects being interrogated, tortured, and even executed. In 1998, U.S. agents apprehended Talaat Fouad Qassem, the reputed leader of an Egyptian extremist organization, in Croatia. Qassem had been traveling to Denmark, where he had been promised political asylum. Egyptian lawyers say that the U.S. agents removed Qassem to a U.S. ship stationed off the Croatian coast. On board, he was questioned by the agents before being taken to Cairo, where a military tribunal had already sentenced him to death in absentia.

Also in 1998, five members of Egyptian Islamic Jihad were taken into custody by Albanian police working in tandem with CIA agents. The five suspects were interrogated for three days before being shipped to Egypt on a CIA-chartered plane. The U.S. alleged that this group of people had been planning to bomb the U.S. embassy in Albania's capital. Two of the five people were put to death.

*The details of this covert and illegal abduction campaign were brought to light in the U.S. by a *Washington Post* article printed on March 11, 2002, entitled, "U.S. Behind Secret Transfer of Terror Suspects." The article cites various U.S. and Indonesian officials (sources unidentified by name) recounting and commenting upon these violations. Although the article appeared on the *Post*'s front page, the story was picked up by only one other corporate media source in the U.S., and the *Post* itself—as of this writing—has not followed up its own story with any new information.

UPDATE BY AUTHOR DON GREENLEES: One of the unanswered questions is what happened to Muhammad Saad Iqbal Madni after he was handed over to the CIA and taken to Cairo? U.S. officials have refused to comment on the case. Indeed, there is still no official confirmation that he was ever placed in the custody of the CIA for extradition to Egypt. Was his interrogation conducted by U.S. or Egyptian personnel? Was he, in fact, ever taken to Egypt? Even alleged terrorists are presumably entitled to some protection under the law. In Iqbal's case, it has not been possible to determine his fate. Rumors circulated among non-U.S. Western intelligence agencies earlier this year that Iqbal had died in interrogation. U.S. officials in Jakarta, requesting anonymity, have denied that allegation.

Given the secrecy surrounding Iqbal's capture in Jakarta and handover to the CIA, it is reasonable to assume he is not the only alleged terrorist to have been placed in the custody of U.S. officials and taken to a third country for interrogation, where the absence of civil rights and U.S. legal protections could afford interrogators more freedom. Soon after the article on Iqbal appeared in the *Weekend Australian*, the *Washington Post* ran an article suggesting there were other cases of individuals being detained by the CIA and sent to countries where interrogation could be more easily carried out. The subject justifies further inquiry. Without the guilt of suspects having been legally ascertained, detentions are clearly open to abuse. How long will suspects be held and on what grounds? What restraint exists on the conduct of the interrogations? These are questions of interest to civil libertarians everywhere, particular in countries where non-democratic rulers could use the crackdown on terrorism as a means of sidelining critics.

The *Weekend Australian* article also sought to highlight the performance of the Indonesian authorities in dealing with the threat of terrorism. The absence of adequate law enforcement and the lack of coordination between law enforcement agencies, the weakness of immigration controls, and the reluctance of the government to take legal action against extremist elements who have broken the law continue to make Indonesia vulnerable to entry by international terrorists. Iqbal's success in entering Indonesia is seen as evidence of this weakness. But a consistent concern of pro-democracy groups in Indonesia is whether many of the hard won civil freedoms of the past four years could be eroded as Jakarta comes under pressure to improve its contribution to fighting potential terrorist threats.

17 Corporate Media Ignores Key Issues of the Anti-Globalization Protests

Source:
COLUMBIA JOURNALISM REVIEW, September/October 2001
Title: "Smoke Gets In Your Eyes: The Globalization Protests and the Befuddled Press"
Author: John Giuffo

Faculty Evaluator: Suzanne Toczyski
Student Researchers: Caroline Hubbard, Cathy Jensen & Derek Fieldsoe

Corporate media coverage: NEW YORK TIMES, February 5, 2002

The U.S. press failed to inform the public of the core underlying issues of the major antiglobalization protests of recent years. Dramatic images such as protesters enshrouded in tear gas, facing down a line of police officers dressed in riot gear, have come to dominate the media coverage and overshadow the actual reasons that thousands of people are taking to the streets.

In July 2001, over 100,000 people went to Genoa to protest the G-8 meetings. However, corporate television gave little recognition to the issues that were being raised by the protesters. CNN showed few protesters actually sharing their views or reasons for protesting. Instead, news correspondents briefly summed up the protest in terms of who was there. This broad summary format was significantly lacking attention to specifics of the meetings or the protests. On Fox networks, the Genoa protesters were all but ignored.

THIS MODERN WORLD   by TOM TOMORROW

A hard look at more than 200 stories by major news outlets including: ABC, CBS, CNN, Fox, NBC, the *Los Angeles Times*, *The New York Times*, the *Washington Post*, *Time*, and *Newsweek*, shows serious weaknesses in the coverage of the four largest protests—the International Monetary Fund meeting in Prague in September 2000; the Hemispheric Free Trade talks in Quebec City in April 2001; the European union summit in Gothenburg, Sweden in June 2001; and the G-8 meeting that took place in Genoa in July of 2001. The problem is not so much the focus on the small percentage of protesters who acted violently, but that the coverage lacks context.

The message that protesters are trying to get across is that they want more democratic control (and less corporate control) over the rules that affect the environment and labor conditions around the world. This includes more democratic control over supranational organizations such as the World Bank, the International Monetary Fund, and the World Trade Organization, whose un-elected leaders, the protesters argue, override democratically determined laws and regulations in the name of "development" and "free trade."

There are many instances of police brutality at these large protests, yet what tends to be emphasized by the mainstream news sources are the few acts of violence perpetrated by the protesters. For example, at the Genoa protest that took place last year, approximately 70 members of an Italian SWAT team barged through the doorway of a site where protesters were organizing. This led to the hospitalization of 61 demonstrators. However, few news sources reported the police violence, and most sources focused on protester violence. CBS News released a Web report that indicated that the protesters were injured during the previous day's events. European news sources and independent news organizations, such as <Indymedia.org> put out full reports of police brutality against the protesters.

An article in *The New York Times*, written by Andrew Jacobs, supports the notion that the media coverage of antiglobalization protests is appalling. Jacobs reports,

THE W.T.O., MEANWHILE, IS MAKING PLANS TO HOLD ITS NEXT MEETING IN THE EMIRATE OF QATAR-- AN ISOLATED COUNTRY WITH NO INCONVENIENT FREEDOM OF ASSEMBLY OR RIGHT TO DISSENT.

IS THAT SO? WE HAD NO IDEA!

WE JUST GOT A REALLY GREAT DEAL ON HOTEL ROOMS THERE!

(FACES DIGITALLY OBSCURED TO PROTECT IDENTITIES OF ANONYMOUS W.T.O. BUREAUCRATS.)

IN SHORT, THE IMPORTANT BUSINESS OF GLOBALIZATION WILL MOST CERTAINLY NOT BE DISRUPTED BY ANY OF THOSE PESKY DEMONSTRATORS THIS TIME AROUND...

CRAZY UNINFORMED PROTESTERS!*

I CAN HARDLY WAIT TO READ THOMAS FRIEDMAN'S LATEST DENUNCIATIONS OF THEIR PATHETIC ANTICS!

I THINK SOMEONE SHOULD WASH OUT THEIR MOUTHS WITH PEPPER SPRAY!

...OR WILL IT?

*SEE FOR YOURSELF JUST HOW "UNINFORMED" THOSE WACKY ACTIVISTS ARE: www.stopftaa.org!

"most press accounts focused on security concerns and the potential for violence…
leaving little room for explanations of why people were protesting in the first place."

UPDATE BY AUTHOR JOHN GIUFFO: We've heard the phrase "September 11 changed everything" so often that it has become a cliché to call it a cliché. But in terms of the global justice movement, 9-11 changed a lot. Support of violence as a legitimate protest tactic was waning before the attacks, but it dropped off the radar afterwards. The drama of the globalization-related protests was play-acted anarchy compared to our glimpse of the real thing that fall morning, and it seems like we've lost our collective stomach for such measures.

The few protests since, such as the New York City World Economic Forum protest in late January, have been relatively violence-free, comparatively under-attended affairs. Before, the violence had usually been the story, but the big story during the New York protests was that there was no story, and that the police had maintained order in a still-shaky city. None of the core issues the movement addressed have changed, but their perceived importance has waned in the swirl of global violence that has wracked the world in the past year. Quite simply, it seems like we've got bigger things to worry about. The coverage reflects that. The number of foreign correspondents at American news organizations has been shrinking for 20 years, and there are only so many left to go around. Protests in Sao Paolo, Brazil lost out to Operations Condor in the mountains of Afghanistan.

There's another complicating factor—what can best be described as a sort of "message drift." One of the movement's main strengths has been its ability to subsume a multitude of complaints under the banner of anti-corporate democratization. But since the conflicts in Afghanistan and the Middle East have drawn away the keyboards and cameras of journalists, the anti-corporate protesters have been willing to share the stage with pacifists and pro-Palestinian protesters. Even IndyMedia, the main organizing news and message site of the movement, in a post to the site on January 11 conflated the economic issues behind the protests with what it called "the violence being committed against the people of Afghanistan."

That's not to say all the media are distracted. Some news organizations have done an admirable job recognizing the need to dedicate space for explanation and detail when covering the protests. A good example is the *Washington Post*, which covered the mid-April World Bank/pro-Palestinian protests relatively comprehensively (arguably because it was a hometown affair), pausing to take time to explain the issues behind the economic and anti-Israel protests.

The global justice movement is very much in flux, and that has been one of the central challenges to it getting its message out. Calls for taking sides in the Middle East and against intervention in Afghanistan and Iraq threaten to drown out other voices advocating for clean air, fair trade, or reregulation in corporate ownership structures. There is a limited amount of space in newspapers, and only so much news airtime on television. The more messages that reporters have to get into their stories, the less they can explore those messages. It would seem the global justice movement has to decide what it wants to be when it grows up.

18 World's Coral Reefs Dying

Source:
HARPER'S, January 2001
Title: "Shoals Of Time: Are We Witnessing The Extinction of the World's Coral Reefs?"
Author: Julia Whitty

Faculty Evaluator: Ervand Peterson
Student Researcher: Connie Lytle

One-quarter of all coral reefs have been destroyed by pollution, sedimentation, over-fishing, and rapid global climate change. Coral reefs have survived enormous changes in our planet's past, but today they are experiencing challenges from a multitude of new fronts. Remaining reefs are in such peril that governments are preparing for the contingency that millions of island residents will need to be relocated.

Corals are among the simplest of invertebrate animals. They are composed of little more than a hollow tube, the gastric cavity, which is surrounded by a fringe of stinging tentacles used to capture prey. Generation after generation of new corals grow atop the limestone skeletons of dead corals, until a reef is formed. The growth is less than one inch per year, and the colonies can live a thousand years or more. Coral colonies occur in the narrow band of equatorial water at the 21°C isotherm, where the delicate balance between sunlight, temperature, salinity, nutrients, and gases meets the exacting requirements of the tiny coral animals, and compose the largest aquatic architecture on the planet.

Ordinarily, more than 6.5 million zooxanthellae inhabit each square inch of coral, and in return these algae contribute the by-products of their photosynthesis: oxygen, carbohydrates, and alkalinity. The corals' calcium carbonate production is considered a likely mediator of atmospheric CO_2, making this collaboration between plant and animal a contributor to the stability of our atmosphere. The reefs contain nearly one-quarter of all marine life and, as they are visibly altered by climatic and sea level changes, are often called "the record keepers of the sea."

Under assault from pollution, coastal development, agricultural runoff, overpopulation, and overfishing, the world's reefs are exhibiting their vulnerability in many ways. Each year new coral diseases are discovered, some caused by such factors as the desertification of Africa, where huge volumes of dust in the atmosphere are dropping viral and fungal spores onto the weakened seas.

In the last two decades, worldwide coral bleaching events associated with higher seawater temperatures have destroyed reefs throughout entire ocean basins. Increasing global temperatures, resulting in a lack of proteins, lipids, and carbohydrates necessary for coral reproductive and skeleton building causes bleached corals. A 1991 bleaching event in French Polynesia led to the death of 25 percent of all Acropora corals. The 1997-98 El Niño killed 70 percent of all corals in the Indian Ocean from Africa to India, and the reefs of the Galapagos Islands have yet to show signs of recovery from the bleaching event 17 years ago. Increases in ultraviolet rays entering the atmosphere have contributed to the bleaching effect in the coral reefs worldwide.

The worldwide trade in aquarium fishing, currently worth $200 million per year, is another source of coral reef destruction. The collection methods of exotic fish include using poisons, primarily sodium cyanide, which destroy entire ecosystems in order to capture the few remaining fish on the perimeter. Blast fishery, also common in such places as the Philippines, is a practice whereby fish for local consumption are collected with explosives, killing the fish at the epicenter, and incapacitating those on the perimeters. The blasts reduce the reefs to rubble, from which they may never recover.

UPDATE BY AUTHOR JULIA WHITTY: Since the publication of this article, I am now working on a book (*The Fragile Edge: Secrets & Struggles of the Coral Reef*) for Houghton Mifflin. Research for this book will take me to Australia, the Philippines, Indonesia, and elsewhere to show important new developments in the science and conservation of reefs. Some of the problems alluded to in the article are already coming to pass, as sea levels continue to rise and island-dwelling people face the loss of their homes and their nations. Elsewhere, conservation efforts are paying off, albeit on a fairly small scale.

I still consider the fate of coral reefs to be vital to our own well-being on Earth. Sadly, this story and other environmental stories rarely make the evening news or the front pages of newspapers. As we fight a "war of national security" against terrorism, I wonder how it is that we fail to see or act upon the threats to global security that face us from the self-induced loss of biodiversity, the destruction of habitats, and global climate change. The "freedoms" and the "way of life" that we fight Al Qaeda for are at least as threatened by our continued misuse of the planet.

Harper's originally offered me this article, so I had no struggle in trying to present it. But I know from years of making nature documentaries that there is strong resistance to telling the environmental truth—even when that truth can reveal important solutions.

Readers interested in learning more can track my coral travels during the autumn 2002 at <www.BlueVoice.org>. I will also be working closely with The Great Barrier Reef Research Foundation, <www.barrierreef.org>.

19 American Companies Exploit the Congo

Sources:
DOLLARS AND SENSE, JulyAugust 2001
Title: "The Business of War in the Democratic Republic Of Congo: Who Benefits?"
Authors: Dena Montague & Frieda Berrigan

VOICE (Pioneer Valley, MA), March/April 2001
Title: "The Matrix: Depopulation and Perception Management (Part 2: Central Africa)"
Author: keith harmon snow

THE VOICE NEWS (Winstead, CT), January 4, 2002
Title: "Central Africa: Hidden Agenda and the Western Press"
Author: keith harmon snow

COVERTACTION QUARTERLY, Summer 2000
Title: "U. S. Military and Corporate Recolonization of the Congo"
Author: Ellen Ray
(Honorable Mention: From *Censored 2001*)

Faculty Evaluator: Philip Beard
Student Researchers: Arinze Anoruo & Chris Salvano

Western multinational corporations' attempts to cash in on the wealth of Congo's resources have resulted in what many have called "Africa's first world war," claiming the lives of over three million people. The Democratic Republic of Congo (DRC) has been labeled "the richest patch of earth on the planet." The valuable abundance of minerals and resources in the DRC has made it the target of attacks from U.S.–supported neighboring African countries Uganda and Rwanda.

The DRC is minerial rich with millions of tons of diamonds, copper, cobalt, zinc, manganese, uranium, niobium, and tantalum (also known as coltan). Coltan has become an increasingly valuable resource to American corporations. Coltan is used to make mobile phones, night vision goggles, fiber optics, and capacitators used to maintain the electrical charge in computer chips. In December of 2000 the shortage of coltan was the main reason that the popular sale of the Sony Play Station 2 video game came to an abrupt halt.

The DRC holds 80 percent of the world's coltan reserves, more than 60 percent of the world's cobalt, and is the world's largest supplier of high-grade copper. With these minerals playing a major part in maintaining U.S. military dominance and economic growth, minerals in the Congo are deemed vital U.S. interests.

Historically, the U.S. government identified sources of materials in Third World countries, and then encouraged U.S. corporations to invest in and facilitate their production. Dating back to the mid-1960s, the U.S. government literally installed the dictatorship of Mobutu Sese Seko, which gave U.S. corporations access to the Congo's minerals for more than 30 years. However, over the years Mobutu began to limit access by Western corporations, and to control the distribution of resources. In 1998, U.S. military-trained leaders of Rwanda and Uganda invaded the mineral-rich areas of the Congo. The invaders installed illegal colonial-style governments that continue to receive millions of dollars in arms and military training from the United States. Our government and a $5 million Citibank loan maintains the rebel presence in the Congo. Their control of mineral-rich areas allows Western corporations, such as American Mineral Fields (AMF), to illegally mine. Rwandan and Ugandan control over this area is beneficial for both governments and for the corporations that continue to exploit the Congo's natural wealth.

American Mineral Fields landed exclusive exploration rights to an estimated 1.4 million tons of copper and 270,000 tons of cobalt. San Francisco-based engineering firm Bechtel Inc. established strong ties in the rebel zones as well. Bechtel drew up an inventory of the Congo's mineral resources free of charge, and also paid for NASA satellite studies of the country for infrared maps of its minerals. Bechtel estimates that the DRC's mineral ores alone are worth $157 billion dollars. Through coltan production, the Rwandans and their allies are bringing in $20 million in revenue a month. Rwanda's diamond exports went from 166 carats in 1998 to 30,500 in 2000. Uganda's diamond exports jumped from approximately 1,500 carats to about 11,300. The final destination for many of these minerals is the U.S..

UPDATE BY AUTHOR DENA MONTAGUE: Nearly four million people dead in four years of war in the Democratic Republic of Congo (DRC), and the world remains silent in the face of an abominable atrocity. The war in the DRC is not only significant because of its infamous status as the world's deadliest war, but also because of the active participation of an international contingent of multinational corporations, terrorist networks, arms brokers, and governments all clamoring for the legendary wealth of the Congo while exacerbating the war.

Ugandan- and Rwandan-backed rebels and the Congolese central government met for nine weeks beginning in March 2002 in Sun City, South Africa to negotiate aspects of the Inter-Congolese dialogue as a part of the Lusaka Peace Accords. In a significant development emerging from the dialogue—Jean Pierre Bemba, a known Mobutuist and leader of Uganda sponsored rebel party, Movement for the Liberation of Congo (MLC), has been appointed prime minister of the DRC in a power-sharing agreement strongly encouraged by Western governments. Rather than being held accountable by the international community for war crimes committed against Congolese civilians and the massive exploitation of Congolese natural resources detailed by the U.N. during the four-year war, Bemba, a multimillionaire, will be leading the country he helped decimate.

In response to its isolation from the power-sharing agreement, Rwandan-backed RCD has formed an alliance with veteran Congolese opposition leader Etienne Tshisekedi. Rwanda has not ceased discussions of an enduring armed partition of the DRC, as it remains in control of approximately one third of the country. The power sharing agreement emerging from Sun City has effectively marginalized civil society groups who have been organizing peacefully for democracy, and instead rewards armed struggle in the country. Meanwhile, Rwanda and Uganda continue to attract international investors as well as military assistance from the U.S. and others. Thousands of Rwandan troops are currently engaged fighting in the eastern region of the country at the continued expense of civilian lives.

The war in the DRC is layered in such a way that it appears as a wartime telenovella. Its complexity tends to distract the layman observer from the fundamental facts. This war is yet another stage in international efforts to control the wealth of the Congo—a story that dates back to the nineteenth century.

The only major U.S. media response to the war in the DRC has been a weeklong *Nightline* report, "Heart of Darkness" that was originally scheduled to air the week of September 11 and was postponed until February. Although the *Nightline* special was significant in drawing attention to the neglected story and the unbearable suffering of the Congolese people, it did little to explain the root causes of the war. Other than the *Nightline* report, only an occasional story on the fledgling peace process appears in major newspapers.

There are few outlets that give a comprehensive account of the war. International Crisis Group has published a series of in-depth reports about the conflict at <www.intl-crisis-group.org/>.

Occasionally the *Washington Post* covers the DRC. Reporter Karl Vick was one of the first to uncover the story of coltan mining. All Africa <www.allafrica.com/> compiles daily reports on the DRC. Other magazines that are less accessible frequently cover the war—*New African Magazine* and *Africa Confidential*.

For an historical perspective on conflict in the Congo, *King Leopold's Ghost* by Adam Hochschild and *The Assassination of Patrice Lumumba* by Ludo De Witte are good sources.

20 Novartis' Gene Research Endangers Global Plant Life

Source:
THE OBSERVER (London), October 8, 2000
Title: "Gene Scientists Disable Plants' Immune Systems"
Author: Antony Barnett

Faculty Evaluator: Albert Wahrhaftig
Student Researchers: Alessandra Diana & Gabrielle Mitchell

Scientists working for Swiss food giant Novartis have developed and patented a method for "switching off" the immune systems of plants, to the outrage of environmentalists and Third World charities who believe the new technology to be the most dangerous use so far of gene modification.

Patents filed by Novartis, manufacturers of Ovaltine, reveal that its scientists expect to be able to use the radical biotechnology for almost every crop on earth. Novartis claims that the new use of genetic modification (GM) will give farmers greater control over disease and boost production. But critics insist that it will make Third World farmers dependent on buying the company's chemicals each year to produce healthy harvests.

A spokeswoman for Novartis said, "We are trying to help farmers, not hinder them. We are looking at ways to improve the way plants fight disease." She agreed that the company had discovered a way of genetically modifying crops so that their immune systems were disabled, but stressed that this was for research purposes only. The process involves transferring a single DNA molecule, described by the firm as the NIM gene, to the plant. This gene then reacts with the plant's immune system, allowing it to be switched on selectively by the use of chemicals when disease threatens. But the patent also describes plants where the entire immune system has been switched off, making them highly prone to disease.

Environmentalists fear the new technology could have a disastrous ecological impact if crops with suppressed immune systems are allowed to cross-pollinate with surrounding plant life. The use of GM technology, which uses chemicals to activate genetic traits, was specifically condemned by the U.N. earlier this year. It recommended that the technology not be field-tested and called for a moratorium on its development until the impact had been fully assessed.

The patent documents seen by *The Observer* suggest that Novartis intends to use the new GM technology on barley, cucumbers, tobacco, rice, chillis, wheat, bananas, and tomatoes. The company cites an extensive list of more than 80 crops, including several cereals, dozens of fruits such as apples, pears, and strawberries, vegetables like beans and lentils, and cash crops like cotton and tea.

Alex Wijeratna of Action Aid, a charity that works with farmers in developing countries, said, "We find it extremely frightening that such a powerful multinational [corporation] is working on this type of technology, which seems aimed at protecting their profits by threatening the rights of poor farmers."

Dr. Sue Mayer, director of Gene Watch, says, "These companies should halt development of these potentially dangerous products until there has been a proper assessment of whether they are good for agriculture."

21 Large U.S Temp Company Undermines Union Jobs and Mistreats Workers

Source:
THE PROGRESSIVE POPULIST, June 1, 2001
Title: "Temps are Ready for Organizing If AFL-CIO Provides the Muscle"
Author: Harry Kelber

Faculty/Community Evaluator: Michael Robinson
Student Researchers: Eduardo Barragan & Connie Lytle

Labor Ready Inc. is a national temporary employment agency that employed over 700,000 people in 2000. Labor Ready has 839 offices in 49 states and in Canada, and stands ready to place temporary workers as strikebreakers in union labor disputes. During the recent Northwest steel strike, it was Labor Ready who provided hundreds of strikebreakers to Kaiser Aluminum in Spokane, Washington.

Labor Ready temps are often paid minimum wage for what can be very rigorous construction work. They receive no health benefits and can be seriously mistreated in their temporary places of employment. Workers are required to arrive at dispatch offices between 5:00 and 6:00 A.M. and wait for daily referrals; however, they are not paid for the waiting time at the dispatch office. Labor Ready workers also have to pay an average of $1.58 when they cash their daily paychecks at the company's cash-dispensing machines. In 1999, the company raked in $7.7 million in fees from these machines. Labor Ready's worker injury rate is three times the national average.

The AFL-CIO Building and Constructions Trade Department (BCTD) has supported class action lawsuits by former Labor Ready employees, and would like to see a national union organizing efforts to protect temporary workers nationwide.

BCTD President, Edward Sullivan stated, "Our organizing committee is wrestling with the growing threat posed by temporary employment agencies, which are selling themselves as 'hiring halls without the union' and sending thousands of construction workers out to jobs every day." Some 75 building and construction trades councils, and more than 100 local unions in 30 states are participating in BCTD's campaign to organize temporary workers. Labor Ready has been forced to close 10 percent of its hiring offices because of union activities, but there is still no noticeable improvement in wages or working conditions nationwide.

There are practical reasons a national union drive is difficult. Many temp workers are unskilled or semiskilled, with hourly wage rates of less than one-third the average union scale. Only about one-third of Labor Ready's employees work in construction. Most workers are used in manufacturing, trucking, landscaping, yard work, and other day-labor assignments. It is very difficult to organize such a transitory labor force.

UPDATE BY AUTHOR HARRY KELBER: As of the summer of 2002, AFL-CIO unions still have not shown any interest in organizing Labor Ready, perhaps the largest employer of temporary manual labor in the United States with more than 750 branch offices that hire out 650,000 workers a year. In fact, the AFL-CIO's official magazine, *America@Work*, and its other publications did not carry my story or any other about the plight of the Labor Ready temps, among the nation's most exploited workers.

The BCTD continues to expose Labor Ready's sleazy business practices, but has steadfastly refused to become involved in attempting to organize the company's employees, even though favorable conditions exist for a successful recruiting campaign.

The AFL-CIO is currently faced with an organizing crisis. It is woefully short of its announced goal to recruit one million new members this year. Labor Ready is an accessible target that is ripe for a multiunion campaign, once that could enlist the support of local unions in each community where a Labor Ready office is located. So why won't the AFL-CIO take on Labor Ready—or at least say why it won't?

22 Fish Farms Threaten Health of Consumers and Aquatic Habitats

Sources:
MOTHER JONES, November/December 2001
Title: "Aquaculture's Troubled Harvest"
Author: Bruce Barcott

PEW OCEANS COMMISSION REPORT on Marine Aquaculture, 2001,
<www.pewoceans.org>
Title: "Marine Aquaculture in the United States: Environmental Impacts and Policy Options"
Authors: Rebecca J. Goldburg, Matthew S. Elliott & Rosamond L. Naylor

Faculty Evaluator: Bill Crowley
Student Researchers: Anthony Sult & Adam Cimino

Farmed fish provide one-third of the seafood consumed by people worldwide. In the U.S., aquaculture supplies almost all of the catfish and trout as well as half of the shrimp and salmon. In the early 1990s, the fledgling aquaculture industry was hailed as a remedy to the problem of marine overfishing and the subsequent decline in jobs for fishermen. unfortunately, aquaculture's harm to people and surrounding environments may be greater than its highly anticipated benefits.

A recent Canadian study found that a single serving of farmed salmon contains three to six times the World Health Organization's recommended daily intake limit for dioxins and PCBs. A salmon farm of 200,000 fish releases an amount of nitrogen, phosphorus, and fecal matter roughly equivalent to the nutrient waste in untreated sewage from 20,000 to 25,000 people. Farmed salmon (usually called Atlantic or cultured Atlantic salmon) are genetically modified to be larger and have a 50 to 70 percent higher metabolic rate. When these super-fish get into the wild they compete unfairly for food resources, causing an increased rate of starvation among wild fish.

There is also a wide range of chemicals used in aquaculture, including antibiotics, parasiticides, pesticides, hormones, anesthetics, minerals, and vitamins. The use of these antibiotics is a health risk for fish as well as people, since it promotes the spread of antibiotic-resistance in both human and fish pathogens.

Canada is a major target for salmon farming. At first, salmon farms were welcomed for the jobs they would bring. Within a few years, however, large foreign corporations bought out many of the smaller operators. As the new operators took control, farms expanded and anchored their net pens in places where wild salmon smolts rested and fed on their way out to sea. Shrimp fishermen began pulling up traps full of back muck—a gooey mixture of feces, excess antibiotic-laden fish feed, and decayed salmon carcasses that had drifted out of the pens.

Other problems persist. Piercing acoustic sirens have been installed over salmon pens to keep seals and sea lions away, and the noise has caused killer whales to flee the Canadian archipelago. To rid their fish of sea lice, farmers dose them with ivermectin, a potent anti-parasitic known to kill some species of shrimp. Farmed fish contracted antibiotic-resistant stains of furunculous, a fatal disease that produces ugly skin ulcers; wild salmon that migrated past their pens also contracted the disease. Said one Canadian fishing guide, "I've been catching salmon up here all my life. I'd never seen a fish with a lesion until the farms came in."

Glen Neidrauer, a game warden who patrols the archipelago for Canada's Department of Fisheries and Oceans, said," I can appreciate the values of the jobs, but why would you jeopardize a place so pristine? We're not just talking fish. All the birds, bears, and sea mammals depend on the wild salmon. I wonder how long you can mess with that until they finally don't return."

COMMENTS BY ERVAND PETERSON, PROFESSOR OF ENVIRONMENTAL STUDIES, SONOMA STATE UNIVERSITY: Human numbers continue to grow exponentially and feeding ourselves is an everexpanding venture. The oceans today are experiencing impacts never before seen. Evidence of overfishing's impacts continues to mount. Aquaculture has been the industrialized technology employed to grow and harvest numerous aquatic resources.

For the past 40 years, beginning in Norway, salmon have been farmed in ocean pens. Environmental regulations in Norway have driven many to the Western Hemisphere. Today the inlets of British Columbia are caged off for the farming of salmon—Atlantic salmon to be accurate. Despite promises to contain the fish, an estimated 40,000 to 1 million have escaped and are spawning in streams native salmon use. Other impacts that have been documented show "dead zones" immediately adjacent to the salmon pens. A pen of 200,000 fish produces as much fecal waste as a city of more than 25,000 people.

We have seen this problem before with land grown livestock. Swine farms are notorious for their environmental impacts. Now we are seeing these impacts from aquaculture in the U.S. and Canada.

UPDATE BY AUTHOR BRUCE BARCOTT: This is merely one answer to the question that will dominate both environmental and consumer reporting in the next decade: What's in our food?

In the case of farmed salmon, the answer is too many antibiotics and a legacy of polluted marine waters. I came away from the story fairly hopeful, because this is an issue where individual consumers, not bought-off politicians, hold the power. The equation is simple, if strangely counterintuitive: Eat wild salmon to save wild salmon. Because the farmed stuff is junk, through and through.

In early 2002, the Canadian government lifted its seven-year moratorium on expanding British Columbia salmon farms. Multinational corporations could add 10 to 15 new B.C. farm sites every year, effectively doubling the industry's footprint over the next decade. Chile continues to dump below-market-price farmed salmon into the U.S., driving down worldwide prices and making it nearly impossible for Alaskan wild salmon fishermen, who operate sustainable, well-managed fisheries, to make a living. Meanwhile, Canadian researcher Michael Easton published a study in May 2002 that found elevated levels of PCBs in British Columbia farmed salmon. "Depending on whether you are a child or not," said Easton, "you would be advised not to eat farmed salmon more than once a week."

Before you get active on this issue, the best thing you can do is eat the stuff. Try a farmed salmon side by side with the real wild thing. You will become well informed with every forkful. The best information, pro and con, starts at Canada's David Suzuki Foundation <www.davidsuzuki.org> and the B.C. Salmon Farmers Association Web sites <www.salmonfarmers.org>.

23 Horses Face Lives of Unnecessary Abuse for Drug Company Profits

Source:
THE ANIMALS' AGENDA, MarchApril 2001
Title: "Pissing their Lives Away"

Faculty Evaluator: Wendy Ostroff
Student Researchers: Kelly Hand, Adam Cimino & Haley Mueller

Premarin, the top-selling hormone replacement therapy (HRT) for menopausal women, is made from pregnant mares' urine (PMU). Estrogen is extracted from the urine and is sold in many different forms to help with the symptoms of menopause. Approximately nine million women are currently taking some form of Premarin and that number is expected to rise due to aging baby boomers. Premarin, made by Wyeth-Ayerst Laboratories, a subsidiary of American Home Products, is the only human estrogen replacement drug that is derived from animal products, most others are derived from soy and vegetables. The patent on Premarin, owned by Wyeth-Ayerst, is about to expire. This may well result in the manufacture of an array of generic substitutes, and is likely to increase the number of horses used in this industry.

Pregnant horses are four-legged drug machines—being repeatedly impregnated and confined to narrow stalls as their urine is collected. Horses are kept inside for six months out of the year. The horses are housed in cramped stalls 8'x 3 1/2'x5'. Horses are hooked up to urine collection bags that are fixed into position just below their tail. These urine collection devises (UCDs) are painful and unhygienic. Urine soaks the skin of the vulva and can cause severe infection and painful lesions. The horses are tied with a short rope to keep them from taking more then a single step in either direction, or from lying down. After several years on line, the mares are shipped to slaughterhouses where they are butchered, so their meat can be exported to Europe or Japan for human consumption.

Today, there are 439 PMU farms still in existence. The majority are in Canada and a few are in North Dakota. In 1999 there were about 55, 000 to 65,000 mares on the "pee lines." Guidelines state that horses should be offered water no less then two times per day. However, PMU farmers prefer to water as little as possible to keep the concentration of estrogen in the urine high. They are paid based on the concentration not the volume of urine collected.

Every spring, each mare gives birth to a foal. These foals spend the first few months with their mothers and then are rounded up in September to allow their mothers to rejoin the lines. Most of these young horses are then taken to feed lots were they are fattened up and sold for slaughter. The meat is then exported to European and Asian markets for human consumption.

Ollie Bracken a retired Manitoba, Canada PMU farmer, stated in a 1995 interview that he retired from PMU farming because, "When you have to see a colt being born and then have to destroy it, it's rough because they're just babies. I just didn't think it was right to continue what I was doing."

According to a former PMU farmer from New York, "piss farms," as he called them, were located in New York and Vermont in the early 1950s. Urine was collected by Wyeth-Ayerst, a subsidiary of American Home Products in Philadelphia, and taken to Montreal, where it was processed into a powdered form and then shipped back to New York to be made into tablets and marketed. Most of the media attention regarding PMU farms has focused primarily on the mass production and slaughter of the foals born to the tens of thousands of mares annually. The heightened European demand for horse meat, due to the effects of mad cow and hoof-and-mouth disease has resulted in a dramatic increase in the number of horses slaughtered, and has caused the price of horse meat to go up.

COMMENTS BY BARBARA SEAMAN, CO-FOUNDER OF THE NATIONAL WOMEN'S HEALTH NETWORK: Premarin, the most popular variety of hormone replacement therapy, was approved as a menopause treatment by the FDA on May 8, 1942. From 1991 to 1999, it was the best-selling drug in the United States. It is now number three, behind Synthroid and Lipitor.

The relationship between Premarin and animal rights presents a valuable model of how industry interests protect themselves on a grand scale without regard to community well-being. In her article, "Pissing Their Lives Away," Susan Wagner writes about how Wyeth-Ayerst, the manufacturer of Premarin, has been exploiting and abusing horses for 60 years. Not just a clever name, Premarin is made from PREgnant MARes urINe. While Wagner raises compelling points about the issue of animal abuse, perhaps the most revealing drug company strategy discussed involves Wyeth-Ayerst's successful blockage of the approval of generic Premarin.

When a drug is approved, drug companies are granted a patent for a limited number of years before other, often smaller, companies are allowed to develop and market generic versions. By the mid 1990s, the patent on Premarin had sat in expiration for more than 25 years. In 1997, a company called Duramed pharmaceuticals applied for approval of a generic, soy-based, nonanimal version of Premarin called Cenestin. Previous to this application, the only condition for generic approval was identical active ingredients. A massive political battle ensued, with Wyeth-Ayerst exerting considerable financial pressure on powerful forces in Washington to intervene on their behalf. The result was the establishment of new, more ambiguous standards for generic drugs, in which testing for total active chemical similarity became the new measuring stick. Since, in 50 years, not all the chemicals in Premarin had been adequately clarified, it would be difficult to determine generic "bio-equivalency." In rejecting Duramed's application, the FDA specifically sited the absence of a chemical called DHES as essential to their conclusions. Previously qualified as an "impurity," DHES was a little understood, animal-specific element present in Premarin. Because the role of DHES in Premarin had not been documented, and Cenestin did not contain DHES, FDA argued that generic approval would be impossible, despite the total lack of evidence that DHES has any active properties. Cenestin was approved shortly after as a new drug rather than a generic.

This outrageous triumph of economic and political influence over patient interests is typical of the tactics employed by drug companies to protect and promote their top-selling drugs. A generic, nonanimal Premarin would be a great thing for HRT consumers. It would provide a lower-priced drug for the same results. It would also begin the important process of converting to the consumption of nonanimal estrogens. Women continue to pay high prices (around $300 a year), and horses continue to suffer, so that Wyeth can continue to reap maximum benefits from a drug that for much of its 60 year history has been one of the top 10 drugs in the United States.

Given the new consensus in the scientific community that neither animal- nor plant-based estrogen may be a healthy choice, perhaps 2002 will prove to be the year when the tide of the estrogen sea turns. If so, perhaps the history of HRT will serve as a model for exposing and controlling corrupt drug company policies. It is a story waiting patiently but imperatively to be told.

UPDATE BY AUTHOR SUSAN WAGNER, PRESIDENT, EQUINE ADVOCATED: Since writing the April 2000 cover story for *The Animals' Agenda*, entitled "Pissing Their Lives Away: How the Drug Industry Harms Horses," there have been many developments with respect to the PMU industry, most of which are negative. We have learned that while Premarin has gone from the most prescribed drug in the United States to second place, its maker, Wyeth Pharmaceuticals (formerly Wyeth-Ayerst Laboratories) took in a record $2 billion last year just from the sale of PMU drugs alone (Premarin, Prempro, and Premphase). This is because it has expanded its market to Third World countries where most women have little to say about what is given to them. Poor women have always been the victims of the drug companies, even in this country where women's clinics purchase large quanties of drugs and dispense them, often without giving their patients a choice and, in the case of PMU drugs, without telling them the origin and main ingredient (horse urine) of the drugs.

Another sad development is that the Canadian province of Ontario, which had banned PMU farming for years, is now allowing it again. The industry was literally forced out of Ontario and had to moved to Manitoba, Alberta and Saskatchewan. Now PMU farming is back in Ontario in a big way and many of the "farmers" are Amish. As president of Equine Advocates, I have been involved with the rescue of many Amish work and buggy horses over the years. I have found that many Amish farmers do not take good care of their animals and frequently unload their horses at slaughter auctions, where they are sold for meat when they can no longer work. It doesn't surprise me that the Amish are involved with the PMU industry. It does surprise me, however, that they have managed to establish farms in Ontario. Activists and environmentalists are trying to have the old law banning PMU farms in that province reinstated. What is also quite disturbing is that the horse urine collected in Ontario is being sold to generic drug companies in the United States awaiting FDA approval to produce generic PMU products, which would ultimately sell for 20 percent less than the name brands. More horses are suffering and dying because of the escalation of PMU production in Ontario and in the United States.

The media, in general, has been reluctant to cover the PMU story because the parent company, Wyeth, formally American Home Products, is a huge conglomerate with great influence over the media. It produces Advil, Robitussin, Solgar Vitamins, Anacin, Centrum, Chap Stick, Dimetapp, Preparation H, Fort Dodge Animal Health Products, QUEST (horse wormers), and numerous other drugs and products. This corporate giant has the clout and financial capability to pressure and silence the media. I am proud that Equine Advocates has been involved in numerous exposés on the subject of PMU production, including local and national television reports and newspaper and magazine articles. Many groups have done a great job in exposing the barbaric practice of using horses as four-legged drug machines, but much more has to be done in order for major changes to take place.

In our view, there is no longer any reason for horses to be used to produce conjugated estrogens (Premarin and other PMU products). This drug can be successfully produced in a lab (Cenestin) and does not possess the more than 30 unknown properties and impurities contained in conjugated estrogens made from horse urine. Ending the use of horses to produce PMU drugs is one of our main goals. Only through education and public awareness can we accomplish that goal. I thank Project Censored for recognizing this story so that more people can become aware of what has been a 60-year catastrophe for horses.

The most positive development is the recent study by the *International Position Paper on Women's Health and Menopause* as reported in a recent article in *The New York Times*. The findings, which will be issued by the National Institutes of Health, challenge and question the benefits of hormone replacement therapy (HRT). The study indicates that the risks of increased blood clots, breast cancer and other very serious conditions may not be worth the risks of taking it and that former claims about HRT preventing heart disease, Alzheimer's, and osteoporosis are questionable.

24 Wal-Mart Takes Union Busting to the State Level

Source:
MADISON CAPITAL TIMES, August 2001
Title: "Wal-Mart Ravages Workers' Rights"
Author: John Nichols
Reprinted ASHEVILLE GLOBAL REPORT, September 6, 2001

Faculty Evaluator: Phil McGough
Student Researcher: Kathy Jensen

Wal-Mart has been pouring a considerable amount of money into a political campaign supporting a law that will reduce the wages and benefits for workers in Oklahoma. Oklahomans voted on the "right-to-work" law in September of 2001. The law bans labor contracts that require workers to pay union dues or representation fees. The law also makes it difficult for unions to negotiate solid contracts. Wal-Mart hopes to use Oklahoma as a model for a renewed campaign to reduce the wages and benefits for workers nationwide.

This campaign will inevitably undermine the ability of unions to effectively organize. The right-to-work law has union members angered and concerned, as expressed by a member of the International Brotherhood of Electrical Workers: "Union members across the country should take note of Wal-Mart's support of measures like 'right-to-work' before they spend any of their union wages at Wal-Mart stores." Right-to-work laws were developed in the 1940s by segregationists to keep African Americans, Latinos, and white workers in the South and Southwest from unionizing. Right to work laws were among the vile legacies of an era when conservatives worked at the state and national level to erect legal barriers to racial progress. Only two states have passed right to work laws since the civil rights era.

In the 21 states with right-to-work laws, the medium household income is $4,882 less than states where workers are free to organize effective unions. These states have higher poverty rates and less health insurance coverage than states without right-to-work laws.

Oklahoma rejected a right-to-work law in 1964, when Martin Luther King Jr. came to campaign against the proposal. This time around, however, powerful right-wing interests combined with Wal-Mart to push the initiative. *The Daily Oklahoman* contributed advertising space and Governor Frank Keating and U.S. Senator Don Nickles campaigned in support of passage.

Author John Nichols writes, "In a sense, it is a good investment for Wal-Mart, which often has a hard time finding workers willing to accept low wages paid at it stores. If the Oklahoma campaign is a success, right-to-work advocates hope to use it as a model for passing similar initiatives in Colorado, Indiana, Kentucky, Montana, New Hampshire, and New Mexico."

UPDATE: On September 25, 2001 the voters of Oklahoma passed the right-to-work law by a 54 percent margin. Wal-Mart contributed $250,000 to the campaign. AFL-CIO has filed legal challenges to the law.

25 Federal Government Bails Out Failing Private Prisons

Source:
THE AMERICAN PROSPECT, September 10, 2001
Title: "Bailing Out Private Jails"
Author: Judith Greene

Faculty Evaluator: Pat Jackson
Student Researchers Erich Lehmann & Michelle Oliva

Corporate media coverage: WALL STREET JOURNAL, November 6, 2001

For close to a decade, the private prison industry was booming because state legislators thought they could be both tough on crime and fiscally conservative by contracting with private prisons. However, private prisons have been rife with more abuse and lawsuits than state-run prisons, leading to a decline in state level support. By last year, not a single state solicited private contracts and many contracts were rolled back or even rescinded as a result of inefficiency and abuses.

The largest private prison in the U.S., The Corrections Corporation of America (CCA), has been criticized for widespread abuses and high rates of escape. In April of 2001, prison guards at Cibola County Correctional Center in New Mexico teargassed 700 inmates who had staged a daylong nonviolent protest of conditions at the facility. Additionally a score of lawsuits have been filed for beatings of prisoners, lack of proper medical treatment, and corruption among staff. Other private companies have similar records. Wackenhut prisons, the second largest private-prison company, has had many similar problems and repeated breakouts of violence.

Problems are often the consequence of companies' attempts to hold down costs. Prisons for profit have resulted in low pay for guards and a high turnover rate of underqualified staff. Whereas guards who work for state-run prisons receive benefits and are usually union members, private prisons tend to hire less-qualified, lower-cost personnel.

While most state correctional officials are aware of the problems, the federal government continues to expand contracts with the private prison industry. Private prison industry officials make significant campaign contributions and their lobbyists have spread their influence widely in Congress. High-ranking private prison company officials have served as directors of the Federal Bureau of Prisons (FBOP) under former presidents Reagan and Bush. U.S. government pending private prison contracts are up to over $4.6 billion for the next 10 years. With the new federal contracts, CCA, which carried more than $1 billion in outstanding debt, was able to avoid bankruptcy and continue in business.

Harsh drug laws have increased the federal prison population, but federal immigration polices are less known. The 1996 Immigration Reform Act expanded the list of crimes for which noncitizens could be deported after serving their sentences. About 36,000 noncitizens are now in federal prisons, close to double what it was only seven years ago. Immigrants make up 9.3 percent of the U.S. population, but disproportionately compose 29 percent of the federal prison population. About half of federal prisoners are Mexican, 10 percent Colombian, 7 percent Cuban, and the rest are a mix of other nationalities. Only 1.5 percent were sentenced for violent offenses compared with 15 percent in state prisons.

The FBOP is now proposing up to 7,500 low-security beds in California, Arizona, New Mexico, Texas, and Oklahoma. Additionally several thousand are being proposed elsewhere in the nation. The private, for-profit prison industry is deemed most likely to receive these upcoming contracts.

Prison reform advocates and correctional officers are fighting the expansion of private prisons. Democratic Congressman Ted Strickland of Ohio, and Republican Congressman John E. Sweeney of New York have introduced federal legislation that would deny contracts with private prisons from the FBOP or by states who contract with private prisons. Nevertheless, the federal government is making sure the private prison industry continues.

UPDATE BY AUTHOR JUDITH GREENE: "Bailing Out Private Jails" questioned the appropriateness of a federal contracting initiative for private prisons designed to segregate immigrant prisoners convicted of low-level, non-violent offenses who face deportation once their sentences are served out. Two months after the article's publication, these concerns were echoed in a front page story in the *Wall Street Journal*.

After public exposure of the critical issues surrounding the immigrant prison contracting initiative, the FBOP awarded one last contract to CCA, but the agency cancelled four more in-the-pipeline contract solicitations that had been slated for awards during 2002. At the state level, the market for new private prisons remained stalled. Facing severe budget constraints, public officials in California and Ohio targeted a number of private prisons for closure. Anti-privatization activists won a hard-fought battle to stop Cornell Companies from obtaining legislative approval for a 1,200-bed private prison they proposed to build. Correctional authorities in Puerto Rico ended two prison management contracts with CCA and slated a third for termination, after they determined that public operation of the prisons would be more cost-effective.

By the summer of 2002, CCA continued to struggle to regain its financial footing, but with 8,500 empty prison beds, the company still had far to go. In the wake of the events of September 11, 2001, private prison company executives expressed hopes that a large-scale increase in detention of undocumented immigrants (if it materialized) would serve to boost the federal market for detention beds, with the Immigration and Naturalization Service (INS) replacing the FBOP as the new target of opportunity.

Prison activists, students, immigration rights advocates, and unionists continue to organize opposition to the spread of private prisons and detention centers, and to diminish the role these companies play in fueling the prison-industrial complex. Some of the key organizations and contacts include:

Kate Rhee, Prison Moratorium Project, 388 Atlantic Avenue 3rd Floor, Brooklyn, NY 11217, Tel: (718) 260-8805, E-mail: <krhee@nomoreprisons.org>, Web sites: <www.nomoreyouthjails.org>, and <www.nomoreprisons.org>; Rose Braz, Critical Resistance, 1212 Broadway, Suite 1400, Oakland, CA 94612, Tel: (510) 444-0484, Fax: (510) 444-2177, E-mail: <Rosebraz@aol.com>, Web site: <www.critical resistance.org>; and Judy Greene, Justice Strategies, 199 Washington Avenue, Brooklyn, NY 11205, Tel: (718) 857-3316, Fax: (718) 857-3315, E-mail: <greenej1 @mindspring.org>.

Project Censored Runners-up 2002

THE HAND THAT RULES THE VISA MACHINE ROCKS THE WORLD

Source: COVERTACTION QUARTERLY, Winter 2001
Author: J. Michael Springmann, Esq.

During the late 1980s the CIA used visa consulates in Saudi Arabia to round up recruits for terrorist training in the United States in order to fight Soviets in Afghanistan. According to then chief of the visa section at the Jeddah Consulate, Michael Springmann, the State Department did not control the consulates in Saudi Arabia; the CIA did. Of some 20 staff members at the consulate in Jeddah, only three people had no ties to any of the U.S. intelligence services.

Between 1987 and 1988, high-level State Department officials repeatedly ordered Mr. Springmann to issue visas to clearly unqualified applicants. Often, when he denied a visa, his decision would simply be reversed by the chief of the consular section. The issuance of these visas, both tourist and business, violated the Immigration and Nationality Act as well as the State Department's own regulations, which states that the adjudicating officer had the first, last, and generally only word on visa issuance or denial.

Also during this time, the Jeddah Consulate was making a considerable amount of money selling alcoholic beverages, illegal in Saudi Arabia, to Saudis and expatriates. These sales were later investigated by the Marine Corps headquarters, but many of the proceeds were never accounted for. It has been alleged that the funds were used to underwrite expenses involved in the CIA recruitment process, such as buying airline tickets for the recruits to travel to the U.S. for terrorist training and back.

By the end of Mr. Springmann's tenure as visa section chief in Jeddah, staff members and applicants who wanted visas went directly to the chief of the consular section for their stamps. Springmann saved copies of the visa applications for which his decision had been reversed or bypassed. Over an 18-month period they totaled nearly a 100.

DOWNED ANIMALS ON YOUR PLATE

Source: <WWW.IMPACTPRESS.COM>, April 5, 2001
Author: Gene Bauston

Downed animals are those that are alive, but so sick and diseased that they are unable to stand. Each year thousands of these animals are slaughtered for human food, posing a health risk to millions of Americans.

It is impossible to transport downed animals humanely. They are dragged with wenches and chains or pushed with tractors and forklifts. These methods cause injuries such as bruises, abrasions, broken bones, and ligaments. As downed animals are incapable of moving, they endure days with no food. Most of them die because of gross neglect or denied basic veterinary attention.

The USDA has failed to prohibit the slaughtering of downed animals, asserting that the law does not prohibit the use of diseased animals for human food.

UPDATE BY AUTHOR GENE BAUSTON: The marketing and slaughter of downed animals, animals too sick even to stand, poses potentially life threatening risks to human consumers, and it results in intolerable animal cruelty. These incapacitated animals are commonly left to suffer for hours or days without receiving food, water or veterinary care, and many die of neglect. Those who survive are inhumanely dragged with chains or pushed with tractors on their way to slaughter. Downed animals are the consequence of cruel and irresponsible farming practices, and most cases of downed animals can be prevented by improving animal care practices. Removing the market for downed animals will help focus attention on improving animal husbandry practices in order to prevent the problem in the first place.

There have been several significant developments since the April/May 2001 article, "Downed Animals: Diseased Food on your Plate," was published in Impact Press. After ten years of lobbying for the Downed Animal Protection Act in Washington, DC, a measure to prohibit the marketing of downed animals at livestock markets finally passed both the U.S. House of Representatives and the U.S. Senate as part of the Farm Bill. The House and Senate Farm Bills were then referred to a conference committee so that differences between House and Senate language could be reconciled. Both the House and Senate downed animal provisions prohibited the marketing of downed animals at livestock markets, and both required that these incapacitated animals be humanely euthanized or provided with veterinary care. But despite the House and Senate versions being nearly identical, and in defiance of the clearly expressed will of Congress, the agribusiness-friendly conference committee completely removed the downed animal protection legislation from the final version of the Farm Bill and replaced it with a study. The Downed Animal Protection Act (H.R. 1421 and S. 267) remains alive in Washington, DC, but faces an uphill battle. Meanwhile, Farm Sanctuary has continued to generate support for its petition before the Food and Drug Administration (FDA) to prevent downed animal slaughter. Over 30,000 comments have now been received by the Agency urging that it grant Farm Sanctuary's petition. Additionally, in November 2001, Farm Sanctuary filed a lawsuit against the United States Department of Agriculture (USDA), asserting that the slaughter of downed animals for human food is a violation of federal law and that the practice must stop.

The mainstream press has been very slow to cover the downed animal issue. When Farm Sanctuary filed its lawsuit against the USDA in November 2001 we publicized the case widely, but were only able to gain coverage on one national television outlet, CNN.

For more information on the effort to prevent the marketing and slaughter of downed animals, please check out Farm Sanctuary's No Downers campaign Web site, at <www.NoDowners.org>, or contact Farm Sanctuary, P.O. Box 150, Watkins Glen, NY 14891; Tel. (607) 583-2225; Fax (607) 583-2041; <www.FarmSanctuary.org>.

WHY BIOTECH COMPANIES ARE CLAMORING FOR NATIVE AMERICAN DNA

Source: SPIRIT OF CRAZY HORSE, November/December 2000
Author: Ron Selden

Biotech research is being done for profit, at the expense of indigenous peoples and their traditions. Tissue, blood, hair, and other samples have been taken without the consent of these native peoples and sold to researchers. The DNA samples are then used to determine who may have come from whom and where.

Researchers for the biotech companies also have special interest in native peoples because some groups have unsual immunities or propensities for various diseases. According to Judy Gobert, chairwoman of the Nevada-based Indigenous Peoples' Council on Biocolonialism, some biotech companies have become so desperate that they have had representatives approach Indian schoolchildren in California and offer them $100 for a single blood sample. Samples are also taken without consent through routine medical exams or through sources who do not reveal that the materials might be sold to third parties.

SECRETS R US

Source: TOWARD FREEDOM, August/September 2001
Author: Greg Guma

On April 20, 2001, Peru's air force mistakenly shot down a private plane carrying U.S. missionaries. ABC initially reported that the plane had been identified as a drug runner by Dyncorp, a CIA subcontractor in the region. However, after two days, the reference to Dyncorp was deleted from ABC's report. The *New York Post* claimed a week later that another CIA firm Aviation Development Corp. actually gave the order to shoot down the missionaries.

Private companies staffed by ex-military officers enjoy almost total freedom in the conducting of the NSA/CIA business worldwide. They constitute a vast foreign policy apparatus that is largely invisible, rarely covered by the corporate press, and not currently subject to congressional oversight. The Freedom of Information Act does not apply to private contractors. The two largest firms, MPRI and Scycorp, currently have operations in Bosnia, Macedonia, Croatia, Colombia, Bolivia, Peru, Nigeria, Equatorial Guinea, and numerous other countries.

THE CHAIN NEVER STOPS

Source: MOTHER JONES, July/August 2001
Author: Eugene Richards

American slaughterhouses are the most dangerous workplaces in the United States. They have the highest injury rate, and the highest rate of serious injury—more than five times the national average.

Changes in what used to be a safer and more lucrative industrial job came in the 1970s when the Iowa Beef Packers (IBP) revolutionized the industry by moving their plants away from union strongholds and bringing in Mexican immigrants to form a new division of labor that eliminated the demand for experienced butchers. Other companies had to adopt IBP's methods or go out of business: wages fell, and unions grew weaker.

Technological innovations allowed cattle to be processed at increasingly faster speeds: 25 years ago, the typical line speed was 175 cows per hour; now it's 400 cows per hour. In the fast-paced production line, surrounded by dangerous machinery, workers are routinely maimed and sometimes fatally injured.

Because many slaughterhouses are self-insured, they have a vested interest in maintaining low workers' comp payments. Injured employees seeking compensation are discouraged on a number of levels—from supervisors whose bonuses are tied to the injury rate of their workers to assignation of injured workers to unpleasant and meaningless tasks.

THE JUDGE AS LYNCH MOB

Source: THE AMERICAN PROSPECT, May 7, 2001
Author: Ken Silverstein

Alabama judges use judicial overrides to disregard juries and impose death sentences. Alabama is one of the few states that allow judges to ignore a jury's recommendation of life without parole and unilaterally impose the death penalty. Thirty-two individuals—about one-sixth of the current population of Alabama's death row—were sent there by judges who overruled the jury.

Judge Ferrill McRae has employed the use of "override" more than any other Alabama magistrate. In six cases, the judge has "enhanced" the jury's decision of life without parole. Judge Ferrill McRae has a reputation for displaying "folksy moralism" in his courtroom. The judge often makes sexist and racial slurs towards the defendants and the officers of the court. Both friends and foe of the judge say that he is famous for his "salty language."

Popular and political support for the death penalty is strong in the South. In Alabama, judges are elected to office, whereas in most states judges are appointed. Alabama has the largest number of people per capita on death row. It is rated by the American Bar Association as having the worst criminal defense system in the country.

'NEW ECONOMY' HIGH-TECH JOBS LOOK MUCH LIKE OLD ECONOMY LOW-WAGE WORK
Source: LABOR NOTES, Thursday, August 9, 2001
Author: Patrick Moran

According to *Labor Notes* magazine, the "new economy" promise of high wages, stellar stock options, and premium benefits has been replaced with mediocre wages, useless stock options, mandatory overtime, and unaffordable family health insurance. The notion that life gets better with the advancements in technology has proven to be untrue for workers in companies such as Microsoft and Amazon.

On Thanksgiving Day, Amazon workers received the "privilege" of having their families come to the warehouse for Thanksgiving dinner. After dinner, their families went home while the workers returned to work. During the holiday rush, a traffic light was installed in the New Castle, Delaware distribution center of Amazon. At the end of their shifts the workers had to take note of the color of the traffic light. Green meant they could go home; yellow implied voluntary overtime; and red signified that they could not go home. Last year some workers were forced to work for 14 straight days during the Christmas rush. Today's high-tech work environment, says *Labor Notes*, bears a striking resemblance to the industrial sweatshops 150 years ago.

The Communication Workers of America (CWA) and its project, Washington Alliance of Technology Workers' (WashTech) began an organizing effort in 1998 to link together high-tech workers in the Seattle area from companies such as Amazon and Microsoft. Also the Prewitt Organization Fund, a non-profit group formed by labor organizers to help workers organize, started the Alliance of New Economy Workers (ANEW) to organize Amazon's distribution center workers worldwide in mid-2000. Yet despite these efforts, most of today's high tech-workers remain without labor representation.

BATTLEGROUND ALASKA
Source: IN THESE TIMES, September 3, 2001
Author: Jeffrey St. Clair

In 1999, a 3,500-acre Kodiak Launch Complex was presented to Alaskans as a commercial spaceport that would provide many high paying jobs for residents, new schools, and a cultural center. The endeavor was to be run by a state-chartered company called the Alaska Aerospace Development Corporation whose goal was to launch telecommunications, remote sensing, and space science payloads into orbit. Soon, however, the corporation claimed to be having financial problems and the project was taken over by the U.S. Air Force. (There is some indication that this may have been the plan all along).

Today the complex on Alaska's Kodiak Island has been converted from an economy boosting aerospace research center into an experimental missile launch site by the United States government. The island is now the main launching point for George W. Bush's "Star Wars" plan to develop satellite defense systems to counter attacks on America.

The greatest misfortune of this conversion is that the rocket boosters, containing magnesium, hydrazine, and radioactive thorium, fall into the ocean and are not recovered. After launch, the exhaust trail of the missiles are toxic as well, with 8,000 pounds of aluminum oxide leaving a trail of poisonous smoke. One of the launch trajectories sends missiles over the fishing villages of Akhiok and Old Harbor, across one of the most pristine salmon spawning grounds in the world.

THE VIOLENCE INITIATIVE PROJECT:
COMING SOON TO A NEIGHBORHOOD NEAR YOU!
Source: THE SHADOW, Fall 2000
Author: Mitchel Cohen

The latest trend in science is to attribute everything one says, does, or has, to genes. New and dangerous genetically engineered drugs are being tested in prisons, mental institutions, Indian reservations, and Third World countries. These venues provide human guinea pigs for what the government considers important research. The Violence Initiative Project is the name given to these experiments.

Scientists running the project are looking for a biological configuration that causes violence and other criminal behavior. DNA samples have been taken from prisoners who have a violent record, to keep on file for comparison at a later date with someone who does not have a predilection towards violence. Children who have older siblings with histories of violence are also subjected to DNA sampling to see if they may share the gene for violence. Most of the subjects of the Violence Initiative Project are African Americans and Latinos.

ARCTIC HEAT WAVE
Source: THE PROGRESSIVE, October 2001
Author: Bruce E. Johansen

In the Canadian Arctic, global warming has caused the ocean's permafrost base to begin to dissolve, causing a wave of ecological change that affects the Native people and their environment.

The change in weather greatly effects Inuit villages and their environment. Swallows, sandflies, and robins now migrate to the Arctic. Mosquitoes and beetles are a common sight where they were virtually unknown a generation ago. The ice-based ecosystem is sustained by upwelling nutrients that feed the plankton, shrimp, and other small organisms. These organisms feed the fish, which in turn feed the seals, which feed the bears. Seals and bears are noticeably suffering from the change in the environment. Because of limited prey, the polar bears around Hudson Bay are 90 to 220 pounds lighter than they were 30 years ago. Many Native people who fish and hunt for their sustenance are similarly deprived of their way of life. Inuit hunters have reported that hunting conditions have grown more dangerous from unpredictable storms and unsually thin ice. Within two or three generations, many Inuit have become urbanized as a result of the changing environment. Six hundred Native people in the village of Shishmaref are watching their village erode into the sea. According to the University of Alaska, mean temperatures in the state have increased by five degrees Fahrenheit during summer and ten degrees in the winter. Life in the Arctic is being permanently altered as a result of global warming.

DIOXIN AND OTHER CHEMICALS IN ALASKA
FOUND TO COME FROM MINNESOTA
Source: THE CIRCLE, August 2001
Author: Winona LaDuke

Inupiat people living in Port Graham, Alaska and the Inuit community in Nunavut, Canada are showing alarmingly high levels of toxic substances in their bodies. Mother's milk in the Arctic contains twice the levels of dioxin as mothers in lower Canada. Yet the closest source of dioxin is over 500 kilometers away.

This danger from pollutants is concentrated for the Inupiat people because they tend to eat traditional foods based on fish. These fish contain concentrated amounts of toxins that collect in fatty tissue over time.

The toxins that are most prevalent in northern climates are called POPs, or persistent organic pollutants. These pollutants are formed from a combination of pesticides, industrial chemicals, and dioxin. The toxins are moved via air and water currents that tend to head toward colder areas. There are over 44,000 sources of dioxin in North America. Dioxins are long-lived and tend to migrate over time. The origin of many of these toxins can be traced to the garbage produced by the emissions from United States incinerators. Two of these incinerators have been found in Red Wing, Minnesota, and La Crosse, Wisconsin.

REACTOR REVIVAL
Source: MOTHER JONES, November/December 2001
Author: Susan Q. Stranahan

The nuclear energy industry, with much support from the Bush Administration, is pushing to extend the life of aging nuclear reactors, despite increasing evidence that as nuclear plants grow old, they also grow unsafe. Old, even defective, nuclear reactor plants are requesting additional funding and license renewals, and these requests are being granted.

The Nuclear Regulatory Commission (NRC) has begun to accept applications to extend licenses to existing power plants, allowing plant owners to squeeze another two decades of funding from their aging facilities. By the end of 2004, companies are expected to seek license renewals for a third of the 103 plants that are now in operation. In the rush to keep these reactors going, regulators are ignoring signs of wear and tear in these aging plants. In a recent study of NRC records, it was discovered that eight reactors were taken out of service because of age-related problems between March 2000 and April 2001. One of the shutdowns took place in North Anna Unit 2 in Virginia, four months before the plant's owner requested an extension from the NRC.

THE POLITICS OF POLLEN
Source: EARTH ISLAND JOURNAL, Spring 2001
Author: Tom Ogren

Deaths from asthma continue to climb each year at alarming epidemic rates. And although in many cities there is less total vegetation than there used to be pollen levels are higher than ever before.

In dioecious (separate sexed) species, there are distinct male and female versions of the same plant. Female trees and shrubs do not produce any pollen, but they do produce messy seeds, fruits, old flowers, and seedpods. Many people consider these by-products to be a litter problem and consequently, female trees and shrubs are rarely used.

In the past 20 years, landscapers have favored using male trees and 4 out of 5 street trees now for sale are male. Female trees are natural pollen traps and air scrubbers. This change in landscaping practices has resulted in huge pollen count increases in our cities.

Five U.S. cities—Tucson, Phoenix, Las Vegas, El Paso, and Albuquerque—have enacted pollen control ordinances. There is now an allergy rating scale available for plants with 1 being the least allergenic and 10 the most allergenic. This system, known as the Ogren Plant Allergy Scale, is used by the USDA to list pollen rates for most major U.S. cities. The list provides our politicians and the public with the information needed to prevent pollen-related illnesses and deaths.

NO RELIEF: BEHIND ARGENTINA'S ECONOMIC MELTDOWN
Source: IN THESE TIMES, February 18th, 2002
Author: David Moberg

Eight years after the military seized power in Argentina in 1976, the country's foreign debt grew to $46 billion dollars. Multiple financial plans have been constructed to help, but the crisis only seems to worsen. In 1991, the government of Carlos Menem pegged the peso's value to the U.S. dollar, causing more strain on Argentina's economy. The Argentine government also privatized government utilities, ended capital controls, privatized social security, opened the economy (including the banking system) to foreign investment, reduced trade barriers, and committed itself to a balanced budget. As a result there was a huge influx of foreign investment ,which currently controls 75 percent of the banking system and 40 percent of the nation's industry. By the year 2000, wages were worth only 30 percent of what they were worth in 1975. The unemployment rate is currently over 20 percent. The Argentine elite have continued to prosper while the middle class and working class have paid dearly; the number of people living in poverty has risen from 1 million to 14 million.

ACADEMIC CASUALTIES OF WITCH HUNT IN SOUTH FLORIDA
Source: WORKING FOR CHANGE, January 16, 2002
Author: Bill Berkowitz

Tenured Florida University professor Dr. Sami Al-Arian was fired by University of South Florida for speaking out after the 9-11 attack.

In late September Dr. Al-Arian appeared on the *O'Reilly Factor*, a Fox TV talk show. During the show, he spoke strongly in defense of his brother-in-law, who was being held without charges under anti-terrorist laws in the U.S.

After the TV interview, Professor Al-Arian received several death threats. The university claimed that he was disruptive presence and threatened student safety.

An emergency meeting of the board of trustees was held in December. During the meeting only trustees, the president, the chief of police and university lawyers were allowed to speak. Dr. Al-Arian was not allowed to be present. The board decided to fire Dr. Al-Arian based on the belief that his presence on campus was a danger to others, and that he had negatively impacted the university's fundraising efforts.

SCANDAL OF SCIENTISTS WHO TAKE MONEY FOR PAPERS GHOSTWRITTEN BY DRUG COMPANIES

Source: THE GUARDIAN (London), February 7, 2002
Author: Sarah Boseley

Scientists are accepting large sums of money from drug companies to put their names to articles that they may not have written endorsing new medicines.

The decline in state and federal funding for research has left scientists dependent on pharmaceutical companies to fund or commission their work. This has given the industry unprecedented control over data and paved the way for papers to be drafted by company employees or commercial agencies. It is alleged that, in some cases, doctors will not have seen the raw data on the drugs, only tables that are compiled by company employees.

Ghostwriting has become especially widespread among fields that require drugs as treatment, such as psychiatry and cardiology. Doctors are plied with expensive gifts and trips to luxurious settings. Additionally, they are paid anywhere from $2,000 to $10,000 dollars to introduce new drugs to other doctors in large presentations. It is becoming increasingly unclear to medical audiences whether the presenter is promoting the drug because he believes in it, or because he is receiving a financial gain.

Some scientific journals propose to demand a signed declaration that the papers scientists submit are indeed their own. Fuller Torrey, director of Stanley Research Foundation, states, "Some of us believe that the present system is approaching a high-class form of professional prostitution."

GAY RIGHTS UNDER ATTACK NATIONWIDE

Source: THE SLANT, October 2001
Author: Patrick Letellier

Members of the far right in the U.S. have developed a strategy of using ballot initiatives to attack anti-discrimination laws affecting gays and lesbians. Nationwide, voters have rejected gay rights at the polls in five of the six places considering them in the past year. Perhaps hardest hit is Michigan, where two gay rights laws have been repealed and several more are under challenge. The only state to survive a referendum thus far is Oregon, which last year managed to narrowly defeat a "no pomo homo" law that sought to prohibit any positive references to homosexuality in schools across the state. According to the National Lesbian and Gay Task Force, at least 10 other cities and states in the U.S. will face anti-gay ballot measures in the next year.

PANAMA-POLLUTED AND ABANDONED

Source: TOWARD FREEDOM, September/October 2000
Author: Ron Chepesiuk

When the U.S. handed the Panama Canal over to the Panamanian government in December of 1999, it left behind a dangerous environmental mess. Years of military training and munitions testing in Panama left hundreds of thousands of unexploded shells, grenades, and land mines over 7,000 hectares of land inhabited by at least 60,000 people. Many of these munitions contain depleted uranium, Agent Orange, and other contaminants that seep into the ground water.

The U.S. Department of Defense (DOD) admits that the cleanup will cost over $3 billion and take 15 to 20 years to complete. Nevertheless, despite protests by environmental groups in Panama, the U.S. maintains that it lived up to its obligation by turning the canal over to Panama and leaving.

U.S. FARMERS EXPLOIT FOREIGN GUEST WORKERS

Source: MOTHER JONES, January 2001
Author: Barry Yeoman

Some 42,000 workers on H-2A visas—mainly from Mexico, Jamaica, and Peru— now harvest crops all over the United States. Farmers often mistreat workers without fear of being penalized. Workers know they can be deported at any time, so they do not complain about rat-infested housing, denials of medical care, unrecorded work hours, and control over their personal mail and shopping opportunities. While standards on paper are high, few inspections occur and workers view complaints as a ticket home.

Studies show that there is actually an agricultural labor surplus in the country, yet the H-2A visa program has remained open. Farmers use numeros tricks to claim that local labor is unavailable. In Idaho, for example, the Snake River farmer's association urged its members to write backbreaking job descriptions to discourage local labor from applying.

THE PRISON AS LABORATORY

Source: IN THESE TIMES, January 7, 2002

Author: Silja J.A. Talvi

The prison has long been a hiding place for human research on inmates, who are often kept in the dark about possible side effects. Prison research is now on the rise, and is violating several federal laws.

Research involving human subjects has become big business. With the high numbers of people currently incarcerated, researchers are eager to test experimental procedures on a variety of chronic medical problems, ranging from asthma to cancer. Prisoners present an ideal type of test group because of the broad array of medical problems that most prisoners possess. In October of 2000, nearly 300 former inmates filed suit against the University of Pennsylvania for injuries, lingering physical illness, and psychological trauma. Many clinical trials have been reported to the Office of Human Research Protections (OHRP) as having violated federal law. Some of the research areas reported include the inducement of labor, obtaining biopsies on inmates, testing experimental vaccines for HIV, and direct injection of a powerful chemotherapy drug into the liver. One of the more shocking studies involved heavily sedating inmates and inserting tubes into their veins and neck to obtain blood. The blood would then be heated up and put back into the inmates, inducing a two-hour-long hyperthermia. Inmates sign a waiver acknowledging possible side effects, and they must waive their right to pursue financial compensation in the event of physical harm. An ongoing problem is the lack of reporting to the OHRP by universities conducting studies.

ENDANGERED WILDLIFE FRIENDS ARE HERE!

Source: PR WATCH, Third Quarter 2001

Author: John Stauber

In 2001, the National Wildlife Federation (NWF) formed a partnership with the oil company BP/Amoco. In gas stations throughout the country, posters carrying both the NWF and the BP/Amoco logos were displayed, inviting patrons to purchase stuffed toys ("Endangered Wildlife Friends") representing endangered animals. The sales, according to the poster, would help raise funds for the NWF. In addition, customers who purchased eight or more gallons of gasoline could also receive a free stuffed animal—bagged in plastic and bearing the label "Made in China."

Philip Kavits, NWF's Vice President of Communications, when questioned about the partnership, initially asserted that the affiliation allowed NWF to "reach a new audience." He later admitted that his organization has no evidence that this stuffed animal campaign raised the public's awareness of environmental issues. He also admitted that he did not know if the "Made in China" logo on the animals meant that the toys were created in sweatshops, although he stated that NWF's partnership with BP/Amoco did not imply an endorsement. According to Kavits, BP/Amoco donated roughly $113,000 dollars to the NWF, although he also stated that the partnership with BP is a "small one compared with others we've done," and "BP is one of a huge number of partners that we've dealt with."

BAYER: NOT JUST ASPIRIN

Source: WASHINGTON FREE PRESS, January/February, 2002
Authors: Kavaljit Singh and Philipp Mimkes,Coalition Against Bayer-Dangers

Though its pharmaceutical division draws most of the media's attention, Bayer pesticides are poisoning the people and environments of Peru, Nepal, and Cambodia. In Peru, 24 children were killed and 18 more severely poisoned when they drank a powdered milk substitute that had been contaminated with the pesticide methyl parathion (the Bayer brand name is Folidol). In Nepal, after pesticides such as DDT and organomercury chlorides were banned, Bayer simply discarded them. The chemicals seeped into the ground water, contaminating water supplies and threatening residents' health. Cambodia also serves as a dumping ground for toxic chemicals that cannot be sold in neighboring countries. Folidol is the most popular pesticide in Cambodia despite the fact that its misuse has caused an outbreak of pests that has devastated rice crops. Bayer recently succeeded in reducing competition when the company was able to reverse Canada's decision to suspend Bayer's patent of the anthrax treatment Cipro.

DIGITAL DIPLOMAS

Source: MOTHER JONES, January/February 2001
Authors: Eyal Press and Jennifer Washburn

Many universities are partnering with corporations to offer diploma programs online, spurring critics to question whether profit instead of education is the ultimate goal. Though touted by proponents as a way to democratize higher education, many critics foresee a two-tiered educational system with prestigious campus-based learning for the elites and distance learning for the working class. Professors may be paid a flat fee for lectures, course materials, and other intellectual property, which can be marketed and distributed at will by the universities and their outside vendors.

Online-learning business venture <unext.com> offers its partner schools an estimated $20 million in royalties, and the option to convert the royalties into shares in an initial public offering, in exchange for the right to market jointly-developed online courses bearing the schools' brand names. University deans and trustees can also be online university shareholders and officers, as was the case in <unext.com>'s deal with the University of Chicago. This is a conflict of interest that makes it unclear if online universities are making decisions based on the best interests of their students or the best interests of their shareholders.

According to a study by a Georgetown professor, students enrolled in online classes are often discouraged by the isolation. Social interaction is important to the students and their prospective employers. Seventy-seven percent of human resources officers surveyed by the employment Web site <vault.com> stated that they did not consider an online degree to be equivalent to a campus-based diploma.

FARMERS FIGHT TO SAVE ORGANIC CROPS
Source: THE PROGRESSIVE, September 2001
Author: Ben Lilliston

The business of organic farming has grown by 20 percent every year since 1990. Organic sales were projected to increase from $5.4 billion in 1998 to more than $9 billion in 2001. Says Ben Lilliston, "According to the Organic Trade Association, the United States exports more than $40 million in organic goods to the uk and an estimated $40 to $60 million to Japan each year." The greatest threat to this booming industry is the activity of neighboring farms planting genetically modified organisms (GMOs). Many crops are "open pollinating," meaning that wind and insects can carry the GMO pollen into organic fields. According to the president of Nature's Path Foods, "There's no wall high enough to keep that stuff contained." The costs associated with trying to keep organic crops free of contamination are mounting. Organic farmers must stagger planting times with neighboring GMO crops, create buffer zones, and pay for special cleaning equipment and after-harvest tests to assure the crop's purity. When the crops have been found contaminated, farmers must sell them on the open market for often half their price as organic. Organic farmers are fighting back, however. They have lobbied legislators resulting in recently proposed bills. They are also filing lawsuits against the EPA and GMO producers such as Monsanto. "We don't want to make enemies," one organic farmer said. "But we want to defend our right to grow GMO-free crops."

THE UNFASHIONABLE MR. LAM
Source: MOTHER JONES, September/October 2001
Author: Elizabeth Kolbert

For the Chinese laborers of New York City, hope for change comes in the form of an unassuming and sensitive man, Wing Lam. Lam is the executive director of the

Chinese Staff and Workers' Association (CSWA), a group that defends the rights of Chinese immigrants working in sweatshops and other businesses that violate U.S. labor laws.

There are no lawyers at CSWA, and Lam has no legal training, yet the group is constantly generating lawsuits against employers, as many as 100 a year. Volunteer lawyers from the Asian American Legal Defense and Education Fund handle most of the lawsuits. Lawyers from big firms that donate their time, pro bono, handle the rest.

Lam's hard work is certainly not appreciated by everyone. In fact, in certain parts of Chinatown, he is openly despised. One restaurant owner accused of labor-law violations told a judge that life in Chinatown would be better if Lam were dead. Despite the vitriol, Lam is persistent. Rallying for change in the way disadvantaged Chinese immigrants are treated in New York City, Lam won't allow anything to stop him, even if it means having to move his office several times a year, and parking his car in a patrolled garage.

Admittedly, Lam can't help everyone who comes to him. The pockets of some businesses run very deep, and a lawsuit against them can be buried in no time. undeterred, he continues his fight for the Chinese who can't fight on their own. His goal is to change the existing labor laws and give those most vulnerable an opportunity to fight back.

COMMENTS BY PROJECT CENSORED NATIONAL JUDGES

ROBIN ANDERSEN, associate professor and chair, Department of Communication and Media Studies, Fordham University:

In the aftermath of the murder of journalist Danny Pearl, some in the media argued that criticizing the Bush Administration's war on terror dishonored his life. I wrote an initial version of this piece for the Media Channel in response to public comments made about the death of Danny Pearl.

A very good friend of mine, a journalist and *Newsweek* photographer named John Hoagland, was killed in El Salvador in 1984. It was devastating. As a grad student I watched him and his colleagues gather the news in Central America, risking their lives daily. I didn't agree with CNN's Aaron Brown when he apologized for spending time on Danny Pearl's story saying, "he's not any more important than anyone else in that situation." Journalists risk their lives so that we can come ever so slightly closer to understanding the world. John and his colleagues actually believed that. I recently reviewed a book for the *Journal of Communication* titled, *Words of Fire: Independent Journalists Who Challenge Dictatorships, Druglords, and Other Enemies of the Free Press* (2001), and while the author got many things wrong in the analysis, he documents the incredible bravery and courage of journalists and editors around the world who expose dictators, corruption, and oppression. They are jailed, killed, and maimed for their trouble.

I'm really mad about Danny Pearl's death, and I'm really mad about Maria Grazia Cutuli, killed in Afghanistan on November 19, 2001. She and her colleagues were courageous journalists trying to document the war on terrorism. I can't help but wonder if the U.S. hadn't made it so difficult to cover, might they still be alive? Later we found out the U.S. knew how dangerous the man who killed Danny really was. The Office of Strategic Influence was set up to brief the foreign press corps with "public diplomacy" spin. The sad irony for foreign press journalists (and the First Amendment) is that real information might have saved all their lives.

Three weeks before Archbishop Romero was killed in El Salvador, I shook his hand in front of his church. Small in stature but incredibly charismatic, he was a real person to me. I saw bodies every morning on the side of the road, the work of death squads. At the time there was plenty of documentation that the killing was being done by the military the U.S. government was supporting. The journalists knew it, but were discouraged from framing the story differently from U.S. geopolitical assertions. Ray Bonner was one of the only journalists to report the El Mozote massacre that killed 900 peasants. For his troubles, his editor, Abe Rosenthal visited Ambassador Deane Hinton at the U.S. Embassy in San Salvador and then recalled Bonner from story and the country. Even before, when Hinton denounced Bonner, it put a chill through the press corps, mostly because they realized that Bonner, out of favor at the embassy, could be considered a target for the paramilitary. On January 13, 2002, *The New York Times Magazine* printed a double-page photograph by Susan Meiselas (a good friend of John's) documenting the ongoing forensic investigation at the site in El Mozote. While the *Times* offered some criticism of U.S. policy, the paper never admitted its own role in discrediting one of it own journalists and putting him at risk. Indeed, it would have been an excellent opportunity for the *Times* also to remember the role played by Elliot Abrams in covering up the massacre. They might also have noted Abrams continuing ties to the Bush Administration detailed in *Censored* #11.

In El Salvador, U.S. foreign policy wasn't an abstraction; it was responsible for killing real people. My friend John stayed in El Salvador way past the time it was safe because he felt connected to the people there and wanted to do something about their suffering. He was a possibly naïve fan of the famous photojournalist, Margaret Bourke-White, and thought documenting the truth would stop the horrors of war. With 20/20 hindsight and a few good documentaries, we know now that the U.S. was wrong, but we still seem to care mostly for the priests and nuns, not the hundreds of thousands of regular people who were killed. Grieving for Danny Pearl isn't different from grieving for all the people the U.S. is responsible for killing.

Whenever I show my students the video *Fear and Favor in the Newsroom*, and the images of dying children in Iraq (estimated at 5,000 a month because of U.S. sanctions, and the subject of *Censored* #5) taken by Jon Alpert but never shown on NBC, they asked, "Why haven't we ever seen these pictures before?" If we are shielded from the news and images of death and destruction caused by our own government's policies, we can't care about their suffering, and we certainly can't make an informed decision about whether to support U.S. government actions around the world.

Journalists risk their lives covering international stories from Central America to Kashmir, and from Afghanistan to the Bosnia. News organizations that ignore the information and images they risk their lives for show their contempt for a free and democratic press. This loss of media democracy is also documented in *Censored* #1. We need Project Censored to spotlight the news left out of the frame, and explain the reasons why it happens.

CARL JENSEN, founder and director emeritus of Project Censored:

I'm often asked what I think is the most important story I've seen censored since Project Censored was started in 1976. To me, the answer is simple: by far the most important *Censored* story of the past 26 years is the monopolization of the media in the United States.

The issue, titled "Media Merger Mania Threatens Free Flow of Information," was first raised by Project Censored in 1985 based on an article by the late Herbert Schiller, professor emeritus of communication, University of California, San Diego.

The issue then was rated the number-one *Censored* story in four subsequent years: 1987—"The Information Monopoly"; 1989—"Global Media Lords Threaten Open Marketplace of Ideas"; 1992—"The Great Media Sell-Out to Reaganism"; and 1995—"Telecommunications Deregulation: Closing Up America's 'Marketplace of Ideas.'"

This year we have another media monopoly story of great import that has been censored—"FCC Moves to Privatize Airwaves." Like its predecessors, it sounds an urgent warning about the dangers of increasing monopolization of the media. Unlike its predecessors, this may well represent the most important warning of all since it may be our last chance to maintain a modicum of diversity of media sources.

As Jeremy Rifkin says in his article, "Global Media Giants Lobby To Privatize Entire Broadcast Spectrum," "…now powerful commercial media are seeking to gain total control over the airwaves."

Unfortunately, the arbiter on this issue is the FCC which is headed by Michael K. Powell, son of Secretary of State Colin Powell, and President Bush's handpicked choice for FCC chairman. While the FCC is charged with regulating the broadcast industry on behalf of the public, Powell's attitude toward this issue was clearly revealed when he recently said, "The oppressor here is regulation."

A lesson from all this, that we have yet to learn, is that until the issue of media monopolization is resolved on behalf of the public, none of the other issues we are all so concerned with can be resolved.

We failed to acknowledge the warnings first issued by Schiller and Ben Bagdikian, author of The *Media Monopoly*. Then we permitted Congress and the Clinton administration to pass the Telecommunications Act. Now we have one final chance, an opportunity to tell the global media lords that enough is enough. Please join with Project Censored and all the other media watchdog groups fighting to preserve what little media diversity we have left.

NORMAN SOLOMON:

The selected *Censored* stories have in common an intrepid willingness to ask tough questions and dig for answers that resonate with the real world. It's a shame that such articles are so conspicuous when seen up against the background of the mainstream media landscape. A sad truth is that the journalism worth celebrating is unsual for its adherence to basic principles of what reporting should be—independent, assertive, and always determined to go beyond official sources as a matter of routine—in sharp contrast to what passes for high-quality reporting in the purportedly finest news outlets of the land. The daily major media stories are dominated by official-source stenography for the powerful, from high government offices to plush corporate suites. But very different sorts of journalism are possible and imperative.

LIANE CLORFENE-CASTEN, president, Chicago Media Watch:

Power corrupts; absolute power corrupts absolutely. When the media become the self-serving gatekeepers that lock out from public scrutiny reports of government and corporate corruption or criminality, then there is little left but the runaway consolidation and nearly complete corruption of media power. Thanks to FCC chair, Michael Powell, and the present administration, the grip—in process since the Telecommunications Act of 1996—has only become tighter. Blather, public relations, and propaganda take the place of significant information, while a corporate agenda now insinuates itself into the classrooms. Children are being trained for the marketplace, not the polling place. Critical thinking and vigorous debate are becoming unpatriotic.

When we have media conglomerations now aligned with the power structure—in all their varied and myriad connections, from regulators to profiteers—we have the perfect blanket that covers over the rapaciousness, the greed, and the immoral indifference to human life that constitutes any definition of evil. With no public scrutiny, both corporations and the government can go about their business of keeping the world safe for Silicon Valley's technologies, for McDonnell Douglas's newest killing machine, for Coca-Cola's and Nike's Third World labor policies and pay structures, or for Occidental Petroleum's pipeline to oil. And this true agenda is being carried out with greater arrogance and abandon because the mainstream media no longer report these crimes or hold the perpetrators accountable. Often the criminal perpetrators—like polluting Disney and GE—are the very corporations that own the media. The agenda is war (anywhere) and missile sales, not peace; profit now, not human health or a concern for the future of this planet.

While the U.S. military is making the world safe for U.S. capitalism, and while it destroys everything in its wake in the process—from local resources to human lives—our own country and indeed the world continues to pay a devastating price. Whole generations in the U.S. and abroad are now suffering, are butchered, starved, and manipulated into poverty and whole generations will continue to suffer and be manipulated by forces beyond their control, unreported and ignored by most media outlets.

As Bob McChesney wisely stated, "The corruption of the system would be difficult to exaggerate."

CHAPTER 2

9-11 Before and Beyond
A CRITICAL ANALYSIS

BY PETER PHILLIPS, TOM LOUGH, ROBERT HACKETT,
KAREN TALBOT, AND PROJECT CENSORED

Corporate media are ignoring many important questions related to 9-11 and have defaulted on their First Amendment obligation to keep the American electorate informed on key societal issues. Corporate news star Dan Rather in a recent interview with Matthew Engel for *The Guardian* admitted that the surge of patriotism after 9-11 resulted in journalists failing to ask the tough questions. Rather stated, "It starts with a feeling of patriotism within oneself. I know the right question, but you know what? This is not exactly the right time to ask it."

When was the right time to question the levels and intensity of civilian deaths during and after the bombings of Afghanistan? According to CNN Chairman Walter Isaacson, there was never a good time. In a memo to his CNN correspondents overseas, Isaacson wrote, "We're entering a period in which there's a lot more reporting and video from Taliban-controlled Afghanistan. You must make sure people [Americans] understand that when they see civilian suffering there, it's in the context of a terrorist attack that caused enormous suffering in the United States." Isaacson later told the *Washington Post*, "…it seems perverse to focus too much on the causalities of hardship in Afghanistan."

Marc Herold, an economics professor at the University of New Hampshire, compiled a summation of the death toll in Afghanistan—saying that over 4,000 civilians died from U.S. bombs—more than died at the World Trade Center on 9-11. Yet only a handful of newspapers covered his story. *Time* magazine reviewed Herold's report, but dismissed it, stating, "In compiling the figures, Herold drew mostly on world press reports of questionable reliability." *Time* went on to cite the Pentagon's unsubstantiated claim that civilian casualties in Afghanistan were the lowest in the history of war.

Other big questions abound. Both the BBC and the *Times of India* published reports several months before 9-11 that the U.S. was then planning an invasion of Afghanistan. The Unocal oil pipeline from the Caspian Sea region was to be built through Afghanistan and the U.S. needed a cooperative government in power. Agence France-Presse in March 2002 reported that the U.S.–installed interim leader of Afghanistan, Hamid Karzai, has worked with the CIA since the 1980s and was once a paid consultant for Unocal.

An explosive post-9-11 report (*Censored* #4) emerged from France regarding how the Bush Administration, shortly after assuming office, slowed down FBI investigations of Al Qaeda and terrorist networks in Afghanistan in order to deal with the Taliban on oil. This slowdown has been related to the resignation of FBI deputy director John O'Neill, expert on the Al Qaeda network and in charge of that investigation. O'Neill later took a job as chief of security at the World Trade Center where he died "helping with rescue efforts."

And we still wonder: What happened to the story in the *San Francisco Chronicle* from September 29, 2001 about how millions of dollars were made on pre-9-11 short-selloptions on United and American Airlines stocks?

Or what about the October 31 report in the French daily *Le Figaro* describing how Osama bin Laden met with a top CIA official while he was in the American Hospital in the United Arab Emirates last July receiving treatment for a chronic kidney infection?

Corporate media today are interlocked and dependent on government sources for news content. Gone are the days of deep investigative reporting teams challenging the powerful. Media consolidation has downsized newsrooms to the point where reporters serve more as stenographers than as researchers. Emerging in the vacuum are hundreds of independent news sources. Independent newspapers, magazines, Web sites, radio, and TV are becoming more widely available. Labeled by the corporate media as having "questionable reliability," emerging news sources are building their own audiences worldwide. For listings and links to independent news sources, see our resource guide in Appendix A.

Chapter 2 is designed to support critical thinking and analysis of issues surrounding the 9-11 tragedy. To lay a frame of understanding of media coverage on 9-11, Robert Hackett from NewsWatch Canada contributes an introductory essay. We then provide short synopses of several important under-covered 9-11 related stories, and finish the chapter with an essay on the policy driving oil interests in central Asia by Karen Talbot.

Covering Up The "War On Terrorism"
THE MASTER FRAME AND THE MEDIA CHILL

BY ROBERT HACKETT

Two weekends after the September 11 atrocity, I watched with appreciation the respected American journalist and media critic James Fallows. He was warning his colleagues in the attack's emotional aftermath that independent journalism was at risk of being swallowed by patriotism. Just one problem: Fallows was speaking not on an American network, but on Canada's main public broadcaster, the CBC.

In Canada, there has been some semblance of debate over fundamental issues, even inspiration and intellectual courage. No one person could track the ocean of coverage, but here are some of the moments I appreciated:

➤A philosophy professor on CBC Radio on September 11, cautioning against the metaphors of Pearl Harbor and war—analogies that imply total mobilization, martial obedience, and much else.

➤Neil MacDonald on CBC's *The National*, questioning the definition of "terrorism," which each state defines differently according to its own perceived interests.

➤Rafe Mair on Vancouver's CKNW radio, one of the country's most listened-to talk shows, interviewing me about the "chill" in American media.

➤CBC television's *CounterSpin* and *Town Hall* programs, and Rex Murphy on radio, accessing Muslim Canadians and other often marginalized voices and viewpoints.

➤Jonathan Manthorpe, one of Canada's most distinguished foreign correspondents, describing how "meddling by Western powers"—dating back to the 1953 coup that installed the Shah of Iran—"fueled the radicalization of the Middle East" (*Vancouver Sun*, September 27, 2001).

➤On Sunday evening radio, Terry Moore discussing, with the president of the Canadian Association for Media Education, how journalism is distorted by jingoism.

At the same time, through the shared trauma of 9-11, close personal and social ties, the influence of American media on Canadian popular culture, and our partial dependence on U.S.–based networks and wire services for foreign news, Canadian journalism is not immune to the silencing pressures on American media. There, voices of dissent and caution were marginalized, even censored.

As the Bush Administration's rhetoric escalated rapidly, from "there has been a terrorist attack" to "an act of war" to "we are at war," the media's dominant narratives, the shared mindset underlying the selection and presentation of news, quickly gelled into a kind of master frame: This is a war (not a campaign or police action) between absolute good and absolute evil.

Like a lightning bolt from Satan, September 11 was an unprovoked attack on Freedom and Democracy. You are either for us, or against us. The American people will unite behind its leaders, use whatever means and make whatever sacrifices are necessary, to crush evil and ensure the triumph of good. This is about "Infinite Justice"—the original brand name of the retaliatory operation.

Frames are unavoidable in journalism, as in any form of effective storytelling. Comprising mostly implicit assumptions about values and reality, they help to construct coherent narratives out of a potential infinity of occurrences and information. The problem is that when they are accepted uncritically, frames can lead journalism to exclude information, which, from another perspective, would be considered relevant. In America's alternative press, but rarely in the dominant media, other frames were in play— that violence begets violence, or that the double standards and hegemonism

of the U.S. government's foreign policy were part of a broader pattern from which the evil acts of September 11 emerged.

Obviously, nothing whatsoever can justify the terror attacks. It ought to go equally without saying that the mass slaughter of innocent civilians in retaliation is not morally acceptable. Yet, ensconced safely within the master frame, some of America's highest-profile media pundits called for just that, including the use of nuclear weapons. A "Rogue's Gallery" of bloodthirsty quotes ("as for cities or countries that host these worms, bomb them into basketball courts") was posted by the New York-based media monitoring group Fairness and Accuracy in Reporting (<ww.fair.org> on September 17.

Perhaps the hotheaded pundits were reflecting the rage of the moment, and their own job of provocation. What is more disquieting is how the frame has shaped the agenda of news reporting.

Topics that fit the frame are highlighted. For example, besides the endlessly repeated visuals of planes smashing into the towers, journalists (sometimes insensitively, sometimes courageously) told tales of human tragedy and heroism in Manhattan. And, understandably so, 9-11 was a made-for-TV atrocity, arousing unparalleled emotions, and offering the human interest, drama, threat, and visuals at which TV excels. But beyond a certain point, the round-the-clock rescue coverage became an alibi for not exploring other topics.

Second, just as previous tyrants (such as Manuel Noriega, Saddam Hussein, and Slobodan Milosevic) popped out of obscurity to become media villains of the month prior to previous U.S.–led interventions, Osama bin Laden and the Taliban regime appeared everywhere. Though initially and responsibly cautious about attributing blame—mindful of the haste with which Middle Eastern

extremists were fingered for the Oklahoma City bombing before it turned out to be the work of home-grown right-wing fanatics—the media soon scrambled to spotlight the Taliban's appalling human rights record—six years after it had seized power. In an unwitting indictment of its own journalism, CNN promoted one of its documentaries as "a side of Afghanistan you have never seen before." In American media, the demonization of foreign villains is selective; by and large, only those who threaten U.S. interests are newsworthy.

Not that these topics were inappropriate. The real problem is the omission of stories that do not fit the master frame. "Silence, rigorously selective, pervades the media coverage," wrote Norman Solomon (author of Chapter 7) whose column is carried in about 15 of America's smaller dailies. "For policymakers in Washington, the practical utility of that silence is enormous. In response to the mass murder committed by hijackers, the righteousness of U.S. military action is clear—as long as double standards go unmentioned."

Borrowing from American media-monitoring and alternative media Web sites (<mediachannel.org>, <fair.org>, <alternet.org>, <znet.org>) here is my list of the "top eight" questions under-covered by the dominant U.S. media:

1) Why did this atrocity happen? As former ABC producer Danny Schechter put it, "There is all too little media reflection on how this attack connects to other things happening in the world. Was it simply aimed, as some officials have been saying, at our culture and way of life or are there specific political factors?"

Squeamishness about this question is understandable; it can wrongly imply that there is some conceivable moral justification for the atrocities. Still, beyond the identity and motives of the hijackers and their backers, U.S. television news has shown remarkably little curiosity about the geopolitical fires that fuel fanaticism and terrorism—not just anti-liberal or anti-modernist tendencies in the Islamic world, but also, as Vancouver political scientist Peter Prontzos says, those of "Washington's own actions, especially in the Middle East, which contribute to widespread anti-Americanism in many parts of the world."

Few North Americans know much of such actions, but independent journalists like British foreign correspondent Robert Fisk and TV producer John Pilger have covered dozens of them, from the deaths of hundreds of thousands of Iraqis in the Gulf War and in the sanctions afterwards, to the Cruise missile attack in August 1998 that destroyed a Sudanese pharmaceutical factory (wrongly suspected as a bin Laden depot) and killed unknown numbers of workers.

2) What are the policy options in response to the attack? From the very beginning, only a unilateral military response was on the media's table. The parade of strategic analysts, "security" experts and former government officials on American network TV defined the issue from the start, and the near total absence of debate in Congress sealed the deal. Even so, Jeff Cohen of the media monitoring group FAIR argues, "It's appalling how little mainstream media have discussed relying on the rule of law—international law—to pursue the foreign terrorists." Multilateral action organized through the United Nations with military action well down the priority list, an approach favored by Canada's New Democratic Party, was ignored or contemptuously dismissed by American media pundits.

3) Was September 11 a case of "blowback"? To what extent were bin Laden's network and the Taliban regime itself made possible in part by previous U.S. funding and training (channeled through the Pakistani security service) for the Afghan resistance to the Soviet invaders in the 1980s? Why did the U.S. government provide $43 million to the Taliban, as part of its drug war, only months prior to the attack? More broadly, what are the implications of the huge international arms trade (63 percent of it from the U.S. in 1997), with much of it flowing to repressive regimes in the Middle East? What lessons should be drawn for future security and foreign policy?

4) Who is the enemy? How far do the intended targets extend? What counts as a victory? And especially, if this is a "war against terrorism" (as distinct from an internationally coordinated police action to bring a specific group of criminals to justice), then what exactly qualifies as "terrorism"? "American news outlets routinely define terrorism the same way that U.S. government officials do," argues Norman Solomon. "Sadly, the evenhanded use of the label would mean sometimes affixing it directly on the U.S. government." The American satirist and film producer Michael Moore (who has been frozen out of U.S. TV newscasts since September 11) cites as one example the U.S. backing for the Nicaraguan Contras, who killed some 30,000 civilians in the 1980s.

5) What is the state of public opinion, not only in the U.S., but also elsewhere in the world? As peace rallies and public doubts at home were arguably scanted, the media were not inaccurate in reporting great support for Bush's military escalation. But they ignored polls (e.g. Reuters, September 21) suggesting that huge majorities in Europe, Latin America and elsewhere favored extraditing and trying the terrorists, rather than bombing their base countries.

6) Was 9-11 really "Islamic" terrorism? Or would it be more correct to describe it, as journalist Christopher Hitchens did, as "fascism with an Islamic face"? Here, the coverage has been ambivalent and probably facing contradictory pressures. On the one hand, the Bush administration was working hard to build a coalition of "moderate" Arab states. "This is not a war against Islam," is a coalition mantra, and to its credit, Bush officials distinguished between terrorism and the legitimate Islamic faith.

On the other hand, the simplistic story lines of commercial TV news demand visible villains. The screens were filled with "dancing Palestinians" and angry crowds in Pakistan. According to an e-mail from a network field assistant in Egypt, Western correspondents are not interested in the voices of sympathetic or moderate Muslims. They parachute in with preconceived story lines, and demand interviews with photogenically raging radicals.

7) What kind of political agendas are piggybacking on the tragedy? Put more bluntly, who benefits in the U.S., the Islamic world, or elsewhere? "How has the national security state's agenda been accelerated, how has their budget been expanded, and what corporations have seen stock value increase after the tragedy?" asks Peter Phillips.

8) Don't talk about the war. After the Gulf War, it became clear that the Patriot missiles were not as accurate as we had been told, most of the bombs weren't "smart," and the Kuwaiti babies torn from incubators by Iraqi troops were inventions of a public relations firm. This time, without even carefully shepherded "pools" of reporters in the combat zone, journalists are even more dependent on Pentagon spoon-feeding and less willing to challenge official information. We hear much about the coalition's military prowess, and as little about "collateral damage" as the Pentagon can get away with. And the list of undercovered, outside-the-frame stories could be expanded—hate crimes (never labeled "terrorism") against Arab Americans, for instance.

Why have American mainstream media been so ready to abandon their once-cherished democratic role as a critical watchdog of the powerful? There is no single explanation. Journalists as well as their audiences are tempted to "rally round the flag" in a time of national crisis, and the political and military leadership on which the media depend as a funnel for information is not about to encourage critical questioning. The 9-11 events themselves made for an emotionally compelling and gut wrenching (but in the long run, dangerously simplistic) story line built around the stuff of legend—heroes, villains, and victims. Schooled in the foundational myths of nationhood, America as the world's beacon of freedom, most TV viewers would not see the master frame as a narrative at all, but simply as "the way things are."

Media corporations themselves have contributed to the current narrowing of public discourse. Drastic cutbacks in international news coverage by U.S. media, in response to corporate demands for larger profits and fragmented audiences, have hardly cultivated an informed citizenry. "Having decided that readers and viewers in post-Cold War America cared more about celebrities, scandals, and local news," writes the *Los Angeles Times*' David Shaw, "news executives have reduced the space and time devoted to foreign coverage by 70 percent to 80 percent during the past 15 to 20 years."

As a result, "the rest of the world knows far more about America than we know about ourselves, let alone what we know about them," laments Nina Burleigh, who as a *Time* magazine reporter was one of the first American journalists to enter Iraq after the Gulf War. "And this triumph of ignorance means that Americans can't even comprehend what motivates those who hate us."

As media corporations converge and commercialize, they develop a corporate culture increasingly hostile to the public service ethos associated with Walter Cronkite and his generation. Years of flak from conservatives, convinced despite all the contrary evidence that the media contributed to defeat in Vietnam, have left the press anxious to prove its patriotism. Contrast Cronkite's legendary speech on TV, that the Vietnam War was not winnable, with Dan Rather's pledge on the David Letterman show: "George Bush is the president...Wherever he wants me to line up, just tell me where."

John MacArthur, publisher of *Harper's* magazine and author of a book on censorship in the Gulf War, makes a depressing observation: "There isn't even the spirit anymore that was in Vietnam, of skepticism, and the sense that the patriotic thing to do is to tell the American people the truth and to try to be impartial and not to be the cat's paw of the government. But when I say this on TV the reaction is overwhelming, there is tremendous hostility to the free press in this country."

Tremendous hostility to the free press—a stunning conclusion from a country gearing up to defeat the enemies of freedom. The master frame exerts its influence in Canada too. The *National Post* promotes it single-mindedly, in both its editorial and news pages. Many Canadian journalists jumped on a bandwagon of vilification against a provocatively outspoken challenge to the master frame from Vancouver professor Sunera Thobani. Several others defended her right to free speech, or pointed out that her critique of "blood-soaked" U.S. foreign policy was hardly unique.

Is there still enough diversity in journalism for it to contribute to public discussion of constructive solutions in a dangerous world, even when they challenge official views or conventional opinion? That is a crucial question both for journalists, and for their audiences.

Reprinted from *MEDIA* magazine, published by the Canadian Association of Journalists, 316B St. Patrick's Building, Carleton University, 1125 Colonel By Drive, Ottawa, Ontario, K1S 2B6. E-mail: <caj@igs.net>.

Undercovered News Stories on 9-11

Project Censored is always careful about covering stories that lean toward conspiracy-based explanations for sociopolitical events. Still, when important questions are raised that create widespread concerns in society, we believe that it is the media's responsibility to investigate and report on the veracity of the issues. The following are persistent and often well-documented news stories related to 9-11. While we cannot verify complete accuracy on each particular story, we believe the stories contain enough substance and information to have at least received wider investigation by the nation's media. The American public deserves to know the full truth about these events.

HAMAD KARZAI AND ZALMAY KHALIZAD: OUR MEN IN AFGHANISTAN

Sources:
INDIGO PUBLICATIONS Intelligence Online
"Oil and Telecommunications in Kabul," January 31, 2002

AGENCE FRANCE-PRESSE, March 13, 2002
"Afghan Leader Karzai Says Moscow No Match for Washington"

AL-WATAN Web site/BBC Monitoring, December 11, 2001
"Saudi Paper Profiles New Afghan Leader"

O'DWYER'S PR DAILY, January 10, 2002
"Bush Picks Ex-Unocal Advisor"

Hamad Karzai, interim leader of Afghanistan, has been working with the CIA since the 1980s and was once a paid consultant for the Unocal oil company.

Karzai's relationship with the CIA began when he lived in Pakistan, acting as the intermediary between the Americans and the Afghan mujahideen fighters. (He helped secure the delivery of U.S. weapons and aid to the fighters.) Karzai eventually became the deputy foreign minister after the collapse of the pro-Soviet government.

In 1994 and 1995, when California-based Unocal was planning the construction of an oil pipeline through Afghanistan, they hired Karzai as a consultant. Unocal, the CIA, and Karzai were early supporters of the (Western-funded) Taliban movement in Afghanistan. The Taliban agreed to Unocal's pipeline deal and in return were promised oil transport tariffs. The Taliban would also provide the needed political stability for the Unocal oil project.

Karzai's administration, now providing the required political stability in Afghanistan, met with U.S. corporate leaders at Washington's Ritz Hotel. On January 28, 2002, Karzai and his delegation were presented with a memo titled "Strategic Plan for a Nation-Wide Telecommunications Infrastructure for Afghanistan." Deputy Secretary of State Richard Armitage also organized a meeting between the Afghan political leaders and several oil company executives. While Unocal executives were not present at this meeting in Washington, executives from ExxonMobil and Vice President Dick Cheney's Halliburton did attend.

Zalmay Khalizad was President Bush's appointee as special envoy to Afghanistan after December 31. He has been called by the *Washington Post* "the top-ranking Muslim in the U.S. government." Khalizad was also a former advisor to Unocal and lobbied the Taliban on behalf of the energy giant.

THE FBI HELPED BIN LADEN FAMILY FLEE U.S. AFTER 9-11

Sources:
THE NEW YORKER, November 12, 2001
"The House of bin Ladin: A Family's and a Nation's Divided Loyalties"
Jane Mayer

THE NEW YORK TIMES, September 30, 2001
"Fearing Harm, bin Laden Kin Fled From U.S.," Patrick E. Tyler

THE TIMES (London), October 1, 2001
"How FBI Helped bin Laden Family Flee U.S.," Katty Kay

In the first days after the attacks on New York and Washington, with all airlines grounded and no commercial flights allowed anywhere in the country, the FBI assisted Saudi Arabia in the evacuation of as many as 24 members of Osama bin Laden's extended family from the United States. Most of the relatives living in the U.S. were younger siblings and cousins of bin Laden attending schools and universities. Immediately after the attack they were taken under FBI escort to Texas. From there they went to Washington, DC, and the safety of the Saudi Embassy. As soon as U.S. airports reopened, the relatives were flown back to Saudi Arabia on a private charter plane, paid for by the Saudi government.

In an interview since the attacks, Saudi Ambassador Bandar bin Sultan also said that private planes carrying the kingdom's deputy defense minister and the governor of Mecca, both members of the royal family, were grounded and initially caught up in the FBI dragnet. Both planes, one jumbo jet carrying 100 family members, and the other 40, were eventually allowed to leave when airports reopened. United States officials apparently needed little persuasion from the Saudi that the family included no material witnesses. Within the eight weeks after the attacks, over 1,000 suspects and potential witnesses were detained by the FBI, yet none of the family members were ever questioned regarding the whereabouts of Osama or the events surrounding September 11.

THE ROLE OF PAKISTAN'S MILITARY INTELLIGENCE AGENCY (ISI) IN THE 9-11 ATTACKS.

Source:
CENTER FOR RESEARCH ON GLOBALIZATION, November 2, 2001
<www.globalresearch.ca>, Michel Chossudovsky

Pakistan Intelligence Services (ISI) chief General Mahmoud Ahmad had connections to terrorist leader Mohamed Atta, and was in the United States before the attacks of

9-11. While in the U.S., he had meetings with the State Department and the Pentagon prior to and following the attacks. ISI has long worked closely with the CIA.

The *Times of India* reported that six months prior to 9-11, $100,000 was wired to WTC hijacker Mohamed Atta from Pakistan by Ahmad Umar Sheikh at the insistence of General Mahmoud. On the Sunday before the bombing in Afghanistan began, Lt. General Mahmoud Ahmad was sacked from his position in a "routine reshuffling."

Still, despite official government reports showing ISI and bin Laden connections, the Bush Administration decided to continue to "cooperate" with the ISI. At the same time, State Department officials were rushed to Islamabad, Pakistan, to put the finishing touches on their war plans.

OSAMA BIN LADEN MET WITH THE CIA IN JULY OF 2001

Source:
LE FIGARO, November 10, 2001
Posted at <globalresearch.ca>

An article in the French daily *Le Figaro* reports that Osama bin Laden underwent surgery in the American Hospital in Dubai in July 2001. During his stay in the hospital, it is reported that he met with a CIA official. Although on the world's "most wanted list," no attempt was made to arrest him during his two-week stay in the hospital. While he was hospitalized, bin Laden received visits from many members of his family, as well as prominent Saudis and Emiratis. During the hospital stay, the local CIA agent, known to many in Dubai, was seen taking the main elevator of the hospital to go to bin Laden's hospital room.

A few days later, the CIA agent bragged to a few friends about having visited bin Laden. Sources say that on July 15, the day after bin Laden returned to Quetta, the CIA agent was called back to headquarters.

9-11 WARNINGS FROM FOREIGN GOVERNMENTS

Source:
WORLD SOCIALIST WEB SITE, <www.wsws.org>
"Was the U.S. Government Alerted to September 11 attack?"
Patrick Martin

The governments of at least four countries—Germany, Egypt, Russia, and Israel—gave specific warnings to the U.S. of an impending terrorist attack in the months preceding September 11. These alerts, while fragmentary, not only combined to foretell the scale of the attack and its main target, but also indicated that hijacked commercial aircraft would be the weapon of choice.

The German intelligence service BND told both U.S. and Israeli intelligence agencies in June that Middle East terrorists were "planning to hijack commercial aircraft to use as weapons to attack important symbols of American and Israeli culture."

The government of Egypt sent an urgent warning to the U.S. on June 13 based on a video made by Osama bin Laden. Egyptian President Hosni Mubarak told the French newspaper *Le Figaro* that the warning was originally delivered just before the G-8 summit in Genoa. It was taken seriously enough that antiaircraft batteries were stationed around Christopher Columbus Airport in the Italian city. According to Mubarak, bin Laden "spoke of assassinating President Bush and other heads of state in Genoa. It was a question of an airplane stuffed with explosives."

Russian intelligence notified the CIA during the summer that 25 terrorist pilots had been specifically training for suicide missions. In an interview on September 15 with MSNBC, Russian President Vladimir Putin confirmed that in August of 2001 he ordered Russian intelligence to warn the U.S. government "in the strongest possible terms" of imminent attacks on airports and government buildings.

U.S. AIR FORCE DELAYS SCRAMBLING INTERCEPTORS ON 9-11

Sources:
GLOBAL OUTLOOK, <www.globalresearch.ca/articles/ZWIZOZAhtml>
Spring 2002, "The Great Deception: Why Did The U.S. Air Force Fail To Act In Time On September 11?," Barry Zwicker

GLOBAL OUTLOOK, <www.globalresearch.ca/ articles/SZA202A>
Spring 2002, "Scrambled Messages on 9-11," George Szamuely

On 9-11, four planes are hijacked and deviate from their flight plans, all while on FAA radar. The planes are all hijacked between 7:45 and 8:10 AM Eastern Time. It is a full hour before the first plane hits the World Trade Center. But it is an hour and 20 minutes later—after the second plane hits—that President Bush becomes officially informed. Then, he gives no orders. He continues to listen to a student talk about her pet goat. It's another 25 minutes until he makes a statement, as Flight 77 is making a beeline for Washington, DC. According to a report by Barry Zwicker, in the almost two hours of total drama, not a single U.S. Air Force interceptor is scrambled (ordered into emergency takeoff and intercept mode). It is standard procedure to call in the air force when radio contact with a commercial passenger jet is lost, if the plane deviates from its flight path, or any such unusual event occurs.

When a chartered Learjet carrying golfer Payne Stewart crashed on October 26, 1999, it was a mere 21 minutes after losing contact with the jet that an F-16 reached the Learjet at 46,000 feet and conducted a visual inspection.

Andrews Air Force Base (AFB) is only 12 miles from the White House. It is a huge installation that is home to Air Force One, the President's plane, as well as two combat-ready squadrons of jet interceptors mandated to ensure the safety of the U.S. Capitol. According to the Andrews AFB Web site on September 11, the base held the 121st Fighter Squadron of the 113th Fighter Wing, equipped with F-16s; and the 321st Marine Fighter Attack Squadron of the 49th Marine Air Group, Detachment A, equipped with FA-18 fighter attack aircraft. These would be the planes to scramble. Instead, Andrews AFB changed its Web site on September 12 to omit mention of the fighters. The Web site now suggests that the base is home to only a single transport squadron.

According to a September 14 report on CBS, the FAA had indeed alerted U.S. Air Defense Units at 8:38 A.M. on Tuesday, and six minutes later, two F-15s received "a scramble order" at Otis Air National Guard Base (ANGB) on Cape Cod. Then, at 9:30 A.M., three F-16s were launched from Langley Air Force Base (AFB) , 150 miles south of Washington.

This story, now the official version, has some logistical holes. First of all, why did it take the FAA so long after the planes had deviated from their flight paths to notify anyone (almost a half an hour)? In addition, F-16s and F-15s can travel at a speed of close to 800 MPH when in scramble mode. As Otis ANGB is 180 miles from Manhattan, it would take them less than 15 minutes to get there. The two F-16 fighters also should have had more than enough time to get from Langley AFB to DC and intercept Flight 77.

CARLYLE GROUP:
THE BUSH-BIN LADEN CONNECTION

Sources:
THE GUARDIAN (London), <www.guardian.co.uk/Print/0,3858,4288516,00.html>
October 31, 2001, "The Ex-President's Club," Oliver Burkeman and Julian Borger

TOMPAINE.COM, <www.tompaine.com/news/2001/10/11/>,* Fall 2001
"Missing the Oil Story," Nina Burleigh

While counseling his son on policies regarding the war on terrorism, former president George Bush is adviser to the Washington, DC-based Carlyle Group. This $12.5 billion private equity firm owns so many defense and aerospace companies that it has essentially become the fifth largest contractor for the U.S. Army.

The roster of the Carlyle Group reads like a who's who of former top-level government officials, including former Secretary of Defense Frank Carlucci, ex-Secretary of State James Baker, former Prime Minister John Major of Britain, and former Prime Minister of South Korea Park Tae Joon. When President George W. Bush was in search of a career in 1990, he was put on the board of Caterair, a Carlyle subsidiary.

Members of the Saudi royal family also hold substantial investments in the Carlyle Group, including Prince Bandar bin Sultan, the Saudi ambassador to the U.S. According to a source close to the royal family, Prince Sultan and his father encouraged wealthy Saudi friends to invest in the Carlyle Group as a favor to Bush Sr. The bin Ladens were some of those wealthy Saudi friends.

While the bin Laden family claims to have disowned son Osama bin Laden, some experts claim that he still maintains connections with the family. In October, the Carlyle Group severed ties with the bin Laden family when it was agreed that the relationship could become embarrassing. The bin Ladens have since divested their holdings in the company.

Through ties to the Carlyle Group, both the Bush and bin Laden families have profited from the jump in U.S. defense spending in the aftermath of the 9-11 attacks. When former government officials use their connections and insights for financial gain, there is a conflict of interest. "[President] George W. Bush could some day benefit financially from his own administration's decisions, through his father's investments," adds Charles Lewis of the Center for Public Integrity.

U.S. PLANNED AN INVASION OF AFGHANISTAN BEFORE 9-11

Sources:
BBC NEWS, <Indiareacts.com>, June 26, 2001
"India in Anti-Taliban Military Plan,"September 18, 2001, George Arney

Jane's Defense Newsletter, March 15, 2001
"India Joins Anti-Taliban Coalition," Rahul Bedi

The U.S. government sub-committee on Asia and the Pacific of the International Relations Committee of the House of Representatives met in February of 1998 to discuss removing the government of Afghanistan from power. The U.S. government told India in June of 2001 that a planned invasion of Afghanistan was set for October. In March of 2001, *Jane's Defense Newsletter* reported the U.S. planned to invade Afghanistan later that year, and BBC reported that the U.S told the Pakistani Foreign Secretary of a planned invasion of Afghanistan in October.

INSIDER STOCK TRADING DISCLOSED
ON COMPANIES IMPACTED BY 9-11

Sources:
PITTSBURGH POST-GAZETTE, September 25, 2001
"How Terrorist Could Have Made Money," Len Boselovis

THE TORONTO SUN, September 29, 2001
"Taking Stock: Proof of Pre-attack Profiteering Hunted," Reuters

USA TODAY, October 4, 2001
"No Evidence of Short-Selling Turned Up Yet," Kevin McCoy and Greg Farrell

SAN FRANCISCO CHRONICLE, October 3, 2001
"Stock-Trading Probe Expands to Canada"

HOUSTON CHRONICLE, October 3, 2001
"SEC Asks 39 Firms to Review Trades"

USA TODAY, October 11, 2001
"Do Terrorists Ply U.S. Stock Markets?"
FROM THE WILDERNESS PUBLICATIONS, <www.copvcia.com>
"Profits of Death—Insider Trading and 9-11," Michael Ruppert

The Securities and Exchange Commission (SEC) asked brokerage and investment firms in the U.S. and Canada to review their computer records from August 27 to September 11, for signs of unsual trading patterns. Regulators were suspicious of heavy "short-selling" in airlines and related stocks in the days before the 9-11 attacks. Short-selling is used by traders who believe a price is going to fall. Trading on 38 firms was being reviewed, including the two airlines united and American that lost planes on 9-11.

Over $4,000,000 was made on stock purchase options on United and American Airlines. Most of the options went unclaimed and expired on October 19. One of the largest options was placed through Deutsche Bank Alex Brown.

Michael Ruppert reports that the number-three person at the CIA is A.B. (Buzzy) Krongard. Krongard was the Chairman of The Bank of Alex Brown. After the Deutsche Bank acquired The Bank of Alex Brown, Krongard headed the investment branch until his appointment to the CIA. Ruppert claims that the CIA monitors the stock market and may have participated in the purchases of options before 9-11.

Corporate media follow-ups on this story after October 2001 are lacking (as of the middle of June 2002).

U.S. GOVERNMENT/CONGRESSIONAL RESPONSES TO 9-11

Source:

THE HIGHTOWER-LOWDOWN, Vol. 4, No. 2, February 2002
"A Load Of Bush Baloney Enacted After 9-11: Looting The Treasury under Cover Of The Flag," Jim Hightower and Phillip Frazer

The U.S. government immediately responded to the 9-11 attacks by doing the following:

➤Pushing through Congress the Patriot Act and a bill enacting secret tribunals—and national ID cards seem to be in the works (*Censored* # 8, 1998). Members of Congress had tried and failed to pass these bills after the 1995 bombing of the Federal Building in Oklahoma City.

➤Awarding federal bailout money to the executives of the airlines, which laid off 140,000 employees ($15 billion); the private beach industry; the brewing industry; Boeing ($23 billion); drug makers (to fight bioterrorism); hospital chains; and insurance companies.

➤Giving $47 billion in tax breaks to AT&T, EDS, Johnson & Johnson, Microsoft, and others in the form of Research and Experiment tax credits.

➤Deciding to use Yucca Mountain as the national nuclear dump and widen Highway I-66, from Washington, DC ,through Virginia.

➤Restoring the businessman's lunch as tax-deductible—a gift to the restaurant industry (fighting terrorism requires solid nourishment).

➤Approving $343 billion for the defense industry, including $8.3 for Star Wars.

Perhaps one of the more ominous post 9-11 developments was the Defense Department's award to the PR firm, Rendon Group, of a $392,000 contract to counter negative portrayals of the us bombing in Afghanistan and abroad. <TomPaine.com> reported that Rendon went beyond wooing foreign journalists to setting up disguised-sources, pro-U.S. Web sites in several foreign languages and blast-faxing foreign media and search engines with pro-U.S. information. Rendon has clients in 78 countries. The company spent over $23 million in the first year of the anti-Saddam campaign, and supplied hundreds of Kuwaitis with American flags to wave as U.S. troops rolled into Kuwait City.

ATTORNEY GENERAL JOHN ASHCROFT URGED GOVERNMENT AGENCIES TO RESIST FREEDOM OF INFORMATION REQUESTS AFTER 9-11

Source:
SAN FRANCISCO CHRONICLE, January 6, 2002
"On the Public Right to Know: The Day Ashcroft Censored Freedom of Information," Editorial

In a memo to federal agencies at the beginning of 2002, Attorney General John Ashcroft vigorously urged them to resist most Freedom of Information Act requests made by American citizens. Ashcroft asked federal agencies to consider whether "institutional, commercial, and personal privacy interests could be implicated by disclosure of the information."

Passed in the post-Watergate era of 1974, the Freedom of Information Act allows journalists, newspapers, historians, and ordinary citizens to request and scrutinize public documents. Government coverup and secrecy can only increase without this law being actively enforced.

WEAPONS OF DESTRUCTION U.S. DROPS WORLD'S BIGGEST NONNUCLEAR BOMB IN AFGHANISTAN

Source:
THE PROGRESSIVE POPULIST, December 1, 2001
"Weapons of Destruction," Laura Flanders

The seven-and-a-half ton BLU-82 Daisy Cutter (nicknamed Big Blue) is the largest non-nuclear device in the U.S. arsenal. Dropped from huge transport aircraft, the Daisy Cutter has the ability to clear a three-mile long path and incinerate an area the size of five football fields. The bomb creates a shock wave and vacuum that destroys the internal organs of anyone nearby. "The intent is to kill people," stated General Peter Pace.

The Geneva Protocol 1, Article 51.2, states: "the civilian population as such, as well as individual civilians , shall not be the object of attack. Acts or threats of violence the primary purpose of which is to spread terror among the civilian population are prohibited."

ANTHRAX SPORES "MADE IN THE U.S.A"

Source:
<WWW.WSWS.ORG>, December 30, 2001
"Anthrax Spores Made in the U.S.A: U.S. Anthrax Attacks Linked
to Army Biological Weapons Plant," Patrick Martin

U.S. anthrax attacks were linked to a U.S. Army biological weapons plant. until the *Baltimore Sun* broke the story on December 12, U.S. officials, including those investigating the anthrax attacks, had maintained that the American military stopped producing germ warfare materials in the late 1960s, before the signing of an international treaty banning the development of such materials. Pentagon spokesmen now claim that the development of weapons-grade anthrax was legal under the treaty because the production of small quantities is permitted for "peaceful and protective" purposes (such as, to prepare countermeasures to a germ warfare attack).

Afghanistan, Central Asia, Georgia
KEY TO OIL PROFITS

BY KAREN TALBOT

By putting various pieces of the puzzle together we begin to get a picture of what really is behind Bush's "war on terrorism." We see that the groundwork for the current us military actions in Afghanistan was being built for several years.

What comes into focus is that the horrific September 11 terrorist attacks have, among other things, provided a new opportunity for the United States. Acting on behalf of giant oil companies, the U.S. has permanently entrenched its military in the former Soviet Republics of Central Asia, and the Caucasus, where there are vast petroleum reserves—the second-largest in the world. Strategically, this also positions U.S. armed might on the western doorstep of China, posing an unprecedented threat not only to those countries but to South Asia and the entire world. The way is now open to jump-start projects for oil and gas pipelines through western Afghanistan and Pakistan, including to Karachi on the Arabian Sea—the most feasible and cheapest route for transporting those fuels to market. Afghanistan itself has untapped oil and gas, as does Pakistan.[1]

The recent deployment of U.S. military personnel in the Pankisi Gorge of Georgia, ostensibly to fight terrorists, is aimed at guaranteeing and protecting the projected Baku-Tbilisi-Ceyhan (Turkey) pipeline designed to bypass Russia and Iran. Meanwhile, U.S. energy companies have been feverishly exploring a section of the Caspian Sea, flouting the legalities and disputes surrounding jurisdiction over these sectors, especially between Azerbaijan and Iran.[2]

Some pundits say Washington merely seeks to guarantee supplies of oil for U.S. consumers, which would explain why Central Asia is in our zone of "national interests." In reality, the U.S. relies heavily on domestic sources and on Venezuela, Canada, and Africa.[3] No, this is about oil corporation *profits* which can be greatly enhanced by selling to energy-hungry South, East, and Southeast Asia, and by outflanking China and Russia for those Central Asian-Caspian Sea Basin energy resources and for the pipelines to transport them to market.

Supplies of natural gas and oil, including those from newly discovered huge oil reserves in Kazakhstan, could easily be piped through existing conduits traversing Russia. But bypassing, and thus hindering, Russian petroleum operations that rely heavily on European customers, would provide Western corporations another benefit. They would gain greater access to the European market. Building the Afghanistan pipelines would also mean spurning an even more direct route to the Arabian Sea through Iran. This would thwart the growing cooperation between Iran, Russia, and the European oil companies, which have invested heavily in Iran's oil and gas sectors, all of whom are pursuing that pipeline corridor. This is a major factor in the growing rivalry between the U.S. and Europe in the ongoing imperial quest for corporate expansion.

THE GREAT OIL GAME

Frank Viviano, in an article in the *San Francisco Chronicle* asserts: "[T]he hidden stakes in the war against terrorism can be summed up in a single word: oil.... It is inevitable that the war against terrorism will be seen by many as a war on behalf of America's Chevron, Exxon, and Arco; France's TotalFinaElf; British Petroleum; Royal Dutch Shell; and other multinational giants, which have hundreds of billions of dollars of investment in the region...developing nations [are] already convinced...of a conspiratorial collaboration between global capital and U.S. military might."[4]

Writing in the Hong Kong-based *Asia Times*, a business-oriented publication, Ranjit Devraj states: "Just as the Gulf War in 1991 was about oil, the new conflict in South and Central Asia is no less about access to the region's abundant petroleum resource."[5]

The very nature of the system inevitably drives corporations to expand or die. This will be done at any cost, no matter the suffering it may bring to human beings or the devastation it unleashes upon the environment. Such are the characteristics of today's imperialism, the main source of war, terrorism, and violence. Commerce in oil remains paramount in this process.

More than ever, these imperial foreign and military policies are being carried out by top U.S. government leaders, from the president and vice president to CIA officials who have direct ties to the corporations and banks that stand to derive superprofits from them. This is particularly true of the oil, energy, banking, and military-aerospace sectors.

UNOCAL AND AFGHANISTAN

A consortium headed by Unocal had for years sought to build a gas pipeline from Turkmenistan's Dauletabad gas field through Afghanistan and Pakistan to the Arabian Sea. Later they put together a larger consortium, the Central Asia Pipeline Project, to carry oil from the Chardzhou oil field essentially following the same route.[6]

John J. Maresca, vice president of Unocal, in testimony before a House of Representatives committee (February 12, 1998), spoke of the tremendous untapped hydrocarbon reserves in the Caspian region and promoted the plan to build a pipeline through Afghanistan as the cheapest route for transporting the oil to Asian markets. He stated that the Taliban controlled the territory through which the pipeline would extend. Pointing out that most nations did not recognize that government, he emphasized that the project could not begin until a recognized government was in place.[7]

Yet a major reason for Washington's support of the Taliban between 1994 and 1997 was the expectation that they would swiftly conquer the whole country, enabling Unocal to build a pipeline through Afghanistan. Pakistan, the U.S., and Saudi Arabia "are responsible for the very existence and maintenance of the Taliban."[8]

In his book *Taliban*, Central Asian expert Ahmed Rashid said: "Impressed by the ruthlessness and willingness of the then-emerging Taliban to cut a pipeline deal, the State Department and Pakistan's Inter-Services Intelligence agency agreed to funnel arms and funding to the Taliban in their war against the ethnically Tajik Northern Alliance. As recently as 1999, U.S. taxpayers paid the entire annual salary of every single Taliban government official..."[9]

Unocal had even secured agreement from the Taliban to build the pipeline, according to Hugh Pope, writing in the *Wall Street Journal*. [10]

The *Washington Post* on May 25, 2001, reported that the U.S. government "pledged another $43 million in assistance to Afghanistan, [the Taliban government] raising total aid this year to $124 million and making the United States the largest humanitarian donor to the country."[11] This was less than four months before the September 11 attacks.

In an article in the British *Daily Mirror*, John Pilger stated: "When the Taliban took Kabul in 1996, Washington said nothing. Why? Because Taliban leaders were soon on their way to Houston, Texas, to be entertained by executives of the oil company, Unocal."

"With secret U.S. government approval, the company offered them a generus cut of the profits of the oil and gas pumped through a pipeline that the Americans wanted to build from the Soviet Central Asia through Afghanistan..."

"Although the deal fell through, it remains an urgent priority of the administration of George W. Bush, which is steeped in the oil industry. Bush's concealed agenda is to exploit the oil and gas reserves in the Caspian basin ... Only if the pipeline runs through Afghanistan can the Americans hope to control it."[12]

TALIBAN WANTED MORE

An Argentine oil company, Bridas, was also in the bidding to build a pipeline. The same month Taliban representatives were being given red carpet treatment by Unocal in Texas, another delegation went to Buenos Aires to meet with Bridas executives. There was an intense campaign by Unocal and Washington to outmaneuver Bridas. The Taliban played one company against the other.[13]

The Taliban and Osama bin Laden were demanding, as part of the deal, that Unocal rebuild the infrastructure in Afghanistan and allow them access to the oil in several places. Unocal rejected this demand.[14]

Nevertheless, the Bush Administration held a series of negotiations with the Taliban early in 2001, despite the developing rift with them over the pipeline scheme. Laila Helms, who was hired as the public relations agent for the Taliban government, brought Rahmatullah Hashimi, an advisor to Mullah Omar, to Washington as recently as March 2001. (Helms is the niece of Richard Helms, former chief of the CIA and former ambassador to Iran.) One of the meetings was held on August 2, just one month before September 11, when Christina Rocca, in charge of Asian Affairs at the State Department, met Taliban Ambassador to Pakistan Abdul Salem Zaef in Islamabad. Rocca has had extensive connections with Afghanistan including supervising the delivery of Stinger missiles to the mujahideen in the 1980s. She had been in charge of contacts with Islamist fundamentalist guerrilla groups for the CIA.[15]

"At one moment during one of the negotiations, U.S. representatives told the Taliban, 'either you accept our offer of a carpet of gold, or we bury you under a carpet of bombs,'" said Jean-Charles Brisard, coauthor of *Bin Laden, the Forbidden Truth*.[16]

When Washington decided to break with the Taliban, they took advantage of the fact that that the U.N. had continued to refuse to recognize their government. Then, of course, the Taliban suddenly became more vulnerable after September 11, for "harboring" Osama bin Laden. Thus it became much easier to win international support for bombing them. Another compelling reason may have been that the Northern Alliance forces, with whom the U.S. would have to join forces, controlled the portion of the country near Turkmenistan, Tajikistan, and Uzbekistan, whose governments were helping to support the Alliance. This offered convenience for the U.S. military to base troops in those countries. The Northern Alliance consists largely of ethnic Uzbeks and Tajiks. The Taliban is made up of Pashtun tribesmen— along with large numbers from Pakistan, Arab countries, and elsewhere— who came to be trained and to fight in Afghanistan as well as in Chechnya, Kashmir, Bosnia, Kosovo, and former Soviet republics in Central Asia.

CIA SPAWNS TALIBAN

All of these disparate mujahideen forces, led by feudal landholders and warlords and Osama bin Laden's organization, were incubated by the CIA in

THIS MODERN WORLD   by TOM TOMORROW

the 1980s when the largest-ever covert operation was carried out in Afghanistan. It was directed against the newly-born government of the Saur Revolution (which gave equal rights to women and set up health care, literacy, housing, job creation, and land reform programs) and then against the Soviets. The mujahideen, who had been trained and armed by the CIA, murdered teachers, doctors, and nurses, tortured women for not wearing the veil, and shot down civilian airliners with U.S.–supplied Stinger missiles.[17]

The story sold to the public by the media is that the Soviets invaded Afghanistan on December 24, 1979, and then in response, the U.S. and some Islamic countries fought back to repel the invasion. Actually, President Jimmy Carter secretly approved CIA efforts to try to topple the government of Afghanistan in July 1979, knowing that the U.S. actions were likely to provoke Soviet intervention. Zbigniew Brzezinski, National Security Adviser in the Carter Administration, confirmed this in an interview with the French publication *Le Nouvel Observateur*.[18]

A remarkable description of CIA operations in Afghanistan can be found in the book, *Victory—The Reagan Administration's Secret Strategy that Hastened the Collapse of the Soviet Union*.[19] The book carries many boastful accounts by William Casey, director of the CIA under President Reagan. It paints a vivid picture of how Casey, himself, convinced the Saudi Arabians to match CIA funding of the mujahideen, and how all the money, and, training were funneled through the Pakistan Intelligence Service (ISI).

According to the book, "The strategy [to bring down the USSR under Reagan] attacked the very heart of the Soviet system and included ... [among several other key operations] substantial financial and military support to the Afghan resistance (sic), as well as supplying the mujahideen person-

nel to take the war into the Soviet Union itself ... [and a] campaign to reduce dramatically Soviet hard currency earnings by driving down the price of oil with Saudi cooperation and limiting natural gas exports to the West...

We learn about the quantities of weapons that were delivered—including Stinger missiles and increasingly sophisticated armaments. "Tens of thousands of arms and ammunition were going through...every year" rising to 65,000 tons by 1985. Approximately 100 Afghans living abroad were schooled in the "art of arms shipping." Two-week courses in "anti-tank and anti-aircraft guns, mine laying and lifting, demolitions, urban warfare, and sabotage were offered for thousands of fighters. Twenty thousand mujahideen were being pumped out every year by these schools dubbed 'CIA U' by some wags..."

"Specially trained units working inside the Soviet Union would be equipped with...rocket launchers and high-tech explosives provided by the CIA. They were to seek out Soviet civilian and military targets for sabotage." This is just a small taste of the details revealed in *Victory*. [20]

NEW MADE-IN-THE-U.S.A. GOVERNMENT

The disparate warlord-led factions, including the Taliban, all part of the CIA-financed mujahideen, have continued to fight each other for years. As always, the ascendancy of one group over another inevitably leads to more fractiousness and warfare.

The newly established "interim" government of Afghanistan, conjured up by George W. and his entourage, purports to include all of these militias along with various Pashtun warlords who are linked with the Taliban.

UNOCAL EMERGES AGAIN

This "interim" government is headed by Hamid Karzai who, according to the Saudi newspaper *Al-Watan*, has been a Central Intelligence Agency covert operator since the 1980s, when he helped the CIA in Afghanistan. Karzai supported the Taliban and was a consultant for Unocal.[21]

George W. Bush's envoy to the new government, Zalmay Khalizad, also worked for Unocal. He drew up the risk analysis for the pipeline in 1997, lobbied for the Taliban, and took part in negotiations with them. After acquiring U.S. citizenship, Khalizad became a special advisor to the State Department during the Reagan Administration and a key liaison with the mujahideen in the 1980s. He was under secretary of defense in the administration of the elder George Bush; headed the Bush-Cheney transition team for the Defense Department; worked for the right-wing think tank Rand Corporation; and was placed on the National Security Council where he reports to National Security Advisor Condoleeza Rice.[22] Rice is an expert on Central Asia, and is a member of the Board of Chevron. Both Khalizad and Rice had long advocated the establishment of U.S. military bases in the region.

ENRON AND OTHER BUSH CONNECTIONS

The connections between the Bush Administration, the oil, energy, and military-industrial corporations, and intrigues in Central Asian and the Caucasus are very intimate ones. Here are only a few:

The proposed Baku-Ceyhan pipeline is represented by the law firm of Baker & Botts. The principal attorney is James Baker, former secretary of state and chief spokesman for the Bush campaign in the struggle over Florida votes.[23]

In 1994, Cheney, as CEO of Halliburton, was a member of Kazakhstan's Oil Advisory Board and helped broker a deal between Chevron and Kazakhstan. Enron Corporation, closely linked with Bush and Cheney, conducted the feasibility study for the $2.5 billion Trans-Caspian pipeline—a joint venture with Turkmenistan, Bechtel Corp, and General Electric.[24]

Moreover, Enron had a $3 billion investment in the Dabhol power plant near Bombay, India, one of its largest-ever projects constituting the single biggest direct foreign investment in India's history. There was massive public opposition to the project in India, ultimately including the Indian government, due to the huge costs to consumers (700 percent more than other projects). Enron's survival depended on getting a cheap source of gas and oil to save the project. This could be solved by building a branch of the proposed natural gas pipeline from Turkmenistan through Afghanistan to terminate in Multan near the India border. In addition, in 1997, Enron announced it was going to spend over $1 billion building and improving the lines between the Dabhol plant and India's pipeline network. In other words the gas would be piped from Multan, Pakistan, to New Delhi, thence to Bombay and the Enron plant.[25]

Enron was expecting also to cash in on the main spur of the pipeline ending on the Pakistan coast from which hydrocarbon supplies would be exported to the other vast Asian markets. Clearly, developments in Afghanistan were critical of Enron. George W. became president just at the point when the India project was in serious trouble. One month later, Vice President Dick Cheney moved into action and held his first secret meeting with Enron CEO Kenneth Lay. The Bush Administration is refusing to reveal the details of this and subsequent consultations with Lay, even in the face of a General Accounting Office suit against Cheney for release of the papers. Nevertheless, it *has* been documented that the vice president's energy task force did change a draft energy proposal to include a provision to boost oil and natural gas production in India in February 2001. The amendment was clearly targeted to help Enron's Dabhol plant. Later, Cheney stepped in to help Enron collect its $64 million debt during a June 27 meeting with India's opposition leader Sonia Gandhi. These are but some revelations concerning the machinations by Bush and his cohorts to help Enron regarding the India deal.[26] Some of the negotiations with the Taliban, such as those led by Christina Rocca, to promote the Trans-Afghan pipeline and thus help save Enron, coincidentally transpired just prior to the September 11 terrorist attacks.

Brown & Root—a business unit of Halliburton Company where Vice President Cheney was CEO until taking office—will be upgrading the U.S. air base in Uzbekistan. According to an article in *Stars and Stripes,* "Brown & Root scouts traveled to Central Asia [including Afghanistan] to check out U.S. bases.... By mid-June [2001] the contractor is expected to take charge of base camp maintenance, airfield services, and fuel supplies. For troops' welfare the company will run the dining halls and laundry service and will oversee the Morale, Welfare, and Recreation program."[27]

Brown & Root perform similar lucrative services at other bases, including those in Bosnia and Kosovo—most notably the giant and permanent Camp Bondsteel in Kosovo located (along with satellite bases) conveniently near the soon-to-be-constructed Trans-Balkan AMBO pipeline.

U.S. BASES IN AFGHANISTAN AND FORMER SOVIET REPUBLICS

"If one looks at the map of the big American bases created for the war in Afghanistan, one is struck by the fact that they are completely identical to the route of the projected oil pipelines to the Indian Ocean," says Uri Averny, a former member of the Israeli Knesset, writing in the daily *Ma'ariv* in Israel.[28]

In the name of conducting the war, the U.S. also won agreement to station troops at former Soviet airfields in Uzbekistan and Tajikistan, and to build a long-term base in Kyrgyzstan. Kazakhstan is next.[29]

The big payoff for the Bush Administration is the entrenchment of a permanent U.S. military presence in oil-rich Central Asia—which is also wide open to another coveted resource-rich region, Siberia. Thus, realization of other goals could be closer at hand: the further balkanization of central Asian and Trans-Caucasus nations into easily controlled emirate-like entities, lacking any real sovereignty; and further military encirclement of China. All of this is icing on the cake—the "cake" being the Trans-Afghanistan pipelines, with their access to and dominance of the South, Southeast, and East Asian markets.

Another major goal of Bush Administration policies appears to be to obstruct or control China's access to the oil and natural gas of Central Asia. China has a rapidly increasing need for those sources of energy. It has relatively few reserves within its borders, the largest being in Tibet. China has joint partnership with U.S. companies for the development of its oil. Nevertheless, as is always the case, those U.S.–based oil conglomerates would much prefer to get their hands on the whole pie and not just a large slice. That includes unfettered access to Chinese consumers.

Potentially vast sources of petroleum and natural gas have been discovered in the South China Sea. A struggle is looming among the littoral states regarding jurisdiction over these offshore reserves, with China laying claim to a large portion of the sea including the Spratly and Paracel Islands. The Philippine government is one of the disputants over this territory. The Philippines are strategically located in this region and adjacent the critically important sea lanes through which oil and other goods are shipped to and from Japan, China, and Korea.

Brown & Root just built the largest offshore oil platform in the world for Shell Philippines.[30] The current U.S. "war on terrorism" military operations in the Philippines are clearly linked to major oil considerations.

Bush's perpetual war is already headed towards Iraq, Somalia, Yemen, and Iran—not so coincidentally, these are all rich in petroleum. So too, the ongoing U.S.–backed brutal Israeli war against the Palestinians continues to be about maintaining U.S. hegemony over the oil-rich Middle East. U.S. military support to Colombia is now openly admitted by the Bush Administration to be aimed at protecting pipelines and putting down the peoples' insurgency. Similarly, the recent U.S.–backed coup attempt against the Chavez government of Venezuela had much to do with controlling that country's petroleum riches.

Increasingly, U.S. and world public opinion is awakening to the hidden agenda of the "war on terrorism" earmarked by the corporate frenzy to plunder oil and other resources, particularly in the petroleum-rich arch stretching from the Middle East to Southeast Asia. The war in Afghanistan is central to reaping super-profits from all that "black gold."

Versions of this updated article appeared in *Global Outlook*, Spring 2002-Issue #1, <www.globalresearch.ca>, and *Correspondence* (Paris), among other publications. It appeared on numerous Web sites and has been translated into other languages.

See also:, "Chechnya: More Blood for Oil," *CovertAction Quarterly*, No. 69, Spring/Summer 2000, "Backing Up Globalization with Military Might,' *CovertAction Quarterly*, No. 68, "Bush Administration Dripping in Oil and Energy Profits," <www.icpj.org>, among other writings on the subject by Karen Talbot.

NOTES

1. "Massive untapped gas reserves are believed to be lying beneath Pakistan's remotest deserts, but they are being held hostage by armed tribal groups demanding a better deal from the central government," reported Agence France-Presse just days before September 11, says Nina Burleigh for <TomPaine.com>.
2. Armen Georgian, "U.S. Eyes Caspian Oil in 'War on Terrorism,'" *Foreign Policy in Focus*, April 30, 2002.
3. U.S. National Security Council, A National Security Strategy for a New Century (Washington, D.C.; White House, October 1998), as reported in Michael T. Klare, *Resource Wars*, New York: Metropolitan Books, Henry Holt, 2001): 32.
4. Frank Viviano, "Energy Future Rides on U.S. War—Conflict Centered in World's Oil Patch," *San Francisco Chronicle*, September 26, 2001.
5. Ranjit Devraj, *Asia Time*.
6. Ishtiaq Ahmad, "U.S.–Taliban Relations: Friend Turns Fiend," Lecturer in International Relations , Eastern Mediterranean University, North Cyprus, Nicosia, October 3, 2001, <www.tehelka.com/channels/currentaffairs/2001/oct/3/ca100301usl.htm>.
7. John J. Maresca, vice president of Unocal, in testimony before a committee of the U.S. House of Representatives, February 12, 1998.
8. Larry P. Goodson, *Afghanistan's Endless War*, University of Washington Press (Seattle and London: 2001): 81.
9. Ted Rall, "It's About Oil," *San Francisco Chronicle*, November 2, 2001: A25.
10. Hugh Pope, "Unocal Group Plans Central Asian Pipeline," *Wall Street Journal*, October 27, 1997.
11. *Washington Post*, May 25, 2001.
12. John Pilger, "This War is a Fraud," *Daily Mirror*, October 29, 2001.
13. Rall, A25.
14. Ahmad, "U.S.–Taliban Relations: Friend Turns Fiend."
15. Ibid.
16. Charles Brisard and Guillaume Dasquie, *Bin Laden, La vérite interdite (Bin Laden, the Forbidden Truth)*. Brisard had worked for the French secret service (DST) and wrote a report for them in 1997 on the Al Qaeda network. Dasquie is a journalist and publisher of the "Intelligence Online." As reported by V.K. Shashikumar, New Delhi, November 21, 2001, <www.tehelka.com/channels/currentaffairs/2001/nov/21/call2112101america.htm>.
17. Phillip Bonosky, *Afghanistan-Washington's Secret War*, Second Editon (New York: International Publishers, 2001).

18. *Le Nouvel Observateur*, January 15-21, 1998. (This is not included in the edition sent to the U.S.) Reported by and translation from original French by Bill Blum, author of "Killing Hope."

19. Peter Schweizer, *Victory—The Reagan Administration's Secret Strategy that Hastened the Collapse of the Soviet Union* (New York: Atlantic Monthly Press, 1994).

20. Ibid.

21. Tim Wheeler, "Bush Calls for Wider War, is Silent on Enron," *People's Weekly World*, February 2, 2002.

22. Patrick Martin, "Oil Company Advisor Named U.S. representative to Afghanistan," January 3, 2002, World Socialist Web site, <www.wsws.org/articles/2002/jan2002/oil-jo3.shtml>.

23. Salim Muwakkil, <OutlookIndia.com>, March 21, 2002.

24. Ibid.

25. Ron Callari, "The Enron-Cheney-Taliban Connection?" *Albion Monitor*, February 28, 2002.

26. Ibid.

27. Rick Scavetta, *Stars and Stripes*, May 2, 2002.

28. Uri Averny, *Ma'ariv* (Israel), February 14, 2002.

29. Michael R. Gordon and C. J. Chivers, "U.S., Tajikistan Make a Deal on Military Cooperation," *San Francisco Chronicle*, November 5, 2001: A4.

30. "Malampaya Topsides Installed in the South China Sea," Kellog Brown and Root Press Release, March 28, 2001, <www.halliburton.com/KBR/KBRNWS/KBRNWS_032801>.

THIS MODERN WORLD

BY TOM TOMORROW

CHAPTER 3

Censored Déjà Vu
WHAT HAPPENED TO LAST YEAR'S MOST CENSORED STORIES

BY PETER PHILLIPS AND THE PROJECT CENSORED WRITING TEAM
Chris Salvano, Krista Arata Eric Garrison, Kevin Cody,
Kerry Beck, Stephen Dietrich, and Kathleen O'Rourke-Christopher

INTRODUCTION
Déjà Vu: East Timor

BY CARL JENSEN

The world applauded on May 20 as tens of thousands of celebrating East Timorese crowded onto a racetrack in their nation's capital to witness the official birth of the Democratic Republic of East Timor as an independent sovereign state.

When United Nations Secretary General Kofi Annan handed power to the country's new president, Jose Alexandre Gusmao, it formally ended four centuries of Portuguese colonial rule, 24 years of oppressive Indonesian occupation, and two years of interim rule by the United Nations.

After taking the oath of office, Gusmao told the crowd, "Today we are a people standing on equal footing with all other peoples of the world. Today we rejoice as an independent nation, governing our own destiny."

Representatives of more than 90 nations including former President Bill Clinton, Indonesian President Megawati Sukarnoputri, Portuguese President Jorge Sampaio, and Australian Prime Minister John Howard, were there to witness the birth of the world's 192nd nation, the first of the new millennium.

Shortly before a peacekeeper lowered the blue U.N. flag and the new flag of East Timor was raised, Kofi Annan told the cheering crowd, "I salute you, people of East Timor, for the courage and perseverance you have shown. That a small nation is able to inspire the world and be the focus of our attention is the highest tribute that I can pay."

Plaudits aside, it was not that easy for East Timor to capture the attention of the world.

In 1979, more than 20 years earlier, East Timor was the number seven *Censored* story of the year, according to Project Censored. The Project revealed that up to 100,000 East Timorese men, women, and children had been slaughtered since Indonesian military forces invaded the tiny territory in 1975 with the support of the United States.

In 1985, Project Censored reported that after 10 years of genocide in East Timor, the world's press did still not cover the tragedy. It was the number three *Censored* story of the year. By then, Amnesty International reported that up to 200,000 East Timorese, a third of the population, had died as a result of Indonesian aggression.

While America's mainstream media recently reported the hard-won independence of East Timor, they neglected to acknowledge the covert involvement of the United States in the region. The United States provided Indonesia with armaments, military training, and political support for its aggression against East Timor. The U.S. officially suspended its military assistance program to Indonesia in 1992, allegedly because of the world attention being paid to the East Timor holocaust.

Critics, responding to questions of why the media had failed to report America's support of Indonesian aggression against East Timor, attributed the press silence to government and corporate interests. They pointed out that the world's leading oil conglomerates were vitally interested in the oil and gas reserves under the Timor Sea. A petroleum industry trade magazine, *Offshore*, reported in May 1996 that companies poised to exploit oil reserves off Indonesia and East Timor included Exxon, Conoco, Chevron, Texaco, Maxus Energy, Marathon, Arco, and Unocal.

A classic example of the cozy relationship between U.S. corporate and political interests and the repressive regime in Indonesia is found in the case of Freeport-McMoRan, one of the world's largest producers of copper and gold.

Freeport-McMoRan is a New Orleans-based company that runs the world's biggest gold mine in the Indonesian rainforest. In 1998, it had access to about 2.8 million acres.

When Indonesia invaded East Timor in 1975, it was with the approval of Secretary of State Henry Kissinger and President Gerald Ford. The approval given to Indonesia's General Suharto by Kissinger and Ford came to be known as "the big wink." In 1995, Kissinger was appointed to the board of directors of Freeport-McMoRan. His firm, Kissinger Associates also is a lobbyist and consultant to Freeport-McMoRan.

In retrospect, we wonder if East Timor would have celebrated its independence on May 20, 2002, if it had not been for the international support given the courageous East Timorese people by individuals like political analyst Noam Chomsky, who wrote the original 1979 source story, "East Timor: The Press Cover-up"; groups like the East Timor Action Network and Amnesty International that wouldn't let the world forget about East Timor; and media watchdog organizations like Project Censored that challenged the press with failing to cover the East Timor issue.

Carl Jensen is professor emeritus of Communication Studies at Sonoma State University and founder and director emeritus of Project Censored.

Here are updates on the most *Censored* stories from *Censored 2001* and other past featured stories.

2001 #1 CENSORED STORY

WORLD BANK AND MULTINATIONAL CORPORATIONS SEEK TO PRIVATIZE WATER

Our finite sources of fresh water (less than one-half of 1 percent of the world's total water stock) are being diverted, depleted, and polluted. If current trends persist, by the year 2025, two-thirds of the world's population will be living in a state of serious water deprivation. Global consumption of water is doubling every 20 years, more than twice the rate of human population growth. According to the United Nations, more than one billion people already lack access to fresh drinking water.

Multinational corporations recognize these trends and are trying to monopolize water supplies around the world. Monsanto, Bechtel, and other global multinationals are seeking control of world water systems and supplies. Monsanto estimates that water will become a multibillion-dollar market in the coming decades.

Governments are signing away their control over domestic water supplies by participating in trade treaties such as the North American Free Trade Agreement (NAFTA) and in institutions such as the World Trade Organization (WTO). These agreements give transnational corporations the unprecedented right to the water of signatory companies.

Grassroots resistance to the privatization of water emerges as companies expand profit-taking. Bechtel was contracted to manage the water system in Cochabamba, Bolivia, after the World Bank required Bolivia to privatize. When Bechtel pushed up the price of water, the entire city went on a general strike. The military killed a seventeen-year-old boy and arrested the water rights leaders. But after four months of unrest, the Bolivian government forced Bechtel out of Cochambamba.

SOURCES: International Forum on Globalization: Special Report, June 1999; Maude Barlow, "The Global Water Crisis and the Commodification of the World's Water Supply," *PRIME*, July 10, 2000, <www.ifg.org/bgsum mary.html>; Jim Shultz, "Just Add Water," *THIS*, July/August 2000; Jim Shultz, "Water Fallout: Bolivians Battle Globalization," *In These Times*, May 15, 2000, <www.inthesetimes.com>; Vandana Shiva, "Monsanto's Billion-Dollar Water Monopoly Plans," *Canadian Dimension*, February 2000, <www.purefood.org/Monsanto/waterfish.cfm>; Jim Shultz, "Water Fallout," *Canadian Dimension*, February 2000; Daniel Zoll, "Trouble on Tap," *San Francisco Bay Guardian*, May 31, 2000, <www.sfbg.com/News/34/35/ bech2.html>; Pratap Chatterjee, "The Earth Wrecker" *San Francisco Bay Guardian*, May 31, 2000, <www.sfbg.com/News/34/35/bech1.html>.

Corporate news coverage: *Toronto Globe & Mail*, May 11, 2000.

UPDATE 2002: Is water a right or a commodity? Murray Dobbin, in *National Editions*, February 8, 2001, says that water, the "most common of elements, the thing of life itself, is rapidly being drawn into the madness and ruin that is corporate globalization." He believes that who controls it and who will die because they can't afford it, will be the most divisive issue of this century. Massive public opposition to corporate globalizers prevails, as water is deemed a means of life.

The clash in the Third World community of Cochabamba, Bolivia, instigated a flood of discourse on water rights and the road to privatization. According to Sophie Tremolet, writing for the *Manchester Guardian Weekly*, "The World Bank places the value of the current water market at more than one trillion dollars" and *Fortune* argues that "water is the best investment sector of the century." *Fortune* estimates the global water market to be a $405 billion-a-year industry. Fresh water supplies are dwindling and less than 1 percent of the earth's water is drinkable. Currently 95 percent of the world's fresh water supply is owned publicly. Corporations see this as a huge profit making opportunity and are acting in concert with global power structures to transfer water rights into private ownership.

The market for water and sanitation services is increasingly global. International conglomerates such as Vivendi and Suez, Lyonnaise des Eaux in France, Thames Water in England, RWE in Germany, and Bechtel and Azurix in the United States are competing for giant contracts to manage and set up provisions for cities' water services, and to acquire rights to local water supplies. Other corporations are trying to buy bulk quantities of water from nations like Canada or Norway and ship it in tankers or huge floating bags to water-scarce regions.

Author Maude Barlow states that the earth's water system will only support one more doubling of demand and this is estimated to occur within 30 years. Water in the future will be as lucrative as oil has been in the twentieth century. Worldwide, more than five million people, mostly children, die every year from drinking poor quality water.

U.S. Global Corporation recently signed an agreement with Sitka, Alaska in which 18 billion gallons of glacier water per year will be exported to China. The water will be bottled and labeled by low-paid Chinese workers and then exported to other countries.

Loans from the World Bank to help fund development projects are conditional, requiring municipal governments receiving the loans to privatize their water systems. This worsens conditions, as in Cochabamba in February of 2000, when the World Bank backed water pricing increases to guarantee that Bechtel would earn a 16 percent profit. As water prices tripled, some people in Cochabamba had to pay 20 percent of their income for water. Residents who were not hooked up to the water system had meters put on their private wells and were forced to pay Bechtel for the water that they drew.

According to author Jim Schultz, after Bechtel was forced out of Bolivia, the company filed a $25 million lawsuit for lost "potential" profits from the Bolivian government. Bechtel's suit was filed with the International Center for Settlement of Investment Disputes, a branch of the World Bank that operates in secrecy. In order to qualify for this legal "arbitration," Bechtel shifted the registration of its subsidiary corporation IWL (International Water Ltd.) to Holland. In the *San Francisco Chronicle*, February 11, 2001, Lewis Dolinsky writes, "under the terms of a bilateral agreement between Bolivia and the Netherlands, where IWL is incorporated, IWL is entitled to out-of-pocket expenses plus unrealized profits projected over the life of the deal."

In the U.S., 86 percent of residential water comes from public utilities and 13 percent comes from private companies. Private water companies are expanding their foothold by establishing operations and maintenance contracts for water delivery and wastewater treatment services. In the past few years dozens of cities like Atlanta, Indianapolis, Jersey City, and Gary, Indiana, have signed such long-term contracts.

According to Maude Barlow, pollution and scarcity are the major problems with water availability and control. Allowing the WTO or globalization treaties like the NAFTA to make decisions about our water supplies and how prices are to be set is a dangerous proposition. Pete Gleick from the *Boston Globe* states that privatization of our water systems runs the risk of turning over control of our most precious resource to "corporations without financial interest in protecting the long-term interests of our local communities or natural ecosystems."

The expanding privatization of water has spurred a growing number of activists, and organizations to respond to the actions of large multinational corporations. Perhaps most notable among these activists is Oscar Olivera, the trade union leader and organizer who played a large role in the ousting of Bechtel and its consortium from Cochabamba. In October of 2001, Olivera was in Washington, DC ,to receive the Letelier-Moffitt Human Rights Award for his actions in Cochabamba and his history of labor organizing in Bolivia. Marcela Olivera, Oscar's sister, made a trip to San Francisco last year to speak on water rights as a spokesperson for the Coordinating Committee for the Defense of Water and Life. Commonly referred to as La Coordinadora, this group consists of the workers, peasants, environmentalists, and human rights groups that took control over the water system in Bolivia when Bechtel was forced out. In an interview with the *San Francisco Chronicle* in February of 2001, Olivera claims, "The [Bolivian] government has taken many actions against many people since April—raided houses, wiretapped phones. Death threats, most recently in October. Harassment is continual."

According to a report by Savannah Blackwell in the *San Francisco Bay Guardian*, November 7, 2001, Bechtel was denied access to San Francisco's water system. The San Francisco Board of Supervisors approved a plan on November 5, 2001, that would end Bechtel's contract with the Public Utilities Commission, which had been leaning toward privatizing the city's water system. Bechtel was working with several other private companies to form the San Francisco Water Alliance. The International Federation of Professional and Technical Engineers, Local 21, protested this action when it was discovered that out of the nearly $8 million that the city had paid to the Alliance, "nearly $5 million went for work that was unnecessary, that duplicated work already performed by city staffers, or that wasn't specialized enough to require the use of a highly paid outside consultant."

Throughout the world, proposals to privatize water systems or let bulk water enter international trade are running into increasing opposition. When water rates doubled and water quality dropped earlier this year in Tucuman, Argentina, the government terminated a 1995 contract with a private concern. The Canadian government has been prompted to pass laws prohibiting the bulk export of its water from Canada. The 1980s privatization of Britain's water system has been heavily modified to allow for stronger government oversight and regulation.

Two-thirds of the world live in areas that are experiencing water "stress," with some 1.4 billion people lacking access to safe water and sanitation. Countries where the crisis is greatest lack not only the water, but the funds needed for building the necessary infrastructure to deliver safe water. Water is generally safe and plentiful in rich countries, but those in developing countries use public taps or water from vendors. The poor pay much more per liter than the rich pay for their piped water. Private vendors or tanker trucks bring water into the slums at great cost to the buyers. In Haiti, Indonesia, and Peru, some of the world's poorest people are buying water of dubious quality from private vendors for as much as 50 or even 100 times what wealthier residents connected to municipal systems pay.

SOURCES: Murray Dobbin, "Water: Right or Commodity?", *National Post*, February 8, 2001. Lewis Dolinsky, "Cochabamba's Water Rebellion— and Beyond," *San Francisco Chronicle*, February 11, 2001. Esther Addley, "Tourist's Water Demands Bleed Resorts Dry," *Guardian Unlimited*, May 12, 2001. South African Municipal Workers Union, "World Water Day of Morning," March 20, 2001, Press statement; Yochi Dreazen and Andrew Caffrey, "The End of Privatization?", *Wall Street Journal*, November 19, 2001; "Bechtel's Legal Action Against Bolivia," Pacific News Service, December 19, 2001; Joan Lowy, "Potable Water Becoming 21st Century's New Gold," Scripps Howard News Service, December 27, 2001; Peter H. Gleick, "A Call For Strict Worldwide Standards," *The Boston Globe*, January 6, 2002.

2001 # 2 CENSORED STORY

OSHA FAILS TO PROTECT U.S. WORKERS

United States labor laws are poorly enforced and fail to meet the basic human rights of U.S. workers. Each year, about 6,000 workers die on the job from accidents and another 50,000 to 70,000 workers die annually from "occupationally acquired diseases." The Occupational Safety and Health Administration (OSHA) is not capable of effectively overseeing U.S. workplaces.

The entire federal and state worker health and safety apparatus involves just 2,300 inspectors, who must cover America's 102 million workers in 6.7 million workplaces. That comes to one inspector for every 44,348 workers. Theoretically, it would take OSHA 110 years to inspect each workplace under its jurisdiction just once.

Titan International, an Illinois-based company, had been under fire at its plant and at other subsidiary locations. Despite a lengthy recent record of safety violations and injuries—including two deaths—Titan's Des Moines plant has stymied five attempts by Iowa OSHA to inspect some 23 complaints lodged by workers. Titan Tire refused entry to OSHA even with an inspection warrant—a violation of law and a direct assault on the integrity of the Occupational Safety and Health Act. Titan was held responsible by the Polk County District Court in Des Moines and was fined Iowa's maximum civil-contempt penalty of just $500.

Titan workers are being maimed across the country. Workers say it is usually the result of decrepit machines, minimal training, and punishing hours. Since May 1999, the United Steelworkers of America (USWA) has been challenging Titan with a slew of unfair labor practice charges. These include, but are not limited to, illegally moving jobs and equipment to avoid a union contract, refusing to bargain in good faith, discriminating against union members, and trying to permanently replace striking workers. union officials say that fines are too low and that companies, even in worker death cases, are only getting slapped on the wrist.

Titan often develops close relationships with job-starved cities. In 1997, Brownsville, Texas, gave Titan $6.5 million in free land, site improvements, and utility and wage subsidies. The state of Texas added $448,000 for job training for 168 workers. Titan received similar subsidies from the state of Virginia to the tune of $500,000.

SOURCE: *The Progressive*, February 2000, christopher D. Cook, "Losing Life and Limb on the Job,"<www.progressive.org/cook0200.htm>.

UPDATE 2002: Titan International Corporation continues to be embroiled in labor and workplace safety issues. *Censored 2001* noted that in November 1999, a heptane chemical spill at Titan Tire's Des Moines, Iowa, plant resulted in a chemical explosion that killed truck driver Douglas Oswald. In March 2000, PR Newswire picked up a news release from the United Steelworkers of America (USWA). The Iowa Occupational Safety and Health Bureau (IOSH) had proposed to fine Titan Tire Corp. $150,000 for a number of "willful" and "serious" violations of the Occupational Safety and Health Act, including Oswald's death.

Coverage of workplace safety issues and OSHA has been significant since last year's book release. In April 2000, the *Boston Globe* reported that workplace deaths were up in Massachusetts from 1998 to 1999. The *Globe* also noted that OSHA only employs 45 inspectors for its 166,986 workplaces in the state.

The *Los Angeles Times*, on August 18, 2000, documented California's dot-com building boom and the fact that construction sites are killing more people than any other industry. According to the article, between 1995 and 2000, 433 people died on construction sites in California. In 1999, there were 747 reported accidents, up nearly 40 percent since 1995. "Let's face it, this is an industry that hasn't been policed in a long time," said Vicky Heza, acting deputy chief of enforcement for Cal-OSHA.

Also in August 2000, Associated Press Newswires reported that OSHA added eight inspectors to its South Florida regional office due to a high number of construction-related deaths in the 10-county area.

In August 2001, Knight Ridder's *Fort Worth Star-Telegram* noted that while workplace deaths decreased nationally in 2000, Texas recorded a 22 percent increase in workplace deaths. The state recorded 572 workers killed in 2000, 33 percent of whom were Hispanic.

Throughout October and November 2001, the *Orange County Register* (Orange County, California) conducted a series of articles highlighting workplace deaths in the county. The articles also examined the failings of Cal-OSHA with these workplace deaths. The *Register* notes that 64 workers died countywide from 1998 to 2000. The paper also documents how Cal-OSHA investigators have taken several days, even months, to show up at a workplace after a worker's death. On November 1, the paper reported that state Senator John Burton began urging California to exempt Cal-OSHA from a new governmental hiring freeze. In a letter to Stephen Smith, head of the Department of Industrial Relations, Burton wrote, "While the heavy workload is no excuse for sloppy practices when lives are at stake, it is recognized that Cal-OSHA has never had the optimal number of investigators." This series of articles by the *Register* prompted a legislative committee to question the heads of the California Health and Safety Administration. The Administration was questioned about issues including skipping interviews with witnesses who do not speak English, the low rate of fines issued against companies, and why some inspectors waited 82 days to begin accident probes.

In May 2002, the *Fort Worth Star-Telegram* reported that OSHA was trying to reduce construction-related dangers to Hispanic workers. In North Texas, there are about 100 OSHA inspectors for about 500,000 construction workers. About 46 percent of these construction workers are Hispanic. In 1999, 54 percent of OSHA-investigated workplace deaths in Texas were Hispanics.

SOURCES: PR Newswire, March 9, 2000; *Boston Globe*, April 28, 2000; *Los Angeles Times*, August 18, 2000; Associated Press Newswires, August 19, 2000; *Fort Worth Star-Telegram*, August 16, 2001; *The Orange County Register*, October 20, 2001; *The Orange County Register*, November 1, 2001; *Orange County Register*, November 26, 2001; *Fort Worth Star-Telegram*, May 29, 2002.

2001 #3 CENSORED STORY
U.S. ARMY'S PSYCHOLOGICAL OPERATIONS PERSONNEL WORKED AT CNN

From June 1999 to March 2000, CNN employed military specialists in "psychological operations" (Psyops) in their Southeast TV bureau and CNN radio division.

CNN had hosted a total of five interns from U.S. Army Psyops, two in television, two in radio, and one in satellite operations. The military/CNN personnel belonged to the airmobile Fourth Psychological Operations Group stationed at Fort Bragg, North Carolina. One of the main tasks of this group of almost 1,200 soldiers and officers is to spread "selected information." The propaganda group was involved in the Gulf War, the war in Bosnia, and the crisis in Kosovo.

CNN and other media coverage of the war in Kosovo and of other media, has attracted criticism for having been one-sided, overly emotional, oversimplified, and

relying too heavily on NATO officials. On the other hand, journalists have complained about the lack of the reliable information from NATO; for almost all of them, it was impossible to be on the battlefield and file first-hand reports. The question remains: Did the military learn from TV people how to hold viewers' attention? Or did the Psyops people teach CNN how to help the U.S. government garner political support?

TV Guide reported in April that Psyops also had team members working at National Public Radio (NPR). This prompted two NPR stories on the program *All Things Considered.* Jeffrey Dvorkin, NPR's vice president for news, stated, "We recruited from the army and got three interns, and that was a mistake. And when we discovered that they were from Psyops branch, we finished the arrangement, and it won't happen again."

SOURCE: Alexander Cockburn, "CNN and PSYOPS," *Counterpunch*, February 16, 2000 and March 1, 2000, <www.counterpunch.org/cnnpsyops.html>.

UPDATE 2002: After the furor that resulted from reports that Psyops Interns were working at CNN and NPR in the early part of 2000, the program was discontinued and the interns were sent back to their U.S. Army base in Fort Bragg, North Carolina. With the events of 9-11, however, U.S. Army Psyops agents were once again deployed from Washington, but this time from the Pentagon's new Office of Strategic Influence (OSI). Their mission was to target foreign media organizations with disinformation campaigns in an effort to convince foreign leaders and citizens to support the U.S. "war on terrorism."

The difference this time is that certain Pentagon officials leaked the OSI plans to *The New York Times.* According to one senior Pentagon official, "Everybody understands using information operations to go after non-friendlies. When people get uncomfortable is when people use the same tools and tactics on friendlies." Once this information became known within the public sphere, Donald Rumsfeld

was forced, on February 26, 2002, to close the OSI program. However, considering the eagerly acquiescent nature of the news networks post-9-11, any disinformation campaign on the part of the Pentagon seemed hardly necessary.

SOURCE: Joel Bleifuss, "Disinformation Follies," *In These Times*, April 1, 2002.

2001 #4 CENSORED STORY
DID THE U.S. DELIBERATELY BOMB
THE CHINESE EMBASSY IN BELGRADE?

Elements within the CIA may have deliberately targeted the Chinese embassy in Belgrade, without NATO approval, because it was serving as a rebroadcast station for the Yugoslavian Army.

The Observer (London) and Copenhagen's *Politiken* reported that, according to senior U.S. and European military sources, NATO knew very well where the Chinese embassy was located and listed it as a "strictly prohibited target" at the beginning of the war. *The Observer* stated that the CIA and its British equivalent, M16, had been listening to communications from the Chinese embassy routinely since it moved to its new site in 1996. The Chinese embassy was taken off the prohibited target list after NATO detected it, sending Yugoslavian army signals to forces in the field. "Nearly everyone involved in NATO air operations (radio) signals command knows that the bombing was deliberate," said Jens Holsoe of *Politiken*, lead investigative reporter on the news team reporting on the story.

President Clinton called the bombing a "tragic mistake" and said it was the result of a mix-up. NATO claimed that they were using old maps and got the address wrong. However, *Observer* reporters quoted a Naples-based flight controller who said the NATO maps that were used during the campaign had correctly identified the Chinese embassy.

A French Ministry of Defense report stated that the flight that targeted the Chinese embassy was not under NATO command, but rather an independent U.S. bombing raid. In July 1999, CIA director George Tenet testified before Congress that of the 900 sites struck by NATO during the bombing campaign, the only one targeted by the CIA was the Chinese embassy.

SOURCES: Joel Bleifuss, "A Tragic Mistake?", *In These Times*, December 12, 1999, <www.inthesetimes.com>; Seth Ackerman, "Mission Implausible," *In These Times*, June 26, 2000, <www.inthesetimes.com/ackerman2415. html>; Yoichi Shimatsu, "Reports Showing U.S. Deliberately Bombed Chinese Embassy Deliberately Ignored by U.S. Media," *Pacific News*, October 20, 1999; "Fairness and Accuracy in Reporting," *New York Times* on Chinese Embassy Bombing: Nothing to Report, February 9, 2000, <www.fair.org/activism/china-response2.html>.

UPDATE 2002: Since 2000, several reports have surfaced indicating that the Chinese embassy bombing on May 7, 1999 was not an accident.

Details of Steven Lee Myers' investigation, reported April 17, 2000 in *The New York Times*, reveal that the CIA Counter-Proliferation Division (CPD) proposed the embassy target, apparently without being solicited by NATO or the Pentagon. This covert operations unit is responsible for the spread of missiles and nuclear, chemical, and biological weapons. Using an unclassified 1997 map of Belgrade provided by the National Imagery and Mapping Agency (NIMA), a CPD analyst is claimed to have set up the targeting, misidentifying the Yugoslav Directorate of Supply and Procurement, a military supply facility. The analyst had downloaded a targeting form from a secure Pentagon computer, filled it out, and sent the joint chiefs of staff what "appeared to be a more advanced proposal than it was," according to Myers. He states that "the reasons are not clear" why the joint chiefs never conducted a thorough review of the target.

The Pentagon blamed the CIA because it is the agency that gave the green light to bomb. Yet logistically the CIA could not have been the sole source of target information. Planning each target involves dozens of military officers in Europe and the U.S. who collect intelligence, calculate the risk of civilian casualties, decide which munitions to use, and mark the Designated Mean Point of Impact (DMPI) where the bomb would do the most damage. Targets are nominated at the Aviano Air Force Base in Italy, verified at NATO headquarters in Belgium, designated on lists sent to the Pentagon for confirmation, and then sent to Washington and other NATO capitals for authorization. The smart bombs are very expensive weapons, indicating that the target was highly valued and there would be ample time taken to study it.

Author Chris Marsden says according to *The Observer* (London) of November 28. 1999, a U.S. B2-bomber that flew from Whiteman Air Force Base in Missouri carried out the bombing. It released the "most accurate air-drop munitions in the world—the JDAM flying bomb," which, says Marsden, is accurate to a range of less than two meters. The JDAM uses "adjustable fins to control its position, which is in turn continually checked and rechecked by fixes from seven satellites." A senior NATO Air Force officer is quoted as saying "far from not knowing the target was an embassy, they must have been given architect's drawings." The bombing was so precise that it demolished the office of the military attaché, killing the three journalists, while leaving the embassy's northern end untouched, which included the front entrance. An American colonel, responding to criticisms by

British, French, and Canadian personnel, said of the supposed mistake, "Bullshit, that was great targeting...we put two JDAMs down into the attaché's office and took out the exact room we wanted. They [the Chinese] won't be using that place for rebro any more, and it will have given that bastard Arkan a headache."

Zeljko Raznatovic (alias Arkan) headed the Serbian militia known as the White Tigers. They were using the embassy to rebroadcast intelligence information. U.K. Foreign Secretary Cook said that the bombing had been meant for the war room. An unnamed NATO intelligence officer, who monitored Yugoslav radio traffic from Macedonia, told *The Observer*: "NATO had been hunting the radio transmitters in Belgrade."

As Mike Head said in his May 10,1999 article, "Of one thing there is no doubt: the most reckless and aggressive elements are exercising enormous influence over American foreign policy, with incalculable consequences for world affairs."

SOURCES: Fairness & Accuracy in Reporting, "*New York Times* Reports on Embassy Bombing Investigation," April 28, 2000, <www.fair.org/activism/embassy-update. html>; Yoichi Shimatsu, "Reports Showing U.S. Deliberately Bombed Chinese Embassy Deliberately Ignored by U.S. Media," *Pacific News Service*, October 24, 1999; Chris Marsden, "Fresh Evidence That NATO's Bombing of Chinese Embassy in Belgrade was Deliberate," World Socialist Web Site, December 1, 1999; Chris Marsden, "British Newspaper Says NATO Deliberately Bombed Chinese Embassy in Belgrade," World Socialist Web Site, October 19,1999; Mike Head, "How Could the Bombing of the Chinese Embassy Have Been a Mistake?", World Socialist Web Site, May 10, 1999; *Counterpunch*, May 12, 1999.

2001 #5 CENSORED STORY
U.S. TAXPAYERS UNDERWRITE GLOBAL NUCLEAR POWER PLANT SALES

The U.S. tax-supported Export-Import Bank (Ex-Im) is backing major U.S. nuclear contractors such as Westinghouse, Bechtel, and General Electric in their efforts to seek foreign markets for nuclear reactors. Between 1959 and 1993, Ex-Im spent $7.7 billion to help sell American-made reactors abroad.

Most countries do not have the capital to buy nuclear power, so contractors, in order to be competitive, provide 100 percent of the financing. Ex-Im offers terms too good for Third World countries and Eastern European buyers to pass up. If the host country defaults on its loan, the Ex-Im steps in with American taxpayer dollars.

Westinghouse built the Bataan nuclear power facility in the Philippines in 1985 at a cost of $1.2 billion, 150 percent above their projections. However, the Bataan plant was never brought on line due to the fact it was near an active volcano. Despite the fact that the plant never generated a single kilowatt of energy, the Philippines still pays about $300,000 a day in interest on the Ex-Im loan that funded the project. Should the Philippines default, U.S. taxpayers will pick up the tab.

The Clinton Administration allowed American contractors to sell reactors to China, claiming the nuclear energy market of China is vital to the U.S. nuclear supply industry. Ex-Im has guaranteed a $322 million loan for two Westinghouse nuclear deals in China. This approval comes despite Beijing's refusal to abide by nonproliferation rules established by the International Atomic Energy Act. The decision to allow the sales was reportedly made over the objections of national security advisor Sandy Berger, who cited Chinese exports of "dual-use" technology to Iran, Iraq, and Pakistan. Estimates are that some 70 nuclear power plants will be built in Asia in the next 25 years.

SOURCE: Ken Silverstein and Ian Urbina , "Pushing the Nuclear Plants: A U.S. Agency Hooks Foreign Clients," *The Progressive*, March 2000, <www.progressive.org>.

UPDATE 2002: American taxpayers continue to finance the construction of foreign nuclear power plants and the upgrade/renovation costs of several aging nuclear plants.

In July of 2000, *Dow Jones International News* reported that the U.S. Ex-Im Bank would guarantee a $77 million loan for upgrading and modernizing the Kozloduy nuclear power plant in Bulgaria. The loan (provided by Citigroup North America and released to Bulgaria's National Electricity Co.) will "finance sales of instrumentation and control equipment, radiation monitoring equipment and related goods," by U.S. company Westinghouse Electric. Ex-Im Bank claims that, "The Kozloduy nuclear safety upgrade will ensure a safe, dependable energy infrastructure for Bulgaria, contributing to the country's economic growth potential and paving the way for increased trade opportunities between our two countries." What Ex-Im Bank and Dow Jones fail to note is that the $77 million is in the form of a U.S. taxpayer subsidy for nuclear power plants.

The $77 million release to Bulgaria's National Electricity Co. is only a portion of the taxpayer subsidized financing for U.S. investment in Southeastern Europe. Overall, throughout 1999 and much of 2000, the Ex-Im Bank has provided approximately $500 million in loans and guarantees in support of U.S. exports to this region.

Ex-Im Bank's original goals were to create U.S. jobs by increasing U.S. exports. However, according to a Congressional Research Service study, "most economists doubt that a nation can improve its welfare over the long run by subsidizing exports." A Congressional Budget Office study concluded, "little evidence exists that Ex-Im

Bank credits create jobs." A General Accounting Office (GAO) study also found that "U.S. subsidies don't just level a playing field, they tilt it in favor of U.S. exporters. Ex-Im Bank provides 100 percent unconditional risk protection on most medium- and long-term coverage that it issues." Another GAO study found that Ex-Im Bank engages in "dual-use" exports. These are exports that have both military and civilian applications. Between 1995-1997, nine loans given to three countries (Indonesia, Venezuela, and Brazil) were used to purchase equipment for their militaries that included aircraft, trucks and radio systems.

In October of 2001, the Ex-Im Bank authorized a $1.78 million loan to engineering company Bechtel to build and put into operation a power plant in Araucaria, Brazil. The plant will receive gas turbines and other equipment from U.S. companies Siemens Westinghouse, Sulzer Bingham Pumps, and ABB Automation Inc. Ex-Im Bank President John Robson says that, "This transaction will support numerous U.S. jobs and help Brazil diversify its energy resources." Yet if previous occurrences are any indication, this remains to be seen.

SOURCES: *Foreign Policy in Focus*, July 31, 1999; *Dow Jones International News*, July 10, 2000; *Nucleonics Week*, July 13, 2000; *U.S. Newswire*, July 26, 2000; *Business News Americas*, October 8, 2001.

2001 #6 CENSORED STORY
INTERNATIONAL REPORT BLAMES U.S. AND OTHERS FOR GENOCIDE IN RWANDA

Bill Clinton and his administration allowed the genocide of 500,000 to 800,000 people in Rwanda in 1994.

The Organization for African unity (OAU) set up a panel comprised of two African heads of state, chairwomen of the Swedish Committee for UNICEF, a former chief justice to the Indian Supreme Court, and a former Canadian ambassador to the U.N. The panel was asked to review the 1994 genocide, the actions preceding the massacre, and the world's response to the killings. The panel concluded that the nations and international bodies that should have attempted to stop the killing chose not to do so. The report condemned the United Nations, Belgium (a former colonial occupier), France (which maintained close relations with Rwanda), and the United States. The report found that after the genocide began, the Clinton Administration chose not to acknowledge that it was taking place. Killings could have been stopped before they began.

Canadian Lieutenant-General Romeo Dallaire, commander of the U.N. peacekeeping troops in Rwanda warned that an extermination campaign was coming. In fact, three days before the genocide started, a Hutu leader told several high-ranking U.N. officials that "the only plausible solution for Rwanda would be the elimination of the Tutsi." While the panel's report states that, "there were a thousand early warnings that something appalling was about to occur in Rwanda," the Clinton Administration took every step possible to avoid acknowledging that genocide was taking place.

Dallaire asked for an additional 3 thousand U.N. troops, which would have brought the total to 5,000, a number likely to have been able to prevent the genocide. However, Madeleine Albright played a key role in the Security Council of the U.N. in blocking the troop expansion. In fact Albright is cited by the report as "tossing up roadblocks…at every stage."

SOURCES: David Corn, "Loyal Opposition: Clinton Allowed Genocide,"AlterNet, July 25, 2000, <www.alternet.org/story.html?StoryID=9494>; Ellen Ray, "The Role of the U.S. Military," *CovertAction Quarterly*, Spring/Summer 2000.

UPDATE 2002: The *Boston Globe* reported on August 30, 2001 that journalist Samantha Power, a seasoned war correspondent now based at Harvard's Carr Center for Human Rights Policy, spent three years investigating the failure of the U.S. government to take the genocide in Rwanda seriously. Her findings are set out in the September 2001 issue of *The Atlantic Monthly*. Anyone who takes seriously the great post-Auschwitz imperative—"Never Again"—will find them heartbreaking and infuriating.

"The U.S. government," Power writes, "knew enough about the genocide early on to save lives, but passed up countless opportunities to intervene." The American response was so minimal that Clinton's Rwanda "apology"—"we…did not do as much as we could have and should have done to try to limit what occurred," he said during a trip to Africa in 1998—was actually a wild exaggeration.

"This implied that the United States had done a good deal but not quite enough," Power says. "In reality the United States…led a successful effort to remove most of the U.N. peacekeepers who were already in Rwanda. It aggressively worked to block the subsequent authorization of U.N. reinforcements. It refused to use its technology to jam radio broadcasts that were a crucial instrument in the coordination and perpetuation of the genocide. And even as, on average, 8,000 Rwandans were being butchered each day, U.S. officials shunned the term 'genocide' for fear of being obliged to act. The United States in fact did virtually nothing 'to try to limit what occurred.'"

The Atlantic Monthly report came only days after The National Security Archive released sixteen declassified U.S. government documents detailing how U.S. policymakers chose to be "bystanders" during the genocide that decimated Rwanda in 1994. The documents showed that, contrary to later public statements, the U.S. lobbied the U.N. for a total withdrawal of forces in Rwanda in April of 1994.

SOURCES: Samantha Power, "Bystanders to Genocide: Why the United States let the Rwandan Tragedy Happen," *Atlantic Monthly*, September 2001; Jeff Jacoby, "Our Indifference To Rwanda Genocide,"*The Boston Globe*, August 30, 2001: A19; "Unwelcome Role: Bystander to Genocide, Rwanda 1994: Washington Did Not Want to Know But Did, Impeding Efforts to Save a People," *The Baltimore Sun*, August 26, 2001: 2C; Neil A. Lewis, "Word for Word/Defining Moments; Did Machete-Wielding Hutus Commit Genocide or Just 'Acts of Genocide'?,"*The New York Times*, August 26, 2001, Section 4: 7; "U.S. Cowardice In Rwanda," *The Boston Globe*, August 24, 2001: A24; Glenda Cooper, "Memos Reveal Rwanda Delay, U.S. Had Early Notice of Genocide, Pentagon Rejected Action," *Washington Post*, August 23, 2001: A20; Neil A. Lewis, "Foreign Papers Show U.S. Knew Of Genocide In Rwanda," *The New York Times*, August 22, 2001: A5.

2001 #7 CENSORED STORY

INDEPENDENT STUDY POINTS TO DANGERS OF GENETICALLY ALTERED FOODS

In 1998, Arpad Pusztai, a researcher at Rowett Research Institute in Aberdeen, Scotland, performed the first independent non-industry sponsored study analyzing genetically engineered food and its effects on mammals. The study had been undertaken to determine whether or not the spliced genes themselves could be damaging to the mammal ingesting them. However, preliminary data from the study suggests something even more startling. The actual process of genetic alteration itself may cause damage to the mammalian digestive and immune systems.

Pusztai's study found that rats fed transgenic potatoes (artificially bioengineered to include a gene from another species) showed evidence of organ damage, thickening of the small intestine, and poor brain development. The transgenic potatoes used in the study had been genetically engineered to contain lectin, a sugar-binding protein, to make the plants pest-resistant. The adverse reactions only occurred in the group that was fed the transgenic potatoes. The control group, fed plain potatoes mixed with lectin from the same source, were normal.

In August 1998 Pusztai appeared on the British television program *The World in Action* to report the findings of his study. In an attempt to quell the resulting public furor, Rowett Institute director Philip James (who had approved Pusztai's TV appearance) said the research didn't exist. He fired Pusztai, broke up his research team, seized the data, and halted six other similar projects. It came out later that Monsanto, a leading U.S. biotech firm, had given the Rowett Institute a $224,000 grant prior to Pusztai's interview and subsequent firing.

SOURCES: Joel Bleifuss, "No Small (Genetic) Potatoes," *In These Times*, January 10, 2000, <www.inthesetimes.com>; Karen Charman, "Genetic Gambling," *Extra!*, May/June 2000; Ben Lilliston, "Don't Ask, Don't Know," *Multinational Monitor*, January-February 2000, <www.essential.org/monitor/mm2000/mm0001.05.html>.

UPDATE 2002: The unknown dangers of genetically modified food is an issue of which Americans are aware. Corporate media continues to choose not to cast light on the issue.

In a thorough national/international search of news databases, no mention of Pusztai's research was found in mainstream newspapers in the United States since the article first appeared in last year's edition of *Censored*.

International articles about Pusztai tended to focus mainly on his firing from the Rowett Institute, rather than on the implications his research on genetically modified crops had presented. Europeans have been much more concerned than Americans regarding genetically engineered foods. Even Prince Charles urged the removal "Frankenfoods" from shelves in England.

On August 8, 2001, *60 Minutes II* did an interview with Pusztai as part of a show featuring a segment about genetically engineered foods. In it, Pusztai's answer to the question, "Do you think genetically engineered foods have moved into the marketplace too quickly [in the U.S.] ,"was an emphatic, "Far, far, too quickly."

The segment also pointed out the resistance in Europe and Japan to these types of foods, which often invokes violence among protesting groups. unfortunately these were small pieces of the entire segment, which promoted an intriguing and positive spin on the matter.

In December 2001, after more than a year of protest by the Northwest Resistance Against Genetic Engineering (NW RAGE), Trader Joe's finally promised to pull all GE ingredients from their house brand products. This is a fairly large step in the fight against genetically modified food. NW RAGE plans to step up their battle by going after Safeway. Grassroots organizer Phil Howard, a member of NW RAGE, states, "This is the first mainstream grocery store chain to drop GE ingredients in response to consumer activism, but it won't be the last." Yet even their successful Trader Joe's campaign found little coverage in the in the corporate media.

For now, it seems, the majority of Americans will continue to be blissfully unaware as to why their cornflakes get a little less soggy these days, and why tomatoes aren't rotting so quickly. Virtually everyone in the U.S. is eating some genetically modified food. The frightening part is we have yet to determine the full extent of the inherent dangers of eating these foods. In response to that concern, Pusztai says, "Well, I think that we don't know what the consequences are or what the effect will be long-term. It's like smoking. You smoke a cigarette, you don't drop dead; but you may develop some real problems in 20, 30, 40 years."

SOURCES: *London AFX News*, February 12, 1999; *The Patriot Ledger*, October 19, 1999; *Times of India*, October 2, 2000; *Toronto Star*, February 13, 2001; *The Portland Alliance*, December 2001

2001 #8 CENSORED STORY
DRUG COMPANIES INFLUENCE DOCTORS AND HEALTH ORGANIZATIONS TO PUSH MEDS

More than 130 million prescriptions were written in 1999 for depression and mental health related symptoms at a cost of $8.58 billion. Physicians know that antidepressants are only part of the answer for mental health, but marketing by drug companies has created the mythology of pills as cure-alls. A 1999 federal research study found that the newer antidepressants were effective in only half of the cases and only outperformed placebos by 18 percent.

Drug companies spend $5 billion annually to send sales representatives to doctors' offices. Sales reps keep FBI-style dossiers on physicians that include information such as the names of family members, golf handicaps, and clothing preferences. Hard sales tactics and small gifts are part of the pitch. In addition, pharmaceutical companies provide perks (such as tickets to sporting events) and outright compensation to doctors for their participation in the prescribing of particular drugs to their mental health patients.

On another front, pharmaceutical companies are reaping big profits by promoting forced drug use through programs at the National Alliance for the Mentally Ill (NAMI). With drug company funding, NAMI promotes a program of in-home forced drug treatment, called the Program of Assertive Community Treatment (PACT). The money is funneled through a suborganization of NAMI called the NAMI Campaign to End Discrimination. Janet Foner, a co-coordinator of Support Coalition International, an activist organization of "psychiatric survivors," says NAMI does a good job in some areas, but argues that the group's corporate sponsors help shape its agenda. "They appear to be a completely independent organization, but they parrot the line of the drug companies in saying that drugs are essential [in treating mental health disorders]."

NAMI has a policy of never disclosing its drug company funding. *Mother Jones* researchers used internal documents to prove that NAMI received $11.72 million from the psychiatric drug industry in just two-and-a-half years. NAMI's leading donor is Eli Lilly and Company, which is the maker of Prozac.

SOURCES: Stephen Pomper, "Drug Rush," *Washington Month*, May 12, 2000; Ken Silverstein, "Prozac.org," *MoJo Wire Magazine* November 1999, <www.motherjones. com/mother_jones/ND99/nami.html>; David Oaks, "NAMI: The Story Behind the Story," *Dendron*, No. 43, Spring 2000, <www.MindFreedom.org/DENDRON/den dron43/namislush/namislush.htm>; Barry Duncan, Scott Miller, and Jacqueline Sparks, "Exposing the Mythmakers," *Networker*, March 2000, <www. familytherapy networker.com/>.

UPDATE: 2002: Considering the serious health consequences of marketing practices by drug companies, and the funding of forced drug use programs like the National Alliance for the Mentally Ill (NAMI), little coverage about these tactics and programs was seen last year. Brief television coverage was found, and London newspapers and *USA Today* provided some print coverage.

The Video Monitoring Services of America noted brief coverage on June 12, 2000 on three separate television stations. *Good Morning Washington* (WJLA), *13 News Daybreak* (WVEC), and *Tampa Bay News* (WFTS) reported that "According to *USA Today*, federal investigators are warning that patients may be getting talked into and misled into participating in a risky drug trial. Drug companies were found to offer money and other incentives to doctors who enroll patients in studies in an effort to speed up commercial development of drugs."

In March 2001, *The Guardian* of London noted that clinical trials remain highly risky. The paper notes that, "the United States government produced a report which revealed that a number of research institutes were not taking risk and ethical considerations fully into account." Research was suspended at Duke University and the University of California, Los Angeles. *The Guardian*, however, does not mention whether these poor ethical considerations meant incentives or monetary compensation to doctors for the patients that they enroll.

In April 2001, *60 Minutes* provided probably the most informative and in-depth coverage from television. They reported how drug companies paid Dr. Robert Fitis an average of $50,000 to $250,000 per clinical study. He apparently ran 30 to 40 at a time. Drug companies paid him more to experiment than to heal. One of Fitis' patients, Tom Parn, was enrolled in a new prostate treatment, which posed a great risk due to Parn's history of heart problems. When Parn was told that he would need a pacemaker as a result of the risky trial, Fitis removed all reference of the new prostate treatment from Parn's record. Fitis lowered standards on qualifications for studies and he eventually began falsifying data.

In December 2001, *The Financial Times* of London noted that a World Health Organization (WHO) official blasted the "growing interference by pharmaceutical companies in the conduct of clinical trials and the publication of their results." WHO's concern, according to the *Times*, reflects growing evidence of "commercial manipulation of trials or their results." In addition, editors of 13 leading medical journals made a joint statement saying "they would refuse to publish studies where the researchers did not appear to have professional independence in the conduct of the trial and interpretation of the results."

SOURCES: Video Monitoring Services, June 12, 2000; *The Guardian*, March 15, 2001; *60 Minutes*, April 1, 2001; *The Financial Times*, December 18, 2001.

2001 #9 CENSORED STORY
EPA PLANS TO DISBURSE TOXIC/RADIOACTIVE WASTES INTO DENVER'S SEWAGE SYSTEM

Between 1950 and 1980, at the Lowry landfill near Denver, millions of gallons of hazardous industrial wastes were dumped into shallow unlined pits. The Environmental Protection Agency (EPA) now plans to pump toxic waste water into Denver's sewer system in order to clean up the Superfund site. The sewage system would then use the sludge from the treated water to fertilize Colorado farmlands.

Citizen groups say that the landfill is widely contaminated with highly radioactive plutonium and other deadly wastes. Adrienne Anderson, an instructor at the University of Boulder, stated that EPA's plan is a way to "legally pump plutonium into the sewer line." Plutonium is widely considered one of the most deadly substances on the planet.

Gwen Hooten, at EPA's region 8 office in Denver, is in charge of the Lowry cleanup. She and other EPA officials deny that the site is poisoned by plutonium or any other nuclear wastes.

SOURCE: Will Fantle, "Plutonium Pancakes," *The Progressive*, May 2000, <www.progressive.org>.

UPDATE 2002: A *Rocky Mountain News* article revealed that after months of protests led by activists, such as Adrienne Anderson, the EPA finally decided to release a 12-page report in late 2001 detailing the various contaminants at the Lowry Landfill. The report titled "Radionuclides and the Lowry landfill Superfund Site" continues to support the EPA's staunch denial of any high radioactive materials in the landfill. In an odd new move, officials say that much of the contamination that was previously reported could have come from decades-old disposal of such items as smoke detectors, gas lanterns, and other consumer-related items.

Anderson herself was quoted in the article as saying that the report is "the unraveling of a complex web of collusion, corruption, and conflicts of interest between EPA, its contractors, and the major dumpers at Lowry." Barry Levene, the regional head of EPA's Superfund program, was also quoted in the article saying the report gives a "more thorough explanation and interpretation" of radionuclide data.

An Associated Press article in September 2001 reported that the metro wastewater site's smear attacks against Anderson from previous years were recently called into question by a judge. Judge David Di Nardi said, "that the district and its board members waged a campaign of defamation against Anderson." Di Nardi proceeded to award Anderson $425,000 in damages for all the illegal actions that had been done to her in recent years by the metro district. The district would also have to put out a one-page ad in the Sunday *Denver Post* and issue an apology for its treatment of Anderson. The judge concluded that the district had also limited access to its records and that Steve Frank, the metro spokesman, had lied under oath about the district's attacks against Anderson. It was reported that the district had circulated inflammatory e-mail attacks against Anderson. Anderson was pleased with the outcome of the trial and was quoted as saying it was "gratifying."

A *Denver Post* article in late September revealed that the metro agency had decided to appeal Judge Di Nardi's earlier rulings. While Anderson may have won a temporary battle, the problems and the controversy around the wastewater plant continue to thrive in the Denver community. A September *Denver Post* editorial pointed out that while the recent report from the metro plant showed minimal damage, there has definitely been damage to the surrounding environment in the groundwater in "contaminated areas".

There is some good news from the cleanup of the Lowry site, though. As the landfill's north face has been covered, a new system has been developed to treat some of the more hazardous aspects of the various landfill gases. unfortunately, it was recently disclosed that some of the contaminated water is moving northwest on an old river that leaves the "containment areas." The EPA has tried to counter their liability by expanding the designated boundaries, but the problem of contaminated water moving downstream still plagues the site and local rural communities.

SOURCES: Todd Hartman, "Plutonium Confirmed at Lowry; Radioactive Contaminants Aren't Threat, Officials Say," *Rocky Mountain News*, August 2001; Associated Press, "Whistle-Blower Wins $425,000 Judgment Against Wastewater District," September 2001; Theo Stein, "Sewage district to contest findings Wastewater critic awarded $450,000," *Denver and the West*, September 2001; Ron Forthofer, "Wayward Water, *"Denver and the West*, August 2001.

SILICON VALLEY USES IMMIGRANT ENGINEERS
TO KEEP SALARIES LOW

Immigrant workers are being exploited by high-tech employers in Silicon Valley. AFL-CIO vice president Linda Chavez-Thompson accuses the industry of using the H1-B visa program to keep foreign workers in a position of dependence. She points out that these workers are often hired under individual contracts, which by U.S. law means they don't have the right to organize. For the high-tech industry this protection against strikes and unions is a key attraction of the H1-B program, especially in the aftermath of the Boeing Corp. engineers who mounted one of the most successful strikes in recent history.

Like other contract labor programs for lower wage and factory laborers, the H1-B program gives employers the power not only to hire and fire workers, but to grant legal immigration status as well. If an employer does not like something a worker does, such as defending themselves by filing discrimination complaints, the employer has the power to deport the worker.

The use of non-union, immigrant labor protects high-tech companies from strikes and union demands. Civil rights groups add that if Silicon Valley companies were interested in increasing the domestic high-tech labor market, they could train American workers—an approach that could also increase minority representation in the high-tech sector. The industry's resistance to such alternatives indicates that its reliance on immigrant workers is not about a domestic labor shortage but about a desire for dependent employees and higher profits.

SOURCES: David Bacon, "Immigrants Find High-tech Servitude in Silicon Valley," *Labor Notes*, September 2000; David Bacon, "Silicon Valley Sweatshops," *Washington Free Press* July 2000.

UPDATE 2002: Since this story first appeared in *Censored 2001*, conditions have only worsened in Silicon Valley. According to a number of reports, "Bridging the situation has declined for immigrant workers, both financially and socially. Kim Singh of the Asian Pacific Publicity Policy Institute of Stanford says, 'What I have seen is rampant discrimination and exploitation...Employers use the laws to their convenience and immigrant workers are denied their rights.'"

Due to the increased costs of living in the Bay Area, immigrants find it harder each year to support themselves in Silicon Valley. Yet spouses are often not allowed to be stationed at the same workplace. Companies such as Hewlett-Packard and Sun Microsystems pay their workers about $25-$30 an hour. The average salary for an American worker is about $75-$175 an hour. In addition, Indian women earn about $10 less an hour than Indian men.

The legal fees for H1-B visa workers can range from $2,500-$3,000 per employee. Employers themselves are required to pay $1,000 to the government for each employee that is hired under the visa program. These costs are part of the rationale for paying Indian workers less than American workers. *Business Week* revealed that, in Silicon Valley, immigrants account for at least a third of the personnel in the computer industry. Many Silicon Valley companies cite H1-B employees as vital to their continued profits.

Companies like TCS in New York claim they have a hard time finding American citizens qualified to work. TCS currently employees about 4,800 workers in the United States; only about 400 of them are actually American citizens. Workers at the John Pickle Company in Tulsa have stated that they worked 12-18 hours a day, earned an hourly wage of $2.31 to $3.17, and were forced to live in a warehouse, sleeping on bunk beds. A.K Shaji, a former worker for the company, said, "we had no freedom...It was work, work, work, and if you were complaining, then they were packing you up, and were shipping you back to India."

Since the terrorist attacks of September 11, the requests for HB-1 visas have dropped between 30 and 50 percent of last year's rates. However, the HB-1 visa program continues to be used as a source of cheap labor.

The AFL-CIO has proposed reforms to laws governing the use of immigrant labor. In an historical move, they called for a general amnesty for undocumented families already here and for employer sanctions to be lifted and immigrants to be given the right to protest unfair and exploitative treatment from employers.

SOURCES: Kenny Bruno, "United Mc Nations," *Dollars and Sense*, October 2000; Daniel Knight, "Perilous Partnerships," *Multinational Monitor*, March 2000, <www.essential.org./monitor/mm20000/00march/economics1.html>; Dee Ann Durbin, "Senate Passes Legislation Allowing More Foreign Workers," Associated Press, October 2000; Sukhjit Purewal, "County Report Cites Immigrants' Problems in Silicon Valley," *India Abroad*, December 2000; Ron Chepesiuk, "Coming to America: The Debate Over the H1-B Visa Program," *Asian Week*, March 2001; Cordula Tutt; "Other Countries Court Laid-Off U.S Tech Workers," *Knight Rider Tribune News Service*, August 2001; Associated Press Newswire, "Workers From India Say Conditions Were Almost Like Slavery," February 2002; PR Newswire, "INS Provides Immigrants with Affordable System," October 2001.

1998 #5 CENSORED STORY

UNITED STATES COMPANIES ARE WORLD LEADERS IN THE MANUFACTURE OF TORTURE DEVICES FOR INTERNAL USE AND EXPORT

In its March 1997 report entitled "Recent Cases of the use of Electroshock Weapons for Torture or Ill-Treatment," Amnesty International lists 100 companies worldwide that produce and sell instruments of torture. Forty-two of these firms are in the United States. This places the U.S. as the leader in the manufacture of stun guns, stun belts, cattle probe-like devices, and other equipment which can cause devastating pain in the hands of torturers.

These weapons are currently in use in the U.S. and are being exported to countries all over the world. The U.S. government is a large purchaser of stun devices—especially stun guns, electroshock batons, and electric shields. The American Civil Liberties Union (ACLU) and Amnesty both claim the devices are unsafe and may encourage sadistic acts by police officers and prison guards—both here and abroad. "Stun belts offer enormous possibilities for abuse and the infliction of gratuitous pain," says Jenni Gainsbourough of the ACLU's National Prison Project. She adds that because use of the belt leaves little physical evidence, this increases the likelihood of sadistic, but hard-to-prove, misuse of these weapons. In June 1996, Amnesty International asked the Federal Bureau of Prisons to suspend the use of electroshock belts, citing the possibility of physical danger to inmates and the potential for misuse.

SOURCE: Anne-Marie Cusac, "Shock Value: U.S. Stun Devices Pose Human-Rights Risk," *The Progressive*, September 1997.

UPDATE 2002: According to the Chinese Human Rights Report on USA, which was published by the Chinese Xinhua News Agency, March 11, 2002, in the United States, close to 100 companies manufacture and export considerable quantities of instruments of torture that are banned in international trade. They have set up sales networks overseas. In its February 26, 2001 report, Amnesty International said some 80 American companies were involved in the manufacture, marketing, and export of instruments of torture, including electric-shock tools, shackles and handcuffs with sawteeth. Many instruments of torture and police tools are high-tech products, which can cause serious harm to the human body. For instance, handcuffs, which tear apart the flesh if the victim slightly exerts himself, are very cruel, as is a high-pressure rope for tying up a person. Although categorically prohibited by U.S. law, the Commerce Department of the United States has given official licenses for exporting such tools. According to statistics, American companies have secured export licenses and sold tools of torture overseas valued at 97 million U.

S. dollars since 1997 under the category of "crime control equipment." It is inconceivable that, while the U.S. State Department is talking about human rights, the U.S. Department of Commerce has given export licenses for products determined to be instruments of torture according to the statutes of the U.S. government.

1999 #25 CENSORED STORY
ABC BROADCASTS SLANTED REPORT ON MUMIA ABU-JAMAL

On May 7 and 8, 1998, KGO-TV, an ABC affiliate in San Francisco, broadcast a two-part series attacking the international movement dedicated to preventing the execution of Mumia Abu-Jamal. Mumia, a black activist, has been on death row in the state of Pennsylvania for 16 years for the killing of a Philadelphia police officer in 1981. KGO claimed to do an objective review of the case. The final broadcast presented a very one-sided story.

SOURCE: C. Clark Kissinger and Leonard Weinglass, "A Case Study in Irresponsible Journalism," *Refuse and Resist.*

UPDATE 2002: There have been numerous developments in the past year regarding the case of death row inmate/political activist Mumia Abu-Jamal. The most recent of these developments came on December 23, 2001, when federal Judge William Yohn decided to overturn the death penalty ruling in Jamal's case. He cited a Supreme Court decision that leaves death penalty sentencing up to the jury as opposed to the judge; the latter made the decision in Jamal's trial. As a result, there will be a new penalty trial for Jamal, who was sentenced to death row in 1981 for the murder of police officer Daniel Faulkner. Neither the prosecution nor the defense are entirely satisfied with the ruling. The prosecution is appealing the most recent decision, while Jamal's lawyers are seeking a new trial all together.

In May of 2000, new affidavits were released regarding this controversial case. Mumia spoke out for the first time, telling his own story about what happened on the night the police officer Faulkner was killed. Statements were also made by Mumia's brother, who was at the scene the night the crime was committed, and a man named Arnold Beverly, who claims to have been the real killer. Beverly said in his affidavit, "I was hired, along with another guy, and paid to shoot and kill Faulkner. I had heard that Faulkner was a problem for the mob and corrupt policemen because he interfered with graft and payoffs..." According to Beverly, he and his accomplice, not Jamal, shot Faulkner. His story corroborates with those told by Jamal and his brother, William Cook. In July of 2001, Judge Yohn refused to take the deposition of Arnold Beverly, citing in part, the Anti-Terrorism and Effective Death Penalty Act, as well as the late timing of the confession. Beverly's signed affidavit was dated June 8, 1999, and was in the possession of Jamal's legal team, but his former attorney Leonard Weinglass, had for an unknown reason, decided not to release the statement, nor make any comments about its release. Mumia has since gotten new legal counsel that has brought this information to the surface.

Jamal's attorneys have also filed with Judge Yohn an article in *The Atlantic Monthly* written by Supreme Court Justice Felix Frankfurter that exposed the case of Sacco and Vanzetti. These two men were innocent Italian immigrants who were executed after a state court refused to hear the confession of the real murderer and grant a new trial. The similarities in the two cases are remarkable, especially the prejudice both Sacco and Vanzetti faced for being anarchists, as well as immigrants, and the prejudice faced by Mumia for being a black political activist. The original trial judge for Mumia's case, Judge Alfred Sabo, was even overheard by a court reporter saying, "fry the ni**er." The hope is that this comparison will justify a new trial. A new trial has yet to be granted, but it appears the filing of *The Atlantic Monthly* article did have some affect. This article was filed in November of 2001, and approximately one month later, Judge Yohn overturned Mumia's death sentence.

SOURCES: *San Francisco Chronicle*, December 23, 2001; *Seattle Times*, December 20, 2001; *Los Angeles Times*, July 22, 2001; Labor Action Committee, "Labor Forums Say—Mumia Is Innocent," November 3, 2001; Carol Seligman, "Major New Developments in the Case of Mumia Abu Jamal," *Socialist Viewpoint*, June 2001; *Daily News* Staff Report, May 8, 2001.

1997 #9 CENSORED STORY
U.S. TROOPS EXPOSED TO DEPLETED URANIUM DURING GULF WAR

Depleted uranium (DU) weapons were used for the first time in a war situation in the Persian Gulf in 1991 and were hailed as a new and incredibly effective weapon by the Department of Defense. Since the Manhattan Project of World War II, numerous government studies have indicated that while DU weapons are highly effective, they are still extremely toxic and need to be handled with special precautionary tools and protective gear.

The effects of depleted uranium exposure, however, are just beginning to be known. DU has now been linked to many illnesses, including the mysterious "Gulf War Syndrome." Despite widespread concern among Gulf War vets and in U.S. communities about the dangers of DU weapons, the Pentagon, Department of Energy, and military defense contractors are all excited about the sales potential of DU weapons as well as the transfer of DU to allies for their own weapons production. According to Nuclear Regulatory Commission shipment records, steady transfers—amounting to several million pounds of DU—have been flowing to U.S. allies over the past decade, with Britain, France, and Canada being the largest recipients.

Dan Fahey, an activist who works with Swords to Plowshares, a veterans' rights organization, cowrote a report, "Radioactive Battlefields of the 1990s: The United States Army's use of Depleted Uranium and Its Consequences for Human Health and the Environment," which was released by the Maine-based Military Toxics Project's Depleted Uranium Citizens' Network in January 1996. Says Fahey, "The health and environmental effects of the 300 tons of DU shot in the Gulf is just a glimpse of the dangers that our society, and the world, will be forced to deal with if and when DU weapons are used in future conflicts. Because DU has a half-life of 4.5 billion years, and because it is extremely difficult and costly to clean up after it has been shot on a testing range or battlefield, DU threatens to pollute future battlefields and poison and kill people for thousands of generations."

SOURCES: Pat Broudy et al, "Radioactive Battlefields Of The 1990s: The United States Army's Use of Depleted Uranium and its Consequences for Human Health and the Environment," *Military Toxics Project's Depleted Uranium Citizen's Network*, January 16, 1996; Gary Cohen, "Radioactive Ammo Lays Them to Waste," *Multinational Monitor*, Jan/Feb 1996; Dan Fahey, "Depleted Uranium: Objective Research and Analysis," *Swords To Plowshares*, November 7, 1995; Bill Triplett," Depleted Uranium: One Man's Weapon, Another Man's Poison," *The VVA Veteran*, March 1996; Kathryn Casa, "Depleted Uranium, First Used In Iraq, Deployed in Bosnia," *National Catholic Reporter*, January 19, 1996.

UPDATE 2002: John LaForge reported in *Nukewatch*, Winter 2001, that opposition has mounted regarding depleted uranium (DU) munitions that have been used as warfare weapons by the United States against Iraq and Kuwait in 1991 and against Bosnia and Kosovo in 1994 and 1995. The U.S. has used the DU, U-238, because of its high density that, when turned into munitions, can pierce through outer shells of tanks made of heavy metal. The problem is that 16 Europeans who participated in military missions in Bosnia and Kosovo have died from leukemia. European Parliament and 11 European governments and major news groups are calling for an investigation into the use of weaponry made with this toxic radioactive waste material.

NATO hastily studied the situation and after one week, proclaimed that DU used in the Balkans can be ruled out as a significant health hazard. Scientists such as Dr. John Boice and physicist Steve Fetter said that, for leukemia to occur, radiation needs to get to the bone marrow. They claim that uranium-238 can not do that.

This has been contradicted by Jean Francois Lacronique, director of France's National Radiation Protection Agency, who says that it has been found stored in bone and from there it can reach bone marrow. Dr. Frank von Hippel says that particles of U-238 can be inhaled and build up in lung tissue, and enter into the bloodstream, and then accumulate in the bone.

Later it was disclosed that plutonium and other nuclear wastes far more radioactive and carcinogenic than uranium-238 were also being used. Dr. von Hippel says that plutonium-239 is roughly 200,00 times more radioactive than U-238. U.S. officials say that the shells contained mere traces of plutonium and that amount wouldn't cause harm. Yet it is one of the most carcinogenic substance known for its power to cause cancer.

NATO officials say that the small levels of plutonium were not "relevant to soldier's health." However, the World Health Organization wants to know just how much plutonium is in contemporary DU ammunition. The U.S. Department of Energy (DOE) says that there are transuraics at low level.

The Hague Conventions of 1907, the Geneva Gas Protocol of 1925, and the Geneva Convention Relative to the Protection of Civilians in Time of War of 1949 all outlaw the use of poisonous gas, and "biological or chemical substances causing death or disability with permanent effects, when in even small quantities they are ingested, enter the lungs or bloodstream or touch the skin." Still, DU has never been declared illegal by any international body.

A shocking study by the Department of Veterans Affairs (DVA) and Johns Hopkins University found that children of veterans of the 1991 Persian Gulf bombardment are two to three times as likely as those of other vets to have birth defects. Persian Gulf vets also reported more miscarriages. Even the U.S. EPA acknowledges that radiation can cause "genetic defects in the children of exposed parents." Toxic, plutonium-contaminated depleted uranium-238 (DU) weapons were Used extensively in the bombardment.

The DVA questioned 21,000 active and retired military, reserve, and National Guard members. Male veterans of the 1991 action reported having infants with birth defects at twice the rate of non-Gulf veterans. Women vets were almost three times more likely to report children with birth defects than non-Gulf veterans.

Official Iraqi figures show an increase in cancer cases from 6,555 in 1989 to 10,931 in 1997, mostly in areas bombed in 1991 by the U.S.–led assault on the Persian Gulf. A team from the World Health Organization arrived in Baghdad last August to begin research on a possible link between cancer and the hundreds of tons of DU munitions used by U.S. and British warplanes. But after a lobbying campaign by the U.S., the U.N. General Assembly (UNGA) voted November 29 to reject a call for a formal U.N. investigation. The vote was 45-54 with 45 abstentions. The UNGA's committee on disarmament and international security had approved the DU study earlier in November.

The Pentagon continues to deny that health problems can be linked with exposure to DU. During a January 4 briefing, Pentagon spokesman Kenneth Bacon was asked, "The Italians have called for a moratorium on the use of depleted uranium munitions. Is that something that the United States would consider doing?" Mr. Bacon answered, "We don't see any health reasons to consider a moratorium at this stage. We will work with our allies, as I said, in health studies, but we see no reason to consider a moratorium now."

In the first move by someone in Congress to investigate the military's use of DU weapons, U.S. Representative Cynthia McKinney (D-GA) has introduced the Depleted Uranium Munitions Suspension and Study Act of 2001. McKinney's bill would: a) suspend the U.S. military's use of DU munitions, pending a certification from the Secretary of HHS that DU munitions will not: 1) pose a long-term residual threat to the health of U.S. or NATO military personnel, and 2) jeopardize the health of civilian populations in the area of use; b) Suspend the foreign sale and export of DU munitions; c) Initiate a GAO investigation of contamination of DU munitions by plutonium; d) Initiate a study of the health effects of DU munitions on current or former U.S. military personnel who may have been exposed and medical personnel who treated such affected personnel.

Additional information is available at <www.nukewatch.com>.

THIS MODERN WORLD
by TOM TOMORROW

CHAPTER 4

Junk Food News and News Abuse

BY KRISTA ARATA AND KATHLEEN O'ROURKE-CHRISTOPHER

"Junk Food News" consists of the cotton candy headlines and soda pop stories that make up the basis for what we often know as news in this country. Media feeds off our desire to escape the humdrum world around us with an emphasis on celebrity "news." Famous lives provide us with a sugar rush and a false reality that radiates in comparison to the darkness that shrouds what's really going on in the world. Genocide, war, big business machinations, and the manipulation of Third World countries can't hold a candle to what Gwyneth Paltrow chooses to wear on Oscar night. We are seemingly a nation obsessed with celebrity.

This is why we write this chapter, and this book, in fact. Our current system of corporate-controlled media isn't doing the job it was created to do: inform the American public of matters requiring national attention. A tabloid mentality has invaded somber news outlets leaving America in the dark about significant issues and events, and promoting our national ignorance. The fluffiest of the fluff that is handed to us by our media is what we call "Junk Food News."

The 23 members of our Media Censorship class brainstormed the initial list of 20 Junk Food stories. To narrow it down to the Top 10, we sent copies of the list to all 150 Project Censored interns, as well as Sonoma State faculty evaluators. In addition, the list went out via e-mail to the thousands people on the Project Censored listserv.

Everyone was asked to pick their personal Top 10, along with the Top 5 News Abuse stories that will be elaborated on later in this chapter. As the votes came flooding in, they were meticulously tallied to determine who would rank supreme in the Junk Food War.

And the "winners" are:

1. Tom Cruise and Nicole Kidman's divorce drama
2. Puff Daddy and Jennifer Lopez's relationship roller-coaster
3. Mariah Carey's fall from sanity
4. The reduction of Pamela Anderson's "liquid assets"
5. Robert Downey Jr.'s frequent and inevitable drug busts
6. The "are they or aren't they" question regarding Britney Spears and Justin Timberlake
7. The constant invasion of the private lives of Prince Charles and his sons
8. The suspicion and confirmation of Rosie O'Donnell's sexuality
9. Dubya's daughter's alcoholic escapades
10. Michael Jordan's wishy-washy decision making skills

Number 1, with an overwhelmingly clear majority of the votes, was the Tom Cruise/Nicole Kidman saga. While the West Bank found itself in the throes of a bloody civil war, our nation took sides in this tawdry battle. There was the Nicole camp—"Tom must have strayed with that tramp Penelope Cruz," his costar in *Vanilla Sky*. And there was the Tom camp—"Nicole obviously cheated with Ewan McGregor," her costar in *Moulin Rouge*.

Number 2 on our list is another frought relationship. Puff Daddy (or is it P. Diddy now?) and Jennifer Lopez headed to Heartbreak Hotel. But the drama was so much more involved this time. First they made headlines by dating—she's Latina and he's African American. Then there was talk of a marriage, which had tongues wagging across the globe. What would one of the most beautiful women in America wear to her wedding? Next came a shooting, in which Puffy was accused of mischief with J.Lo as a witness. The final blow came when, during Puffy's trial, J.Lo dumped him, and the rumor mill churned about her supposed involvement with a backup dancer in her crew while she was with Puffy. Eventually, Puffy was acquitted and J.Lo married the dancer, and they all lived happily ever after.

Number 3 brought us Mariah Carey. Poor Mariah, the weight of being an megasuperstar proved to be too much for her. Her first feature film flopped faster and harder than *Howard the Duck*. The corresponding soundtrack CDs were used as Frisbees in backyards around America, and she had herself a mental breakdown. When she came out of it—although that may be debatable as of yet—her record company paid her to go away! She was given millions upon millions of dollars to take her "talent" elsewhere. Next, in the number 4 spot, we have Pamela Anderson's breasts again. We last featured them in "Junk Food News" in 1999 in the number 5 position. Her breasts have taken a step up the Junk Food ladder, while taking several steps down in size (or did they?).

Number 5 this year went to Robert Downey Jr. and his drug addiction. Being a drug addict is nothing to joke about. But when you're being arrested for it every other day, going to court twice a month, and being let off with a slap on the wrist, reality seems warped. Here we have a clear case of someone who needs help, but because he's a celebrity, he's allowed to break the rules. When he should have been sent to rehab or jail, he was allowed to go home and get high again.

Barely missing the Top 5 dishonor roll was the innocent relationship between Justin Timberlake (of *NSync) and Britney Spears at number 6. When their "togetherness" was finally confirmed, the entire world breathed a sigh of "we knew it." Then we all wanted to know if they had consummated it yet. Britney professed to be a virgin, insinuating that Justin wasn't getting any. How much was true, we will never know, but why do we care in the first place?

Lucky number 7…the private lives of Prince Charles and his sons. So what if Charlie was publicly out with Camilla Parker Bowles? Haven't they been eyeing each other since before Princess Diana was in the picture? Why was Prince William's sex life of utmost importance to America? He's a young man with urges just like any young man. Then there's Prince Harry: smoking pot, getting drunk, failing school. You'd think he had recently experienced a horrific tragedy, cast in the permanent shadow of his devastatingly handsome brother, and consistently hounded by the media.

The coveted number 8 position is held by Rosie O'Donnell. The inclusion of this entry on the Junk Food list was the topic of some controversy. We should preface this entry by saying this: the sole purpose of the Junk Food list is not to be humorous. It's meant to highlight the various stories that were overcovered and sensationalized and took precedent over more pressing matters in society. Rosie's sexuality and her ability to come out is no laughing matter, especially to members of the gay/lesbian community. The fact that it was sensationalized points to the contention that our society has a long way to go in terms of sensitivity to and understanding of gay and lesbian issues.

The escapades of George W. Bush's daughters held our number 9 position. The media had a field day with their underage drinking and naughty behavior. But instead of using this story as a tool to teach younger kids to be smarter than that, it was used as a superfluous reason to bash Dubya. And we heard about it for weeks.

Last, but most certainly not least, Michael Jordan squeaked into the Top 10 in the last position. Number 10 belonged to #23, with his cycle of retirements, comebacks, and his newest tribulation: his separation from his wife. Even that held no water as they quickly got back together. It seems that indecisiveness runs in the Jordan family.

Corporate media has built a successful entertainment dynasty on Junk Food News in our society. They repeat the message that money and status consistently overshadow ethics and morality. This message treats us all as passive voyeurs in the drama of life, status, and power.

NEWS ABUSE

News Abuse is a new addition to our Junk Food News chapter. News Abuse highlights those stories that had the emotional aspects to them that the corporate media fed on like jackals to a fresh kill. It would have been inappropriate to include these stories with the preceding ones because of their sensitive nature, but we felt it was just as important to show the abuse of journalistic reporting in this area as well. Our concern with the bastardization of these stories was significant enough for us to include them in a separate but equal forum with Junk Food News.

Media's knack for going straight to the emotional center of a story and turning it into a tabloid headline is often at the victim's expense. Even the lives of readers are manipulated by the repeated hashing out of unfortunate situations in life. Innocent bystanders' worlds are disrupted by the bombardment of relentless reporting of someone else's tragedy. Needless fear and rage can occur in the witnessing public.

We presented voters with a list of some of these "Headlines of a more serious nature." Results of our poll produced the following top five News Abuse stories for 2001-2002:

1. Gary Condit/Chandra Levy scandal
2. John Walker—American Taliban
3. Anthrax Scares
4. San Francisco dog mauling case
5. Summer Shark Attacks

Since April 30, 2001, and well into the time before 9-11, the Chandra Levy case had nearly uninterrupted news coverage. The case drew national attention when the name of Representative Gary Condit, (D-CA), who represents Modesto, surfaced in the investigation. Until the disappearance of the former intern in May, Condit was a name few people outside California's 18th District had ever heard. Because of this case, he has become the nexus of a media frenzy surrounding the young woman's disappearance and the eventual finding of her body. Within days, the congressman's political life began to unravel, which made this story even juicier. Pundits began to wonder what would happen at election time and as November elections emerged, Condit's loss was a media event.

The focus of the coverage centered on the nature of Levy's relationship with Condit, who initially denied any involvement in her disappearance. Six weeks after Levy disappeared, Condit had become the center of intense media interest. Not a day went by that the story didn't appear somewhere in the media. He was everywhere it seemed, and he had the same thing to say every time, which wasn't much.

Chandra became a celebrity in her own right. She was scrutinized and dissected in front of and by the whole world. Was she a spy? Was she pregnant? Was she threatening to tell his wife? Why didn't she do something about her hair? But the tawdriness of this drama outweighed everything else. Dozens of other young women have disappeared or lost their lives since she was reported missing, but their disappearances haven't gotten the same coverage because they don't have that "dirty-little-secret" quality to them. The illicit affair between an older married politician and his young impressionable intern, on the other hand, became a media circus.

The media has had a heyday with the mysterious disappearance and have blown it out of proportion. One can go to a search engine such as Google and get 54,800 hits on Chandra Levy, suggesting that the story may be the biggest News Abuse story of all time.

Another story that was overtly sensationalized was the John Lindh Walker Taliban tale. Politicians were at odds in their views on how to deal with this young man. Many were found crying for his blood, and that attitude sits well with a large majority of their constituents. Others called for understanding and compassion. At age 20, he is one of the most hated men in America. Pictures of Walker captured and tied up have been in circulation and some appear to be souvenir photographs with Special Forces troops shown "posing with their prisoner" and a profanity written across Walker's blindfold. Shall we mention that the Geneva Convention prohibits activities that might humiliate prisoners?

U. S. Attorney General John Ashcroft said, "The United States does not casually or capriciously charge one of its own citizens with providing support to terrorists. We are compelled to do so today by the inescapable fact of September 11—a day that reminded us in no uncertain terms that we have enemies in the world and that these enemies seek to destroy us." And at a news conference on January 15, 2002, Ashcroft said that Walker identified himself as "a Muslim who wanted to go to the front lines to fight.... Terrorists did not compel John Walker Lindh to join them. He chose to." Bill Jones, a friend of Walker's family, told *Good Morning America* on December 4, 2001, "as far as we're concerned, he's a victim of the Taliban." Walker's family believes he was subjected to intense propaganda from Islamic extremists. In December 2001, Eugene Fidell, president of the National Institute of Military Justice said that, in the case of Walker, "It's irresponsible to speculate what will happen because we don't know all the facts yet." The real question, however, is until we get the facts, shouldn't we too reserve judgment on Walker? Aren't we being subjected to intense propaganda like he was by our own media machine? Some say that the media's focus on Walker substituted for the lack of eagerly awaited reports on the finding and killing of Osama bin Laden.

Following close behind Walker we had the number 3 story, the anthrax scares. This was a case of The War of the Worlds gone crazy. Media has had us all running scared, afraid to open our mail and buying up Cipro. In reality, until the events of 9-11, there hadn't been a case of inhalation anthrax in the United States since 1978. There were only 18 cases of inhalation anthrax in the U.S. from 1900 through 1978 and 224 U.S. cases of skin infection between 1944 and 1994. Anthrax as a disease in animals has been around for tens of thousands of years but rarely does anthrax cause serious disease in humans. These facts were generally overlooked.

Anthrax has been called the perfect germ for bioterrorism as related to the ability for control of mass spreading of the disease among the population. It isn't contagious; only those exposed to a release of spores get sick. Thus, there's no chance that a release of the germs will boomerang and kill unintended victims. In October 2001, the National Center for Infectious Diseases, Division of Bacterial and Mycotic Diseases, stated that the recent exposures to anthrax appeared to have come from letters containing powdered anthrax spores, but there was no cause for panic.

Still there was an extensive media scare about the dangers of "catching" anthrax. Reports of anthrax-laced letters sent to members of Congress in Washington and to television network offices in New York started a panic that multiplied when anthrax-by-mail attacks ended up killing five and sickening at least thirteen. In October of 2001, an assistant to NBC anchorman Tom Brokaw contracted the skin form of anthrax after opening a "threatening" letter to her boss that contained a suspicious powder. Bob Stevens, 63, a photo editor for *The Sun*, was the first person in 25 years in the United States to die of the inhalation form of anthrax. Many New Yorkers and other people across the nation started stockpiling Cipro, the antibiotic that they think will treat anthrax.

Overemphasizing the incidents of anthrax exposure caused fear and anxiety within our nation. For instance, reporting that the governor of New York, George Pataki was taking Cipro, even though he had never even been tested for exposure to anthrax, only helped to increase the public panic of those seeking prescriptions for the antibiotic. People were hoarding it as though doomsday was approaching.

The number 4 pick for most abused serious news item was the San Francisco dog-mauling case, the ongoing saga of two attorneys, Marjorie Knoller and Robert Noel, whose dog attacked and killed Diane Whipple outside her Pacific Heights apartment. Again the media coverage was relentless. How many times did we have to relive how Knoller's and Noel's dogs, Bane and Hera, horribly mutilated Diane in January 2001, a scene so horrific that rescue workers needed counseling? Over and over again, we bared the tragic loss with Whipple's partner, Sharon Smith.

This story was repeatedly covered in the San Francisco Bay Area and soon became a nationwide daily soap opera. There were startling "revelations" at every turn: the dogs really belonged to inmates in prison, the inmates ran an illegal dog-fighting ring, Noel and Knoller had sex with the dogs, Knoller prodded Hera to attack Whipple, and on and on. Although the public originally thought of this as an accident, when Noel and Knoller placed blame on the victim, defended their murderous canines, and so candidly and publicly displayed a lack of remorse, they became their own worst enemies in the courtroom. They broke one cardinal rule of their profession after another. Lawyers were watching from the sidelines, wincing every time they opened their mouths.

A key element of the case, mostly ignored by the corporate media, was the stunning legal gains for gay and lesbian partners. The legal rights married couples enjoy has now been extended in the courts to lesbian couples and a clear precedent has been set. A personal rights victory is perhaps one small gain from this over-sensationalized personal tragedy.

"Summer Shark Attacks" was rated number 5 for our News Abuse list. Out of 79 shark attacks reported worldwide in 2001, 51 occurred in the United States, and 34 in Florida. New Smyrna Beach on the Florida east coast was named the shark attack capital of the world as 21 documented attacks were recorded there last year. By August 27, 2001, there were 10 bites in 8 days and beach patrol officials closed a quarter-mile stretch of the beach, eerily reminiscent of *Jaws*. This is when the news media ran the shark attack stories in abundance, even though minor shark attacks are fairly common in this popular surfing area. Six of seven attacks in one week in April occurred on this same stretch of beach. Joe Wooden, deputy beach chief for Volusia County, reported that sharks are drawn to the area because it is rich in baitfish. Shark attacks occurred because so many surfers were out splashing around in the water, not because sharks were getting more aggressive.

Suspense and drama built up as headlines flashed in horror-like fashion. George Burgess, director of the International Shark Attack Files at the University of Florida, said, "I don't think it indicates we're under siege or anything like that, for the results are almost inevitable given the conditions."

The question is why then the endless reporting of these particular incidents? Because it had a scary humans-under-attack factor that played upon the fears of a nation still reeling from the movie *Jaws*.

Spear fisherman Kent Bonde had a chunk of his calf bitten off by a Bahamian shark, but he doesn't blame the shark. He says, "We are not part of their menu. It's their ocean. We are taking a calculated risk." But it was not that information that was reported. We heard all about what Dr. Tamara Burke, an emergency room physician at Rand Memorial Hospital in Freeport, had to say. After this second attack in two weeks in the Bahamas she advised everyone to stay out of the water. Because it is quite unusual to get two shark bites in waters off the same island in two weeks, he felt that a "phenomenon" was going on "that we don't understand yet." And news hype picked up again when Jessie Arbogast, an eight-year-old boy was attacked by a shark in July in Pensacola, Florida and ended up having his severed arm reattached.

CNN had labeled this the "Year of the Shark." No doubt they were hurting for other news coverage. In reality, the notion of a shark stalking humans is pure fiction, in spite of what was being said in the media. It may sound logical, "but it's not biologically logical," said Samuel Gruber, a University of Miami professor and internationally renowned shark authority. Shark attacks, scientists say, are almost always random, and this year's total, despite the "Summer of the Shark" media stories, is fairly typical. There were deaths from shark attack injuries—one in Virginia Beach, Virginia and another in Avon, North Carolina, but coastal residents, tourism officials, and beach-goers were trying to be calm about the situation. "It's causing a panic that doesn't need to be caused," said Terri Behling, spokeswoman for the Center for Shark Research at Mote Marine Laboratory in Sarasota.

As you have seen, these last five stories needed to be handled with kid gloves. There is nothing humorous about a dog gruesomely mauling a young woman to death and it certainly isn't funny that another young woman has turned up murdered after being missing for a year. We want to emphasize that while these stories were important, the corporate media has used their high emotional content to build news ratings by over sensationalizing the most shocking aspects of each story. All five News Abuse stories were turned into lurid tabloid news, and not one got the thorough, meaningful coverage it deserved. They were developed like movies with a focus on the genre-specific aspect. We had a horror movie (shark attacks), a mystery (Chandra Levy), a thriller (anthrax scares), a spy movie (John Walker), and a drama (dog mauling). It is a real wonder we weren't encouraged to treat them like entertainment, with popcorn ads in between showings and dancing soda pop on our screens.

THIS MODERN WORLD

by TOM TOMORROW

THIS WEEK: YOUR COMPREHENSIVE CARTOON GUIDE TO THE ENRON ~~COLLAPSE!~~

EVERYTHING* YOU NEED TO KNOW IN FIVE EASY PANELS!

*AS DEFINED BY CARTOONIST AND SUBJECT TO LIMITATIONS OF AVAILABLE SPACE. TERMS AND CONDITIONS APPLY. COMPREHENSION MAY VARY.

1. NEW ECONOMY HYPE

BEFORE INVESTING IN COMPANIES CLAIMING TO SPIN STRAW INTO GOLD... YOU MIGHT WANT TO MAKE SURE THEY AT LEAST HAVE SOME *STRAW*.

OUR REVENUE MODEL IS MUCH TOO COMPLICATED TO *EXPLAIN!*

NO PROBLEMO! I'LL TAKE A *THOUSAND* SHARES!

2. DEREGULATION MANIA

OOPS! AS IT TURNS OUT, CORPORATIONS *CAN'T* ALWAYS BE TRUSTED TO POLICE THEMSELVES. WHO *KNEW*?!

SO WE OVERSTATED OUR VALUE BY $600 MILLION. WHAT'S THE BIG *DEAL*?

YOU NEVER MADE A MISTAKE BALANCING YOUR *CHECKBOOK?*

3. THE REVOLVING DOOR

IN 1993, WHILE WORKING FOR AN OVERSIGHT COMMISSION, WENDY GRAMM (WIFE OF PHIL) HELPED EXEMPT ENRON FROM REGULATIONS. FIVE WEEKS LATER--*COINCIDENTALLY ENOUGH*-- SHE JOINED ENRON'S BOARD.

WHAT AN *UNEXPECTED* TURN OF EVENTS!

IT'S CERTAINLY FUNNY HOW LIFE WORKS OUT SOMETIMES!

4. MONEY-N-POLITICS

ENRON WAS A MAJOR BUSH CONTRIBUTOR...NUMEROUS BUSHIES ARE FORMER ENRON EXECS AND/OR SHAREHOLDERS...AND ENRON CEO *KEN LAY* WAS A KEY PLAYER ON DICK CHENEY'S SECRETIVE *ENERGY TASK FORCE*. *YOU* FIGURE IT OUT.

YOUR COUNTRY APPRECIATES YOUR *SERVICE*, KEN!

JUST DOING MY *PATRIOTIC DUTY*, MR. VICE PRESIDENT!

WINK!
WINK!

5. POLITICAL RELATIVISM

EXECS WALKED AWAY WITH MILLIONS; SHAREHOLDERS GOT THE SHAFT. IF THIS HAD HAPPENED UNDER A *DEMOCRATIC* ADMINISTRATION, THE SPECIAL PROSECUTORS WOULD BE LINED UP DOWN THE *BLOCK* BY NOW.

WELL WE CAN'T AFFORD A DIVISIVE INVESTIGATION DURING *WARTIME!*

AND SINCE WAR ON TERROR IS SCHEDULED TO LAST *INDEFINITELY*--

--YOU GET THE IDEA.

CHAPTER 5

Rebuild Democracy with Grassroots Community News

BY PETER PHILLIPS AND THE PROJECT CENSORED WRITING TEAM
Chris Salvano, Eric Garrison, Kevin Cody, Kerry Beck,
and Stephen Dietrich

Fifty-five million non-voters in the U.S. cynically understand that it takes money to access our two-party system and have opted out of the national voting charade. They sense that citizen participation means little in the current political decision-making process.

Our collective cynicism was greatly reinforced with the recent revelations that two-thirds of U.S. Senators and close to half of the House of Representatives accepted financial donations from Enron. Politicians are quick to claim that campaign contributions have no impact on their voting records or constituent representation, but the public knows better.

Those of us who still vote intuitively recognize that money in politics negates grassroots democracy. Voters and nonvoters alike mistrust political-corporate elites who pontificate the virtues of privatization and globalization, while supporting cutbacks in social spending and the need for personal belt-tightening. We resent being told to lower our expectations while the political insiders laugh and wink behind their tax-free Cayman Island bank accounts, lobbied legislative victories, and White House visits. There is that deep uneasy feeling inside us as we recognize the money sickness within the bowels of our political system.

How do we connect with each other? How do we find citizen-based popular agreement and action? How do we fight personal cynicism and paralyzing despair? What steps of social action are needed to heal this systemic illness?

Certainly the corporate media are not the ones to answer these questions. The National Association of Broadcasters—corporate media united—is one of the principle lobby groups working against campaign finance reform. It is the corporate media that reap the profits from the billions of dollars spent on candidate advertising "donated" by the moneyed insiders. Television news and the national print media chains do not encourage grassroots citizen action. Their role as corporate-political insiders is to keep us at home and entertained instead of active and involved. They think that if they scare us enough with stories of the evil ones, we will hide away and not question our declining freedoms, lessening access, and loss of civil liberties.

Our choice of social action is quite evident. We must find the mechanisms for communicating with each other. We must build our own media systems from the bottom up. We must empower thousands of voices to tell real news stories, stories that speak truth to power.

Imagine real news originating from local communities that tells our stories of democratic action and positive social change. Imagine real news that offers meaningful information and sociopolitical understandings for working people. Grassroots real news would empower and reawaken the democratic spirit of working people in America and challenge the hegemonic top-down corporate entertainment news system. Real news would not be measured with Arbitron ratings. It would not be there for the selling of materialism or elitist propaganda. Real news is measured in collective movement for human betterment. Real news stimulates democratic activism and helps us find the foundations for shared action. Real news ignites, shapes policy for equality, and stands up to the robber-baron power brokers.

So how do we build this grassroots Real News system? Partially it is already there in the form of thousands of independent noncorporate newspapers, magazines, Web sites, radio stations, and local cable access TV shows. But we need more of these and greater access for working people nationally. The Internet gives us new tools for accessing real news, yet we need to create other more expansive outlets at the local level.

This transformation is the job for the activist in each of us This chapter is dedicated to the activists who reach out, find alternative sources of real news, and develop systems for sharing that news with their local communities. Activists everywhere can find like-minded partners to help create local listservs, newspapers, or radio/TV shows. Support the independent media that already exists and encourage the multidimensional sharing of real news stories. There will be no political reform without media transformation.

Microradio and Media Activism
BY KEVIN CODY AND STEPHEN DIETRICH

Commercial interest and consequent governmental regulation of the public airwaves has marginalized the voice of the people and their respective communities. At present, radio is primarily a source of entertainment rather then a source of news or a venue for enlightened dialogue. In national corporate radio, voices from local communities are virtually nonexistent.

Local radio is a way to bring communities together by giving them a voice of their own, a voice that has the potential to reach large numbers of people. Church groups, schools, city council, activist coalitions, and environmental groups can all find an outlet on the airwaves to create public discourse—an absolutely vital element to democracy. Information accessed via the alternative press, or school, or your own community can be disseminated through truly democratic means through community-based radio stations.

At present, there is a large part of the picture that corporate-based media tends to leave out of its representation of society. It is up to the local activist to fill in these gaps by "becoming the media," as Jello Biafra urges us to do. Local activists can simply take the power into our own hands, creating a multidimensional perspective on our society, culture, and politics. Public access to the radio airwaves is at an all-time low, and just starting to again become a practical source of alternative/independent media.

Two forms of local radio have emerged in the past decade. Hundreds of illegal microradio stations are operating throughout the U.S. These grassroots garage-style stations transmit to only a few miles radius, but in urban areas, this can represent thousands of potential listeners. To counter the illegal microradio stations, the Federal Communications Commission (FCC) is now allowing a limited number of microradio licenses in local communities. Lawyers and lawsuits have pressured the FCC to issue licenses to Low Power FM radio stations (LPFMS). The microradio movement is on its way to reestablishing the long lost legacy of public radio.

The microradio/Low Power FM movement is not just a cause for political action; it is also a means by which to open the lines of communication to invigorate our democracy. Microradio or LPFMS, as defined by the FCC , is the broadcasting of a station between 10 and 100 watts that can reach a radius of between 1 and 3.5 miles. These stations must be noncommercial, and would be licensed only to "noncommercial government or private education organizations, associations or entities, and government or non-profit entities providing local public safety or transportation services" (FCC Web site, <www.fcc.gov/mmb/prd/lpfm.html>). Individuals are not eligible for a license. The means of acquiring a license is covered below. If licensing does not work, and an activist opts for the route of civil disobedience, they face FFC sanctions and criminal penalties.

A brief history of microradio will help explain the current state of affairs. The Radio Act of 1912 was a response to the growing number of pioneers who were broadcasting over the airwaves. It required everyone doing so to obtain a license. Radio as a form of individual and group expression boomed during the following years, into the 1920s, with tens of thousands of people broadcasting their own unique programs. Commercial radio stations were also popular at this time, although outnumbered two-to-one by noncommercial stations (Ruggiero, p.16). The Radio Act of 1927 formed the Federal Radio Commission (FRC), which would become the Federal Communication Commission in 1934. The intent of the law was to regulate the airwaves "in the public interest, convenience, and necessity." The FRC was responsible for reallocating funds and interpreting the Radio Act of 1927. The little-known CBS and NBC radio networks that "barely existed in 1927 were quickly able to dominate the licensing process so that by 1931 they and their affiliated stations accounted for 70 percent of all wattage…and 97 percent of nighttime broadcasting" (McChesney, 192). The radio advertising industry was created after 1927, and reached levels of over $100 million by 1929 (McChesney, 192).

Privatization is the taking over of economic segments once considered open to the public domain. And with profits to be made in radio, privatization mushroomed. Educational and non-profit stations sharply declined after 1927. College radio was cut in half in just a few years, and by 1930 non-profit broadcasting was "effectively nonexistent for most Americans" (McChesney, 193). There were groups like the National Committee on Education by Radio (NCER) that voiced the large opposition towards commercial, profit driven radio, but eventually their voices were muted by the power of the private radio industry.

In 1948 there was a resurgence of low-power stations as the FCC decides to grant "Class D" licenses to colleges and local communities. But the tables then turned once more in 1978 when the FCC, with pressure from the National Public Radio, who was looking to monopolize audiences, completely banned all stations broadcasting with fewer than 100 watts. A typical commercial station is usually around 6,000 watts or more. After other acts were passed that encouraged the consolidation of stations by allowing one corporation to own more media outlets, activists desiring radio access turned to illegal pirate radio because it was basically the only way to access public airwaves.

After mounting public pressure and numerous court cases, the FCC has succumbed to granting LPFM licenses, albeit to a select few that have endured the application process. Most recently, a court case overthrew a portion of the Radio Broadcasting Act of 2000. *Ruggiero v. Federal Communications Commission (FCC)* overturned the portion of the act that prohibited anyone who had operated without a license from ever operating one again. As of May 6, 2002, this decision was "vacated," or retracted, and is going back to the U.S. Federal Court of Appeals for the DC circuit to be heard by the eight judges no later than September 2002. The case of Free Radio Berkeley is among the many cases that have sparked ongoing courtroom battles to return the airwaves to the public.

Free Radio Berkeley was founded without an FCC license on April 11, 1993, as a way to challenge the FCC and to promote free speech in the local community. Legal problems have plagued Free Radio Berkeley since its inception and they were finally silenced by a court injunction in June of 1998. Their mission, which was essentially to provide community news, discussions and interviews, information, a wide range of music, and more has now been taken up by Berkeley Liberation Radio. Free Radio Berkeley has evolved into another entity, promoting free speech radio with training and education called IRATE (International Radio Action Training Education). Visit the Web site at <www.freeradio.org/frb/irate.html>.

There are basically three major ways to get involved in microradio: 1) Apply for an LPFM license from the FCC; 2) Forgo the license and operate on your own pirate radio station in the spirit of civil disobedience; and 3) Take action in the growing political movement to reclaim the airwaves and support community-based radio. If you choose radio as your means for a creative and informative outlet, there are a number of actions to take, varying in their direct effectiveness. If you choose the first option, applying for a license from the FCC, go to their Web site at <www.fcc.gov.lpfm> or call (888) CALL-FCC. There is a rotating schedule of when you can apply depending on what state you live in, so it could take months before your turn comes; and then there is a five-day window for accepting applications. This process is long and arduous and does not guarantee you will get a license. Currently, the FCC has not announced any new filing windows for new applications to be accepted.

Another avenue would be to start your own pirate radio station. Whether you make a station at home or simply use your computer to broadcast over the Internet, access to the airwaves is not as remote a possibility as would otherwise be expected. While broadcasting over the Internet is not always considered to be "pirate," recent developments in copyright laws may make this more of an illegal venture. Information on broadcasting over the Internet can be accessed via <www.microradio.net>. Currently there is a debate over royalties for the songs that are played on Internet radio stations and in 2001 the U.S. Copyright Office created the "Copyright Arbitration Royalty Panel" (CARP) to resolve the issue. For more information on this struggle visit <www.SaveInternetRadio.org> put together by the Radio and Internet Newsletter (RAIN).

An excellent source for finding out everything you need to know to run your own pirate radio station is *Micropower Broadcasting-A Technical Primer* by Stephen Dunifer. It includes how to find a frequency, the necessary equipment, and the overall costs, which runs between $1,000 and $1,500. The primer can be found online at <www.radio4all.org/how-to.html>. Another comprehensive book on microradio, complete with a resource guide, is *Seizing the Airwaves: A Free-Radio Handbook*. This book was edited by Ron Sakolsky and Stephen Dunifer, and can be ordered from Free Radio Berkeley, 1442A Walnut Street #406, Berkeley, CA 94709. Books like this have enabled hundreds of people to start their own pirate radio stations all over the United States.

Freak Radio Santa Cruz is an example of a pirate radio station that has been continuously broadcasting for seven years without a FCC license. They base their operations on direct action and civil disobedience in defense of free speech. Freak Radio offers a wide variety of music, news, and culture along with updates from grassroots politics and local community news.

The South Eastern Association of Microbroadcasters (SEAM) is a group of nine pirate broadcasters, one of which is Free Radio Asheville in North Carolina, another station committed to grassroots community news.

Pirate radio stations offer an array of programming including alternative music often not well represented on the corporate-owned stations. In an e-mail interview, Sean, an operator of a pirate radio station in Texas said, "On our station we play mostly electronica, hip-hop, and other forms of music that you do not hear on the corporate radio stations or on television. We want to do more of the public access type of thing on our station so that the community's voice could be heard more."

San Francisco Liberation Radio tries to provide this type of a community voice by opening the discourse on topics such as social justice, progressive and local politics, along with local independent music.

A third option in microradio is getting involved politically. The Microradio Empowerment Coalition was built to strengthen the political sway of the movement. There are numerous groups involved in the coalition, such as Fairness and Accuracy in Reporting and the Media Education Foundation. The Prometheus Radio Project and Paper Tiger are there to fight in the struggle for more publicly owned radio. The National Lawyers Guild has a Committee on Democratic Communications (CDC) that is very active in the microradio campaign and can be found on the web at <www.nlgcdc.org>. Their Web site, along with <www.radio4all.org>, can connect you to the growing network of activist movements seeking to take back the airwaves. Progressive community radio stations across the country, and all over the world serve as great examples of the power the airwaves have to create a more democratic society.

KPFA in Berkeley, an internationally-known community radio station, originated from the Pacifica Foundation in 1949. The founder of Pacifica, Lewis Hill, pioneered the idea of listener sponsored radio, a concept that was not taken seriously at first.

The mission that followed this radical new idea was:

➤to encourage and provide outlets for the creative skills and energies of the community;

➤to serve the cultural welfare of the community;

➤to promote the study of political and economic problems, and of the causes of religious, philosophical, and racial antagonisms;

➤and to obtain access to sources of news not commonly brought together in the same medium.

This format proved to be quite successful and has lead the Pacific Network to create stations in Berkeley, California; Washington, DC; New York City; Houston, Texas; and Los Angeles, California. Pacifica is affiliated with some 60 community based radio stations.

One such station is KBOO, based in Portland, Oregon. Through a continuous effort since its inception in 1964, KBOO has increased listenership to over 50,000 and now has affiliate stations in the local area. The programming is all produced by a staff of volunteers and seven employees, with an annual budget of around $600,000 which is generated through listener sponsorship. KBOO's model of programming includes "filling needs that other media do not, [and] providing programming to diverse communities and unserved or underserved groups." KBOO is one of many stations that are part of a worldwide movement for community radio.

The World Association of Community Radio Broadcasters (AMARC) is an international nongovernmental organization built to tie together community radio stations all over the world. AMARC currently has almost 3,000 members and associates in 106 countries with every continent represented on the International Board. This movement that AMARC is a part of is a piece of the worldwide movement for free speech and community empowerment.

With the wide reach and accessibility of radio, communities and individuals can take power into their own hands to create a more local and diverse environment. While the approaches to microradio and/or community radio are varied in form and legality, their potential to bring democracy and free speech to the community is infinite. Many of the Web sites that we covered are in the resource guide in the back of this book. This can help you to elaborate on how to create your own form of media, which can then be used to create a community in which a forum for diversity of opinion and thought is available to everyone.

SOURCES:

McChesney, Robert W. Rich Media, *Poor Democracy: Communication Politics in Dubious Times*, New York: New York Press, 1999.

Ruggiero, Greg. *Microradio & Democracy: (Low) Power to the People.* New York: Seven Stories Press in association with Open Media, 1999.

Federal Communications Commission, <www.fcc.gov>.

Radio 4 All, <www.radio4all.org>.

National Lawyers Guild Committee on Democratic Communications, <www.nlgcdc.org>.

KBOO, <www.kboo.fm/history.php>.

Free Radio, International Radio Training Education, <www.SaveInternetRadio.org>, <www.freeradio.org/frb/irate.html>.

MicroRadio.Net, <www.microradio.net>.

Media for All:
Public Access Cable TV

BY KERRY BECK

Public cable access television is one of the most effective and far-reaching mediums available to groups and individuals to disseminate information directly to their communities. Public access television offers free air space for community residents to produce their own shows. Public cable access programming is broadcast locally to thousands of television sets each day. Local grassroots participation is often encouraged by public access stations because they rely on community producers for their programming content. Because of the broad spectrum of people and levels of experience brought to public cable access programs, the shows are of varying degrees of quality. Higher quality programs of interest to audiences beyond a local community are often cycled around to local cable TV stations outside the area (usually at the initiative of the show's producer). Thus local programs have potential to be viewed by expanded audiences and for information to travel even further. A high-quality program may be broadcast or distributed to outlying public access stations and beyond, enabling a producer's message to reach hundreds of thousands of viewers.

Project Censored interviewed four veteran local cable access producers. Joan Levinson of Berkeley Community Media, Will Stapp, former producer of *Chicken Scratch* a weekly public affairs program that aired on Petaluma Community Access television, Dan Bluthardt of Petaluma Cable Access, and John Moriarty, producer and host of the long-running Stockton Cable Access program *Talking It Through*, shared their experiences in creating and airing programs for public cable access. In addition to sharing pragmatic wisdom earned through their various experiences, this process also enabled the construction of a practical guide to the general processes involved in public access program production.

With persistence and determination, virtually anyone can create a public access TV program. It is not necessary for participants to be technical experts or professional journalists to successfully produce and air programs on local cable access channels. Public cable access channels are available for use by people of varying degrees of expertise. Programming for public access stations is a product of community residents. As such, public access stations are in the business of assisting and training local residents in the process of television production, thus empowering them to create and air their own TV shows.

A public cable access station is usually created as part of the contract between a city and a cable company. As part of the contract that allows the cable company to lay cable in the streets and to conduct business in the community, cities may require the cable company to provide a public access station and funding for facilities, equipment, and programs that assist residents in the production of programs for broadcast. By negotiating such contracts, residents are empowered to utilize the television forum while cable companies are able to offer unique local programming (not available via satellite) to its customers.

Once the station has been created, residents are empowered to participate in program production. The production of a local cable TV show begins with an idea: You have a story to tell. You may want to produce and host the show yourself or solicit the aid of one or more people with experience to fulfill these roles. Many knowledgeable, experienced people are willing to help and to share their expertise. They are an invaluable resource and can provide information that you might not find in your local station's educational literature. Lack of experience does not exclude you from utilizing public access TV to share your story. If you have a good story and access to knowledgeable, articulate people to tell it, you can bring your ideas to a local cable station and ask them to help you produce a program. Approach the station or program manager to discuss your story idea. Keep in mind that these stations operate on low budgets and are largely dependent on volunteer efforts for programming. As such they are generally receptive to new ideas and volunteers. Perhaps because of this unique quality and position, public access stations generally allow producers to determine program content independently. Programs are subject to FCC regulations and standards

THIS MODERN WORLD   by TOM TOMORROW

for content, but a serious producer with an important message to convey will usually be able to do so while remaining within the guidelines of the FCC.[1] With the cooperation of the station, you will be on your way to creating a program.

Before any interview or program production takes place, a producer must be familiar with the necessary equipment and procurement procedures. Each station will have its own set of guidelines for volunteer producers to follow. Most offer workshops to help train novice producers to use equipment and various production techniques. Training and certification is usually required of anyone wishing to use the expensive equipment. These workshops are a good place to begin networking with other certified participants and begin forming crews. Alternately, you may find opportunity to participate on another producer's program, which will allow you to gain experience and insight that you can later apply to your own project. Producing TV shows for public access is labor intensive and challenging, but your production processes will become more streamlined and your show quality will improve as you gain experience.

If you are planning a weekly program, it may be difficult to locate guests and crew initially. As a producer you will be responsible for securing your own crew for each program. Most of the work is done by volunteers. Shows generally require teams of at least five or six people to function as lighting technicians, sound engineers, editors, camera persons, on-camera storytellers, hosts, interviewers, and producers. If you are planning a weekly program, you may want to keep the names of several reliable backup crew members on file to accommodate volunteers' often fluctuating schedules. You may also want to consider creating a production group collective with volunteers from multiple programs where members do production work for one another's programs. This allows each production a larger pool of reli-

able prospective crew members. If your efforts are successful and you are able to produce a consistently good program, eventually guests will become more readily available. In some cases, after a show has become established as a respected forum for the exchange of ideas, a producer will be approached by community members with ideas for topics for individual shows. John Moriarty's *Talking It Through* has become an essential platform for community voices that might otherwise go unheard in the Stockton, California area, as well as being a forum for local political discussions. Political candidates and concerned citizens alike will often request to appear on the program because it is recognized as an important community resource for the open exchange of ideas.

Initially, however, a new program will not likely be approached by prospective guests. It is the crucial responsibility of the producer to solicit people who can speak informatively, articulately, and succinctly to an issue. Often the producer will request that you seek an alternate point of view to include in the presentation of your story, or suggest other methods of improving your presentation. Brief and concise communication is key to producing an effective program. If your topic expert tends to be verbose or stray from the focus of your program, you may want to seek the service of a host who is adept at exercising some control over the interview's direction. An effective producer will insure that the expert's attention remains focused on the subject of the program or will find a skilled host to do so.

While public cable access is a viable means of conveying one's message, it is to some extent flawed. Television is a passive medium. Producer Will Stapp expressed concern about television as an effective organizing tool. Stapp explained, "I don't think it [television] activates people." Television is a "pacifying medium, and not necessarily a good community builder." Still, despite these expressed reservations, after producing some 80 shows, he affirmed that he enjoyed the experience and would be willing to do it again. His advice to new producers, "Keep it simple and develop a committed team."

Beyond its capacity to distribute information, participation in public access television and the creation of a finished product is rewarding in personal satisfaction. Time and resources are rarely available to research the program's reception. After a program is aired, it is virtually impossible to discern who (if indeed anyone) has been watching. Since programming is local, one will occasionally be recognized by peers and neighbors, confirming that there is an audience. But public cable access television is largely an act of faith. Trust in the value of the message you are working to convey, persist in your endeavor, and most importantly, says veteran producer John Moriarty, "respect your guests and treasure your crew members." He stresses the importance of remembering that the crews are volunteers with other obligations and must be valued for their dedication to the task of enabling free expression.

Adhering to these guidelines, a motivated individual with an idea and a crew can produce high-quality, effective, and rewarding public access television programs. In doing so, one person is empowered and consequently empowers others through the practice of free speech and enabling the independent flow of information that might otherwise be censored by the corporate media.

A wealth of information about public cable access television is available on the Internet. Many programmers and organizations maintain Web sites with specific information about programs, local stations, and services. Below are some of the most comprehensive Web sites for information about public access television:

<www.fstv.org>

Free Speech TV provides a nationwide platform for those voices traditionally absent from mainstream media. FSTV airs full time via direct broadcast satellite and part time on a network of 35 community access cable stations.

<http://world.std.com/~rghm/>

Web Space for Comparative Study of U.S. PEG (Public, Educational, and Government) Access Centers.
This site provides a directory of public access TV centers with Web sites.

<http://dmoz.org/Arts/Television/Cable_TV/Public_Access/>

This site offers community edited listings of public access TV as well as other alternative media references.

<http://dir.whatuseek.com/Arts/Television/Cable_TV/Public_Access/>

Similar to the previous Web site, this is another informative community edited Web site that provides annotated links to public access resource, program, and station Web sites.

<www.sfctc.org/usaccess.htm>

A comprehensive and regularly updated listing of U.S. public access TV stations.

<http://dirs.educationworld.net/cat/2169/>

This site provides annotated references and links to public access resources, stations, and program Web sites.

<http://papertiger.org/>

Paper Tiger Television (PTTV) is an open, non-profit, volunteer video collective. Through the production and distribution of our public access series, media literacy/video production workshops, community screenings, and grassroots advocacy, PTTV works to challenge and expose the corporate control of mainstream media.

NOTE

1. See FCC Web site for further information on broadcast regulations at <http://www.fcc.gov/mb/>.

Indy Media Activism: Grassroots News

BY ERIC GARRISON

In December of 1999, in the wake of protests against the World Trade Organization (WTO), something happened that had never happened before in the history of alternative media. A collective movement of journalists and citizens decided to unite and make a difference globally. Before 1999 there had been a few ways of accessing alternative and global news, but never in a unified way. At the start of the protests, many journalists and concerned citizens decided to do something about it. The collective group decided to form their own Seattle Independent Media Center (S-IMC) to engage in grassroots media coverage of the WTO protests. Once it was established, the S-IMC started a printed publication called *The Blind Spot* and a new Web site, <www.indymedia.org>. Once the Web site went up and began to cover the WTO protests, the numbers of visitors to the site started to increase daily. At one point during the height of the Seattle protests, the number visiting the site mushroomed to about 1.4 million over a 24-hour period.

While the IMC group effort has started with a bang, it is now making an explosion throughout the IndyMedia news circuit worldwide. There are now a total of 80 independent but connected IMCs that operate from Italy to Colombia on a worldwide basis. Also being planned is a global council for mutual decision making between the IMCs. This planned global council will work to expand the format of the IMCs and ensure its long-term survival and success.

The IMC has now become so accessible that basically anybody can publish or write on the Web. As long as it's considered newsworthy, news pieces are often ported to the front pages of various IMC Web sites. Writing articles isn't the only way to publish on the IMC Web sites; a person can also submit video feeds, audio portions of interviews, or even show their own newsreels. This report is a guide for media activists, not just on how to get published, but also on where to look and how to get started. Open publishing is a great way to begin and will multiply your chances for publishing activist news.

OPEN PUBLISHING

Sue Supriano is a media activist in charge of both audio and out reach for the San Francisco IMC. When not doing work for the IMC she can be heard on her own shows, *Radio for Peace International* and *The Planet,* both of which are respectively broadcast from Costa Rica and WBCQ in Maine. While many of her shows can be heard on microradio, they can also be heard on the Internet at <www.radio4all.org> and <www.luver.org>. When interviewed Supriano commented on open publishing:

"We prefer news, but anything can go up on the Web site. What goes on the front page is news—priority news specifically. There's a collective of people, and everything is democratic and open. Decisions are made democratically, collectively, and by consensus. It's the people that run it that make the decisions, it's collective really, and not hierarchical. Anybody can open publish. *Open publishing* means someone can sit in their room and think of something they want to write."

Open publishing is the basis for which most of Independent Media Centers are founded. A person will find on most of the IMC Web pages a "publish" link and simple instructions on how to get a story published. The story should, however, be news, delivered in a clear and honest way that presents both sides of the story. Stories other than news can be published; they will just be relegated to other sections of the site.

For example, a recent police scandal in Sonoma County had police officers claiming that there was drug possession at a college party. Many of the students who actually attended the party, as well as some of the neighbors who witnessed it, said exactly the opposite of what the police stated. In a case of open publishing, a person can give his or her own report on the matter. The policeman in question at the party could be interviewed, as well as some of the neighbors and college students at the actual college party in question. Once both sides were taken into consideration, the reporter could write a summary of the events and post the report to their local IMC, in this case the San Francisco Chapter at <www.sfindy-media.org>. Publishing a written work, though, isn't the only way to report things. A person can also report in either audio or video.

VIDEO

While IMC is definitely a good place to start for publishing, there are several viable alternatives as well. Eric Galatas, a producer at Free Speech TV offers some useful advice on how to present news stories in a video format for both the Internet and your own community:

"The best way for a person to present news stories on TV is to use your own public access channels. Begin to talk about issues in your own area once you start talking about news. Public access TV and radio used to cost between $80,000 and $100,000 to operate. Now if you have about $1,000, you can run your own local show. Two to three thousand dollars will afford additional editing equipment for a more polished production. On the other hand, you can borrow a camera from another person. For those who are interested but unfamiliar with operating video, a great Web site, <http://satellite.indy media.org> has a production guide on how to operate with cameras and how to start your own newsreel. You can edit from this site as well.

"If you can't afford such equipment, your local IMC may have equipment for you to borrow when you develop newsreels. Sometimes local cable channels will even run your newsreel and develop it within their own programs, Free Speech TV itself currently run segments from over 35 news stations that are across the country. If none of these options seem viable, you can always publish your own news stories through <http://Print.indymedia.org>."

Free Speech TV itself is one of the first full-time networks dedicated to alternative media and "social change." Free Speech TV also has offered hosting in the past for the S-IMC's audio and video content. Because of recent FCC rulings, Free Speech TV (FSTV) may soon have the ability to be on air 24 hours a day, 7 days a week. FSTV receives about 200,000 visitors each day to its programs nationwide and is on cable systems that reach approximately seven million homes. Free Speech TV also has a newsreel of its weekly news at w<ww.freespeech.org/>. If video seems a complicated option, one can always choose to do audio interviews.

AUDIO

While there are many ways to publish through the IMC Web sites, sometimes a simple audio interview speaks more effectively than a written one. For audio, a person can do many things to get published on the IMC Web sites. The most widely used option is Real Media. The most economically way of utilizing Real Media is to spend about $10 on a computer microphone and then conduct your interviews through the Internet, on a phone, or in person. Other options are to have a tape recorder handy, the necessary adapter and simple programs such as Cool Edit 96. Equipment for this generally runs from about $1 to $50. There are more detailed instructions with extensive notes and links on how to operate Real Media and audio equipment at <www.indymedia.org/tutorial.php3>.

Once a reporter has learned to utilize audio, he or she can then become full-fledged media reporter for their local community. In the case of public accusation against the police in Sonoma County, a media reporter could record both sides of the interviews and then mix the audio content together with software programs like Cool Edit. The resulting interview could then be posted to their local IMC Web site. Now that the reader has basic knowledge of alternative media in their minds, what if they want to form their own independent media center?

LISTSERVS

Another very effective way of pursuing and reporting news is through the format known as listservs. Listservs are e-mail servers that allow a person (or group of people) to send out news stories to as many people as are willing to receive them. Listservs can average about 1,000 to 2,000 subscribers. Fortunately, a person doesn't need a large budget nor do they need extensive knowledge of the Internet to create a listserv. Web sites such as IndyMedia have the technology to enable people to have their own listervs. By visiting the IndyMedia listserv page at <http://lists.indymedia.org>, one can get an idea of the listservs currently in use and the categories currently offered.

Local Northern California IndyMedia activist Attila Nagy runs a sociopolitical news listserv from his own home:

"My own listserv started out with just a few hundred people and quickly expanded to the approximate 1,000 who are on it today. Instead of spending a couple hundred dollars for pamphlets or fliers, listservs are a quick and free alternative. You can just keep adding names to your server as people discover your listserv distribution. Most e-mail programs work. The program I use is Eudora Light, which has been easy for me to use and does the job quite adequately. The only email program I wouldn't recommend is Outlook Express, as that program is the virus carrier of choice for many hackers.

"One of the great things about a listserv is that it's very close to the concept of open publishing. That is, you can write about anything you want. If there's some kind of scandal going on in your area or your just want to spread the word about a local rally, you can send it out on the listserv. Some listservs deal with local news, while others such as <www.mediachannel .org>, deal with national and international news. That's the best thing about listservs, be it local or international; it's anything you want to write about. I encourage everyone to try this free and easy option."

Attila's listserv, which deals with Northern California, national, and international news, can be reached at <zenekar@sonic.net>.

IMCS IN YOUR AREA

If an IMC is not accessible in your local area, you can always find information on how to form one at <http://newimc.indymedia.org>. There is also advice on how to put together an IMC at <http://process.indymedia.org>. Once an individual or group decides to form an IMC, a mission statement must be created that includes both an overall goal and a general editorial policy on how the IMC will be managed effectively. One can get a better idea of IMCs by looking at some local examples such as the San Francisco IMC's mission statement:

➤To cover local events that are ignored or poorly covered by corporate media.

➤To seek out and provide coverage underscoring the global nature of people's struggles for social, economic, and environmental justice directly from their perspective.

➤To encourage, facilitate, and support the creation of independent newsgatherings and organizations.

Once a group has shown sincere effort they can then e-mail the new IMC working group at <new-imc@indymedia.org>.

To spread the word about what is currently going on at the IMC Web site, a person can download a summary of the week's news at <http://print.indymedia.org> and release it as a pamphlet in their community.

CONCLUSIONS: MAKING A GLOBAL GROUP EFFORT

Sue Supriano has some good closing words on the IMC group effort:

"Indy media has infinite possibilities. A person can do photographs, video, or audio; it's not hard. If they have ideas and follow through with them in a quality way, it'll be much more useful because of its quality. The advantage of the indie media and the Internet is that you can download the material to print in a newsletter, or even put it on radio. It really opens up all these possibilities. There's a job for anybody, you don't have to be a media major to get involved. You can do fundraising, or design fliers, or get them copied, or pass them out, or you can raise money, spread the word! Go to demonstrations. Write press releases, flood the press, and spread publicity for yourself. Participate in the global decision making."

IMCs are here to stay and will continue to evolve as a global phenomenon—offering individuals and groups the opportunity to communicate via many forms of media.

A special thanks to Eric Galatas, Sue Supriano, and Attila Nagy for their help and advice in the formation of this tutorial.

Developing Independent Newspapers
BY CHRIS SALVANO

The purpose of the following interviews is to provide a glimpse into the growing independent newspaper movement. Four newspapers (*Onward* in Gainesville, Florida; *Asheville Global Report* in Asheville, North Carolina; *Connections* in Stockton, California; and the *San Francisco Bay View* in San Francisco) were chosen to provide an understanding of issues, people, and geographical locations associated with this movement. In addition, we intend to provide an understanding of how and why these individuals organized to start an independent newspaper, how they maintain readership and distribution, how they decide what's an important story, and what continuous challenges or obstacles they encounter.

Each newspaper has a different history, focus, methodology, and different resources at their disposal. However, all newspapers had one common goal: To provide an independent forum for discussing issues and events that the corporate media marginalize or ignore. Moreover, each newspaper stressed one common theme during these interviews: People are losing their voices within the corporate media system. These and many other media sources across the country are actively working to counter this dangerous trend within our society.

ONWARD (Gainesville, Florida)

Onward is an independent quarterly newspaper that began operation in August 2000. Its three editors, Rob Augman, Dan Berger, and Tom Thomson, organized the start-up of the paper. According to the collective, *Onward* is a newspaper intending to facilitate both a report of anarchist actions worldwide and to foster an analysis of current events from an anarchist perspective.

Anarchism, in brief, espouses the dissolution of all forms of hierarchy and the abolition of economic systems that set one class above another. Instead, anarchist cooperative structures present a future based on solidarity, mutual aid, freedom, and direct participatory democracy.

Augman, Berger, and Thomson began this anarchist-oriented paper because they were concerned about the lack of mainstream coverage of the growing movement against capitalist globalization, and the role of anarchist organizations within that movement. In 1999, "Much of the housing and actions in Seattle were organized by anarchists," explains Augman. At that time, he adds, "there weren't enough forums for anarchist ideas, discussions, and actions." They started the *Onward* newspaper in order to provide that forum. The twenty-page quarterly prints about 2,500 copies and began with an initial mailing and distribution of about 500 newspapers. The paper began with a low budget, says Augman, and was initially financed with a couple hundred dollars of the editors' own money.

Augman, Berger, and Thomson have worked to increase the paper's distribution through continuous contacts with other people and organizations throughout the country. There is even some distribution outside of the United States, says Augman, due to these contact efforts. By 2002, *Onward*'s mailing has grown to 1,300 copies. The paper, according to Augman, is found mostly in information shops, alternative bookstores and is distributed through people in the anti-globalization movement.

Augman, Berger, and Thomson are still with the paper today, and form the core group of the newspaper's editorial and decision-making process. They decided *Onward* should contain first-hand articles about what other anarchist groups and individuals were doing. When asked how they organized people to get the newspaper started, and to keep it going, Augman described how the editors "focused on making contacts with people in the left movement in general and with anarchists in particular. We wanted first-hand reports from anarchists around the country and the world."

As far as the ongoing effort needed to keep the paper circulating, Augman states that "many volunteers and friends make themselves available to help," with each issue of the paper. Friends, local and from around the country, volunteer to help with mailings and make important suggestions about the layout of the newspaper. "They also help with the Web page, distribute the paper, and provide feedback about the newspaper and the Web site," he adds. With the exception of a paid printer, the newspaper relies entirely on dedicated volunteer labor.

Onward's news gathering consists of first-hand news reports from individuals around the country, and from outside the United States. Through the editors' organizing efforts, the newspaper has regular contacts in Richmond, Virginia; Orlando, Florida; Albuquerque, New Mexico; Texas; and Ohio. These people, according to Augman, help fill the pages of the newspaper each issue by regularly contributing articles. They also help with donations, help increase distribution, and they "provide advice and ideas to help advance the newspaper."

Fundraising for the newspaper is achieved in several different ways. The editors, in addition to selling newspapers and accepting donations, organize a variety of local activities to help pay for the newspaper. As Augman informed me, benefit concerts by local musicians, film festivals, and plays all help to raise funds for *Onward*. The latest fundraiser was a play based on the life of union/labor organizer and anarchist Emma Goldman.

Augman doesn't consider *Onward* a "Gainesville paper" because it focuses on broader issues of the anarchist community. However, he says, the newspaper is trying to become more community-oriented and is "trying to cultivate more connections to Gainesville issues." The newspaper has recently become free in the Gainesville area and as Augman notes, the newspaper will always be free to prison inmates.

Independent newspapers face several challenges and obstacles to maintain their circulation. According to Augman, a big challenge *Onward* faces is "getting the paper to people not associated with social movements," such as anarchism. People like your neighbors, for example. Like with other newspapers, funding provides an ongoing challenge for the independent press. "*Onward* funds itself and wants to give the papers free to everyone," says Augman. However, "there is a financial restraint that ends up restricting the paper's access to a broader audience. That's the biggest problem," he says.

For media activists who want to start their own newspaper, the major advice that Augman gives is to make contacts with lots of people. "Contacts, contacts, contacts!" he stresses. "Contact with other people serves the purpose of getting their input about issues, ideas, and it also helps the distribution of the paper," he adds. "The paper is there as a forum for ideas. It needs the people."

ONWARD, P.O. Box 2671, Gainesville, FL 32602-2671
Tel: (352) 377-6865
Web site: <www.onwardnewspaper.org>
E-mail: <info@onwardnewspaper.org>

SAN FRANCISCO BAY VIEW (San Francisco, California)

The *San Francisco Bay View* is a free independent weekly newspaper that is run by editor Mary Ratcliff and her husband, and publisher Willie Ratcliff. They bought the newspaper in 1992 from its previous owner, Mohammad Al-Karim, who started the *Bay View* in 1976. According to Willie Ratcliff, "Mohammad was having problems getting [the paper] out," and, "we wanted to carry on the dream of the paper."

The newspaper focuses mostly on issues of economic and environmental racism in the San Francisco neighborhood of Bay View Hunters Point, and throughout the entire Bay Area as well. One of the largest problems of the African-American community, says Ratcliff, is that of economic inequality. "We're here," he adds, "to support the poor and people of color." In addition, there are several hundred polluted sites in this San Francisco neighborhood, including the city's main sewage treatment plant, an aging power plant, and the Hunters Point naval shipyard. The naval shipyard is one of the nation's most polluted Superfund sites, resulting in rampant health problems. This neighborhood has "the highest cancer rate, asthma rate, and breast cancer rate for women under 40 in the state," says Ratcliff. One of the main focuses of the newspaper is to "politicize and educate the community about these health issues." The paper also acts to put pressure on the polluters and government regulators to resolve these health and safety problems.

The local corporate media has not done much to address these issues of environmental racism in the African-American community, says Ratcliff. "The *San Francisco Chronicle* is not talking about these community issues. They're part of the problem," he adds. The importance of the *Bay View* is that "we're putting issues in the interest of women and people of color."

In 1992, the Ratcliffs began publishing the *Bay View* twice a month and helped increase its distribution. In 1998, the newspaper began publishing as a weekly, and it now pays local individuals to distribute about 20,000 copies throughout the Bay Area. The papers are delivered primarily into African-American neighborhoods in Oakland, Berkeley, and Richmond, as well as San Francisco. It's also distributed into community centers, information shops, churches, and colleges. Distribution, says Ratcliff, also includes about 500 annual subscriptions that are mailed all over the country.

Funding for the *Bay View* has fluctuated over the years. until 1998, Willie Ratcliff's construction company subsidized the paper. Since then, advertising covers most of the costs. But, he adds, the paper lost some money last year and probably will lose money again this year.

The major cost of the *Bay View* is printing, which comes to nearly $1,700 each month. Other costs include a rent-controlled office, layout, and paying the distributors and the freelance writers. The newspaper has one paid, part-time employee who does the layout and maintains the Web site.

The *Bay View* gathers news and articles by several different methods. The paper is a member of the National Newspaper Publishers Association (NNPA), the San Francisco Neighborhood Newspaper Association, and New California Media, among others. The NNPA is a coalition of African-American weeklies throughout the country, which, according to Ratcliff, allows the *Bay View* to engage in news-sharing programs with other African-American communities.

While the *Bay View* focuses mostly on community-oriented issues of economic and environmental racism, it does include coverage of national and international issues from freelance writers. "We've been covering the war in the Middle East, the American bombing range in Vieques, the coup in Venezuela, and we wrote about our support of Representative Cynthia McKinney's call for an investigation into the events of 9-11," says Ratcliff.

The *Bay View* also receives about 1,200 news articles via e-mail each week from individuals and organizations. These help the newspaper fill the pages of each issue.

As the other interviews pointed out, financing independent newspapers to keep them circulating provides a constant challenge. As Ratcliff states, there is "always a challenge with money. Computer problems too."

His advice to those interested in starting their own independent newspaper is, "Be truthful, no propaganda bullshit. You're going up against the big papers that want you to go along with the status quo. The mainstream press has been toeing the line since 9-11. When a paper does that, what do you expect to gain?"

SAN FRANCISCO BAY VIEW, 4908 Third Street, San Francisco, CA 94124
Tel: (415) 671-0449 Fax: (415) 822-8971
Web site: <www.sfbayview.com>
E-mail: <editor@sfbayview.com>

ASHEVILLE GLOBAL REPORT (Asheville, North Carolina)

The *Asheville Global Report (AGR)* is a free independent weekly newspaper that began operation in January 1999. Three people, Brendon Conley, Bob Brown, and Clare Hanrahan, began meeting once a week to discuss what issues to include in a newspaper. The group felt strongly about social and environmental justice, and decided to provide a cross section of local, national, and international stories concerning these issues. The editors decided to follow the mainstream model for structure and layout of *AGR*. It is divided into topical sections such as "Environment" and "Labor" (as opposed to the mainstream papers' "Business" section).

Conley, one of the *AGR*'s founders and currently one of its four editors, says that at the time of the paper's founding the three editors were motivated because they believed that "the mainstream press was not covering people's movements and social issues." Conley views the *AGR* as having the "original mission of newspapers: be the voice of the people. Mainstream press has abandoned that."

When the *AGR* began circulating in January 1999, Conley, Brown, and Hanrahan relied on available resources to produce their paper. The *AGR*, began as an eight-page newsletter, with layout done on computer. The group was photocopying about 100 copies of the newsletter and distributing it throughout the Asheville area.

Through fundraising efforts, the *AGR* was able to secure enough funding and resources to expand the newsletter. In June 1999, the paper hired a local Asheville printer and began publishing a 16-page weekly, which it still maintains and distributes today. As Conley notes, "The layout of the newspaper has become more complex; we now have advertising and nonprofit business status." Today, the *AGR* distributes 1,500 to 2,000 copies each week, mostly in the Asheville area. The newspaper also continues to be available for free with over 100 back issues available on its Web site.

The entire staff of the *AGR* is composed of about 12 individuals, including its editors (and board of directors) Brendon Conley, Sachie Godwin, Kendra Sarvadi, and Eamon Martin. All staff members, who help with editing, layout, distribution, and mailings, dedicate their time and effort on a volunteer basis. In addition, according to editor Sachie Godwin, volunteers that dedicate about 10 or more hours per week are eligible for a small weekly stipend.

Funding for the *AGR* has been expanded from donations and fundraising events, and now also includes grant writing. With a continuous process of fundraising, the *AGR* is currently able to maintain an annual budget of about $20,000. Major costs for the newspaper, according to Godwin, are rent, printing, and bulk mailings. Printing costs are the largest expense of the paper, about one-third of its total budget.

Godwin also informed me that the *AGR* is beginning to award small stipends to people who provide exclusive stories for the paper. Staff members and freelance reporters can receive a stipend of $20 per story (more for longer stories), and possible compensation for travel expenses.

The *AGR* uses several different methods of newsgathering to fill its pages every week. It maintains contacts with other independent media organizations to help promote news-sharing capabilities. The group also monitors activist-oriented Web sites searching for first-hand reports of important issues. The paper also accepts unsolicited submissions of exclusive stories from individuals and organizations. As stated above, the paper actively works to assign local, regional, and even national stories (when possible) to *AGR* reporters. Conley informed me that several of these *AGR*-assigned stories appear in the newspaper each week. In addition, Godwin maintains and updates the Web site on a weekly basis.

Deciding what's an important story is a decision made by the editors on a collaborative, if not consensual, basis. Conley notes that the *AGR*'s philosophy is "to focus on what people are doing; people in unions, organizations, and movements."

Maintaining an independent, volunteer-run, weekly newspaper for over three years is a challenge in itself. Conley, however, notes that fundraising is probably the most challenging obstacle of the weekly paper. "Raising money is always a challenge. It needs to be done; it's essential," says Conley. His financial advice to people interested in starting a newsletter or newspaper is to "do everything to raise money. Don't rely on just donations or grants. Do a little bit of everything." Another constant challenge is that of the internal dynamics of the staff. "People have made a long-term commitment to this paper. A dozen or so people treat it as a job." The internal dynamics, he says, has pretty much worked out with the *AGR*.

As far as content is concerned, Conley's advice is to keep the opinions and person-bashing to a minimum. "We try to avoid too much editorializing," he adds. He believes the paper is best served presenting the information not just to activists, but more broadly to people who don't consider themselves political activists. Provide the information to the people and let them draw their own conclusions, says Conley.

The important thing, he adds, is to recognize that the independent media movement is as essential as all other movements. "People are losing their voice," says Conley of the content of corporate media. "People can and should protest" about corporate media and its current trend of ownership consolidation. But, he adds, "the real way to fight that is to create an alternative."

ASHEVILLE GLOBAL REPORT, P.O. Box 1504, Asheville, NC 28802
Tel and Fax: (828) 236-3103
Web site: <www.agrnews.org>
E-mail: <editors@agrnews.org>

CONNECTIONS (Stockton, California)

Connections is a free independent monthly newspaper (10 issues per year) that evolved out of the Peace and Justice Center Network of San Joaquin County. The Network, says layout artist Laurie Litman, had been mailing a newsletter and "we wanted to upgrade." In 1986, the organization began publishing and circulating a 12-page newspaper. "The newsprint allowed more room for community issues and advertising," says Litman. And it wasn't as expensive as we had anticipated, she adds.

The *Connections* newspaper includes a cross section of local, national, and international stories. According to Litman, the newspaper and its editors tend to focus coverage on issues concerning peace, justice, and the environment. The editor, Bruce Giudici, also writes extensively about the influence of campaign contributions on local elections and local policy.

Connections is now a 20-page publication. It currently circulates about 10,000 copies of the newspaper each issue, and has a consistent distribution of about 2,000 copies in San Joaquin County.

As Litman notes, the newspaper relies on a crew of volunteers to help distribute the paper each month. About a dozen people associated with the Peace and Justice Center Network make themselves available to help get the free newspaper into the communities throughout the county.

Connections maintains most of its funding through several donation requests throughout the year. The newspaper utilizes its Peace and Justice enter Network database and does a mass mailing to these individuals about two or three times per year, says Litman. This raises enough money to keep the *Connections* newspaper circulating on a monthly basis. Advertising also helps buffer the newspaper's expenses each month. Advertising revenue covers about half of the costs of the paper, says Litman. The major costs of *Connections*, she says, are the printing costs and the bulk-mailing costs.

Connections makes its newspaper available for free and in turn makes several donation requests throughout the year "to be more inclusive," says Litman. When asked if she believes that distributing the newspaper in this manner is a better approach to increasing the paper's readership and distribution, she is emphatic: "It's absolutely helping distribution."

According to Litman, the biggest challenge of *Connections* is "quality of content and the timeliness of writing." However, after 15 years, not much is unforeseen she says. "We've got it down to a science."

Another challenge for the newspaper, says Litman, has been the burnout factor. The time required for layout, graphic design, editing, and distribution is a huge task. It's a big commitment for an entirely volunteer staff, especially the editor. As Litman explains, once the editor has chosen the content for each issue, it takes her between eight and twelve hours just to do layout for the newspaper. "Finding salespeople and advertising representatives" has also proven to be a constant challenge for *Connections*, says Litman.

For people who want to organize an independent newspaper, Litman reminds un of the importance of these community-based media resources. "They're basic and they're needed," she says. "How do you get that information to mainstream people?"

CONNECTIONS, Peace and Justice Network of San Joaquin County
P.O. Box 4123, Stockton, CA 95204
Tel: (209) 467-4455
Web site: <www.pjnsjc.org>
E-mail: <dsteele@igc.apc.org>

By looking at the patterns of corporate newspaper ownership, we begin to see the importance of independently owned newspapers. Currently six corporations (Gannett, Knight Ridder, E.W. Scripps, Advance, Lee Enterprises, and *The New York Times*) own about 278 daily newspapers in this country. Many of these daily newspapers receive national and international exposure. In addition to these "big six," five other corporations (Liberty Group Publishing, CNHI, Hollinger, Media News Group, and Pulitzer) control an additional 729 newspapers. This group of newspapers receives mostly regional exposure rather than national exposure. Other corporations can be added to list: Dow Jones (24 newspapers), Cox (15 newspapers), Hearst Corporation (20 newspapers), and so on.

However, when a dozen corporations control the flow of information for over 1,000 domestic newspapers (dailies and weeklies), voices of the poor, people of color, and women get drowned out. As evidenced by the four newspapers interviewed, issues concerning social justice, economic and environmental racism, the "labor side" of business, and the movement against corporate globalization become marginalized or ignored by mainstream corporate media. With the trend of media consolidation continuing under the current FCC administration, the role of independent newspapers such as *Onward, Asheville Global Report, Connections*, the *San Francisco Bay View*, and hundreds of others like them nationwide becomes all the more important for the maintenance of democratic institutions within our society.

THIS MODERN WORLD

by TOM TOMORROW

CHAPTER 6

The Big Ten Media Giants

BY MARK CRISPIN MILLER

The corporate press routinely kills or underplays important news, not because there are dishonest people managing the system, or incompetent reporters working in it. There are always such bad apples in the mix, of course, but in the mainstream there are also gifted journalists who try to do their best, and even some executives who would prefer to see the people well-informed. Although the integrity and skill of those who do the work, and of those who oversee it, is of course immeasurably important, the corporate news as it is sponsored and produced today would still be fragmentary, simplistic, fundamentally irrelevant and largely idiotic even if the folks responsible were, without exception, paragons of journalistic probity—for that system, finally, is itself the problem. Those who do good work within it do so largely by resisting it, while those who churn out garbage day and night are doing only what the system asks of them.

The charts reproduced here—a blueprint of the U.S. media landscape at the start of 2002—should help explain the problem, once we point out those crucial factors that no chart alone can properly explain. We must note first of all that those 10 mammoth parent companies† are very heavily indebted—the high price of their recent radical expansion, and the reason why they must *continue* to expand, so as to keep their stock price high. While forcing them to buy up everything in sight, the corporations' heavy debt also requires them to impose on all their properties, from book publishers and movie studios to magazines and music labels, a certain simple two-part formula for beefing up the bottom line. On the one hand, it is imperative

AOL/TIME WARNER

Janus Capital Corporation owns 6%
Revenues: $36.2 billion

MAGAZINES

More than 64, including the 3 bestselling: *Time, Life* and *People; MAD Magazine*, DC Comics (87.5% w/12.5% AT&T); IPC, leading consumer magazine publisher in Britain

MOVIES

Warner Bros., New Line, and Fine Line Features (75% w/25% AT&T); library of MGM, RKO and pre-1950 Warner Bros. films; Warner Home Video (75% w/25% AT&T); theaters: UCI (50% w/50% Viacom); WF Cinema Holdings (50% w/50% Viacom)

MUSIC

More than 40 labels including Warner Bros., Atlantic, Elektra, London-Sire and Rhino Records; manufactures, packages, and distributes the company's CDs, tapes and DVDs, majority interest in Alternative Distribution Alliance; Quincy Jones Entertainment Co. (37.5% w/ 12.5% AT&T and 50% Quincy Jones), Columbia House (50% w/50% Sony); Music publisher Warner/Chappell

BOOKS

Warner Books, Little, Brown, Time-Life Books, Book-of-the-Month Club (50% w/ Bertelsmann)

TELEVISION

NETWORKS
WB (50% w/17% AT&T, 22% Tribune Co. and 11% WB officers), HBO and Cinemax, (75% w/25% AT&T), Comedy Central (37.5% w/12.5% AT&T and 50% Viacom), Court TV (37.5% w/12.5% AT&T and 50% Liberty), E! and Style (7.5% w/AT&T, Liberty, Disney, and Comcast), TBS, TNT, Cartoon Network, Turner Classic Movies, CNN, Headline News, CNNfn and CNN/Sports Illustrated; TVKO (75% w/25% AT&T); Music Choice (w/Sony, EMI, AT&T, and others); wholly and partially-owned channels in Europe, Asia, and South America

CABLE
Second largest provider with 12.8 million customers in wholly and partially owned systems (most with AT&T)

PRODUCTION / PROGRAMMING
Warner Bros., Warner Bros. Animation, Telepictures, Castle Rock; library of 6,500 movies, 32,000 TV shows, and 13,500 cartoons (all 75% w/25% AT&T); Other: TiVo (18% w/GE, Liberty, News Corp. and others); digital video recording

THEME PARKS

Warner Bros. Movie World Theme Park and hotel in Australia (w/AT&T and Village Roadshow)

INTERNET

America Online, CompuServe, Netscape, ICQ, and AOL Instant Messenger; websites include: MusicNet (20% w/20% Bertelsmann, 20% EMI and RealNetworks), digitalcity, moviefone, mapquest, and music sites Spinner.com, Winamp, and SHOUTcast; stakes in Amazon.com (2%), Dr. Koop (10%); RoadRunner cable modems (majority stake w/ AT&T and Advance-Newhouse)

SPORTS

Atlanta Braves, Atlanta Hawks, Atlanta Thrashers, Goodwill Games, Phillips Arena

OTHER

Time Warner Telecom (37%), Warner Bros. Studio Stores (75% w/25% AT&T), licenses rights to DC Comics, Hanna-Barbera characters, other WB properties (75% w/25% AT&T); stake in Sportsline Radio

---

GENERAL ELECTRIC

Revenues: $129.9 billion

INTERNET

Includes stakes of 47% in Snap and NBC.com; CNBC.com (10%), Salon.com (10%), Autobytel.com Inc. (10%), and polo.com (50% W/Polo Ralph Lauren Media)

SPORTS/ LIVE VENUE

New York Knicks, New York Rangers, New York Liberty, New England Seawolves, Hartford Wolfpack, Madison Square Garden, management of Hartford Civic Center (all 16% w/44% Cablevision and 40% News Corp); Radio City Music Hall (16% w/44% Cablevision and 40% News Corp), World Wrestling Federation Entertainment (3% w/3% Viacom and others)

OTHER

Aircraft engines; GE, Hotpoint, and other appliances; light bulbs; operates 14 communications satellites; cars, computers, equipment for refineries, ammonia plants and nuclear reactors, MR and CT scanners, X-ray, and ultrasound machines; health, accident, and long-term care insurance; investment and retirement plans, mortgages, home equity and commercial real estate loans, car loans, credit card application processing, sales authorization, and collection services for retailers in 23 countries; owns stock in companies in retail, financial services, telecommunications, healthcare, food and beverages, cable and broadcasting industries; leases almost 1,000 aircraft, 190,000 railcars, and about 1 million cars, trucks, and tractor trailers

TELEVISION

NETWORKS
NBC, CNBC, MSNBC (50% w/50% Microsoft), A&E, History and Biography channels (all 25% w/37.5% Disney and 37.5% Hearst); Snap TV (80%); AMC, Bravo, WE, and Independent Film Channel (all w/Cablevision and MGM); stakes in regional news, sports, and entertainment channels with News Corp., AT&T, and Cablevision; international channels include NBC and CNBC channels in Europe and Asia, Canal de Noticias NBC and TV Azteca (joint venture)

STATIONS
13 stations, plus 32% stake in Paxson, owner of TV stations and PAX TV, a national programming network

PRODUCTION / PROGRAMMING
NBC Productions; Radio City Television, Bravo Original Programming, IFC Productions, and Next Wave Films (16-26% w/Cablevision); Satellite DBS provider (13% w/37% Cablevision and 50% Loral); TiVo (w/AOL-TW, News Corp., Viacom, and Liberty)

VIACOM, INC.

National Amusements owns 68%
Revenues: $20 billion

MOVIES

Paramount Pictures, Nickelodeon Movies, MTV Films, BET Arabesque Films; Blockbuster (82%); About 1,800 screens in theaters the US, Canada, Europe, Asia, and South America through Famous Players, UCI (50% w/50% AOL-TW); WF Cinema Holdings (50% w/50% AOL-TW)

BOOKS

Simon & Schuster, Pocket Books, Scribner, The Free Press, Arabesque Books; divisions in Britain and Australia

INTERNET

MTVi (90% w/10% Liberty) includes MTV.com and VH1.com; Nickelodeon Online (w/AT&T); stakes also in iWon, Sportsline.com, MarketWatch.com, hollywood.com, storerunner.com, Thirdage.com, and Webvan; web design

RADIO

184 Infinity radio stations; CBS Radio Network; Westwood One (18%) and Sportsline Radio (20% w/Reuters and AOL-TW)

TELEVISION

NETWORKS

CBS, UPN, MTV, MTV2, VH1, Showtime, Nickelodeon, Noggin (50% w/Sesame Workshop), Nickelodeon GAS, TV Land, Comedy Central (50% w/37.5% AOL-TW and 12.5% AT&T), TNN, CMT, The Movie Channel, Sundance Channel (50% w/Vivendi and Robert Redford), FLIX, BET and BET, on Jazz. stakes in channels throughout Europe, and in India, Africa, Asia, and Russia

STATIONS

39, including two each in Philadelphia, Boston, Dallas, and Detroit; operates 2 others.

PRODUCTION

CBS Enterprises (includes King World and CBS Broadcast International), Paramount, Spelling, Big Ticket, Viacom Productions, Nickelodeon Studios, MTV Productions, Nicktoons Animation; other TV: TiVo (w/AOL-TW, News Corp., Liberty, and GE)

THEME PARKS / VENUE

Paramount theme parks in the US and Canada; Star Trek: The Experience at the Las Vegas Hilton; jazz restaurant in Las Vegas; theme-based restaurants and dance clubs in Largo, MD, Memphis, and at Disney World; World Wrestling Federation Entertainment (3% w/3% GE and others); House of Blues Entertainment (w/that company)

OTHER

Exclusive advertising rights on buses, subways, trains, kiosks, billboards, and other venues in New York, LA, Chicago, San Francisco, Philadelphia, Detroit, Houston, Atlanta, and 82 other US cities and in cities in Mexico, Canada, Britain, Ireland, and throughout Europe; BET Financial Services; BET Design Studio (w/G-III Apparel Group, Ltd.); licenses Viacom-owned properties and third-party clients including the U.S. Postal Service, Jeep, and Red Dog Beer; Famous Music holds copyright to more than 100,000 musical works

MAGAZINES

BET Weekend (w/New York Daily News), Emerge, Heart & Soul, Nickelodeon Magazine

---

WALT DISNEY COMPANY

Revenues: $25.4 billion

SPORTS

Mighty Ducks, Anaheim Angels

MAGAZINES

US Weekly (50% w/Wenner Media), Discover, Family Fun, Disney Adventures, ESPN The Magazine (80% w/20% Hearst), Talk (50% w/50% Hearst)

RESORTS / THEMED ENTERTAINMENT

Disney World, Disneyland, Disney Cruise Line, Disney Vacation Club, Tokyo Disney (royalties on revenues), Disneyland Paris (39%), Hong Kong Disneyland (planned for 2005); ESPN Zone (80% w/Hearst)

BOOKS

Hyperion, Talk Miramax, Disney Children's Book Group, ESPN Books, ABC Daytime Press

TELEVISION

NETWORKS

ABC; Disney Channel; Toon Disney; Soap Net; ESPN, ESPN2, ESPN Classic, ESPNEWS, and ESPN Regional Television (all 80% w/20% Hearst); A&E, History, and Biography channels (all 37.5% w/37.5% Hearst and 25% GE); Lifetime and Lifetime Movie Network (50% w/50% Hearst); E! and Style (40% w/40% Comcast, 10% Liberty, 7.5% AOL-TW, and 2.5% AT&T), Fox Family Channel; Disney and ESPN channels in more than 140 countries, plus stakes in other channels

STATIONS

10 stations

PRODUCTION

Buena Vista, Touchstone, Walt Disney, ABC Entertainment, ABC News Productions, Saban

MOVIES

Walt Disney Pictures, Touchstone Pictures, Hollywood Pictures, Miramax Film Corp., Dimension, Buena Vista International

RADIO

Stations: 50; networks: ABC Radio Network, Radio Disney, ESPN Radio (80% w/20% Hearst)

OTHER

Theatrical productions of Beauty and the Beast, The Lion King, The Hunchback of Notre Dame, and Aida; New Amsterdam Theatre on Broadway; 741 stores and Disney catalogue; licenses characters for clothes, toys, etc., and for teaching aids; videos/films for schools; stakes in sites including NFL.com and Movies.com (50% w/News Corp.); markets cell art from Disney animated films; Celebration, FL, a 4,900-acre town

LIBERTY MEDIA CORP.

Janus Corporation owns 5%

Spun off from AT&T in August 2001; assets valued at $42 billion
Owns 4% of AOL Time Warner; 1% of Viacom; 18% of News Corporation

MAGAZINES

PRIMEDIA (5%) 101 magazines including *American Baby*, *Modern Bride*, *Seventeen*; regional and specialty publications including *Texas Monthly* and *Country Sampler* through 12% stake in Emmis; *TV Guide* (4% w/38.5% News Corp.)

MOVIES

Studios USA, USA Films, October Films, Gramercy Pictures, Interscope Communications, and Propaganda (all 21% w/43% Vivendi and Barry Diller)

SPORTS

Denver Nuggets, Colorado Avalanche, Pepsi Center in Denver (6.5% w/93.5% Stan Kroenke)

MUSIC

DMX, Inc. (84%) canned music to more than 29 million US subscribers

INTERNET

Ticketmaster, Citysearch, Hotel Reservations Network and others (21% w/Vivendi and Barry Diller); MTVi (10% w/90%Viacom)

OTHER

Sprint (21%), Motorola (4%), calling cards, long distance, phone service via cable, and Omnipoint (4%); stakes also in wireless and telephony services in Japan, Central and South America, and throughout Europe; Ticketmaster (21% w/43% Vivendi and Barry Diller); Avis Rent A Car (6%), Coldwell Banker (6%) and Century 21 (6%); Antec Corporation (18% w/others) makes broadband network products; The Nature Company Stores and Discovery Channel Stores (49% w/25% Cox Communications, 25% Advance/Newhouse); art gallery in New York; includes consolidated assets and non consolidated assets in Starz Encore Media Group, Discovery Communications and QVC.

RADIO

Stakes in 21 stations in US; 49 stations in Canada

TELEVISION

NETWORKS

Discovery and The Learning Channel (49% w/25% Cox, 25% Advance/Newhouse); stakes of 49% in Animal Planet, Discovery Health and other Discovery channels; USA Network, Sci-Fi Channel, and HSN (all 21% w/43% Vivendi and Barry Diller); Fox international sports channels (w/News Corp); International Channel (90%); Crown Media Holdings (14% w/47% Hallmark, 10% National Interfaith Cable Coalition, 8% JP Morgan and Jim Henson Co.) includes Odyssey Channel, Hallmark Entertainment Network and Kermit Channel; Telemundo (35% w/34% Sony; sale to GE pending), QVC (43% w/57% Comcast); Starz; E! and Style (10% w/Disney, Comcast, AOL-TW and AT&T); TV Guide Channel, TV Guide Interactive and TV Guide Sneak Prevue (4% w/38.5% News Corp.); other international holdings include stakes in more than 8 cable and satellite channels and systems

STATIONS

Stakes in 14 stations

CABLE AND SATELLITE

19 million cable customers in Europe; largest cable operator in Japan

PRODUCTION

MacNeil/Lehrer Productions (67%); Ascent Entertainment—TV, pay-per-view and Internet access to Days Inn, Ramada, and other chains through stakes in Cendant Corp. and On Command; stakes in production and postproduction firms in US and Australia; TiVo (w/AOL-TW, News Corp., Viacom, and GE)

TELEVISION

NETWORKS

FOX, FX, FMC, Fox News Channel, National Geographic Channel (67% w/33% National Geographic Society); Speedvision and Outdoor Life (34% w/Comcast, 34% AT&T and others), Fox international sports channels (w/Liberty), Golf Channel (31% w/Comcast, Times Mirror, and Arnold Palmer), Health Network (through stake in WedMD), Television Games Network (horse racing and betting), TV Guide Channel, TV Guide Interactive and TV Guide Sneak Prevue (38.5% w/4% Liberty); internationally, extensive holdings in cable, broadcast, and satellite TV systems and channels in Asia, Europe, Latin America, and Australia including BSkyB, STAR TV, and Channel V (87% w/13% EMI)

STATIONS

26, including 2 each in New York, LA, and Dallas; 58% stake in 7 other stations

CABLE AND SATELLITE

Sells satellite TV to individuals, hotels, and apartment complexes; Primestar

PRODUCTION

Includes Twentieth Century Fox, Regency Television (50% w/50% Monarchy Enterprises), Greenblatt Janollari, XYZ Entertainment (50% Foxtel [partnership "between News Corp., Telstra Corp., and Publishing and Broadcasting Ltd.] w/Liberty and others) and Main Event Television (33.3% each Singtel and Foxtel, and 27% Liberty); TiVo (w/AOL-TW, Viacom, Liberty, and GE)

NEWS CORPORATION

Murdoch family controls 30%. AT&T Owns 8%

Revenue: $11.6 billion

BOOKS

HarperCollins; Zondervan, largest commercial Bible imprint

NEWSPAPERS

NY Post; in Britain: the *Sun*, the *Times*, *News of the World*; the *Australian*, the *Daily Telegraph*, the *Herald Sun*, and others in New Zealand

MOVIES

Twentieth Century Fox, Fox 2000, Fox Searchlight, Fox Animation Studios, Fox Studios Australia (w/Lend Lease Corporation); New Regency (20%); Fox Home Entertainment; Fox film library

OTHER

Weekly Standard; *TV Guide* (38.5% w/4% Liberty Media); stakes in internet sites including ChinaByte.com and broadsystem.com; licenses *Simpsons*, *X-Files*, and other Fox properties

SPORTS

New York Knicks, New York Rangers, New York Liberty, New England Seawolves, Hartford Wolfpack, Madison Square Garden, management of Hartford Civic Center (all 40% w/44% Cablevision and 16% GE); Los Angeles Dodgers and Staples Center, Dodger Stadium and Dodgertown; National Rugby League (50%)

MUSIC

Rawkus (80%) Festival Mushroom group

VIVENDI UNIVERSAL

Liberty Media owns 3.6%*

Revenues: $37.2 billion

* Based on announced merger agreement
** Stake will decrease if proposed EchoStar DirecTV merger is approved

BOOKS

Leading publisher in France of literature; Houghton Mifflin publishers; medical and reference books and CDs

MAGAZINES

L'Express and L'Expansion, France's most influential news and business magazines; information technology and medical journals

INTERNET

Vizzavi (50% w/50% Vodafone) Internet access portal in France, Britain, Germany, Italy; stakes in sites include Get Music (50% w/Bertelsmann); iWON.com game site (42%)

THEME PARKS

Universal City Hollywood and adjacent CityWalk, retail/entertainment complex; Universal Studios (50%) in Orlando, FL; 25% in nearby hotels and water park; Universal Studios Japan (24% w/US J Co.); Universal Studios Port Aventura and nearby hotels in Spain (37%); SEGA GameWorks (27%); 12 entertainment centers in the US

TELEVISION

NETWORKS

USA Network, Sci-Fi Channel (93% w/Liberty and Barry Diller); HSN (proposed structure: 12% w/18% Liberty and Barry Diller*); Sundance Channel (w/Viacom and Robert Redford); international: CANAL+ (49%) 30 channels in 14 countries including BskyB (23%); CANALSATELLITE and MultiThematiques channels in Europe (w/Lagardere)

CABLE AND SATELLITE

15.3 million subscribers in 11 countries; EchoStar (10%**), CANAL+ interactive services on digital TV

PRODUCTION

Universal Studios; CANAL+ (49%)

MOVIES

Universal Studios; StudioCanal, PolyGram Films, Gramercy Pictures, Interscope Communications and Propaganda (all 93% w/Liberty and Barry Diller*); CANAL+ (49%); World's second-largest film library; PolyGram Home Video (93% w/Liberty and Barry Diller*); United Cinemas International Multiplex BV and Cinema International Corporation (49%)

OTHER

Cell phone service in France through Cegetel (44% w/26% British Telecom and 15% Vodafone); cell phones also in Morocco, Monaco, Poland, Hungary, Spain, and Kenya; Ticketmaster (proposed structure: 12% w/18% Liberty and Barry Diller*); 151 recycling facilities, 119 landfill sites and 83 incineration plants worldwide; commercial and industrial cleaning; street cleaning; water and waste-water facilities for municipalities; sells bottled water; operates 26 passenger rail networks in Europe; rail cargo services; 186 bus lines for cities in Europe and Australia; manages 65,000 heating systems in Europe; provides electrical and mechanical equipment, maintenance, and secretarial services; Spencer Gifts, DAPY, GLOW stores; Universal Studios Stores and SPIRIT Halloween Superstores names; 220 advertising agencies in 65 countries (11%)

MUSIC

27% of US music sales; labels include Interscope, Geffen, A&M, Island, Def Jam, MCA, Mercury, Motown, Universal, and Pressplay (w/Sony)

NEWSPAPERS

Free papers in France

BERTELSMANN

Groupe Bruxelles owns 25%

Revenues: $16.5 billion

TELEVISION

Europe's biggest broadcaster with stakes of 35-100% in 22 TV channels in Europe; Also, Europe's largest film producer

INTERNET

Lycos in Europe (18%) and Fireball search engines; MusicNet (20% w/20% AOL/TW, 20% EMI and RealNetworks) music downloads; option to take majority control of Napster; Get Music (50% w/50% Vivendi); barnesandnoble.com (40% with Barnes and Noble); The Travel Channel and ANDSOLD in Germany; partial ownership in digital media and internet connection services primarily in Europe

BOOKS

Largest US trade book publisher; imprints include Random House, Knopf, Vintage, The Modern Library, Bantam Doubleday Dell, Delacorte; imprints in Europe including BertelsmannSpringer (74.9%); book clubs include Literary Guild Mystery Guild and Book-of-the-Month Club (50% w/50% AOL-TW)

MUSIC

20% of US music sales with over 200 labels in 54 countries including Arista, BMG Classics, RCA, and Windham Hill Group. Also, music publishing and the largest music distributor

NEWSPAPERS

11 dailies in Germany and Eastern Europe (74.9% through Gruner + Jahr)

MAGAZINES

One of the largest publishers in the US and Europe through Gruner + Jahr, publisher of 80 magazines worldwide. US holdings include *Family Circle, YM, Parents, Homestyle, Fast Company, Inc., Fitness, Rosie's McCall's* (all 74.9% with 25.1% Jahr Family)

RADIO

CLT-UFA (80%) with 18 stations in Europe

OTHER

Graphic design, greeting cards, trading cards

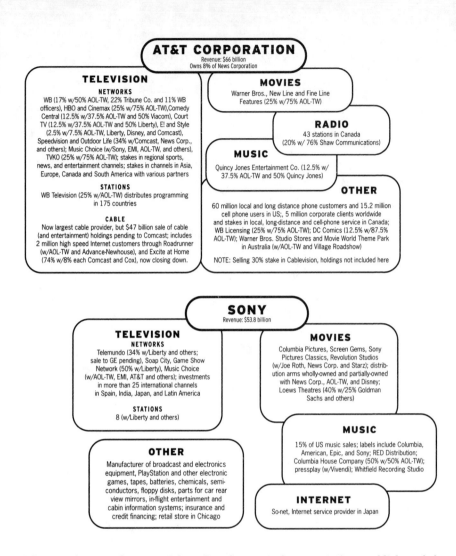

AT&T CORPORATION
Revenue: $66 billion
Owns 8% of News Corporation

TELEVISION

NETWORKS

WB (17% w/50% AOL-TW, 22% Tribune Co. and 11% WB officers), HBO and Cinemax (25% w/75% AOL-TW),Comedy Central (12.5% w/37.5% AOL-TW and 50% Viacom), Court TV (12.5% w/37.5% AOL-TW and 50% Liberty), E! and Style (2.5% w/7.5% AOL-TW, Liberty, Disney, and Comcast), Speedvision and Outdoor Life (34% w/Comcast, News Corp., and others); Music Choice (w/Sony, EMI, AOL-TW, and others), TVKO (25% w/75% AOL-TW); stakes in regional sports, news, and entertainment channels; stakes in channels in Asia, Europe, Canada and South America with various partners

STATIONS

WB Television (25% w/AOL-TW) distributes programming in 175 countries

CABLE

Now largest cable provider, but $47 billion sale of cable (and entertainment) holdings pending to Comcast; includes 2 million high speed Internet customers through Roadrunner (w/AOL-TW and Advance-Newhouse), and Excite at Home (74% w/8% each Comcast and Cox), now closing down.

MOVIES

Warner Bros., New Line and Fine Line Features (25% w/75% AOL-TW)

RADIO

43 stations in Canada (20% w/ 76% Shaw Communications)

MUSIC

Quincy Jones Entertainment Co. (12.5% w/ 37.5% AOL-TW and 50% Quincy Jones)

OTHER

60 million local and long distance phone customers and 15.2 million cell phone users in US;, 5 million corporate clients worldwide and stakes in local, long-distance and cell-phone service in Canada; WB Licensing (25% w/75% AOL-TW); DC Comics (12.5% w/87.5% AOL-TW); Warner Bros. Studio Stores and Movie World Theme Park in Australia (w/AOL-TW and Village Roadshow)

NOTE: Selling 30% stake in Cablevision, holdings not included here

SONY
Revenue: $53.8 billion

TELEVISION

NETWORKS

Telemundo (34% w/Liberty and others; sale to GE pending), Soap City, Game Show Network (50% w/Liberty), Music Choice (w/AOL-TW, EMI, AT&T and others); investments in more than 25 international channels in Spain, India, Japan, and Latin America

STATIONS

8 (w/Liberty and others)

MOVIES

Columbia Pictures, Screen Gems, Sony Pictures Classics, Revolution Studios (w/Joe Roth, News Corp. and Starz); distribution arms wholly-owned and partially-owned with News Corp., AOL-TW, and Disney; Loews Theatres (40% w/25% Goldman Sachs and others)

MUSIC

15% of US music sales; labels include Columbia, American, Epic, and Sony; RED Distribution; Columbia House Company (50% w/50% AOL-TW); pressplay (w/Vivendi); Whitfield Recording Studio

OTHER

Manufacturer of broadcast and electronics equipment, PlayStation and other electronic games, tapes, batteries, chemicals, semiconductors, floppy disks, parts for car rear view mirrors, in-flight entertainment and cabin information systems; insurance and credit financing; retail store in Chicago

INTERNET

So-net, Internet service provider in Japan

† It is worth noting that nine of them (Bertelsmann is the exception) are publicly traded transnational corporations, mainly owned by banks, insurance companies, pension funds, and other institutional investors. AT&T itself owns a considerable percentage of several other of the media corporations, as does the Capitol Group, a secretive investment enterprise whose manager is Gordon Crawford. Swashbucklers like Bill Gates and Warren Buffett also hold a lot of media stock. There is, in short, no basis to the very stubborn claim—still commonplace on both the left and right—that the Jews own the U.S. media. Although many Jews do work in Hollywood per se, it is not they who call the shots, but the large shareholders, who do the hiring and the firing of the CEOs according to how well the stock is doing. It makes no difference whether that top manager is Gentile, like AOL Time Warner's Richard Parsons, or Jewish, like Disney's Michael Eisner. In this regard the media cartel is just like any other sector of the corporate universe—a realm whose workings are determined by the needs of capital, and not by any ethnic group.

that each division go primarily for short-term profits—hyping *only* what is *sure* to sell, as much as possible and right away. Such product tends to be as coarse and stupid as the corporate marketers think most of us to be, since they believe devoutly in the bad old axiom that one can't fail by under-estimating the intelligence of the American people. And as they sink as low as possible in making both their "journalistic" and "creative" judgments, so do the parents keep on slashing costs, to make their wares as inexpensive (to themselves) as they are gross and titillating. (That those corporations are still broke despite their endless bottom-feeding would suggest that that taste-free approach is *not* the way to wealth.)

In the entertainment sphere, that killer combination of low standards and low budgets has brought us a new universe of tacky goods—TV programs like *Fear Factor* and *Temptation Island*, endless music that you can't remember, sitcoms that you couldn't laugh at if your life depended on it, magazines that tell you only what to buy, explosive movies that don't make a lick of sense, and so on. As bad as all of that may be, however, it is in the realm of journalism that the corporate formula is most destructive. At best, the sys-tematic over-focus on mere gossip and celebrity—e.g., the O.J. trial, the death of Lady Di, the plane crash that killed JFK Jr.—crowds out the sort of news that people really need to know if they're to live and thrive in a democracy. At worst, such unrelenting over-concentration on the trivial will often suit the purposes of right-wing propagandists, who have the know-how—and the power—to exploit that tendency for partisan advantage, as they did through-out the Nineties and beyond, fabricating countless Clinton "scandals" (while ignoring most of Clinton's *policies*), then going after Democrat Gary Condit with the same crackpot intensity. Such tawdry tales were just right for the parents' penny-pinching news divisions, since such stuff was full of fascinating dirt, but didn't cost a dime, requiring only that a lot of true believers come and vent their colorful and uninformed opinions in the studio. Indeed, the Clinton/Condit episodes would never have distracted the republic if it were not for the parents' all-news cable channels—Fox, CNN, and MSNBC, all three benefiting big-time from those cheap and dirty "stories."

Since 9-11 it has been rightly noted (although not frequently enough) that all such mean and groundless blather harmed the nation, preserving us in ignorance while Al Qaeda planned its operations and our government was fast asleep or worse. And yet the defects of the corporate press were no less flagrant after 9-11 than they had been prior to the catastrophe. Even after the attacks had shaken them from their obsession with *Survivor* and the fate of Chandra Levy, the reporters kept on favoring alarmist hearsay over any actual investigation. Where it had been All Condit All the Time it suddenly was now All Anthrax All the Time, yet without any inquiry into the anthrax terror's evident domestic basis. (Once it lost its power to spook, the story simply disappeared, although the perp—presumably American—is still at large.) Likewise, the corporate press obligingly reechoed every fresh scare by the Bush Administration, while largely overlooking the more complex and important story of how and why Bush/Cheney had ignored such dangers in the first place. Thus even after 9-11 did the corporate press persist in its postmodern tendency to go for easy hits while cheaping out on genuine journalism. (As we shall see, there are also other reasons for the media's quickness to bend over for Bush/Cheney.)

While it slights some stories automatically for reasons of economy, the corporate press also deliberately avoids all kinds of news because of various conflicts of interest, of which there are two categories. First, the media machine looks carefully away from countless stories that would give serious heartburn to its major advertisers—which tendency is hardly new, of course, since the commercial press has done just that from the beginning of its history, as Upton Sinclair noted over 80 years ago, and as other muckrakers reported earlier than that. If anything, the advertisers' clout is even heavier today than it was back in the age of Pulitzer or that of Paley, now that the audience has grown enormously, the spectacle is overcrowded with competing messages, the advertising revenues are therefore astronomical, and Viacom et al. are desperately dependent on that income. And so the bad old days are with us still, imposing routine blackouts all around us Just as, for decades, the tobacco companies imposed a lethal silence on the risks of smoking, so do powerful advertisers of all kinds now frequently get special treatment by the media, as this book amply demonstrates.

And yet the situation is far worse today, because the media cartel, while pandering as ever to its advertisers, also routinely kills news stories that refer—or would refer—to the cartel's *own* interests. The parent companies, in other words, are also highly self-protective advertisers; and those busy entities no longer deal in broadcasting alone, but are involved in many different, often controversial businesses, including defense electronics, nuclear facilities, waste management, financial services, and outdoor advertising. (Of course, the media per se are also controversial businesses.) Thus would the news divisions of the media cartel be heavily muzzled even if the outside advertisers had no influence. As it is, the cartel's journalists must observe a complex code of *omertà* that shields the advertisers and the parent companies alike. In 1998, for example, Fox Television, at the urging of Monsanto, infamously fired two of its telejournalists at WTVT-TV in Florida for refusing to whitewash their report about the toxic impact of Monsanto's bovine growth hormone. (The reporters sued and finally won.) Less controversial by far has been the network's perfect silence on its own and/or News Corporation's various misdeeds—the latter's heavy lobbying for special treatment by the government; the copious misinformation vented by Sean Hannity and Bill O'Reilly, Fox News Channel's leading lights; the crucial role played by Fox employee John Ellis, George W. Bush's cousin, in the theft of the 2000 presidential election; and so on. Likewise, GE's gross environmental record has gone unreported on NBC, CNBC, and MSNBC (which GE owns or co-owns), as did the parent's deep involvement in the pricey Joint Strike Fighter (its engines manufactured by GE). A story on the dark side of Disneyland was spiked at ABC News (which Disney owns). Likewise, nor did CNN report on its own use of Pentagon psy-war specialists to help shape its coverage of the war in Kosovo. And, across the board, the TV news divisions failed to note their parents' deep involvement in the drafting and the stealthy passage of the Telecommunications Act of 1996, which gave those corporations everything they'd ever wanted, at great cost to the public.

Thus the parents benefit immensely from their news divisions' frequent sins of omission. Meanwhile, the reporters also push the parents' interests positively, by airing countless cross-promotional items suited up as "news." Thus Rupert Murdoch's *TV Guide* ran (at least) two cover stories on Fox TV's *Teenage Mutant Ninja Turtles*—barely mentioning the long, loud controversy over that show's violent effect on little viewers; thus CBS News devoted lots of airtime to the latest happenings on the CBS hit show *Survivor*; and thus the <pets.com> sock puppet made a number of cute cameo appearances on various ABC news programs (Disney owns both that Web site and the network). Such instances of "synergy" are both too numerous and, often, too well-camouflaged for anyone to track them adequately. In any case, such covert propaganda merely serves to keep us uninformed, by tacitly whitewashing all the firms concerned, and taking up more airtime that might otherwise be used to tell us something.

Finally, the giant outfits represented here also suppress the truth out of their overeagerness to please the government. Those mighty private players do not comprise a salutary counterforce to state authority, as they would do in Russia—on the contrary. The larger they have grown, in fact, the *closer* their relations with the government, which has the power to give them highly profitable breaks of many kinds. (For obvious reasons, both parties have rolled over for them—and yet Bush/Cheney is especially intent on making them completely unaccountable.) Thus have we lately seen the media machine itself black out a staggering number of important stories that have been duly covered in the foreign press and on the Web. Before 9-11, the corporate news machine conspicuously laid off George W. Bush, despite his obvious limitations and extremely iffy record, including his team's flagrant theft of the election—and all this at a time when Bush did not enjoy much popularity. After 9-11, once the people had been terrorized into near-reverence for the president, the journalists became about as docile and supportive as the press in Riyadh or Havana. Although we are the primary targets of Al Qaeda and its peers, the people of France, Britain, Germany, and India know more than we do about 9-11, the progress of the "war on terrorism," the links between the Bush and the bin Laden families, the dealings of the Carlyle Group, the situation in Afghanistan, and the truth about the anthrax mailings in the fall of 2001. And even though, in this charged atmosphere, we stand to lose the very freedoms that make this democracy worth fighting for, our press has told us next to nothing of that danger, underplaying or ignoring countless inroads on our liberty that have been recently attempted by the White House, the Department of Justice, and the Pentagon, with only slight congressional resistance and the likely acquiescence of the Supreme Court. Thus has our corporate press, fixated on its own commercial interest, failed absolutely to perform its crucial function of protecting us from governmental tyranny.

And yet, although such silence is outrageous from a civic point of view, legally it is not only proper but exemplary—as is the cartel's rampant budget-cutting, brazen bottom-feeding, cringing deference to its advertisers, systematic self-promotion, and all other means of goosing up (or trying to goose up) the bottom line. It is, by law, the fiduciary obligation of the cartel's managers to serve their shareholders above all else—which means that they must serve their shareholders *alone*. If the reporters finally were to let us have the news, the whole news, and nothing but the news, it would be good for us and for those journalists, and very good for this imperiled democracy, but it would not be good for business—and in the world the corporations have now made for us, that is the only thing that counts. In such a world, the media will not even report the problem, much less air a full debate about it—and so that necessary job is up to us.

A special thanks *The Nation* for allowing us to reprint these charts from their Web site at <www.thenation.com/special/bigten.html>.

CHAPTER 7

Media War and the Rigors of Self-Censorship

BY NORMAN SOLOMON

Eight months after the World Trade Center suddenly disappeared from Manhattan's skyline, Dan Rather told a BBC television interviewer that American journalists were intimidated in the wake of September 11. Making what he called "an obscene comparison," the CBS news anchor commented, "There was a time in South Africa that people would put flaming tires around people's necks if they dissented. And in some ways the fear is that you will be 'necklaced' here, you will have a flaming tire of lack of patriotism put around your neck. Now it is that fear that keeps journalists from asking the toughest of the tough questions." Rather added that "I do not except myself from this criticism," and he went on: "What we are talking about here—whether one wants to recognize it or not, or call it by its proper name or not—is a form of self-censorship. I worry that patriotism run amok will trample the very values that the country seeks to defend."

Self-censorship has always been one of journalism's most ineffable hazards. It is obscured and murky—exercised privately and perhaps unconsciously—while the effects are enormous and ongoing in news media. At times of national crisis and military action, the constrictions on journalism become even tighter.

Like some of his colleagues, Dan Rather may engage in a bit of belated hand-wringing, after consistently marching in wartime step—helping the nation's Fourth Estate to function largely as a fourth branch of government. When he appeared on David Letterman's program six days after September 11, Rather pledged to back up the commander-in-chief. "George Bush is the president, he makes the decisions," the newsman said. And, speaking as "one American," Rather said about the president, "Wherever he wants me to line up, just tell me where. And he'll make the call."

We stared at televisions and tried to comprehend the horrific terrorism that occurred on September 11, 2001. Much of what we saw on the screens was ghastly and all too real, terrible anguish and sorrow.

At the same time, we witnessed an onslaught of media deception. "The greatest triumphs of propaganda have been accomplished, not by doing something, but by refraining from doing," Aldous Huxley observed long ago. "Great is truth, but still greater, from a practical point of view, is silence about truth."

Despite the nonstop media din, a silence—rigorously selective—pervaded the mainstream news coverage. For policymakers in Washington, the practical utility of that silence was huge. In response to the mass murder committed by hijackers, the righteousness of U.S. military action was clear—as long as double standards went unmentioned.

While rescue crews braved intense smoke and grisly rubble, ABC News analyst Vincent Cannistraro helped to put it all in perspective for millions of TV viewers. Cannistraro is a former high-ranking official of the Central Intelligence Agency who was in charge of the CIA's work with the Contras in Nicaragua during the early 1980s. After moving to the National Security Council in 1984, he became a supervisor of covert aid to Afghan guerrillas. In other words, Cannistraro has a long history of assisting terrorists—first, Contra soldiers who routinely killed Nicaraguan civilians; then, mujahideen rebels in Afghanistan… like Osama bin Laden.

How can a longtime associate of terrorists now be credibly denouncing "terrorism"? It's easy. All that's required is for media coverage to remain in a kind of history-free zone that has no use for any facets of reality that are not presently convenient to acknowledge.

In his book *1984*, George Orwell described the mental dynamics: "The process has to be conscious, or it would not be carried out with sufficient precision, but it also has to be unconscious, or it would bring with it a feeling of falsity and hence of guilt…. To tell deliberate lies while genuinely believing in them, to forget any fact that has become inconvenient, and then, when it becomes necessary again, to draw it back from oblivion for just so long as it is needed, to deny the existence of objective reality and all the while to take account of the reality which one denies—all this is indispensably necessary."

Secretary of State Colin Powell denounced "people who feel that with the destruction of buildings, with the murder of people, they can somehow achieve a political purpose." He was describing the terrorists who had struck his country hours earlier. But Powell was also aptly describing a long line of top officials in Washington. Surely U.S. policymakers believed that they could "achieve a political purpose"—with "the destruction of buildings, with the murder of people"—when launching missiles at Baghdad or Belgrade. But media scrutiny of atrocities committed by the U.S. government is rare. Only some cruelties merit the spotlight. Only some victims deserve empathy. Only certain crimes against humanity are worth our tears.

"This will be a monumental struggle of good versus evil," President Bush proclaimed. The media reactions to such rhetoric were overwhelmingly favorable. Yet the heart-wrenching voices on the USA's airwaves were, in human terms, no less or more important than voices we've never heard. The victims of terrorism in America have deserved our deep compassion. So have the faraway victims of America—human beings whose humanity has gone unrecognized by U.S. media.

With the overwhelming bulk of news organizations accustomed to serving as amplification systems for Washington's warriors in times of crisis, the White House found itself in a strong position to retool and lubricate the machinery of domestic propaganda after September 11, 2001. When confronted with claims about "coded messages" that Osama bin Laden and his henchmen might be sending via taped statements (as though other means like the Internet did not exist), TV network executives fell right into line.

Tapes of Al Qaeda leaders provided a useful wedge for the administration to hammer away at the wisdom of (government-assisted) self-censorship. Network execs from ABC, CBS, NBC, Fox, and CNN were deferential in an October 10 conference call with Condoleezza Rice. The conversation was "very collegial," Ari Fleischer told the White House press corps. The result was an agreement, *The New York Times* reported, to "abridge any future videotaped statements from Osama bin Laden or his followers to remove language the government considers inflammatory." It was, the *Times* added, "the first time in memory that the networks had agreed to a joint arrangement to limit their prospective news coverage." News Corp. magnate Rupert Murdoch, speaking for Fox, promised: "We'll do whatever is our patriotic duty." CNN, owned by the world's largest media conglomerate AOL Time Warner, was eager to present itself as a team player: "In deciding what to air, CNN will consider guidance from appropriate authorities."

"Guidance" from the "appropriate authorities" was exactly what the president's strategists had in mind—brandishing a club without quite needing to swing it. As longtime White House reporter Helen Thomas noted in a column, "To most people, a 'request' to the television networks from the White House in wartime carries with it the weight of a government command. The major networks obviously saw it that way…" The country's TV news behemoths snapped to attention and saluted. "I think they gave away a precedent, in effect," said James Naughton, president of the Poynter Institute for Media Studies. "And now it's going to be hard for them not to do whatever else the government asks."

Some ominous steps were underway. "The U.S. State Department contacted the Voice of America, a broadcast organization funded by the federal government, and expressed concern about the radio broadcast of an exclusive interview with Taliban leader Mullah Mohammed Omar," according to the Committee to Protect Journalists, based in New York. As a follow-up, VOA head Robert Reilly "distributed a memo barring interviews with officials from 'nations that sponsor terrorism.'"

In early October, while the U.S. government prepared for extensive bombing of Afghanistan, efforts increased to pressure media outlets—at home and abroad. Colin Powell urged the Emir of Qatar to lean on the Qatar-based Al Jazeera satellite TV network. A correspondent for the *San Francisco Chronicle*, reporting from Cairo, remarked on "the sight of the United States, the defender of freedom and occasional critic of Arab state repression, lobbying one of the most moderate Arab leaders to rein in one of the region's few sources of independent news."

What was the global impact of such measures? The Committee to Protect Journalists included this assessment in its "Attacks on the Press" annual report: "The actions taken by the Bush Administration seemed to embolden repressive governments around the world to crack down on their own domestic media. In Russia, a presidential adviser said President Vladimir Putin planned to study U.S. limitations on reporting about terrorists in order to develop rules for Russian media."

While the bombing of Afghanistan continued, Uncle Sam proved to be quite a role model for how avowedly democratic nations can serve rather explosive notice on specific news outlets. The Pentagon implemented a devastating November 13 missile attack on the Al Jazeera bureau in Kabul. Months later, the Committee to Protect Journalists expressed skepticism about the official explanations: "The U.S. military described the building as a 'known' Al Qaeda facility without providing any evidence. Despite the fact that the facility had housed the Al Jazeera office for nearly two years and had several satellite dishes mounted on its roof, the U.S. military claimed it had no indications the building was used as Al Jazeera's Kabul bureau."

That's one of many ways for governments to "dispatch" news.

During the first two days of October 2001, CNN's Web site displayed an odd little announcement. "There have been false reports that CNN has not used the word 'terrorist' to refer to those who attacked the World Trade Center and Pentagon," the notice said. "In fact, CNN has consistently and repeatedly referred to the attackers and hijackers as terrorists, and it will continue to do so."

The CNN disclaimer was accurate—and, by conventional media standards, reassuring. But it bypassed a basic question that festers beneath American media coverage: Exactly what qualifies as "terrorism"?

For this country's mainstream journalists, that's a non-question about a no-brainer. More than ever, the proper function of the "terrorist" label seems obvious. "A group of people commandeered airliners and used them as guided missiles against thousands of people," said NBC News executive Bill Wheatley. "If that doesn't fit the definition of terrorism, what does?"

True enough. At the same time, it's notable that American news outlets routinely define terrorism the same way that U.S. government officials do. Usually, editors assume that reporters don't need any formal directive because the appropriate usage is simply understood. The *Wall Street Journal* does provide some guidelines, telling its staff that the word terrorist "should be used carefully, and specifically, to describe those people and nongovernmental organizations that plan and execute acts of violence against civilian or noncombatant targets." In newsrooms across the United States, media professionals would agree.

But—in sharp contrast—Reuters has stuck to a distinctive approach for decades. "As part of a policy to avoid the use of emotive words," the global news service says, "we do not use terms like 'terrorist' and 'freedom fighter' unless they are in a direct quote or are otherwise attributable to a third party. We do not characterize the subjects of news stories but instead report their actions, identity, and background so that readers can make their own decisions based on the facts." During the autumn of 2001, the Reuters management took a lot of heat for maintaining this policy—and for reiterating it in an internal memo, which included the observation that "one man's terrorist is another man's freedom fighter." In a clarifying statement, released on October 2, the top execs at Reuters explained: "Our policy is to avoid the use of emotional terms and not make value judgments concerning the facts we attempt to report accurately and fairly."

Reuters reports from 160 countries, and the "terrorist" label is highly contentious in quite a few of them. Behind the scenes, many governments have pressured Reuters to flatly describe their enemies as terrorists in news dispatches. From the vantage point of government leaders in Ankara or Jerusalem or Moscow, for example, journalists shouldn't hesitate to describe their violent foes as terrorists. But why should reporters oblige by pinning that tag on Kurdish combatants in Turkey, or Palestinian militants in occupied territories, or rebels in Chechnya? Unless we buy into the absurd pretense that governments don't engage in "terrorism," the circumscribed use of the term by U.S. media makes no sense. Turkish military forces have certainly terrorized and killed many civilians; the same is true of Israeli forces and Russian troops. As a result, plenty of Kurds, Palestinians, and Chechens are grieving.

American reporters could plausibly expand their working definition of terrorism to include all organized acts of terror and murder committed against civilians. But such consistency would meet with fierce opposition in high Washington places.

During the 1980s, with a nonevasive standard for terrorism, news accounts would have routinely referred to the Nicaraguan Contra guerrillas—in addition to the Salvadoran and Guatemalan governments—as U.S.–backed "terrorists." Today, for instance, such a standard would require news coverage of terrorism in the Middle East to include the Israeli assaults with bullets and missiles that take the lives of Palestinian children and other civilians.

It's entirely appropriate for news outlets to describe the September 11 hijackers as "terrorists"—if those outlets are willing to utilize the "terrorist" label with integrity across the board. Evenhanded use of the "terrorist" label would mean sometimes affixing it directly on the U.S. government. During the past decade, from Iraq to Sudan to Yugoslavia to Afghanistan, the Pentagon's missiles have destroyed the lives of civilians just as innocent as those who perished on September 11. If journalists dare not call that "terrorism," then maybe the word should be retired from the media lexicon.

At the Pentagon, the Office of Strategic Influence went from obscurity to infamy to oblivion during a spin cycle that lasted just seven days in late February 2002. Coming to terms with a week of negative coverage after news broke that the Pentagon office might purposely deceive foreign media, a somber defense secretary announced: "It is being closed down." But for Donald Rumsfeld and his colleagues along the Potomac, the inky cloud of bad publicity had a big silver lining.

Orders to shut the controversial office came a day after President Bush proclaimed zero tolerance for lies from U.S. officials. "We'll tell the American people the truth," he vowed. Would the Defense Department try to deceive journalists? The question in the air was distasteful, and the answer from Rumsfeld could only offer comfort: "This is something the Pentagon has not done, is not doing, and would not condone." A retired Air Force general was likewise reassuring when the Office of Strategic Influence crashed and burned. "I'm absolutely convinced that in no way would top officials of the administration ever have approved lying to the media," said Donald Shepperd, working as a CNN military analyst.

After Rumsfeld ceremoniously disbanded the office, amid profuse pledges of veracity, *Newsday* columnist Ellis Henican astutely wrote: "But don't worry, Rumsfeld's people were whispering yesterday around the Pentagon. They'll keep on spreading whatever stories they think they have to— to foreigners especially. Call it the free flow of misinformation. Who needs a formal office for that?" The whole brouhaha must have caused quite a few laughs in high places behind the Pentagon's thick walls.

In American news outlets, some of the attacks on the Office of Strategic Influence actually reinforced the notion that the U.S. government has no rational motive for hiding truth, since its real endeavors can proudly stand the light of day—an easy misconception that would hardly displease the propagandists who concocted the Office of Strategic Influence in the first place. At the end of a tough *New York Times* piece, titled "Office of Strategic Mendacity," columnist Maureen Dowd applied an oily salve to the PR wounds she'd just inflicted. "Our cause is just," she concluded. "So why not just tell the truth?"

Why not just tell the truth? Because—whether the issue is support for human rights abusers or civilian deaths courtesy of U.S. taxpayers—"the truth" would often indicate that the Pentagon's cause is not just. That's why not.

As soon as Rumsfeld declared the Office of Strategic Influence to be null and void, some public-relations dividends began to flow. The *Chicago Tribune* quoted Lucy Dalglish, executive director of the Reporters Committee for Freedom of the Press, generously praising officials at the Pentagon: "This is good news for the public. Now we can have more confidence that what they're telling us is true." But anyone would be ill-advised to have "confidence" in the truthfulness of Pentagon pronouncements—or to trust that officials aren't hiding key facts with the simple tactic of withholding information, letting silence effectively tell whoppers.

Deceptive propaganda can only succeed to the extent that journalists are gullible—or believe that they must pretend to be—while encouraging the public to go along with the charade. Four centuries ago, the French cardinal and statesman Richelieu remarked that concealing true intentions "is the art of kings." ("*Savoir dissimuler est le savoir des rois.*") For kings and presidents, the illusion of credibility is crucial. Manipulation hinges on deference from courtiers and scribes, reporters and pundits.

In the spring of 2002, Thomas Friedman won a Pulitzer Prize for commentary. The award came after many months when the syndicated *New York Times* columnist was on television more than ever, sharing his outlooks with viewers of *Meet the Press, Face the Nation, Washington Week in Review,* and other programs. "In the post-9-11 environment, the talk shows can't get enough of Friedman," a *Washington Post* profile noted.

Another media triumph came for Friedman in early 2002 with the debut of "Tom's Journal" on the *NewsHour with Jim Lehrer.* A news release from the influential PBS program described it as a "one-on-one debriefing of Friedman by Lehrer or one of the program's senior correspondents." Friedman was scheduled to appear perhaps a dozen times per year, after returning from major trips abroad.

If he were as fervent about stopping wars as starting them, it's hard to imagine that a regular feature like "Tom's Journal" would be airing on the *NewsHour.*

Friedman has been a zealous advocate of "bombing Iraq, over and over and over again" (in the words of a January 1998 column). When he offered a pithy list of prescriptions for Washington's policymakers in 1999, it included: "Blow up a different power station in Iraq every week, so no one knows when the lights will go off or who's in charge."

In an introduction to the book *Iraq Under Siege*, editor Anthony Arnove points out: "Every power station that is targeted means more food and medicine that will not be refrigerated, hospitals that will lack electricity, water that will be contaminated, and people who will die." But Friedman-style bravado goes over big with editors and network producers who share his disinterest in counting such human costs. Many journalists seem eager to fawn over their stratospheric colleague. "Nobody understands the world the way he does," NBC's Tim Russert claims.

Sometimes, Friedman has fixated on four words in particular. "My motto is very simple: Give war a chance," he told Diane Sawyer in late 2001 on *Good Morning America*. It was the same motto that he'd used two-and-a-half years earlier in a Fox News interview. Different war; different enemy; different network; same solution. In the spring of 1999, as bombardment of Yugoslavia went on, Friedman recycled "Give war a chance" from one column to another. "Twelve days of surgical bombing was never going to turn Serbia around," he wrote in early April. "Let's see what 12 weeks of less than surgical bombing does. Give war a chance." Another column included this gleeful approach for threatening civilians in Yugoslavia with protracted terror: "Every week you ravage Kosovo is another decade we will set your country back by pulverizing you. You want 1950? We can do 1950. You want 1389? We can do 1389 too." In November 2001, his column was in a similar groove: "Let's all take a deep breath and repeat after me: Give war a chance. This is Afghanistan we're talking about."

Friedman seems to be crazy about wisps of craziness in high Washington places. He has a penchant for touting insanity as a helpful ingredient of U.S. foreign policy and some kind of passion for indications of derangement among those who call the military shots. During an October 13, 2001 appearance on CNBC, he said: "I was a critic of Rumsfeld before, but there's one thing…that I do like about Rumsfeld. He's just a little bit crazy, OK? He's just a little bit crazy, and in this kind of war, they always count on being able to out-crazy us, and I'm glad we got some guy on our bench that our quarterback—who's just a little bit crazy, not totally, but you never know what that guy's going to do, and I say that's my guy."

And Friedman doesn't just talk that way. He also writes that way. "There is a lot about the Bush team's foreign policy I don't like," a Friedman column declared in mid-February 2002, "but their willingness to restore our deterrence, and to be as crazy as some of our enemies, is one thing they have right."

Is Thomas Friedman clever? Perhaps. But not nearly as profound as a few words from W.H. Auden: "Those to whom evil is done / Do evil in return."

In the fall of 2001, Pentagon reporters sought—and got—more frequent news conferences. "Let's hear it for the essential daily briefing, however hollow and empty it might be," Secretary Rumsfeld said in the middle of October. "We'll do it."

After that, Rumsfeld regularly helped with the propaganda chores. Airing live on such cable networks as MSNBC, CNN, and Fox, his performances won profuse media accolades. A news report by CNN called him "a virtual rock star." A *Wall Street Journal* essay—by TV critic Claudia Rosett, a member of the newspaper's editorial board—described Rumsfeld as "a gent who in our country's hour of need has turned out to be one [of] the classiest acts on camera." Published on the last day of 2001, Rosett's article was a fitting climax to a media season of slathering over the well-heeled boots of the man in charge of the Pentagon. During the closing weeks of the year, she noted approvingly, "in print and on the air, we've been hearing about Don Rumsfeld, sex symbol, the new hunk of home-front airtime."

Deep into the mass-media groove, the *Wall Street Journal* piece declared: "The basic source of Mr. Rumsfeld's charm is that he talks straight. He doesn't expend his energy on spin…" Now there's an example of some prodigious spinning. Actually, Rumsfeld—who excels at sticking to the lines of the day—is a fine practitioner of spin in the minimalist style, with deception accomplished mostly by what's left unsaid. Yet for some, Rumsfeld's dissembling style is a source of continual delight. "These briefings, beamed out live, have become, to my mind, the best new show on television," Rosett gushed. "It's a rare one that doesn't contain, at some point, some variation on his wry trademark reply when asked to discuss matters he'd rather not go into: 'I could, but I won't.'"

One of the subjects that Rumsfeld would "rather not go into" was civilian deaths in Afghanistan.

Just before 2001 ended, University of New Hampshire professor Marc Herold released a report calculating that 3,767 Afghan civilians had been killed by the bombing from October 7 to December 10. (That figure was later revised to between 2,650 and 2,970 civilians.) Ignored by major U.S. media, the report got a bit more attention in Britain. "The price in blood that has already been paid for America's war against terror is only now start-ing to become clear," an editor at *The Guardian* in London wrote on Decem-ber 20. Seumas Milne explained that Herold's research was "based on corroborated reports from aid agencies, the U.N., eyewitnesses, TV stations, newspapers, and news agencies around the world." Milne added: "Of course, Herold's total is only an estimate. But what is impressive about his work is not only the meticulous cross-checking, but the conservative assump-tions he applies to each reported incident. The figure does not include those who died later of bomb injuries; nor those killed in the past 10 days [Decem-ber 10-20]; nor those who have died from cold and hunger because of the interruption of aid supplies or because they were forced to become refugees by the bombardment."

But the civilian deaths caused by American military action held little interest among the people in charge of major U.S.–based media outlets. After the first weeks of bombing, CNN chair Walter Isaacson sent a memo to the network's international correspondents telling them that it "seems perverse to focus too much on the casualties or hardship in Afghanistan." Interviewed by a *Washington Post* reporter on October 30, Isaacson explained: "I want to make sure we're not used as a propaganda platform." He added: "We're entering a period in which there's a lot more reporting and video from Tal-iban-controlled Afghanistan. You want to make sure people understand that when they see civilian suffering there, it's in the context of a terrorist attack that caused enormous suffering in the United States."

Meanwhile, a separate memo went out to CNN anchors from the network's head of standards and practices, Rick Davis, who supplied helpful exam-ples of appropriate language to use on the air: "'We must keep in mind, after seeing reports like this from Taliban-controlled areas, that these U.S. military actions are in response to a terrorist attack that killed close to 5,000 innocent people in the U.S.' or, 'We must keep in mind, after seeing reports like this, that the Taliban regime in Afghanistan continues to harbor ter-rorists who have praised the September 11 attacks that killed close to 5,000 innocent people in the U.S.,' or 'The Pentagon has repeatedly stressed that it is trying to minimize civilian casualties in Afghanistan, even as the Tal-iban regime continues to harbor terrorists who are connected to the Sep-tember 11 attacks that claimed thousands of innocent lives in the U.S.'"

The memo was clear about the mandatory nature of the instructions: "Even though it may start sounding rote, it is important that we make this point each time."

News accounts keep telling us about "the war on terrorism." Journalists have gotten into the habit of shortening it to "the war on terror"—perhaps the most demagogic term in recent memory. The comfort zone of media coverage excludes unauthorized ironies, much preferring to accept that the U.S. government can keep making war on "terror" by using high-tech weapons that inevitably terrorize large numbers of people. Just about any measures deemed appropriate by top officials in Washington fit snugly under the rubric of an ongoing war that may never end.

Irony, while hardly dead, is mainly confined to solitary reflection. If insights run counter to the prevailing dogma, then access to mainstream media is apt to be scant or nonexistent. The need for independent thought has never been greater. At this point, facile phrases about war on "terrorism" or "terror" are written in invisible ink on a blank check for militarism. They can be roughly translated as "pay to the order of the president"—to be cashed with vast quantities of human blood.

A line from *King Lear*, in Act 4, is hauntingly appropriate: "'Tis the time's plague when madmen lead the blind." The observation fits the current era, and not only with reference to the murderous qualities of the Al Qaeda network. Few media outlets—and certainly none of the major national brands—have been willing to scrutinize the unhinged aspects of the adulated leadership in the White House.

After September 11, 2001, many journalists commented that the United States is unaccustomed to the role of victim. Left unsaid is how accustomed we are to being victimizers while preening ourselves as a nation of worldly do-gooders. The 3,000 human beings who lost their lives at the World Trade Center have cast an enormous shadow—as they should. But what about the uncounted people killed, one way or another, by U.S. policies?

The list of countries that the Pentagon has attacked in recent decades is long. The list of governments using American-supplied weapons to repress and massacre is even longer. And there's quieter slaughter, on a grand scale: During every hour, more than 1,000 children in the world die from preventable diseases. Basic nutrition, medical care, and sanitation would save their lives. A fraction of the Pentagon budget would suffice.

But we still live in a society with the kind of priorities that Martin Luther King Jr. described a long time ago—spending "military funds with alacrity and generosity" but providing anti-poverty funds "with miserliness." If he were alive now, his voice would still cry out against "the glaring contrast of poverty and wealth." King would have good reason to reiterate words from his speech on April 4, 1967, when he denounced "capitalists of the

West investing huge sums of money in Asia, Africa, and South America, only to take the profits out with no concern for the social betterment of the countries."

Today, advocates for humanitarian causes might see the United States as a place where "madmen lead the blind." But that's kind of a harsh way to describe the situation. Our lack of vision is in the context of a media system that mostly keeps us in the dark.

In American media's echo chamber, much of the genuine anguish from September 11 segued into a lot of braying about national greatness. Like many other pundits now in their glory days on cable TV networks, Chris Matthews knows how to dodge difficult truths. "Patriotism is more important than politics," he proclaimed one day in December 2001. What "unites us" is "democracy, freedom, human rights, the right to pursue happiness." And what about the "right to pursue happiness" for the kids dying from lack of food or clean water or medicine, while Matthews and thousands of other journalists fawn over the U.S. military?

Anyone watching TV news has seen lots of idolatry lavished on the latest Pentagon weapons. Uncle Sam's immense military power and Washington's role as the number-one arms dealer on the planet add up to a colossal drain of resources—and a powerful means of enforcing the bonds between the U.S. government and scores of regimes that combine repression with oligarchy, amid rampant poverty.

Winners get to write history, and that starts with the news. Victory in Afghanistan became ample justification for going to war in the first place; the message that overwhelming might makes right is ever-present, even if no one quite says so out loud. And when human flesh goes up in flames and human bodies shatter—but not on our TV screens—did it ever really happen?

Several decades ago, peace activist A.J. Muste observed: "The problem after a war is with the victor. He thinks he has just proved that war and violence pay. Who will now teach him a lesson?"

Norman Solomon is the author of many books including *The Habits of Highly Deceptive Media*. His syndicated column focuses on media and politics.

THIS MODERN WORLD

by TOM TOMORROW

CHAPTER 8

Power Sources

ON PARTY, GENDER, RACE AND CLASS, TV NEWS
LOOKS TO THE MOST POWERFUL GROUPS

BY INA HOWARD

On an average weeknight, *ABC World News Tonight*, *CBS Evening News*, and *NBC Nightly News* are tuned in by approximately one-quarter of television-viewing homes in the U.S. (Nielsen Media Research, 2001)—about two-thirds of the U.S. public that claims to follow current events regularly (Pew Research Center, 2000). In 22 minutes they deliver snapshots of national and international news that not only frame current events for the public, but influence story selection at local affiliate stations, at radio outlets, and in print media. In addition to putting topics on the nation's agenda, the networks help set the range of debate on those issues by selecting sources who ostensibly represent the interests and opinions of the population.

In this role as agenda setters and debate arbiters, the networks' broadcasts profoundly affect the democratic process. While conservatives from Spiro Agnew to Bernard Goldberg have accused the news media of using this influence to promote liberal ideals, a comprehensive analysis of the sources used on the big three networks' evening news in 2001 suggests otherwise.

Instead of a liberal bias, the study found, source selection favored the elite interests that the corporate owners of these shows depend on for advertising revenue, regulatory support, and access to information. Network news demonstrated a clear tendency to showcase the opinions of the most powerful political and economic actors, while giving limited access to those voices that would be most likely to challenge them. Based on the criterion of who got to speak, the broadcast networks functioned much more as venues for the claims and opinions of the powerful than as democratic forums for public discussion or education.

METHODOLOGY

This study was based on data compiled by Media Tenor Ltd., a nonpartisan, international media analysis firm with an office in New York City. This information was gathered on a continuous basis from each report that appeared on *ABC World News Tonight*, *NBC Nightly News*, and *CBS Evening News* in 2001. If special programming preempted a news show's broadcast in New York City, transcripts were analyzed when available. For this study, data was analyzed for reports from January 1 through December 31, 2001, which included 14,632 sources in 18,765 individual reports.

Sources were defined as any person quoted directly or indirectly for a total of five seconds within a single news report. For each of these sources, professional or social distinction, partisan affiliation, gender, and race or nationality (when determinable) were recorded.

PARTISAN IMBALANCE

In 2001, the voices of Washington's elite politicians were the dominant sources of opinion on the network evening news, making up one in three Americans (and more than one in four of all sources) who were quoted on all topics throughout the year. On the partisan level, the news programs provided a generous platform for sources from the Republican Party—the party in power in the White House for almost the entire year—while giving much less access to the opposition Democrats, and virtually no time to third party or independent politicians. Of sources that had an identifiable partisan affiliation, 75 percent were Republican and only 24 percent Democrats. A mere 1 percent were third-party representatives or independents.

The three networks varied only slightly in their selection of partisan sources. CBS had the most Republicans and the fewest Democrats (76 percent versus 23 percent); NBC (75 percent versus 25 percent); and ABC (73 percent versus 27 percent) were marginally less imbalanced. CBS had the most independents (1.2 percent), followed by ABC (0.7 percent); and NBC (an almost invisible 0.2 percent).

Small as they are, these latter figures may overstate the presence of independent politicians on the nightly news. Senator James Jeffords, the centrist Vermont Republican who broke with his party in May (giving Democrats control of the Senate), made up 83 percent of the independent sources who were quoted throughout the year, suggesting that networks highlighted independent politicians mainly when they impacted the fates of the two major parties. The only avowedly antiestablishment independent who appeared in 2001, Ralph Nader, made up 3 percent of independent or third-party sources—0.03 percent of all politicians quoted.

Although the attacks of September 11 exacerbated the tilt towards Republicans, the difference was pronounced beforehand as well. Prior to the attacks, Republicans made up 68 percent, Democrats 31 percent, and independents 1 percent of partisan sources. Afterward, Republican sources surged to 87 percent, with Democrats (13 percent) and independents (0.1 percent) falling even further behind.

PARTISAN AFFILIATION OF SOURCES, WHERE IDENTIFIABLE

	REPUBLICAN	DEMOCRAT	THIRD PARTY/INDEPENDENT
ABC	73 percent	27 percent	0.7 percent
CBS	76 percent	23 percent	1.2 percent
NBC	75 percent	25 percent	0.2 percent
Total	75 percent	24 percent	1 percent

TOTAL PARTISAN SOURCES BEFORE & AFTER SEPTEMBER 11

	REPUBLICAN	DEMOCRAT	THIRD PARTY/INDEPENDENT
Before 9-11	68 percent	31 percent	1 percent
After 9-11	87 percent	13 percent	0.1 percent

DISPELLING "DEMOCRATIC BIAS"

While these figures ought to dispel the persistent notion that network news has a liberal or pro-Democratic bias, they do not in themselves necessarily prove a conservative or Republican bias. Rather, they may reflect the networks' definition of news that prioritizes the actions and opinions of the executive branch. Members of the Bush Administration (and Clinton Administration, for the preinauguration period in January), including the president, vice president, cabinet members, and official spokespeople, made up 17 percent of all U.S. sources and 62 percent of all partisan sources. When these are set aside, the remaining partisan sources showed a rough parity between the two major parties, with 51 percent Republicans, 48 percent Democrats, and 2 percent third-party members or independents appearing as sources.

This breakdown suggests that in 2001 there was a strong advantage on the nightly news for the party that held the White House; after the administration had its say, there was roughly one source from its own party to defend it for every representative from the opposition party that might criticize it. Unfortunately, complete data does not exist from 2000 or earlier to compare whether the same ratio held true during a Democratic Administration.

The leading topics on which partisan sources were quoted, however, imply that the disparities in sourcing could indicate a more substantial bias than mere reverence for the presidency. Partisan sources from both parties were most likely to appear in stories on domestic politicking, such as speeches or debates in Congress. After that area of coverage, however, their next most common appearances were qualitatively very different: Republicans appeared in reports on the widely supported war in Afghanistan, while 12 percent of the reports in which Democrats were quoted focused on corruption and scandals, in most cases defending themselves or other party members. Republicans, by contrast, were presented in such reports in only 1 percent of their total appearances. By focusing so much on largely non-political scandals (e.g., Chandra Levy, White House gifts) involving the party out of power, the networks bolstered the Republican image—not only by showcasing Democratic "character" questions, but by reserving the vast majority of Republican quotes for more dignified policy discussions, thereby disassociating the party from the "dirty politics" of scandal-mongering.

The top individual sources on the news reflect the emphasis given to the administration at the expense of the opposition. George W. Bush alone made up 9 percent of all sources and 33 percent of partisan sources, putting him far ahead of any other individual voices for the year. The next most common sources were Al Qaeda leader Osama bin Laden (2 percent), former President Bill Clinton, Secretary of State Colin Powell, Attorney General John Ashcroft, Defense Secretary Donald Rumsfeld, Palestinian Authority President Yassir Arafat, Vice President Dick Cheney, Senate Majority Leader Tom Daschle, and New York Mayor Rudolph Giuliani (with 1 percent each).

Clinton faded from prominence shortly after the Bush inauguration (80 percent of his appearances occurred in the first four months of the year), leaving Daschle as the only other top 10 source from the domestic opposition party. The remaining top U.S. sources were all members of the Bush Administration, with the exception of the Republican mayor of New York (89 percent of whose appearances occurred after September 11).

WOMEN'S RESTRICTED ROLE

After U.S. politicians, "Unclassified citizens"—a category that can be used as a proxy for ordinary Americans—were the most common individual type of source, providing 20 percent of all quotes. While it's valuable to hear the voices of ordinary citizens on the nightly news, the context in which most of their soundbites appeared makes it unlikely that their viewpoints did much to shape the nation's political debate: They were more often presented in human interest stories, crime reports, and entertainment news than in all "hard" news topics combined, leaving discussion of most policy issues to "expert" political and economic elites.

While women made up only 19 percent of the total sources, they represented more than double that share—40 percent—of the ordinary citizens in the news. This reflects a tendency to quote men as the vast majority of authoritative voices while presenting women as non-experts; women made up only 9 percent of the professional and political voices that were presented. More than half of the women (52 percent) who appeared on the news were presented as average citizens, whereas only 14 percent of male sources were.

The balance was roughly equal among networks. NBC, with 18 percent, had slightly more female sources (of whom 53 percent were nonauthorities), while ABC and CBS both presented 14 percent (of whom 48 percent and 55 percent, respectively, were ordinary citizens).

Even in coverage of gender-related policies (which made up 0.2 percent of coverage), women made up only 43 percent of the sources. On such issues as equal opportunity, gender equality, and discrimination, partisan sources made up 24 percent of the total; 71 percent of these were Republicans and 29 percent Democrats. All of these partisan sources were men. Women were presented as non-expert citizens 77 percent of the time in gender stories. Men, by contrast, spoke as experts in their fields 100 percent of the time in such stories.

Ordinary citizens (all women) made up 33 percent of sources on gender policies, followed by George W. Bush (17 percent), company representatives (10 percent, all men), Alan Greenspan (10 percent), soldiers (7 percent, all men), writers (7 percent, half men, half women), and other groups that constituted 3 percent or less of the total each. In keeping with other areas of coverage, white Americans clearly dominated the quoted sources, making up 89 percent of sources for whom race was determinable.

Two women from the Middle East represented the only non–U.S. women quoted on issues of gender policy. It's noteworthy that the Taliban's oppression of women did not become a topic for the evening news in 2001 until First Lady Laura Bush "introduced" the long-recognized problem during the U.S. bombing of Afghanistan in mid-November.

GENDER OF SOURCES

	MEN	**WOMEN**
ABC	86 percent	14 percent
CBS	86 percent	14 percent
NBC	82 percent	18 percent
Total	85 percent	15 percent

RACIAL UNDERREPRESENTATION

The racial balance of all sources was firmly tilted towards the historically most powerful segment of society as well. Among U.S. sources for whom race was determinable, whites made up 92 percent of the total, blacks 7 percent, Latinos and Arab Americans 0.6 percent each, and Asian Americans 0.2 percent. (According to the 2000 census, the U.S. population is 69 percent non-Hispanic white, 13 percent Hispanic, 12 percent black, and 4 percent Asian.) A single source who appeared on NBC (July 26, 2002) constituted the entire representation of Native Americans on the nightly news in 2001—0.008 percent of total sources.

Among all sources, white Americans constituted 67 percent of the total, followed by Middle Easterners (9 percent), black Americans (5 percent), and Northern Europeans (mostly English) at 3 percent. No other racial or regional group made up more than 2 percent of the total.

The networks presented a remarkably similar distribution of races among U.S. sources. On all three networks, 92 percent of racially categorized U.S. sources were white, while 7 percent were black. Latinos were the next most quoted sources on all networks (0.6 percent on NBC, 0.5 percent on ABC, and 0.7 percent on CBS), followed by Arab Americans (0.6 percent, 0.5 percent and 0.7 percent respectively) and Asian Americans (0.2 percent, 0.3 percent, and 0.3 percent respectively).

As with the network's presentation of women as non-experts, racial minorities were disproportionately presented as ordinary citizens rather than as authorities or experts. Nonwhite U.S. sources made up 16 percent of average citizens and 11 percent of expert sources.

When race, gender, and nationality are considered together, white American men clearly dominated the evening news, making up 62 percent of all sources, far ahead of the next most commonly quoted sources: white American women (12 percent), Middle Eastern men (6 percent), black American men (4 percent), and Northern European men (2 percent).

Even on racial issues like affirmative action, racism, and asylum policy (which made up 0.9 percent of overall coverage), the majority group was still afforded far greater opportunity to televise their opinions than the populations most directly affected by those issues were. White Americans made up 68 percent of sources on such stories, followed by residents of Latin America (14 percent), African Americans (7 percent), U.S. Latinos, and people of the Middle East (3 percent each).

Among U.S. sources quoted on minority policies, whites made up 87 percent, far ahead of blacks (8 percent), Latinos (4 percent), and Asians (1 percent). Even in reports specifically on racism, 59 percent of quoted sources were white Americans, 29 percent were African Americans, and 6 percent were Asian Americans, with no Arab Americans, Latinos, Native Americans, or other minority groups quoted at all.

Of partisan sources quoted in racial stories, 84 percent were Republicans, a group so dominant that they made up more than one in four overall sources on these issues throughout the year. Democrats made up the remainder, with no independents or third-party representatives quoted at all.

RACE OF U.S. SOURCES, WHERE IDENTIFIABLE

	WHITE	BLACK	LATINO	ARAB AMERICAN	ASIAN AMERICAN	NATIVE AMERICAN
ABC	92%	7%	0.5%	0.5%	0.3%	0%
CBS	92%	7%	0.7%	0.7%	0.3%	0%
NBC	92%	7%	0.6%	0.6%	0.2%	0.024%
Total	92%	7%	0.6%	0.6%	0.2%	0.008%

WHO ARE THE EXPERTS?

After ordinary citizens, the next largest categories of sources on the nightly news were various professional or expert voices of industry, science, or government. The most common among these were corporate representatives, providing 7 percent of all sources, along with economists and academics, also at 7 percent. The visibility of these categories reflects the networks' heavy coverage of business and financial stories; the economists were unlikely to provide perspectives that challenged the corporate spokespersons, since they generally came from major investment banks such as Goldman Sachs and Morgan Stanley, from conservative think tanks such as the Heritage Foundation, or from elite business schools such as those at Princeton and Stanford.

Nonpartisan government employees and officials—such as FDA and EPA representatives, National Security Council spokespersons, and mail carriers (especially in the midst of the anthrax attacks)—were the next most quoted sources (6 percent). Medical doctors provided 5 percent of soundbites, reflecting the nightly news' interest in health issues. No other professional or social group provided more than 4 percent of the total.

Representatives of nongovernmental organizations, which might have provided an alternative perspective to the U.S. government, business community or establishment experts, made up only 3 percent of the sources. Not all of these were from organizations that were likely to challenge the status quo, however; groups represented ranged from the United Nations and Human Rights Watch to the Christian Coalition and the National Rifle Association.

Organized labor was granted even less access to the airwaves. Even as the country lost 2.4 million jobs in 2001, Union representatives made up less than 0.2 percent of sources on the evening news, making company representatives 35 times more likely to be heard.

This lack of interest in labor was reflected not only in sourcing but in topic selection: The unemployment rate, layoffs, strikes, wage levels, workplace discrimination, and all other labor issues combined were only 1 percent of total coverage. By contrast, other business and economic issues made up 14 percent of the total. Product reports alone were twice as likely to appear on the news as labor-related stories, making up 2 percent of overall coverage.

Even on labor stories, union representatives were rarely heard, making up a mere 2 percent of quoted sources. This was far behind corporate and business association representatives (26 percent), economists (19 percent), and politicians from the major parties (15 percent). Of the partisan sources presented on labor issues, 89 percent were Republicans and 11 percent were Democrats.

CONCLUSION

Journalists sometimes claim that they do not make the news, but merely report what is newsworthy; at the same time, media owners argue that they do not make the news but simply give the people "what they want" through the machinations of the media marketplace. Both arguments are as irresponsible as they are false. International news programs cannot cover every newsworthy story, independent of how the term is defined, because of limited resources and format restrictions. The filtering process that is intrinsic to those limitations is the lever through which journalists and media owners do make the news.

The selection of sources is one of the primary elements in the news-making process. Sources who are allowed to appear on the news are able to defend themselves directly, to present their own opinions overtly, to deflect criticisms onto opponents (who may not be able to defend themselves), and to achieve a level of credibility that those without access to the eyes and ears of America will never have. While the political inclinations of journalists might well be taken into account when considering bias in the evening news, a news anchor's intimations, or an abstract principle vaguely inserted into an interview question, will not drive voting behavior or dispel deeply entrenched stereotypes. The citizens, politicians, and advocates whose televised images are familiar, and whose ideas are clearly tied to those images through their first-person repetitions of key messages, most potently influence public opinion and action.

This study was performed to provide an objective quantification of news sources in order to underlie informed, democratic debate about how news content affects public perceptions, political initiatives, and social interactions. In order to provide a democratic forum for public debate and education, a balance of opinions and agendas must be granted access to the nation's national news programs and it is hoped that such efforts might lead in that direction.

Thank you to Fairness and Accuracy in Report (FAIR), <www.fair.org/>, for allowing us to reprint this chapter.

THIS MODERN WORLD

by TOM TOMORROW

CHAPTER 9

Truth About Afghan Civilian Casualties Comes Only Through American Lenses for the U.S. Corporate Media
[OUR MODERN-DAY DIDYMUS]

BY MARC W. HEROLD

Award-winning reporter Anthony Lloyd of The Times *[London] wrote recently, "seldom in a modern conflict has 'fact' been so manipulated as it is by the Western media and coalition forces in Afghanistan today."*[1]

ABSTRACT: The U.S. and allies' bombing campaign upon Afghanistan has resulted in well over 3,000 civilian impact deaths, the indirect deaths of tens of thousands of internally displaced persons, and thousands of injured in an agricultural society where limbs are crucial. In addition, the landscape and environment have been polluted with cluster bombs and depleted uranium. The intense bombing campaign destroyed urban and village residences, bridges, mosques, electricity and water supplies, communication systems, cratered roads, and so on. Unlike with the victims of September 11, the dead Afghan civilians remain largely uncounted, faceless, de facto unworthy bodies.

One evening in early February after an hour long phone conversation, an Associated Press foreign desk editor blurted out, "but why, Professor

Herold did you publish your report on the Internet? Is that what people do nowadays?" Her exasperation was evident in that I had not respected the corporate media as gatekeeper to truth, but had independently and without their sanction released my dossier on civilian victims of the U.S. air war on December 10.[2] That is, the A.P. had not "independently verified the truth" of my dossier.

1. PREFACE : HARBINGER OF TOMORROW?

The British bombed the 'restless natives' of Afghanistan intermittently between 1915 and 1919 and even considered using poison gas against them during 1919 and 1920.[3] Bombing the Pathans' irrigation ditches, which cut water supplies and emptied terraces' topsoil, was deemed more effective than destroying their villages.[4] The Pathans were temporarily subdued, because food and water were difficult to secure in the bleak, dry region that still remains wretchedly poor. Sir John Maffrey, chief of colonial Britain's Northwest Frontier Province—now Pakistan's troubled tribal zone along the Afghan border—was told by regional air force headquarters that international law did not apply "against savage tribes who do not conform to codes of civilized warfare."[5]

The first air attacks in support of British and colonial ground columns took place in early May, upon Afghan forces in Dakka just over the Khyber Pass. The *New York Times* reported the attacks were met with "good results."[6] The "good result" here was primarily demoralizing the Afghans, evidence for which was claimed to be the exaggerated casualties [600] reported by the Afghans.[7] This was followed by a bombing attack carried out by Bristol F2-Bs upon Jalalabad after which "large portions of the town are reported to be burnt out."[8] On May 24, the Handley Page strategic bomber hit Kabul and the Afghan amir's palace. Soon thereafter, the Afghan amir sued for peace.

2. THE HIDDEN DETAILS OF THE U.S BOMBING CAMPAIGN

Eighty-two years later, at 9:00 P.M. on October 7, the United States and Britain renewed the air assault upon Afghanistan, setting in motion many processes that would devastate the people, the land, and the environment of Afghanistan. Far from suing for peace, Mullah Omar in Kandahar declared a holy war.

My report argues that the main reason that so many civilians have died in Afghanistan is less because of targeting errors, faulty intelligence, equipment malfunction (as argued by Conetta, 2002) and more from the decision of U.S. military planners to employ highly destructive bombs upon what were perceived to be "targets" in areas populated by civilians, whether residential neighborhoods or villages.[9] The bombing campaign took a very heavy toll upon urban infrastructure, destroying buildings, communication systems, water and electricity supplies, fuel storage depots, and cratering innumerable roads. In the third phase of the air war, Afghan fuel trucks became a favored target.

On February 13, Peshawar's daily newspaper, *The Frontier Post*, got it more right than all the U.S. media war pundits, headlining a brief article as follows:

PROXIMITY TO TALIBAN WAS FATAL!
The bomb craters are like enormous footsteps a few hundred yards apart, marching in the direction of a Taliban radio transmitter. Along the way, four men died…a fatal proximity to a site considered militarily useful to Afghanistan's Taliban or Osama.

Hundreds of individual stories exist, as yet mostly untold, of how proximity to what U.S. war planners deemed a military "target," is at the heart of why so many innocent Afghan civilians died. Ghulam and Rabia Hazrat lived on the outskirts of Kabul near a Taliban military base. One day, a U.S. missile landed in the family's courtyard and the neighborhood was showered with cluster bombs. Mrs. Hazrat remembers:

"There was no warning. I was in the kitchen making dough when I heard a big explosion. I came out and saw a big cloud of dust and saw my children lying on the ground. Two of them were dead and two died later in the hospital."[10]

Along with the U.S. military planner's decision to bomb perceived military targets in urban areas, the use of weapons with great destructive blast and fragmentation power (see Table 1) necessarily results in heavy civilian casualties. The weapon of choice during the first three weeks of the air campaign was the 500-lb. bomb that has a lethal blast range of 20 meters; later, the 2000-lb. bomb became the weapon of choice with a lethal blast range of 34 meters. The JDAM technology consists of a $21,000 kit produced by Boeing that transforms 1,000- and 2,000-lb. conventional "dumb" bombs into "smart" bombs that rely upon the global positioning system. When global positioning updates are available the JDAM-outfitted bomb can strike within 13 meters (43 feet) of its target. When updates are not available due to jamming or other problems, it can "still hit within 30 meters [or 98 feet]."[11] The B1-B bombers flying out of Diego Garcia in the Indian

Ocean, can carry 24 to 30 Mark 84 2,000-lb JDAM bombs. Each bomb is 14 feet long and will destroy military targets within a 40-foot radius from the point of impact. Using only an inertial guidance system (INS), the Mark 84 bomb has a circular error radius of 30 meters, but with a GPS guidance unit, this gets reduced to 13 meters.

Table 1. DATA ON WEAPONS SYSTEMS USED IN AFGHAN AERIAL WAR THEATER

CHARACTERISTICS	MARK 82 500-LB. PAVEWAY II BOMB	MARK 83 1,000-LB. JDAM BOMB	CBU-87 1,000-LB. CLUSTER BOMB	MARK 84 2,000 LB. JDAM BOMB
Officially reported accuracy range	9 meters	13-30 meters, 39 feet in tests	N.A.	13-30 meters, 39 feet in tests
Fragmentation range		3,000 feet	N.A.	3,000 feet
Blast shrapnel range		600 foot radius	500 feet	1,200 foot radius
Effective casualty radius*	About 60 meters radius		Disperses 202 bomblets, each with 300 steel fragments	Safety at least 400 meters from impact site
Lethal blast range**	About 20 meters radius		250 feet or 76 meters	110 feet or 34 meters
Crater upon impact	12 feet or 4 meters	35 feet wide	Footprint is 200 x 400 meters	50 feet wide and 36 feet deep
Price per unit	$19,000	$25,000	$12,400	$25,000
Manufacturers	Texas Instruments and Raytheon	Boeing Corp. and Lockheed Martin	Aerojet/ Honeywell	Boeing Corp. and Lockheed Martin

* meaning 50 percent of exposed persons will die
**meaning 100 percent mortality within this range

Afghan civilians in proximity to alleged military installations will die, and must die, as "collateral damage" of U.S. air attacks aiming to destroy these installations in order to make future military operations in the sky or on the ground less likely to result in U.S. military casualties. The military facilities of the Taliban were mostly inherited from the Soviet-supported government of the 1980s that had concentrated its military infrastructure in cities, which could be better defended against the rural insurgency of the mujahideen. This reality is compounded insofar as the Taliban maintained dispersed facilities: smaller units spread out. U.S. military strategists and their bombers, thus, engaged in a very widespread high intensity of bombing. Such intense urban bombing causes high levels of civilian casualties. From the point of view of U.S. policymakers and their mainstream media boosters, the "cost" of a dead Afghan civilian is zero as long as these civilian deaths can be hidden from the general U.S. public's view. The "benefits" of saving future lives of U.S. military personnel are enormous, given the U.S. public's post-Vietnam aversion to returning body bags.

The documented Afghan civilians killed were not participating in warmaking activities (e.g., working in munitions factories, and so on.) and, therefore, had not forfeited their right to immunity from attack.[12] In effect, as an astute scholar has noted, I am turning Michael Walzer's notion of "due care"[13] upside down: that is, far from acknowledging a positive responsibility to protect innocent Afghans from the misery of war, U.S. military strategists chose to impose levels of harm upon innocent Afghan civilians to reduce present and possible future dangers faced by U.S. forces.

Table 2. CIVILIAN CASUALTIES* OF THE U.S. AIR WAR IN AFGHANISTAN

TIME PERIOD	LOW ESTIMATE	HIGH ESTIMATE
October	1,061	1,238
November	1,012	1,106
December–present	864	1,045
No date available	177	177
TOTAL	**3,108**	**3,560**

*includes only impact deaths. Data derived from Appendix 4. Daily Casualty Count at : <http://pubpages.unh.edu/~mwherold>.

The 14,000 tons of bombs dropped upon Afghanistan between October and February killed a conservatively estimated 3,100 to 3,500 civilians upon impact, or what I call impact deaths. These do not include persons dying later from injuries, from exploding cluster bombs[15], from hunger, disease, and cold as U.S. bombing hampered relief efforts[14], and so on. Table 2 "counts the dead" during the U.S. bombing campaign. From the data I have, about 70 percent of these casualties are women and children.

Analysis of civilian casualty data reveals two other important characteristics of the U.S. air war: 1. Most civilian deaths were registered in regions of high population density;[16] and 2. The elevated number of civilian deaths is the result of a very large number of small death tolls in many bombing attacks. This fits well with the fact that most fighter planes were carrying out 3 to 4 bombing attacks per sortie.

The U.S. air war upon Afghanistan was played out in five phases, though without any overall grand plan. The air war was adjusted to the shifting realities on the ground. The five sequential phases were:

➤Bombing of perceived military facilities in urban areas, airports, and outlying camps (October 7 – 20);

➤The battle for the central plains area, the Shomali Plain campaign and the carpet-bombing aroind Kunduz, Khanabad, and Mazar (October 21– November 25);

➤The bombing campaign around Kandahar and the southern provinces (November 26–December 10);

➤The Tora Bora campaign (November 27–December 10);

➤The bombing of selected sites believed to harbor Al Qaeda or Taliban leadership (December 20–present).

Beginning in the Balkan wars of the 1990s, military and media propagandists began arguing that casualties among civilian populations do not count so to speak (pious public relations statements aside) if they are unpremeditated, that is, "we're the good guys, so if we killed some innocent people, well, we didn't do it on purpose. The bad guys, on the other hand, are being bad intentionally." In Afghanistan, the war is touted not to be against Afghans, but against Al Qaeda and the Taliban and, moreover, the devilish Taliban just hide amongst human shields.

A very different interpretation might read:

> But where the likelihood of "errors" in a bombing raid has a probability of over 90 percent, the damage is intentional even if the particular victims were not targeted. If somebody throws a bomb at an individual in a crowded theater, and 100 bystanders are also killed, would we say that the bomb thrower was not clearly guilty of killing the 100 because their deaths were "unintended" and the damage was "collateral"? The propaganda agencies reserve such purr word excuses for "humanitarian" bombing.[17]

But a bigger factor is at work here. The stark asymmetry in which "bodies count" and therefore merit great efforts at uncovering them, whereas in other places similar "bodies" are neglected, is a topic of enormous significance but beyond the scope of this research. Sometimes, civilian victims are "worthy" and other times "unworthy." The zeal—nay even inventive overzealousness—in uncovering bodies killed by Serbs, the recounting of the most horrific witness accounts, and the ensuing indignation, is precisely matched by the utter neglect and great skepticism towards any who might count the Afghan civilians who died under U.S. bombs. Contrast this with Human Rights Watch's report on worthy Chechan bodies, which depicts the Russian war on Chechnya as seen through the drawings of children in Chechnya.[18] Similar neglect was evident for the 500 to 3,500 civilians who died in the El Chorillos slum of Panama City in the 1989 U.S. invasion. They happened to be overwhelmingly poor blacks living next to the Panamanian military headquarters. Our good propaganda system—deployed by the U.S ideological and propaganda collective—simply made Panamanian and Afghan civilian victims "unworthy" of note...unworthy bodies not to be really counted by the collective U.S. corporate mainstream press, our modern-day Didymus. The Afghan bombing victims and survivors' fate was well-captured in a *New York Times* article, describing the December 1 attack upon the mountain village of Madoo where 82 villagers succumbed: "Perhaps someday there will be a reckoning for this tiny village of 15 houses, all of them obliterated into splintered wood and dust by American bombs...but more likely, Madoo will not learn whether the bombs fell by mistake or on purpose, and the matter will be forgotten amid the larger consequences of war. It is left an anonymous hamlet with anonymous people buried in anonymous graves."[19]

Mahtab, 20, a refugee, lives in a squatter's camp in Peshawar. The bombing made her leave Kabul on October 18. Her house was hit during a raid and her mother-in-law was killed by shrapnel, she said: "It pierced her heart."[20]

3. THE CRACK IN THE U.S CORPORATE WALL OF SILENCE

On December 10, 2001, my study documenting 3,500 Afghans who died under U.S. bombs since October 7 was released, being published on the Internet by the San Francisco-based Media Alliance. At the same time, I was interviewed by Amy Goodman on the *Democracy Now* radio show. Exactly 10 days later, the major British daily newspaper, *The Guardian*, featured a prominent article on my study by Seumas Milne with the title,

"The Innocent Dead in a Coward's War."[21] The corporate wall of silence had been cracked. Two days later, a major Australian newspaper summarized my report, even citing particular bombing incidents,[22] followed another two days later by a story in *The Financial Times* by Simon Briscoe.[23]

The *Guardian* story in effect meant that the report could no longer be ignored. On December 26, Kevin Canfield, staff writer at the Hartford daily, *Hartford Courant*, wrote a detailed, factual, front-page account of my dossier, noting that it "has caused a stir abroad and is starting to be noticed stateside."[24] On January 3, 2002, the world's premier news agency, BBC News, ran a feature story in its online journal, "Afghanistan's Civilian Deaths Mount," describing my research report's findings.[25] The following day, Canada's major daily, the *Toronto Globe & Mail*, featured a front-page article by Murray Campbell, "Thousands of Afghans Likely Killed in Bombings," paraphrasing my report.[26] This was followed by mention in the *Washington Post* and the *Boston Herald*, though buried in the back pages.[27]

The dossier on civilian casualties has been translated into German, Italian, and Japanese. In addition, I have had hundreds of radio interviews, invitations for national TV appearances (turned down), TV shows in Germany and California, public speaking engagements from Boston to Iowa to California, and research reported in major dailies and weeklies in New Zealand, Australia, India, Pakistan, Hong Kong, Egypt, Italy, Germany, Switzerland, Norway, Portugal, Spain, Britain, Ireland, France, Brazil, Canada, and the United States, including *Der Spiegel*, *Corriere della Sera*, *Il Manifesto*, forum in *Le Monde*, *The Guardian*, *BBC News Online*, *The Financial Times*, *Irish Times*, *South China Morning News*, *Pravda*, *Publico* daily (Portugal), Switzerland's two major dailies *Tages Anzeiger and Neues Zuricher Zeitung*, *La Vanguardia* (Spain), *Die Zeit* (Hamburg) and *Die Tageszeitung-TAZ* (Berlin), *Tribune de Geneve*, *Ny Tid* (Norway), *Al-Ahram Weekly*, *New Zealand Herald*, *Sydney Morning Herald*, *Jornal do Brasil* and *Correio Braziliense* (Brasilia) and *Jornal Hora do Povo* (Sao Paulo), *Time*, *U.S. Catholic*, *The New York Times*, *Wall Street Journal*, *Village Voice*, *The Progressive*, *Earth Island Journal*, *Harper's*, *Hartford Courant*, *Boston Herald*, *Des Moines Register*, UT *Daily Texan*, *St. Louis Post Dispatch* (letter to editor), *San Francisco Chronicle*, PaxChristi USA, ZNet, <Wired.com>, *Counterpunch*, *Toronto Globe & Mail* and the Center for Research on Globalization (Montreal), Cyberpresse (Toronto), as well as all the local newspapers, to mention just a few. My research was mentioned at this year's World Social Forum in Porto Alegre (Brazil). Professors of journalism interviewed me and wrote up articles in the *Houston Chronicle*,[28] the *San Francisco*

Chronicle,[29] and the *American Journalism Review.* My research formed the basis of pointed questions posed in a press conference held by Secretary of Defense Rumsfeld (USA) and in a debate in the House of Commons to Geoffrey Hoon (U.K).

The only alternative report issued to-date that counts civilian casualties of the Afghan air war, is that by Carl Conetta of the Cambridge-based Project on Defense Alternatives.[30] While agreeing with several factors mentioned in the study that have caused a higher civilian casualty rate—the mix of weapons used, the nature of intelligence sources, and the campaign's specific objectives—I also harbor reservations. As argued in my dossier, the high civilian impact deaths are primarily caused by a decision of U.S. military planners to carry out bombing upon certain targets with certain weapons, regardless of whether these munitions were precision-guided or not.[31]

The most glaring problem in the PDA report, in my view, is the author's choice to rely only upon so-called Western sources. This has two major consequences: 1. It necessarily dramatically under-reports casualties given that relatively few Western reporters were on hand; and 2. It implicitly reinforces a very ethnocentric perspective that says "only Western sources can be trusted" and all others "must be independently verified." I, on the other hand, carried out numerous "checks" to see whether, for example, the independent Islamabad Afghan Islamic Press could be trusted. In every instance, I found it could be. The same holds for the Iranian news agency, IRNA. I also rely on a number of outstanding Australian journals and reports of NGOs (e.g., RAWA and so on), which are neglected in the PDA report. Given that I cast my net wider (and in so doing, reported far more incidents), I naturally develop a higher (and more accurate) count.

A third major problem with the PDA report is that the author does not provide his disaggregated detailed data. I do at my university site at <http://pubpages.unh.edu/~mwherold>. Moreover, I am continually updating and revising my database and its accompanying essay. Fourthly, the PDA report relies far too much, in my view, upon the mainstream corporate press, which, as I show in my dossier's Appendix 2, engages in misrepresentation on this matter of casualties.

4. THE CRITICISMS OF MY DOSSIER HAVE FALLEN INTO SIX GENERAL CATEGORIES.[32]

CLAIM: Reported civilians might be Taliban in civilian dress. This argument (Fleeson, 2002), falsely extrapolates from the Vietnam and other guerrilla war experiences. The Taliban military was not a guerrilla army after 1996, but rather functioned as well-defined militia and military units, living in facilities separate from the population. This is not the same as in Indochina 30 years ago. Certainly, the Taliban moved around in relatively small military units, but they did not live amongst the people. Moreover, the overwhelming number of documented civilian casualties (impact deaths) took place in living facilities in either closer or further proximity from perceived military units that were bombed by U.S. planes. Others took place in vehicles, hospitals, schools, mosques, marketplaces, and so on, upon which U.S. bombs fell. A somewhat related claim is that Taliban soldiers hid out in civilian homes. While undoubtedly, some terrified fleeing Taliban, for example, around Kunduz and Khanabad, sought temporary safety in civilian homes, simple "logic" suggests that Taliban were precisely fleeing areas of heavy bombing. As Holger Jensen, international editor of *Foreign Affairs*, cautioned: "the 'human shield' gambit is an old propaganda ploy, often used to vilify the enemy and justify the killing of civilians. During the Gulf War, it explained away the deaths of hundreds of Iraqi women and children in a bomb shelter said to be a top secret headquarters of the Iraqi military. It wasn't. In Afghanistan so far, it has justified the bombing of Red Cross facilities and a home for the elderly."[33]

CLAIM: Impossible to account for civilian casualties in the general confusion. The reality of city neighborhoods and village life in Afghanistan is one where there are dense social interactions/networks and large extended families. People know each other. Geographic mobility is minimal. Therefore, when two houses are obliterated, people know who lived there. Most of the impact deaths occurred in relatively small bombing incidents (small number of bombs). This assertion is often made by persons seeking to avoid the topic of civilian casualties.

CLAIM: Herold's figures will be revised downwards just as those at the WTC have been. The reality at the WTC and the Afghan neighborhoods could not be more dissimilar. In the WTC, thousands of people worked in a couple large structures and did not know each other—alone in a crowd. In the city neighborhood or the typical village in Afghanistan, people know each other by name. Hence, whereas in New York, the sight of crumbling skyscrapers brought forth initial estimates of 20,000 deaths, months later after reconstructing who was in which office, the casualty toll has been cut to below 3,000. In Afghanistan, the initial reports of survivors, witnesses, and such will be largely accurate insofar as they knew who lived where. I suspect that the overall civilian casualty toll in Afghanistan will rise as accounts of unreported bombing incidents come forth, as has already happened (e.g., the village of Esferghich in the Shomali Plain, and so on).

CLAIM: Newspaper articles might all be relying upon a single report of a news wire agency. My response is provided in footnote to the database. Since the publication of the above tabulation, a question has been raised about whether the sources for a particular incident I cite might all be relying upon a single news agency report. As far as I know—and frequently newspaper articles do not mention the particular news press release or particular possible on-site reporter—I have not deliberately engaged in such practice. I do believe that if separate newspaper stories report a particular story (without expressing reservations), then this reflects a de facto judgment by the newspaper staff about the veracity of the report and I count this as a separate source. Frequently, different sources mention different civilian casualty figures and most of the time, I have chosen the lowest number. I might add that if reports give different figures, they most likely do not come from the same source. Whenever possible, I have tried to locate first-hand reports, or statements by persons present (and still alive!) at a bombing incident. If a "story" presents a more detailed account, I have lent it greater credibility.

CLAIM: A war in which fewer bombs are dropped and more of those dropped are "precision-guided" cannot result in higher civilian casualties. I call this claim one of mistaken analogy. How is William Arkin's common logic flawed?[34] Mr. Arkin argues that in a war where fewer munitions are dropped and more of those dropped are "precision-guided," this must lead to lower civilian casualties than in other wars. It almost sounds good. The critical assumption being made here is that of *ceteris paribus* (incidentally one very dear to economists, a breed of which I form a part). Were everything else the same, then Mr. Arkin might just have a case. But, reality in Afghanistan differed markedly from Iraq and Serbia.

The decision by U.S. military planners to carry out a bombing campaign first (partly—I will leave out the isolated training camps in mountains and frontier regions) in urban centers, and secondly to hit Taliban front-line positions weaving their ways through inhabited villages in the central plains and north, and later massively bomb villages around Tora Bora and in Paktia Province, not to mention the week-long campaign in later November in the Kandahar region when U.S. planes hit just about anything moving on highways around Kandahar, Uzurgan, and Helmand Provinces, led to extremely high civilian impact deaths. Anyone even vaguely familiar with the lethal blast range and the effective casualty radius of the U.S. bombers' favored munitions—the "precision-guided" 500- and 2,000-lb. JDAM bombs—full well realizes that the damage caused by a building possibly hit in Kabul or Kandahar, a village possibly hit in the Shomali Plains, and so on, necessarily extends beyond the impact site (even if the bomb does fall on target). U.S. planes hit many targets per sortie in Afghanistan and this fact, along with the use of powerful munitions, led to a cascading number of civilian deaths. The bombing in Iraq and in Serbia was focused to a far greater extent upon relatively large perceived military targets and physical infrastructure (of which Afghanistan had very little) and the armies of both Iraq and Serbia were of a much more traditional organization than the decentralized Taliban militia and batallions. This point is alluded to by retired Air Force General Merrill McPeak, the top Air Force general during the Persian Gulf War, who in a much cited remark, warned that because the conflict in Afghanistan is far less structured than in the Gulf War, civilian casualties may be harder to prevent.[35] He stressed how civilian and military sites often blended together.

My point is that to make assumptions of *ceteris paribus* and not to admit the specificity of the U.S. aerial campaign waged upon Afghanistan merely contributes to greater confusion than explanation.

CLAIM: Herold's sources are unreliable. One who makes this assertion is saying the reporters for major newspapers and newswire services whom I quote are either dupes or liars. Fleeson (2002), for example, approvingly cites a couple American reporters, one of whom says the Pakistani press "is very often inaccurate—inaccurate with precision in numbers and inaccurate with precision in facts." I have relied upon established, reputable news media sources complemented with the occasional NGO report. Many of the reporters have lived in the area and speak local languages. If my critics wish to argue that such experienced people have been misled by Taliban news reports, I suggest that they write the editors of these newspapers and present documentation to that effect. One editorial in a mainstream corporate newspaper alleged that I employed "hearsay" as a source. My database is publicly available and I defy anyone to locate an instance of hearsay being used. A somewhat similar rhetorical ploy is used by Karen DeYoung of the *Washington Post*, who cites my study in the same paragraph wherein she dismisses Taliban claims as having little basis in fact.[36] The next paragraphs lay out the "correct approach" as being to either plead ignorance in the face of confusion, or to rely upon a future study by Human Rights Watch. John Donnelly of the *Boston Globe* cites my dossier but then adds, "much of that report included single source accounts from the Afghan Islamic Press."[37] A perusal of my publicly database indicates that is incorrect (less than one-tenth of my sources are "single source accounts from the Afghan Islamic Press"). Moreover, as mentioned in the dossier, the AIP has actually proven to be very accurate (see my detailed story of the reporting on the Asmani Kilai incident).[38]

The reliability of Pakistani news sources has been questioned by my detractors. Let us examine how two incidents were reported by the independent Pakistani press and the U.S. corporate media. On the evening of November 16, U.S. planes dropped three bombs upon buildings in Khost, seeking to kill a prominent Taliban leader, Maulvi Jalaluddin Haqqani. Bombs fell upon Haqqani's religious seminary (*madrassa*) and the Light of Koran mosque. Both Reuters and Behroz Khan (in the Pakistani daily, *The News International*) reported that 15 to 34 religious students were killed in the mosque.[39] The Pentagon conceded that one of the three bombs dropped on Khost had strayed and possibly killed some civilians. Nothing else was mentioned in the U.S. press until February 2, when John Burns published an article in *The New York Times* mentioning the mosque incident, as well as the related bombing of another guesthouse nearby in Zani Khel, in which 20 innocent people were killed.[40] The Zani Khel incident is also mentioned by Reuters, *Arabia News,* and Behroz Khan, citing respectively "19 members of one family" being killed in the raid, and "18 persons, including six bodyguards of Taliban Minister..., Haqqani and the entire family of his host...." In other words, Pakistani/Reuters reported 18 to 19 deaths, while *The New York Times* reported 20.

About one month later, U.S. war planes attacked a convoy en route to the inauguration ceremony of the new prime minister in Kabul. On December 21, the Pakistani *News International*, the Afghan Islamic Press, and the BBC reported that at least 15 civilians had died in Asmani Kilai, a number raised to 65 during the next 24 hours. Subsequent reports cited civilian casualties of "at least 60."[41] Once again, the early reports emanating from Pakistan proved to be correct.

5. SOME SPECIFIC EXAMPLES OF MIS-REPRESENTING AFGHAN CIVILIAN CASUALTIES BY THE U.S. MAINSTREAM CORPORATE PRESS

Twenty-four hours after a CIA drone fired Hellfire missiles upon "three tall Afghan men" near Zhawar Killi on February 4, I had been contacted by two mainstream staff reporters who were writing "stories" about civilian casualties in Afghanistan. Chip Cummins of the *Wall Street Journal* phoned my office mid-afternoon of February 5 and a bit later a very persistent Cindy Roberts of the New York office of the Associated Press contacted me. Both reporters subsequently published articles and I will examine these as typical exemplars of the corporate mainstream reporting on civilian casualties caused by the U.S. air war.[42]

The Cummins column presents an accurate summary of my report, though noting that it had "drawn sharp criticism," after mentioning that a Human Rights Watch (HRW) "research" team led by William M. Arkin will visit Afghanistan in March to investigate about 100 "credible" reports of civilian deaths. Apparently in early December, the HRW privately estimated such deaths at between 100 and 350. The use of nuanced wording is a method to de-legitimize accounts. My report is associated with "sharp criticism" whereas the word "credible" is associated with Human Rights Watch.[43] In an article in the *San Francisco Chronicle* which reported on my study, the reporter uses the descriptive adjective "controversial,"[44] whereas Barry Bearak et. al. in *The New York Times* eschew all such negative bracketing and simply present the results of the Herold and Conetta reports.[45]

But Cummins then pulls out the major, standard critique when he notes that "human-rights groups have said it [my report] is flawed because it relies on second- and third-hand reporting." This argument can be answered in at least two ways: I have done nothing different than most news reporters do and it collapses into the Doubting Thomas position. Most news reporters are far away from events they describe and rely upon wire reports, phone conversations, conversations with eyewitnesses, and so on. The news reports I cite have been compiled using just such procedures. The second retort involves rejecting an old view that asserts that one must see (or be there to see) in order to know the truth: "Now Thomas (called Didymus), one of the Twelve, was not with the disciples when Jesus came. So the other disciples told him, 'We have seen the Lord!' But he said to them, 'Unless I see the nail marks in his hands and put my finger where the nails were, and put my hand into his side, I will not believe it.'"

Unless I, a Westerner, see the Afghan civilian dismembered bodies and graves, I will not believe the deaths occurred. A towering example of a modern-day Didymus is military analyst, one-time army intelligence officer and consultant to Human Rights Watch, the feisty William Arkin, who with indignant righteousness constantly inveighs the mantra that an accurate count can only be gotten by on-site visits, preferably by himself. A professor of journalism concurs with Arkin.[46]

A more vicious attack upon my dossier chronicling Afghan civilian casualties was launched by Associated Press writers Laura King and Deb Riechmann, and foreign desk editor Cindy Roberts, who provided background materials to the first two. King begins, "although estimates have placed the civilian dead in the thousands, a review by the Associated Press suggests the toll may be in the mid-hundreds, a figure reached by examining hospital records, visiting bomb sites, and interviewing eyewitnesses and officials."[47]

We are then told how the Kabul civilian death toll was calculated from hospital tallies, yet most dead Afghans were never brought to hospitals to be counted. The author also mentions that "AP reporters visited these [bombed] areas during the course of the war and gathered data on civilian casualties. Their reporting and other reliable counts—by no means complete—suggest a civilian death toll ranging from 500 to 600."

A month earlier, Michael Evans, defense editor of *The Times* (London) had noted the steadily rising civilian casualties notwithstanding the use of "precision weapons," noting that conservative estimates put the death toll at 1,000, though "it may be considerably higher. One recent unofficial report by an American academic said that the death toll among civilians could be closer to 4,000."[48]

Where detailed information is provided by the AP—the bombing incidents of the Khair Khana neighborhood in Kabul on October 21 and Darul Aman on October 23—it does not contravene our estimates. In the former example, King mentions how the original Taliban Bakhtar agency reporter cited eight civilian deaths, but this supposedly got adjusted upwards by the Taliban officials to thirty. My data base reports figures of 9 to 18, listing more than a dozen sources which a reader might consult. In the Darul Aman bombing, on October 23, military deaths were reported as civilian ones, but my report indicates 25 to 34 Pakistani soldiers dying in this bombing attack.[49]

The next step in King's attack is to quote a one-time Bakhtar news reporter, Mohammed Ismail, who states that the Taliban higher-ups doctored civilian casualty figures upwards. Examples cited by King include the October 21 bombing of Khair Khana and the October 23 attack of Darul Aman—examples that then get replayed in the corporate mainstream press with Fleeson mentioning these three items in April and Zucchino in June.[50] But why should we believe Mr. Ismail today, who has been promoted by the Kabul government? We are informed that "Afghanistan was almost completely closed to the outside world and figures could not be verified." Death tolls, allegedly, took on a life of their own once "they were electronically indexed and archived. In some cases, they served as the basis for academic research." In other words, let us be clear here, the studies by Herold and Conetta stand accused of naively relying upon electronically archived, doctored Taliban data. The *San Francisco Chronicle* article, for example, cited unnamed critics of my dossier who asserted that I relied "on casualty reports from sources such as the Al Jazeera TV network and the Pakistan-based Afghan Islamic Press, which U.S. officials say sometimes based their reports on false information put out by the Taliban."[51] The weekly *Time* magazine cited my report and immediately qualified it as "drawing mostly on world-press reports of questionable reliability."[52]

Luckily, this will be corrected but we must wait for a "full and reasonably accurate estimate of civilian casualties" in the reports of Afghan aid agencies (AREA and Afghan Red Crescent) and by Human Rights Watch (again), which has collected information on 300 bombing incidents of which only about a third have "real credibility." But some sentences later, an AREA official admits that as time passes, the difficulty of compiling an estimate of actual civilian deaths increases—physical evidence disappears, witnesses and families become harder to find, and peoples' recollections get confused. This latter point is very important and emphasizes why we believe that the most accurate counting of the dead is made shortly after a bombing incident.

The women of the AP and Fleeson (2002) are simply wrong when they whine about "the almost complete absence of outside reporters" in Afghanistan. Many credible, experienced reporters often speaking local languages were in Afghanistan writing wire reports, compiling information for newspaper reports, and writing independent stories (e.g., Rahimullah Yusufzai,[53] Jonathan Neale,[54] and so on). Two full-time reporters and staff for Al Jazeera were in Kabul and Kandahar. Three British reporters for *The Independent* were both in Afghanistan and in the border areas, continually filing stories (Robert Fisk, Richard Lloyd Parry, and Justin Huggler) as were reporters for *The Guardian*. Reporters for the Pakistani press filed reports and elsewhere I have verified that these early reports by local news persons were later corroborated as being accurate—the mainstream corporate press discovered the real, old news.[55] The prestigious Committee for the Protection of Journalists (the CPJ) noted in its annual report 2001 for Asia that although the Taliban were hostile to (most) foreign journalists, some journalists did slip into the country, Al Jazeera was "another crucial source of information about the consequences of the U.S. bombing campaign, and local wire service agency reporters (like Amir Shah of the AP, Sayed Salahuddin of Reuters, Amir Latif of Islam Online in Kandahar, Said Mohammad Azam of Agence France-Presse, and so on) were a consistent source of reliable information.[56]

We are never told what the AP's universe of covered bombing incidents was, who these AP reporters were (besides the Canadian Kathy Gannon whose reports I used), presented with refutable evidence, or why new Afghan officials should be credible? We are simply asked to believe.

The AP report is not serious research, but merely a postmodern pastiche of convenient anecdotes.

To admit the difficulty involved in counting civilian casualties from U.S. bombing in Afghanistan need not deter from attempting to carry out such a research project. Not to do so merely leaves the field of discourse filled with pious words of the Pentagon and its cohorts. A report in *Cox Newspapers* pointed out some of the alleged particularities of Afghanistan, making a counting of the dead difficult: "among the problems: the remote areas of Afghanistan that were targeted; the lack of international humanitarian workers and journalists in the country to serve as impartial witnesses; and cultural practices that make it difficult to discern the size of households and thus the number of deaths."[57]

As the Appendix 5 in my dossier indicates, the vast bulk of civilian impact deaths did not occur in remote regions. The lament about absence of impartial observers, besides being wrong, implicitly assumes that locals and news reporters are biased.

Sometimes, Afghan "cultural practices" are pointed to as making a counting of the dead neigh impossible (Fleeson, 2002). The Muslim practice of burying the dead immediately thwarts matching bodies with personal testimonies. The poor cannot afford gravestones.[58] Pascal Du Port of the International Committee of the Red Cross in Afghanistan, said, "People weren't taking bodies to hospitals or government, but burying them very quickly.... It's very difficult for anyone to know how many died and how many were wounded...."

But, can Muslims count or not? They can count bodies before burying them. The absence of municipal records often makes knowing the population of a village difficult.[59] Yet we do know that the average Afghan family size is about seven to eight and cultural practices of the extended family are no different there from in Southeast Asia or in Latin America.

All kinds of specious tricks, logical horrors, innuendo, unsubstantiated claims, untenable inference, and sophist's sleights of hand are used by the mainstream to advance the Bush "war on terror."[60] One of the corporate media's major assignments has been to diminish the significance of those irritating claims of civilian casualties caused by U.S. bombs.

A portfolio of such "tricks" includes the following:

➤Admit "some" casualties but immediately emphasize that the Taliban have a motive to inflate the number for propaganda purposes. Never ask whether the "other side" might have a motive to deflate.

➤Bury the details of air strikes upon civilians in a story about something else and/or print the story in the later pages of the newspaper, e.g., the Cummins story appeared on page 18. For example, unlike in British newspapers where the gory details were presented, *The New York Times* gave only cursory coverage to the U.S. attack upon the village of Qalaye Niazi on December 29, prompting FAIR to issue an action alert against *The New York Times*.[61]

➤Admit "some" casualties but solemnly inveigh these were accidental, unintentional. But if civilian deaths are necessarily inevitable given the weapons used in certain contexts, can we really say they are accidental?

➤Emphasize that claims of civilian casualties are "unverified" and "could not be independently confirmed." But, U.S. and U.K. claims that they weren't targeting civilians and were using precision weapons are equally unverified. The point here is that what the powerful say need not be verified but must simply be assumed as truth, a point I will return to below. Moreover, much past evidence exists that U.S. bombs have targeted civilian infrastructure, just as they have in Afghanistan.

➤In the face of a specific number cited for civilian deaths in a particular incident, merely assert a much smaller "more likely" number without providing any backup to the assertion.

➤Avoid dealing with specific details and rather talk/write in the catch phrases that resonate with a programmed general public.

➤Employ innuendo and guilt by association whenever needed to diminish the credibility of a report on civilian casualties. For example, Kenneth Roth (executive director of Human Rights Watch) sarcastically writes how the Internet has allowed me to gather data on civilian casualties "without ever leaving my desk in New Hampshire," with the obvious implication that a Human Rights Watch team dispatched to Afghanistan will by virtue of being on-the-scene, collect accurate information.[62] I relied upon data collected by persons—like Sayed Salahuddin, Kathy Gannon, Mohammed Bashir, Behroz Khan and countless others—who were close to the bombing attacks. I trust their reporting.

➤Use deprecating language to "qualify" what is considered to be irritating analysis. A good illustration of that was when *The New York Times* recently contrasted my dossier with that put together by the Project on Defense Alternatives. *The New York Times* solemnly intoned the latter research had "used a more stringent distillation of media accounts" when in fact, the appropriate characterization is "used a less inclusive" compilation of media accounts.[63] The choice by Carl Conetta lead researcher of the PDA. study to only employ "Western" sources certainly made the study more acceptable and respectable in a nation increasingly hostile to persons of Arab and South Asian nationality.

Credible or hearsay? The counting of the dead caused by U.S. bombs is a messy, inexact task. As explained elsewhere, I have relied upon a variety of sources. Criticisms have been levied at my dossier, which merit correction. One argues that no or very few credible journalists were in Afghanistan for many weeks and hence accurate reporting was impossible. Besides simply presuming without evidence that Ambassador Zaeff, Bakhter News Agency, and Pakistani sources are liars, this is simply factually not true. Luke Harding in Islamabad, of *The Guardian*, noted on October 12 that "the three main news agencies, Reuters, Associated Press, and Agence France-Presse, all have reputable Afghan correspondents in Kabul."[64]

Persons like Sayed Salahuddin, Mohammed Bashir, and Zeeshan Haidar, reported regularly for the major news wire services. British and Pakistani journalists were in the border areas and often in Afghanistan filing news stories, for example, people like Richard Lloyd Parry and Behroz Khan. Harding continues, "another important source of news is the Afghan Islamic Press (AIP) agency, run buy one man, Sharafat Ali, from the Pakistani border town of Peshawar. AIP has excellent Taliban contacts. But most of its reports have a pro-Taliban slant, and need to be treated with some caution."

Precisely! One might similarly say of the *Washington Post*, "most of its reports have a pro-Washington slant, and need to be treated with some caution."

I traced the reporting of U.S. bomb attacks by the Afghan Islamic Press in a number of cases and found its original estimates to be highly accurate. Others have also deemed the AIP to issue "credible" news bulletins. For example, Masood Farivar wrote in a prestigious CPJ (Committee to Protect Journalists) Press Freedom Report (December 1999), "the old resistance organs have been replaced by new independent publications. Two new agencies, Afghan Islamic Press and Sahaar News Agency, feed reasonably credible news bulletins to Western wire services...."[65]

This assessment was echoed recently by John Burns writing in *The New York Times*: "The Afghan Islamic Press, a private news agency with a credible record of reporting on Afghan fighting…"[66]

At the very least, the AIP provides a counterweight to those many experienced Western journalists' who for three months packed the Pentagon's press room and regurgitated Pentagon statements as "truths." A model of reporting might be Reuters, which recognizes that interested parties have incentives to bias reporting, but relies on the expertise and integrity of its individual reporters to verify sources.

In a long exploration of "the civilian casualty conundrum," Professor Lucinda Fleeson (2002) presents the standard critique of reports by Herold and Conetta. She asserts that U.S. war correspondents, having "higher reporting standards than the foreign media" (notwithstanding that for months this U.S. media was content to serve as stenographers of Donald Rumsfeld and Colonel Hagenbeck), chose in the face of a dearth of 'hard data on casualties' to remain largely mute. But Herold and Conetta forged ahead, largely using Internet data to derive spurious overall counts. Fleeson assaults these writers for not engaging in painstaking reconstruction of bombing gone awry [sic!] and for uncritically accepting second-hand accounts. She goes on to claim these studies suffer from multiple counting of the same incident reported by different sources. In fact, Fleeson doesn't realize the elementary difference between multiple sources mentioning one incident (possibly all relying upon one original dispatch or eyewitness account), and counting the same bombing incident many times as separate incidents. A casual perusal of my Appendix 4, would clearly reveal no such multiple counting.

During a visit by Fleeson at her own expense, to the University of New Hampshire to "check me out first-hand," I learned of her methods and preferences. She had asked me for my raw data for various days, including bombings in the Shomali Plain and Kapisa Valley area on October 27. Whereas Kate Rowlands, a staff member in the Italian medical agency, Emergency, who had lived in the area for years, reported first-hand eyewitness accounts of eight to nine people dying in the three villages of Kikhahil, Ghanikheil, and Raqi, Ms. Fleeson preferred to rely upon the casualty estimate of a *Washington Post* reporter, William Branigan, who had just dropped into Raqi. Similar veneration of Western reporters by Fleeson gets revealed in her approval of the Laura King AP report, and especially her awe before William M. Arkin—"probably the world's leading expert in civilian casualties"—and Human Rights Watch.

A Washington-based military analyst and frequent radio commentator, Arkin has sought to minimize the importance of and public discomfort felt about civilian casualties from the U.S. air war.[67] Arkin makes three points: 1. Civilian deaths are to be expected given that the air campaign will last more than a few weeks because the Pentagon wants to destroy everything the Taliban may use (e.g., barracks, vehicle parks, and so on); 2. The public and even military and government officials overstate civilian deaths especially after a war; and 3. There is a popular myth that a ground war both guarantees military success and is less dangerous to non-combatants. With regards to the second point, Arkin cites 3,200 civilian deaths in the Persian Gulf War's 43 days, and 500 civilian deaths in Yugoslavia in 78 days of NATO bombing. In the Gulf War, 9 percent of the firepower used were "smart weapons," compared to 35 percent in Yugoslavia. Arkin then turns to Afghanistan, arguing that targets are in its less populated areas and the percentage of smart weapons will be much higher. Hence, we need not be overly concerned about civilian "collateral damage."

As it turns out, on the very day Mr. Arkin wrote his piece, U.S. bombs killed 71 to 105 civilians in four Afghan provinces.[68] A F-18 dropped a 1,000-lb. cluster bomb on a 100-bed military hospital in Heart, killing 25, bombs killed 10 to 19 in two residential districts of Kabul and 21 to 32 in the city of Tarin Kot in the Uruzgan Mountains, 23 in the farming village of Doori located six hours away from Kandahar, and four more Afghan civilians perished in Parvan and Kandahar provinces. On October 21, the U.S. also began carpet-bombing Taliban front-line positions around Bagram in the Shomali Valley north of Kabul.

A month later, the same William Arkin urged the Pentagon to hit more Taliban buildings, bridges, electrical power, and oil storage facilities.[69] He notes that by mid-November, the Pentagon had dropped some 6,000 bombs and missiles—that is, about 12 weapons an hour on a country the size of Texas. We are informed by Bill Arkin that U.S. planes did not hit the Kajakai hydroelectric complex in Helmand province on October 31, yet eyewitnesses report seven U.S raids hitting nearby cars and the power station. The city lights went out in Lashkargah and Kandahar, yet Arkin, siding with the Pentagon, asserts the U.S. target was "nearby caves."

I am reminded of "Wild Bill" Hickok, "in the service of upstanding justice," about whom has been said, "It would be learned of 'Wild Bill' Hickok in later years that he had a certain bent toward straining the truth now and then when it was to his advantage to do so. Of course in this situation he figured that it was right and proper to get creative in the service of upstanding justice…"[70]

Fleeson waxes lyrical before Arkin's use of population density maps, his Fujitsu laptop computer, and his GPS maps, complemented with alleged on-site investigations (of bomb craters, destroyed structures, graveyards, and interviews). Contrast all that with Fleeson's patronizing and de-legitimizing language about Herold's handwritten notes on 3 x 5 cards, his use of foreign graduate students, and the general chaos Fleeson observed in the professor's office (not to mention gratuitous comments about my health). Conetta gets dismissed for using a method relying entirely upon induction. When one examines the utterances of Arkin, his agenda is quickly revealed. For example, in late January on CNBC's *Hardball*, Arkin steadfastly defended the Pentagon's attack of Hazar Qadam village on January 24, despite mounting reports of a misdirected attack, confidently responding that the only people being snookered in Afghanistan are the reporters who come up with these stories of flawed attacks.[71]

How might data on civilian casualties be collected? I need first reiterate that the only civilian casualties covered in this study are those that occurred upon impact of the aerial device, or what I call impact deaths. I omit all deaths resulting later from injuries, diseases, lack of hospital treatment or of clean water, later cluster bomblet explosions, and so on. In general, data can be gathered from the following seven sources:

1. Computer-based simulation modeling exercises (which the Pentagon allegedly employed);
2. Death certificates (though these are not common in Afghanistan);
3. Graves (though these are often not identified as single or as multiple and many bodies have likely simply disappeared). I have numerous reports that mention survivors burying parts of many dead in a single grave;
4. Hospital records (which are mostly unavailable and do not report impact deaths);
5. Body counts (which are difficult after major blasts);
6. Accounts of relatives and survivors;
7. Assessments by journalists and/or others who visited the incident scene shortly after the impact deaths.

A challenge might be raised that survivor accounts in the immediate aftermath of the bombing incident might be especially inaccurate, confused by the emotional severity from the immediate tragedy, which results in unintentional exaggeration. Stories gathered later might be freer of such "immediate post-impact exaggeration" bias, which leads to distress inflation. I argue that information gathered months later from those still residing in the area "hit" will more than likely be downward-biased as people will have focused upon their immediate family and friend victims, or what I call "post-trauma centripetal memory loss" as time passes (the idea being that memory focuses over time upon central personal relationships to the exclusion of others).

The overwhelming number of U.S, air attacks in Afghanistan has been either upon homes or public spaces in cities or upon small villages in rural or mountain regions, where people know each other. Thus, relying upon personal accounts and journalists' assessments taken shortly after the impact deaths will tend to be accurate, or at least more accurate than other forms of data collection. Most of the reports cited in this study follow this approach, being based upon journalists assessments, upon wire press releases, upon reports by NGOs, and upon reported first-hand accounts.

The literature on civilian casualties caused by the U.S. bombing is completely silent on the psychology of those being bombed. Military strategist, George Quester, has advanced an interesting hypothesis linking aerial bombing with psycho-political behaviors of the bombed.[72] Quester suggests that the critical intervening variable is not a population's stoicism, but rather its expectations concerning the bombing. If the effects of bombing exceed expectations, that is, is a surprise, then a population will react by opposing its government and/or by defeatism. Quester's expectancy hypothesis argues a bombed population will act in a way its aggressor wishes if the destructiveness of the aerial attacks exceeds the population's expectations. Certainly, the British bombings of Afghanistan in 1919 had that effect with the amir quickly suing for peace. The situation in 2001 is more complex. The successful mujahideen war against the Soviets in the 1980s and their ability to withstand ferocious Soviet bombing undoubtedly created an expectation in both Taliban officialdom and the Afghan population that a similar resistance could be mounted against the Americans. This sense of invincibility of the Taliban was compounded by the ease with which the Taliban came to power in 1996. But the great effectiveness of U.S. bombing, quickly obliterating Taliban military targets, and the complete ineffectiveness of Taliban air defenses, set in motion a two-fold process. On the one hand, the Taliban had to under-report the numbers of bombing victims in order to offset likely popular defeatism (caused by Quester's expectancy hypothesis). On the other hand, Taliban and their allied troops suffered disastrously under U.S. bombs that, according to Quester's hypothesis, would lead them to capitulate or defect. That happened. As regards the Afghan civilian population and the world public (especially Muslim) opinion, the Taliban under-reported the number of bombing victims, a deception that was possible given the disruption of information flows amongst the Afghan population.

A comment in "liberal" *The Nation* (February 4, 2002) by Michael Massing[73] employs the journalistic trick of selective quotation to discredit my dossier, by putting in quotations my use of the term criminal to describe some U.S. bombing and my assertion that mainstream corporate media engaged in some lying. I make the latter claim and support it with detail in my Appendix 2.[74] Massing objects to my use of the word "criminal" in describing some U.S. bombing incidents. I employ this word having in mind the U.S. bombing of civilian installations and infrastructure in Afghanistan. An organization undoubtedly dear to my critic, Human Rights Watch, castigates NATO for doing just that in its bombing of Serbian civilian facilities in 1999 (e.g., radio stations, bridges, and so on) and for hitting military targets close to civilian areas without giving adequate prior warning. I also have in mind U.S. violation of the practice of proportionate response in Afghanistan.[75]

Mr. Massing decided to verify my account by focusing upon one incident, the October 11 bombing raid on the village of Karam near Jalalabad. My publicly available data base cites civilian impact death figures for Karam of 100 to 200, listing half a dozen sources (more available upon request). Massing chooses rather to consult sources in Lexis-Nexis, that is, sources from the mainstream corporate press. Let us see what he finds. Karam is cited six times. Four articles provide some detail of the Karam incident—three in the British press and one in the *St. Petersberg Times*. Two articles (in *The Telegraph* and *The Independent* by its Washington correspondent) merely recite the Taliban figure of 200 casualties. The column in the Floridian *The St. Petersberg Times* (October 13, 2001) mentions an unnamed Pakistani on temporary assignment for *The New York Times*, who quoted a villager in Karam saying 53 persons had died. By far the greatest detail is given in Richard Lloyd Parry's article in *The Independent*, upon which I have partly relied in coming to my estimate, as well as from a detailed account by Jason Burke from Peshawar for *The Observer*.[76] Parry, a senior reporter for the London-based *Independent* newspaper, was in the border area and wrote from Peshawar (Pakistan). But I also cite reports from Agence France-Presse and from the Peshawar-based daily, *The Frontier Post*.[77] Yet another source I used though did not cite, provided refugee confirmation of 100 and some civilian casualties, independent from Taliban sources.[78]

Let me now elaborate upon why I used a figure of 100 to 160 civilian impact deaths in Karam. Karam is a small village in a valley, comprised once of some 60 mud brick and rock dwellings. Each dwelling houses six people (about the average family size in Afghanistan). Apparently, 60 to 70 poor, landless families have lived there since the 1990s, joined by nomads during the winter. Reports stressed that 40 to 45 of the homes were flattened. Two U.S. fighter jets made repeated runs upon Karam at 3:45 A.M., precisely during prayer time on Wednesday/Thursday night. Reporters visiting later reported upon craters each 3 to 4 feet deep and 10 to 12 feet wide. Parry cites Danish Karwakhel, an Afghan who lives in Kabul and is a correspondent for *Wahadat*, a Pakistani-Pashto language daily. Karwakhel, who passed through the village on his way from Kabul to Pakistan, noted that 40 of the 60 huts had been flattened and about 100 civilian deaths had occurred with many still missing. Articles in *The Frontier Post* newspaper of Peshawar provide very similar figures.

Mr. Massing chooses to ignore all this, blithely concluding, "Herold's estimates seem to be on the high side but substantial enough to warrant a closer look." How gracious. I have documented hundreds of bombing incidents, read over 1000 newspaper accounts on such, publicly divulged my sources, and committed the apparent sin of relying upon reports in major daily newspapers and newswire services from outside the United States (and not included in the LexisNexis database).

Truth apparently comes only when wrapped in red, white, and blue and blessed by LexisNexis, according to Michael Massing and others in the ideologico-propaganda establishment. Let us recall Mahtab, the refugee in Peshawar, who said, "she is angry at America, and when she is told that the United States is trying to minimize civilian casualties, she answered with a list of neighborhoods where innocents have been killed: Khuja Bughra, Maidan Hawai, and others. Her patience wore away quickly at this subject. "It is easier to understand if it is you being bombed," she said."[79]

Yes, it is easier to understand if it is *you being bombed*.

Marc W. Herold is a Professor in the Departments of Economics and Women's Studies at Whittemore School of Business & Economics, University of New Hampshire, Durham, NH 03824.

NOTES

1. Anthony Lloyd, "Don't Believe All the Major Tells You," *The Times* (London), May 10, 2002.

2. The original dossier was published on the Internet on December 10, by San Francisco-based Media Alliance, "Who Will Count the Dead? U.S. Media Fail to Report Civilian Casualties in Afghanistan," Media File 21, 1, December 2001, <www.media-alliance.org/mediafile/20-5>. Subsequently, updated and revised versions have appeared at the Cursor Web site at <www.cursor.org/stories/civilian_deaths.htm>. The daily civilian casualties data base is available at <http://pubpages.unh.edu/~mwherold>.

3. Edward M. Spiers, "Gas and the North-West Frontier," *Journal of Strategic Studies* 6, 4, 1983: 94-112.

4. Sven Lindqvist, A History of Bombing (New York: The Free Press, 2000): 42.

5. From Richard S. Ehrlich, "Bombing Afghanistan," <http://zolatimes.com/V5.41/afghan_bombing.html>, also printed in *The Bangkok Post*.

6. "Afghan Terror: Effect of Air Raids," *The Times*, May 24, 1919: 12; and *The New York Times*, May 13, 1919:2.

7. Llyod, "Don't Believe all the Mayor Tells You," *The Times*.

8. "Kabul Bombed," *The Times* (May 29, 1919): 11. Also described in Robert Strausz-Hupe, "The Anglo-Afghan War of 1919," *Military Affairs* 7,2 (Summer 1943): 89-96.

9. The only other report to-date counting civilian casualties emphasizes the former elements. The report, while useful, is, in my opinion questionable, insofar as it employs only so-called Western sources for information on bombing incidents and the author has not published his disaggregated day-by-day count of casualties as I have. The report is Carl Conetta, *Operation Enduring Freedom: Why a Higher Rate of Civilian Bombing Casualties* (Cambridge, MA.: Project on Defense Alternatives, Briefing Report #11, January 18, 2002).

10. Carlotta Gall, "Shattered Afghan Families Demand U.S. Compensation," *The New York Times*, April 8, 2002: A11.

11. Loren Thompson, *What Works? VIII. The Joint Direct Attack Munition: Making Acquisition Reform a Reality* (Arlington, VA: Lexington Institute, November 1999).

12. Nicholas J. Wheeler, "Protecting Afghan Civilians From the Hell of War" (New York: Social Science Research Center Viewpoint Essay #9, December 2001): 5-6.

13. Michael Walzer, *Just and Unjust Wars: A Moral Argument with Historical Illustrations* (London: Allen Lane, 1977): 156.

14. On U.S. cluster bombs in Afghanistan, see my "Above the Law and Below Morality: Data on 11 Weeks of U.S. Cluster-Bombing of Afghanistan ("shining like a diamond, death comes in *a little yellow soda can*") at <www.cursor.org/stories/abovethelaw.htm>.

15. This subject is explored in my "Rubble Rousers: U.S. Bombing and the Afghan Refugee Crisis," at <www.cursor.org/stories/rubble.htm>.

16. See my Appendix 5. The Spatial Distribution of Afghan Civilian Casualties Caused by the U.S. Air War, in Marc W. Herold, *A Dossier on Civilian Victims of United States' Aerial Bombing of Afghanistan: A Comprehensive Accounting* (revised) (Durham, NH: monograph, Departments of Economics and Women's Studies, University of New Hampshire, March 2002), <www.cursor.org/stories/civilian_deaths.htm>.

17. Edward S. Herman, "Kosovo and DoubleSpeak," *ZNet Commentary*, June 15, 1999. Also Norman Solomon, "Orwellian Logic 101—A Few Simple Lessons," at <www.fair.org/

media-beat/980827.html> and Euan Ferguson, "Language of Conflict," *The Observer*, September 2001.

18. Human Rights Watch, "The War Through My Eyes—Children's Drawings of Chechnya" (New York: Human Rights Watch, 1999-2000).

19. Barry Bearak, "In The Village Where Civilians Died, Anger Cannot be Buried," *The New York Times*, December 16, 2001: B1.

20. Barry Bearak," Escaping Afghanistan, Children Pay the Price," *The New York Times*, October 31, 2001.

21. Seumas Milne, "The Innocent Dead in a Coward's War," *The Guardian*, December 20, 2001, <www.guardian.co.uk/afghanistan/story/0,1284,622000,00.html>.

22. Miles Kemp, "Innocence A Victim in Afghanistan. Justice?" *National News Pty. Ltd. The Advertiser*, December 22, 2001.

23. Simon Briscoe, "Afghan Civilian Death Toll Rises," *The Financial Times*, December 24, 2001: 7.

24. Kevin Canfield, "No Winners in Battle To Gauge Cost of War," *The Hartford Courant*, December 26, 2001: A1.

25. "Afghanistan's Civilian Deaths Mount," *BBC News Online*, January 3, 2002 at 16:14 GMT.

26. Murray Campbell, "Thousands of Afghans Likely Killed in Bombings," *Toronto Globe & Mail*, January 4, 2002: A1 and A8.

27. Karen DeYoung, "More Bombing Casualties Alleged. U.N. Aide 'Concerned'; Rumsfeld Defends Airstrike Targeting," *Washington Post*, January 4, 2002: A18 ; Stephanie Schorow, "Net Life; N.H. Professor Shines Light on Bombs' Toll Among Afghan Civilians," *Boston Herald*, January 15, 2002: 40.

28. Robert Jensen and Rahul Mahajan, "We Can't Just Forget About Dead Afghans," *The Houston Chronicle*, December 20, 2001 at <www.chron.com/CDA/story.hts/editorial/outlook/1181572>.

29. Roberto J. Gonzalez, "Ignorance is Not Bliss. Lack of Reporting Civilian Casualties From the War in Afghanistan is Keeping Americans in the Dark—And Endangering Their Future," *San Francisco Chronicle*, January 2, 2002.

30. "Operation Enduring Freedom: Why a Higher Rate of Civilian Casualties" (Cambridge, MA: Project on Defense Alternatives Briefing Report #11, 18 January 2002).

31. Granted use of dumb bombs might well have resulted in far higher casualties.

32. I leave aside the silly ad hominem type jabs made by some, for example, Jim Wooten, "Left Using Cynicism to Spin War," *The Atlanta Journal*, January 8, 2002. For a prime exemplar of derogatory, sexist, and racist commentary undeserving of a response, see the opinion piece by Kevin Myers, "An Irishman's Diary," *The Irish Times*, January 22, 2002 at: <http://scripts.ireland.com/search/highlight.plx?TextRes=Anpercent20Irishmanpercent27spercent20diary&Path=/newspaper/opinion/2002/0122/2371354307dijan22.html>.

33. Holger Jensen, "Propaganda War Escalates Along With Military Action," *Rocky Mountain News*, Denver, CO, November 8, 2001: 33A.

34. Arkin's view is uncritically presented in Zachary Coile, "Smart Bombs Put U.S. Strikes Under Greater Scrutiny," *San Francisco Chronicle*, January 13, 2002: A6.

35. Mentioned in Nancy Benac, "Death Toll Inching Up in Afghan War," *Washington Post*, December 5, 2001.

36. Karen DeYoung, "More Bombing Casualties Are Alleged. U.N. Aide 'Concerned'; Rumsfeld Defends Airstrike Targeting," *Washington Post*, January 4, 2002: A18. Note the significance of the term in quotation marks.

37. John Donnelly, "U.S. is Probing Cause, Degree of Civilian Toll," *Boston Globe*, January 19, 2001: A12.

38. Available as "An Average Day: 65 Afghan Civilians Killed by U.S. Bombs on December 20," at <www.cursor.org/stories/ontarget.htm>.

39. Reuters, "U.S. Bombs Kill 62 in Eastern Afghan Town," *Deccan Herald*, November 18, 2001; Behroz Khan, ""U.S. Planes Heavily Bomb Frontlines," *The News International*, November 19, 2001; and *Arabia News*, November 18, 2001, citing the Afghan Islamic Press.

40. John F. Burns, "Villagers Add to Reports of Raids Gone Astray," *The New York Times*, February 2, 2002: A9.

41. "15 Killed in U.S. Bombing Raid on Afghan Village," *The News International*, December 21, 2001, and "Confusion Over U.S. Bombing Raid," *BBC News Online*, December 21, 2001. Later reports noted 50 to 65 killed. See Mohammed Bashir, Reuters, "Locals Reject U.S. Account of Afghan Convoy Attack," December 22, 2001, Paul Harris and Peter Beaumont, "Up to 60 Die as U.S. Bombs Tribal Leaders By Mistake," *The Observer*, December 23, 2001, and the *Sunday Herald*, December 23, 2001, which reported the killing of 65.

42. Chip Cummins, "Human-Rights Group to Estimate Civilians Killed in U.S. Campaign," *Wall Street Journal*, February 7, 2002: A18; and Laura King, "Review: Afghan Civilian Deaths Lower," Associated Press, February 11, 2002, in *Yahoo!News Online*. Shorter versions of the King piece were fairly widely reproduced, see Laura King, "Taliban Doctored Civilian Casualty Toll," *Detroit News*, February 12, 2002.

43. No mention here that HRW's report on Yugoslav civilian deaths during the Serbian bombing campaign has been roundly criticized as counting only about one-third of the true civilian deaths.

44. Zachary Coile, "Smart Bombs Put U.S. Strikes Under Greater Scrutiny. Pentagon Tabulates Offensives But Not the Toll on Civilians," *San Francisco Chronicle*, January 13, 2002.

45. Barry Bearak, Eric Schmitt, and Craig S. Smith, "Uncertain Toll in the Fog of War: Civilian Deaths in Afghanistan," *The New York Times*, February 10, 2002: A1 and A14.

46. See Lucinda Fleeson, "The Civilian Casualty Conundrum," *American Journalism Review* 24, 3, April 2002.

47. King, "Review: Afghan Civilian Deaths Lower," Associated Press. Applies to quotes that follow as well.

48. Michael Evans, "'Precision Weapons' Fail to Prevent Mass Civilian Casualties," *The Times* (London), January 2, 2002.

49. These two incidents, in turn, get recycled and replayed in the corporate mainstream. On October 24, the Pakistani daily, *Dawn*, clearly noted that the Darul Aman attack had killed 34 Pakistanis, see "Bodies of Pakistanis to Arrive in Kabul Today," *Dawn*, October 24, 2001.

50. For example, David Zucchino cites the same two cases in his "In the Taliban's Eyes, Bad News was Good," *Los Angeles Times*, June 3, 2002.

51. Coile, *San Francisco Chronicle*.

52. Hannah Bloch et. al., "How Bad Are Civilian Casualties?" *Time*, January 14, 2002: 24.

53. Rahimullah Yusufzai, "Report: The Scripted War," Muzzling the Media [no date], <www.himalmag.com/2002/february/report_2.htm>.

54. A superb historical account setting the bombing campaign in context is provided by Jonathan Neale, who was in Afghanistan during the U.S. bombing campaign. See his "The Long Torment of Afghanistan," *International Socialism Journal* 93, Winter 2001, <www.isj1text.ble.org.uk/pubs/isj93/neale.htm>.

55. See Marc W. Herold, " U.S. Media Discovers the Real, Old News" posted February 17, 2002, <www.cursor.org/stories/oldnews.htm>.

56. Committee for Protection of Journalists, "Asia 2001: Afghanistan," (New York: CPJ Report, 2002).

57. Margaret Coker, "Counting Civilian Deaths is a Difficult Task," *Washington Cox Newspapers*, January 27, 2001.

58. The point about burying the dead quickly is made even by reporters concerned with civilian casualties; see the late Anthony Shahid, "Victims of Circumstance," *Middle East Report* 222, Spring 2002: 13.

59. These examples are mentioned by Craig Nelson, "U.S. Silence and Power of Weaponry Conceal Scale of Civilian Toll," *Sydney Morning Herald* , January 26, 2002.

60. The phrases are from Stephens Gowans, "Media Signs on to the War for the Hearts and Minds of the World, and Muslims in Particular," Media Monitors Network, October 17, 2001, <www.mediamonitors.net/gowans32.html>.

61. Fairness and Accuracy In Reporting [(AIR), "Action Alert: *NYT* Buries Story of Airstrikes on Afghan Civilians," *Action Alert,* January 9, 2002, <www.fair.org/activism/nyt-niazi-kala.html>.

62. Kenneth Roth, "Letter: Casualties of War," *The Guardian*, February 15, 2002.

63. Barry Bearak et. al.: A1 and A14.

64. Luke Harding, "Voice of the Taliban Keeps Up PR Offensive," *The Guardian*, October 12, 2001.

65. Masood Farivar, "Dateline Afghanistan: Journalism Under the Taliban," CPJ Briefings: Press Freedom Reports from around the Worldm December 1999.

66. John F. Burns, "In a Shift, U.S. Uses Airstrikes to Help Kabul," *The New York Times*, February 19, 2002: A1.

67. William M. Arkin, "Civilian Casualties and the Air War," *Washington Post*, October 21, 2001.

68. See Marc W. Herold, Appendix 4, at <http://pubpages.unh.edu/~mwherold> under October 21.

69. William M. Arkin, "Bad News in the Good News," *Washington Post*, November 12, 2001.

70. From <www.abacom.com/~jkrause/hickok.html>.

71. See Bill Berkowitz, "Bombs 'r' Us Cluster-Bombing Afghanistan and the Critics of the 'War on Terrorism,'" *Working for Change*, February 11, 2002, <www.workingfor-change.com/article.cfm?ItemID=12795>.

72. George C. Quester, "The Psychological Effects of Bombing on Civilian Populations: Wars of the Past," in Betty Glad (Ed.), *Psychological Dimensions of Wars* (Newbury Park, CA.: Sage, 1990): 201-214.

73. "Grief Without Portraits," *The Nation*, February 4, 2002: 6-8.

74. The database with daily casualty counts ban be found at <http://pubpages.unh.edu/~mwherold> and the accompanying essay at <www.cursor.org/stories/civilian_ deaths.htm>.

75. See articles by law professor Brian J. Foley, "U.S. Campaign Against Afghanistan Not Self-Defense Under International Law," *Counterpunch*, November 6, 2001, and the article by a former prosecutor at the Nuremberg War Crimes Trial, Walter J. Rocker, "War Crimes Law Applies to U.S. Too," *Chicago Tribune*, May 23, 1999.

76. Richard Lloyd Parry, "Witnesses Confirm That Dozens Were Killed in Bombing," *The Independent*, October 13, 2001, and Jason Burke, "U.S Admits Lethal Blunders," *The Observer*, October 14, 2001.

77. "Refugees Confirm Taliban's Casualties Report," *Frontier Post*, October 14, 2001, and "Afghanistan's Female Bombing Victims," *Frontier Post*, October 17, 2001.

78. Alex Spillius and Imtiaz Khan, "Refugees Back Taliban's Casualty Figures," The Telegraph, October 13, 2001.

79. Barry Bearak, "Escaping Afghanistan, Children Pay the Price," *The New York Times*, October 31, 2001.

CHAPTER 10

Leave No Child Untested

HOW NEW YORK STATE EXAMS CENSORED LITERATURE

BY JEANNE HEIFETZ

I have never been a professional journalist, but one of my first jobs after college was as a fact-checker for *American Heritage* magazine (no relation to the Heritage Foundation, by the way). After a writer turned in a piece, my job was to make sure it was accurate. Some writers, bless them, gave me a complete list of footnotes. Others would hand me a stack of books and say, "It's all in there somewhere." Still others, when queried about a particular fact, would shrug and say, "It came to me in a dream" or "I've always known that." Needless to say, "It came to me in a dream" is a fact-checker's nightmare. But the job gave me invaluable experience in pre-Internet research methods, and a healthy skepticism for the printed word.

I first turned that skepticism on the New York State Regents Exams because my stepdaughter, Rosa, was attending an alternative high school in New York City, one of 32 schools around New York State—the New York Performance Standards Consortium—that had achieved national recognition. These small schools offered a second chance—and sometimes a last chance—to kids who weren't making it in large, factory-style high schools. They had a terrific track record of educating largely low-income kids and sending over 90 percent of them on to college. An earlier, more enlightened Commissioner of Education, Thomas Sobol, had recognized their success by granting them a waiver from standardized tests so that they could assess students through meaningful in-depth projects undertaken over time: for example, to design, execute, and write up an original science experiment, and then defend their work before a panel of examiners.

But in my stepdaughter's sophomore year, these schools came under threat from the current, benighted commissioner, Rick Mills. Like many in the so-called "Standards" movement, he insisted that standardized testing for all was a way of raising expectations for kids and the *only* way to measure whether students had met the State Learning Standards. For those of us who cared deeply about the alternative schools, these tests were a terrifying prospect. We knew that their superficial, "If this is Tuesday, we must be studying the Civil War" approach to learning was never going to engage kids, or get them ready for college. The kind of preparation kids need for college and work is complex, and we knew that to work, assessments have to be complex, too.

The first test to be implemented, in June 1999, was the English Language Arts exam, a six-hour, two-day affair. (By 2003 students would have to pass five such tests to graduate.) The censorship began on the very first exam, but I didn't discover it right away, and wasn't even looking for censorship when I found it. I was just trying to figure out whether these exams were a reasonable way—I knew they weren't the only way—to measure the State Learning Standards.

The first clue came on the January 2001, exam, which contained a "speech" attributed to Anne Lamott. From what I knew of Lamott, the idea of her delivering a formal speech on writing dialogue was completely out of character. The logical source of the "speech" was her book on writing, *Bird By Bird*, which I had on my shelf. Looking at the two side by side, I saw that the State Education Department (SED) had indeed lifted her chapter on dialogue—but not all of it. They'd cut and pasted and rearranged, which was horrifying enough; they'd also quietly excised anything even mildly controversial.

The SED seemed bent on removing every bit of personality from Lamott's writing. For example, Lamott says she doesn't want characters "to think all the time on paper. It's bad enough that *I* have to think all the time **without having someone else dump all his or her obsessive-compulsive, paranoid thinking on me, too.**" The altered sentence (**the words in bold have been cut from the test**) is flat instead of crisp and funny and memorable. The SED had taken a book about writing by a teacher of writing, cut it up so that the writer's own voice was unrecognizable, and then had the temerity to say that this altered work was something Lamott had actually said in public. And in what I would discover was their consistent m.o., they didn't use ellipses or brackets to indicate where they had done their dirty work.

A tiny cut was the most telling: when Lamott observes that when you finally give characters their own voices, "sometimes what they are saying and how they are saying it will finally show you who they are and what is really happening. Whoa—they're not getting married after all! **She's gay!** And you had no idea!" Now this was clearly censorship. At the time, I surmised that the SED had cut **"She's gay"** in the belief that homosexuality was a risqué topic for high-school students. This made no sense given the high-school students I knew, but I assumed it had been done with some more conservative students—or parents—in mind. Still, Lamott was right: I had no idea what was "really happening." I could never imagine that "obsessive-compulsive paranoid thinking" might have been removed as an inappropriate description of a disability, any more than I could have predicted that I would later find a **"skinny** Italian boy" and a **"fat** Portuguese" in Ernesto Galarza's list of his elementary school classmates turned into "a thin Italian boy" and a "heavy Portuguese."

On the next exam, one of the compare-and-contrast passages came from Isaac Bashevis Singer (or Isaac Singer, as they called him, as though this unrecognizable work must come from a different writer). Again, the title wasn't given, but I guessed the selection had to come from his memoir, *In My Father's Court*, and took that off the shelf. The chapter they had used was about the relationship of Jews and Gentiles in his native Poland. On the exam, all references to Jews and Gentiles had been removed. This time they hadn't just taken out incidental (if critical) details: they had cut out the story's heart. The SED seemed completely indifferent to the effect of censorship on the meaning of the literature students were being asked to analyze. I was beginning to realize that to the State Education Department, literature could—and should—be manipulated to serve the needs of the test. The test was certainly not there to serve literature. The two examples I'd found so far weren't flukes. They were part of a pattern. The pattern was hiding in plain sight. The tests were publicly available. Although the titles of the works were almost never given, the authors' names were, and a person willing to put the time and energy into finding the source material could do so. Some of it required a little detective work: a "speech" by Pittsburgh Steelers' coach Chuck Noll turned up in an anthology of writing by football coaches for businessmen. Kofi Annan mentioned San Francisco in his speech; the Commonwealth Club of San Francisco is famous for its lecture series. And so on. In the end, I was able to locate the sources of 25 of the 26 pieces of prose used on the 10 exams that had been given up to that point (the one I never found was a piece of science writing on leatherback turtles). Even the State Education Department seemed to have scruples about changing poetry, so the four poems they'd included had escaped almost unscathed. That they didn't treat the choices of prose writers with equal respect only shows how little they understand about literature. Of the 25 pieces of prose, 20 had been censored. An additional four had been altered, but not in ways that rose to the level of censorship. One had been left untouched. The SED had cut references to sex, nudity, ethnicity, religion, drinking, violence, and criminal activity. Worried about the tender sensibilities of teenagers, they had cut mild profanity and graphic language: "**Hell**" had become "Heck"; "**damn**" was gone, and "I felt **like I was going to puke**" had become "I felt sick."

I wondered who these censors were. Was there a committee? A lone censor working under cover of darkness? Could there possibly be a regulation specifying what to cut? Well, yes. After I'd found the 20 censored works—from which you could deduce what the prohibited topics must be—I found the censorship template on the SED's Web site: the "Sensitivity Review Guidelines." These included the categories I could have predicted: gender; ethnicity; disability; age; violence; graphic language; controversial topics like war and death (that knocks an awful lot of great literature right off the list); but also socioeconomic considerations; and consideration for English Language Learners (looking at the exams you'd have to conclude these last two had never been applied). They also included all-encompassing guidelines like "Does the material require a student to take a position that challenges parental authority?" and "Does the material assume values not shared by all test takers?" Between those two, you could eliminate just about anything, and that's what makes them so dangerous.

The SED would later defend its censorship on the grounds of student comfort (although how students can be comfortable in an exam that determines whether they graduate from high school is another question). However, some of the censorship seems entirely self-serving. It's hard to see whose feelings might be hurt by an accurate representation of political controversy.

To give just a few examples (**again, words cut or altered by the SED are in bold**): The SED censors half of U.N. Secretary General Kofi Annan's observation that polls show "strong American support for the organization at the grass-roots level **regardless of what is said and done on Capitol Hill.**" The unpaid American debt to the U.N. was the subject of the speech he actually gave, but not of the speech as it appeared on the exam. Apparently talking about the anti–U.N. forces in Congress is controversial, even if you are the Secretary General. Poet, playwright, and fiction writer Samuel Hazo's actual speech to the Pennsylvania Music Educators' Association was a no-holds-barred argument for federal funding of the arts. In its original form, his speech contains much to threaten the world view of a State Education Department that seems bent on turning out drones, not independent thinkers. Hazo contrasts "bottom-line" thinkers who care only about their budgets with those who focus on the "top-line": "The top-line is concerned with visions, not costs—**with potentiality, not restriction, with courage, not cowardice—with support, not suppression**—with what is in the best interest of the young, regardless of the bearable burden it places on their elders." Since it's hard to imagine these words offending a test taker, presumably the reference to cowardice and restriction and suppression hit the SED too close to home.

If only the SED had been able to follow Chuck Noll's example (a passage censored on the test): "**Likewise, I did not attempt to censor what our players said to the media. I didn't threaten them with fines if they said something inflammatory. I said they were responsible for their own words. If they said something dumb, they had to deal with the consequences. It wasn't junior high school.**"

What the State Education Department seemed to be counting on was that 1) no one looking at the tests had ever read the originals (what did this say about their expectations of students?); 2) no one cared enough about the tests to spend the time examining them (if you make a single test the determinant of whether students graduate from high school, you can be sure a lot of people will care what's on them); and 3) that no one cared enough about the literature to object to the changes—in short, that everyone shared the State Education Department's view that it was more important to create a sterile testing environment with no possible distractions than to honor the writers' work and to give students an opportunity to wrestle with a real piece of literature.

I could speak out as a parent and a reader who cared about literature, but no one had a greater right to protest the censorship than the authors themselves. The SED had completely disregarded their choices, both of what to say and how to say it, and then sent this crudely doctored version out into the world with their names on it. Since many of the works were memoirs, not just the authors' words but their lives had been rewritten. I couldn't imagine for an instant that any of them had given permission for these cuts. If I could show them what the SED was doing to their work, I was sure the writers would be furious.

Here, too, research skills helped. I found some authors through the universities where they teach, others through their editors or agents. For authors who were no longer living, I tried to find a colleague, agent, editor or scholar of their work who would speak on their behalf. For example, in the case of William Maxwell, the novelist and much-beloved fiction editor of *The New Yorker*, who had recently died, I contacted Alec Wilkinson, who had just written a memoir of his relationship to Maxwell. Wilkinson put me in touch with Maxwell's literary executor, and that was the first inkling I had that I was not alone in discovering something wrong with the exams. Maxwell's executor, Michael Steinman, told me that Maxwell's elder daughter, Kate, worked in a tutoring center for low-income kids in New York City. In the course of preparing a student for the Regents Exam, she had come across her father's mangled work on a previous exam (this, by the way, is one of the insidious ways the censorship gets perpetuated, because old exams are recycled as test-prep materials.) She had been particularly incensed that the rewriting of her father's work meant that the multiple-choice questions after the passage now required the student to misunderstand what her father had written. To get the question right, she later told me, you would have to get her father's work wrong.

Michael Steinman laughed when I told him my project of taking on the State Education Department. "Good luck—I don't know whether it's more accurate to describe their attitude as stupid obstinacy or obstinate stupidity." It turned out that Kate Maxwell had asked him to take this issue up with the SED through her father's publisher, Random House. Over a year's worth of correspondence had gone back and forth; the SED's final position was that this editing without permission was perfectly acceptable under the "fair use" portion of copyright law. This answered a question that had been plaguing me: was it possible any publisher had given permission for this butchery? No publisher I'd contacted had been able to find any record of a permission request (in any case, they assured me, they only grant permission for unaltered excerpts). Now I knew there was no record because the SED didn't think it needed to ask.

As I later learned, "fair use" does allow a not-for-profit educational use of a piece of writing without charge, but does not entitle the user to edit or distort the work without permission. It was only logical—if the user could edit the work at will, how much would have to be changed before the author's rights (what I later learned were called the author's "moral rights" to the work) had been violated? In this case the answer was obvious: the SED had long since crossed that line.

The writers and academics I reached were even angrier than I had anticipated. For the writers, of course, had a sense of helplessness: they had no control over how their work was being rewritten. Frank Conroy's response in a letter to Commissioner Mills was typical: "Who are these people who think they have a right to 'tidy up' my prose? The New York State Political Police? The Correct Theme Authority? What does their training have to do with literature. Has New York State turned into Mississippi? Print my work as written, or don't print it at all. You should be ashamed of yourself, sir." Conroy, took this up as a personal mission, getting his current publisher involved even though he had not published the earlier censored book.

In addition to tracking down the writers, I sent the evidence of the censorship to free-speech and literary organizations like the National Coalition Against Censorship and PEN American Center. NCAC brought the NYCLU on board, and other organizations soon joined our campaign to bring the censorship and its disdain for writers and students to light.

The co-chair of the New York Performance Standards Consortium, Ann Cook, brought the story to *The New York Times*, which put it on the front page of the Sunday paper. Suddenly, a project that had only a month or two before consisted of me feeding quarters into the copy machine at the Brooklyn Public Library was now prompting calls from CNN and the BBC. Censorship hits journalists where they live, and I don't think any of the reporters claimed to be objective on the topic. On the day of the press conference, the State Education Department was still lamely trying to defend the practice on the grounds of student discomfort; by midweek they had rescinded the practice altogether.

The State Education Commissioner, Richard P. Mills, put out a press release stating that he had "looked carefully at the Education Department's current practices and the concerns of the writers and have directed that these changes be made." A person might reasonably wonder why the Commissioner had never looked at the "practices" of his department until the media made his life miserable. Robert Bennett, Chancellor of the State Board of Regents, said in the same press release, "This is the right thing to do. It's important for students to have the literary passages without changes in the author's words." Again, one might reasonably ask why it was the right thing to do *after* the media got wind of the story, but not before.

Perhaps the most poignant response to the story came from Maureen Roszkowski, an English teacher who posted the following comment to the National Council of Teachers of English listserv: "More than the tests are at issue here. This kind of intellectual bastardization of these authors' works makes it nearly impossible for me to teach, never mind teach to any test. How can I, subsequent to this news, and the yet untold similar stories, convince young authors in the classroom that words matter? How do I get them to take their own writing seriously when it is obvious that these 'educators' do not respect the most able of the craft?"

The few people who defended the Sensitivity Review Guidelines accepted the state's claim that the texts had been altered to make sure all students would do well on the test. Testmakers do measure bias on exams, but they use statistics, not "Sensitivity Review Guidelines." If two groups of students with matched skill levels perform very differently on a given question in a field test, and if those two groups vary along some critical dimension—typically gender, ethnicity, or income—that question is examined for bias. However, since the SED cannot possibly conduct field tests on the effect of individual words or sentences in literary passages, if it found statistical evidence of bias on an essay question, it would have to eliminate the entire passage. Removing "sensitive" words is censorship, not science.

The State Education Department repudiated its policy of censoring texts, but not the Sensitivity Review Guidelines, so things may actually get worse. It's easy to document censorship when you can show what's been cut from an original text. It's much harder when controversial selections can be rejected in their entirety even before they make it onto the exam.

"NO CHILD LEFT BEHIND"

Censorship on testing is not just an issue for New York State. Testing is big business in the United States, and it's about to become even bigger with the passage of President Bush's Elementary and Secondary Education Act, otherwise known as the "No Child Left Behind" act.

I had it easy. The high-stakes tests in my state were publicly available on the State Education Department's Web site. Others have taken up the challenge of making high-stakes tests public at the risk of losing their jobs, going to jail, or getting sued:

James Hope, a fourth-grade teacher in Gwinnett County, Georgia, who was his school's Teacher of the Year in 2000–01, posted six flawed items to a Web site maintained by parents opposed to their district's Gateway test. Hope was threatened with jail and had his teaching license revoked. James appealed the revocation, and the district allowed him to continue teaching during the appeal. The judge on his suspension hearing said Hope's actions "do not exemplify honesty and integrity" and violate a code of ethics for teachers dealing with standardized tests. His teaching certificate was suspended for six months.

Teresa Glenn of North Carolina paraphrased a few bad test items and criticized the state's end-of-grade tests in general on an e-mail discussion list for teachers maintained by the North Carolina Board of Public Instruction. Her post was forwarded to her principal and to the superintendent, and Teresa was suspended without pay for five days.

George Schmidt, a 29-year veteran high-school English teacher in Chicago, published six pilot forms of the Chicago Academic Standards Exams (CASE) in his newspaper, *Substance*. The tests appeared at his office in a plain, brown envelope; Schmidt thought the test items were awful and, rather than write an editorial to that effect, published them in his paper. Independent experts declared the CASE tests unprofessional, simplistic, and error-ridden, but Schmidt was suspended and later fired, then sued for over $1.3 million, the alleged cost of replacing the published tests.

David and Terry Knight, parents of six students in Gwinnett County, Georgia, belonged to a parents' group that opposed the county's standardized Gateway test. After a copy of the test was sent to the media, the school district's police force conducted a criminal investigation in the course of which they threatened the Knights with jail, and told Terry Knight that her children could be taken away from her if she didn't cooperate. The experience prompted the Knights to move out of state, while the district superintendent has been appointed to a committee to draft federal regulations for state standards and testing, the only district school superintendent in the country given that honor.

Two members of the Gwinnett County, Georgia, school police traveled to Vermont to threaten teacher and writer Susan Ohanian, whom they accused of helping provide Georgia media with copies of the tests. The cops threatened Ohanian with extradition for a felony, punishable by five years in jail and a $50,000 fine; they said they would "go easy" on her if she implicated one of the Georgia parents. She was later asked to provide fingerprints and a writing sample, even though Georgia law does not entitle police to ask for a writing sample.

What about these tests could possibly be so vital that government agencies will threaten teachers and parents with jail to keep it hidden? We need to make sure that any test that determines the future of thousands of students across the country is exposed to the light of day.

The work isn't over.

APPENDIX 1

Works altered by the New York State Education Department on English Language Arts Regents Exams:

Edward Abbey, *Desert Solitude* (January 2001)

Mortimer J. Adler, "How to Mark a Book" (from *How to Read a Book*) (June 2001)

Kofi Annan, Speech to the Commonwealth Club of California, April 20, 1998 (August 2001)

Roger Ascham, "Toxophilus" (January 2000)

Anton Chekhov, "An Upheaval" (June 2001)

Frank Conroy, *Stop-Time* (June 2000)

Annie Dillard, *An American Childhood* (August 2001)

Ernesto Galarza, *Barrio Boy* (June 1999)

Samuel Hazo, "Strike Down the Band" (August 2000)

John Holt, *Learning All the Time* (June 1999)

June Jordan, "Ah, Momma" (August 1999)

B.B. King, *Blues All Around Me* (June 2000)

Anne Lamott, "Dialogue"(from *Bird by Bird*) (January 2001)

William Maxwell, *So Long, See You Tomorrow* (June 2000)

Chuck Noll, "Staying the Best" (January 2000)

Lise Pelletier, "Life As It Is In Pinegrove Correctional Centre on a Monday Morning" (April 2000)

Carol Saline, *Mothers and Daughters* (August 1999)

Isaac Bashevis Singer, *In My Father's Court* (June 2001)

Margaret A. Whitney "Playing to Win"(August 2000)

Elie Wiesel, "What Really Makes U.S. Free"(April 2000)

Works used with minor alterations (but without indication of changes):

Annie Dillard, *The Writing Life* (January 2001)

Dale Fetherling "The Sounds of Silence" (August 1999)

Jack London, "The Story of an Eyewitness"(January 2000)

Lynn Sherr, *Failure Is Impossible* (April 2001)

Works used without alteration:

Roger Jack, "The Pebble People" (January 2002)

APPENDIX 2

Representative Samples of Literary Works Altered on New York State Regents English Language Arts Examinations: **Altered or deleted text is in bold.**

Ernesto Galarza's[1] memoir, *Barrio Boy:*

Original: "Almost tiptoeing across the office, I maneuvered myself to keep my mother between me and the **gringo** lady."

Regents: "Almost tiptoeing across the office, I maneuvered to keep my mother between me and the **American** lady."

Original: "Off the school grounds we traded the same insults we heard from our elders. On the playground, we were sure to be marched up to the principal's office for calling someone **a wop, a chink, a dago, or a greaser.**" (After describing the school as "not so much a melting pot as a griddle where Miss Hopley and her helpers warmed knowledge into us and roasted social hatreds out of us.")

Regents: "Off the school grounds we traded the same insults we heard from our elders. On the playground, we were sure to be marched up to the principal's office for calling someone **a bad name.**"

Annie Dillard's memoir, *An American Childhood:*

"From the nearest library, I learned every sort of surprising thing—some of it, though not much of it—from the books themselves.

"The Homewood branch of Pittsburgh's Carnegie Library system was in a Negro section of town—Homewood. This branch was our nearest library; Mother drove me to it every two weeks for many years, until I could drive there myself. I only very rarely saw other white people there."

"Beside the farthest wall, and under leaded windows set ten feet from the floor, so that no human being could ever see anything from them—next to the wall, and at the farthest remove from the idle librarians at their curved wooden counter, and from the oak bench where my mother waited in her camel's-hair coat chatting with the librarians or reading—stood the last and darkest and most obscure of the tall nonfiction stacks: **NEGRO HISTORY and** NATURAL HISTORY."[2]

Isaac Bashevis Singer's memoir, *In My Father's Court:*

"She was a small woman, old and wrinkled. When she started washing for us she was already past seventy. Most **Jewish** women of her age were sickly, weak, broken in body. All the old women in our street had bent backs and leaned on sticks when they walked. But this washwoman, small and thin as she was, possessed a strength that came from generations of peasant forebears."

The washwoman cleaned "featherbed covers, pillowcases, sheets, **and the men's fringed garments. Yes, the Gentile woman washed these holy garments as well.**"

(The following material was deleted completely from the exam.)

"**And now at last the body, which had long been no more than a broken shard supported only by the force of honesty and duty, had fallen. The soul passed into those spheres where all holy souls meet, regardless of the roles they played on this earth, in whatever tongue, of whatever creed.**"

Samuel Hazo's "Strike Down the Band":

"Like poetry, music puts us in touch with our feelings **and through our feelings, with our very souls.**"

"I contend that nothing promotes the general welfare and seeks the blessings of peace better than the arts—**even more than religions, which, for some reason in our time, tend more toward divisiveness than unity.**"

Elie Weisel's essay, "What Really Makes U.S. Free":

"Man, **who was created in God's image**, wants to be free **as God is free**: free to choose between good and evil, love and vengeance, life and death."

Frank Conroy's memoir, *Stop-Time:*

(The following material was deleted completely from the exam.)

"**It was easy to undress. We wore only blue jeans. I remember a mild shock at the absence of anything but air against my skin.**"

"**If we saw a king snake, all six feet wrapped black and shiny in the shade of a palmetto, we'd break off a pine branch and kill it, smashing the small head till the blood ran.**"

B.B. King's autobiography, *Blues All Around Me*:[3]

"My great-grandmother, who'd **also** been a slave, talked about the old days. **She'd [She would]** talk about the beginnings of the blues. She said that, sure, singing helped the day go by. Singing about sadness unburdens your soul. But the blues hollerers shouted about more than being sad. They were also delivering messages in musical code. If the master was coming, you might sing a hidden warning to the other field hands. Maybe you'd want to get out of his way or hide. **That was important for the women because the master could have anything he wanted. If he liked a woman, he could take her sexually. And the woman had only two choices: Do what the master demands or kill herself. There was no in-between.** The blues could warn you what was coming. I could see the blues was about survival."

A speech by U.N. Secretary General Kofi Annan to the Commonwealth Club of California:

Polls "show strong American support for the organization at the grass-roots level **regardless of what is said and done on Capitol Hill.**"

Chuck Noll's "Staying the Best":

Halfback Frenchy Fuqua drew the most attention. He liked to wear platform shoes with plastic heels that he filled with water and goldfish selected to match the rest of his outfit.

The writers, who knew me as a conservative guy, asked what I thought of Frenchy's attire. I'm sure they thought I was seething but, really, I wasn't.

I said it was fine. Frenchy liked it. The other players got a kick out of it. So what was the harm?

"An Upheaval," by Anton Chekhov:

"A maid-servant came into the room.
'Liza, you don't know why they have been rummaging in my room?' the governess asked her.
'Mistress has lost a brooch worth two thousand,' said Liza.
'Yes, but why have they been rummaging in my room?'
'They've been searching every one, miss. They've searched all my things, too. They stripped us all naked and searched us . . . . God knows, miss, I never went near her toilet-table, let alone touching the brooch. I shall say the same at the police-station.'

'But . . . why have they been rummaging here?' the governess still wondered.

'A brooch has been stolen, I tell you. The mistress [She] has been rummaging in everything with her own hands. She even searched Mihailo, the porter, herself. It's a perfect disgrace!" (The ellipses are Chekhov's; the essay topic is "the nature of human dignity.")

APPENDIX 3: THE WRITERS RESPOND

"The practice of altering literary texts—often drastically—without indicating that the resultant texts are abridgements or adaptations or (to be truly honest) expurgated versions of what the author originally intended (and ultimately achieved though his or her careful craft) represents a kind of academic dishonesty for which Columbia students are subject to dismissal."

———

"What I see here is unthinkable. And this falsification is performed in the name of education? As part of the ultimate test of what our students have learned?"

———

"As educators we must set and maintain standards of behavior and honesty for the students under our charge. Not only do they deserve it, but our society cannot endure unless these values are instilled and upheld. I implore you to put a stop to the scandalous practice of censoring literary texts, ostensibly in the interest of our students. It is dishonest. It is dangerous. It is an embarrassment. It is the practice of fools."—From a letter by Cathy Popkin, Lionel Trilling Professor In the Humanities, Columbia University, and a Chekhov scholar

"To rewrite the offensive text so as to make it inoffensive, by a governmental or any other standards, is an astonishing presumption.

"Such a practice offends against another governmental standard that some of us still value highly: the First Amendment. By what right does a government agency deny to the authors of literary works the right to speak in their own words and their own voices?

"Beyond that, such a practice insinuates into the teaching of literature a fundamental disrespect for writers, their art, and their work. And it obtrudes a blatant dishonesty between an education system and its students."—From a letter by Wendell Berry, writing on behalf of the late Edward Abbey

"The exam asks students to express opinions, make arguments, and analyze literary style based on texts that have been substantially changed, often in ways that omit critical points or alter their mood and spirit profoundly. I am deeply disturbed to find this happening in a country that prides itself on freedom of expression."—From a letter by Nader F. Dareshori, CEO of Houghton Mifflin, writing to Patricia Schroeder, President and CEO, Association of American Publishers

"Given that Mr. Holt's work had as its core principle the belief in treating young people with respect and taking them seriously as learners, it seems particularly inappropriate to offer an abridged and misleading sample of his work to students on the Regents Exam."—From a letter by Susannah Sheffer, colleague of the late John Holt

"If they want to run pap on the Regents, I'd sure rather it was written AS PAP, not by some honest writer censored to paphood."—From an e-mail by Annie Dillard to Judy Blume, to be read at press conference, June 3, 2002

"Apparently there were several references to 'God' and the 'soul' that upset your resident censor. How you deal with this person is none of my business, but it is my business to ask if you have a policy of altering an author's language to suit your purposes whatever they may be.

"I gather that there were other authors whose remarks or writings were altered or censored to conform to unspoken testing standards. I find this repugnant and, if I may use the phrase, unworthy of the literary and political traditions of our country. I have no intention of getting into a tug-of-war of political correctness here, but I think it is ethically correct, as well as educationally correct, to ask an author's permission before you make a correction in his work, particularly if such bowdlerism distorts or otherwise interferes with the work's meaning. What possible answer can you give to this?"—From a letter by Samuel Hazo

"I am, frankly, astonished that seasoned academics like yourselves would misrepresent passages of literature ostensibly for political and moral reasons. If you as educators of the next generation do not impose a strict literary law and order on yourselves, how can you possibly teach children the value of individual expression or literary honor? How, indeed, will the children in your charge learn not to cheat and doctor information to suit their purposes, as you have done?

"Those of you who study history should know that tolerance has never resulted from censorship but is cultivated through free access to all ideas, politically correct or otherwise."—From a letter by Lynne McTaggart

"The cuts and changes made in Mr. Singer's story 'The Washerwoman' are so bizarre and disturbing that they boggle the mind; it is inexplicable that a story by a writer known for exploring the world of his forefathers in his work should have his story altered—effectively censored—by nameless bureaucrats who, in removing virtually all references to Jewish life and traditions, have effectively destroyed the texture, the depth, and, above all, the deep humanity of this great writer's work."

"It is not only an offense to writers and publishers when great writing is damaged in this manner; it also deprives students of the rare chance to be exposed to and appreciate literature within an environment intended to foster that interest. That is the greater offense—and one for which the New York State Board of Regents is wholly responsible."—From a letter by Linda Rosenberg, Vice President and Associate Publisher, Farrar, Straus & Giroux

NOTES
1. Erroneously identified on the exam as Ernesto Gallarzo.
2. The relevance of race to the passage becomes obvious in the last paragraph: "The people of Homewood, some of whom lived in visible poverty, on crowded streets among burned-out houses, they dreamed of ponds and streams. They were saving to buy microscopes. In their bedrooms they fashioned plankton nets. But their hopes were even more vain than mine, for I was a child, and anything might happen; they were adults, living in Homewood. There was neither pond nor stream on the streetcar routes. The Homewood residents whom I knew had little money and little free time. The marble floor was beginning to chill me. It was not fair."
3. Pieces of six chapters presented to students as a single speech.

APPENDIX A

Project Censored's Guide to Independent Media Resources and Activism

INDEPENDENT PRESS PUBLICATIONS

ABORIGINAL VOICES
116 Spadina Avenue
Suite 201
Toronto, ON M5V 2K6 Canada
Tel: (800) 324-6067
(416) 703-4577
Fax: (416) 703-4581
E-mail: info@aboriginalvoices.com
Web site: <www.cmpa.ca/si2.html>

A magazine focusing on indigenous
art, literature, culture, media and
entertainment.

ADBUSTERS: A MAGAZINE
OF MEDIA AND ENVIRONMENTAL
STRATEGIES
A Journal of The Media Foundation
1243 West Seventh Avenue
Vancouver, BC Canada

Tel: (604) 736-9401
(800) 663-1243
Fax: (604) 737-6021
E-mail: adbusters@adbusters.org
Web site: <www.adbusters.org>

Provides strategies for fighting mind
pollution from advertising.

THE ADVOCATE
P.O. Box 4371
Los Angeles, CA 90078
Fax: (323) 467-0173
Editorial Fax: (323) 467-6805
E-mail: newsroom@advocate.com
Web site: <www.advocate.com>

Leading national gay and lesbian
news magazine.

AGAINST THE CURRENT
Published by Solidarity
7012 Michigan Avenue
Detroit, MI 48210-2872
Tel: (313) 841-0160
Fax: (313) 841-8884
E-mail: efc@igc.apc.org or solidarity
@igc.org
Web site: <www.igc.apc.org/solidarity>

Promoting dialogue among activists,
organizers, and serious scholars of the
left, from the general perspective of
"socialism from below."

ALBION MONITOR (AM)
P.O. Box 1733
Sebastopol, CA 95473
Tel: (707) 823-0100
E-mail: editor@monitor.net
Web site: <www.monitor.net/
monitor/0106a/default.html>

AM is an online biweekly with
a nationwide readership. News
and commentary from both alternative
and mainstream sources, primarily
covering environmental, human rights,
and politics. Syndicated and other
copyrighted material available to
subscribers only.

ALLIANCE FOR COMMUNITY
MEDIA
666 11th Street, NW, Suite 740
Washington, DC 20001-45429
Tel: (202) 393-2650
Fax: (202) 393-2653
E-mail: acm@alliancecm.org
Web site: <www.alliancecm.org>

Journal covering topics such as legal,
community, censorship, technical,
professional, advocacy—for cable
access, Internet, and electronic media.

ALTERNATIVE PRESS REVIEW
Published by A.A.L. Press
P.O. BOX 4710
Arlington , VA 22204
Tel: (573) 442-4352
Fax: (703) 553-0565
E-mail: editors@altpr.org
Web site: <www.altpr.org>

Publishes a wide variety of the best
essays from radical zines, tabloids,
books, and magazines—publishes
a selection of short and lively
article excerpts, along with reviews,
commentary, and columns on the
alternative press scene and other
alternative media.

ALTERNET
77 Federal Street
San Francisco, CA 94107
Tel: (415) 284-1420
Fax: (415) 284-1414
E-mail: info@alternet.org
Web site: <www.alternet.org>

A news service for the alternative
press, supporting independent
journalism and best known for
sponsoring the Media & Democracy
Congress.

AMERICAN CIVIL LIBERTIES
125 Broad Street, 18th floor
New York, NY 10004-2400
Tel: (212) 549-2500
Fax: (212) 549-2646
E-mail: aclu@aclu.org
Web site: <www.aclu.org>

Provides information regarding issues
of civil liberties including online
information on Internet free speech
issues.

AMERICAN JOURNALISM REVIEW
1117 Journalism Building
College Park, MD 20742-7111
Tel: (301) 405-8323
Fax: (301) 405-8323
E-mail: editor@ajr.umd.edu
Web site: <www.ajr.org>

American Journalism Review is a monthly, national magazine that covers trends in the industry ethics and news in print, broadcast, and online journalism.

THE AMERICAN PROSPECT
"A journal for the liberal imagination"
5 Broad Street
Boston, MA 02109
Tel: (888) MUST-READ
(617) 547-2950
Fax: (617) 547-3896
E-mail: letters@prospect.org
Web site: <www.prospect.org>.

A bimonthly publication covering areas of concern such as political, social, and cultural issues.

ANARCHY: A JOURNAL
OF DESIRE ARMED
C.A.L. Press
P.O. Box 1446
Colombia, MO 65205-1446
Tel: (573) 442-4352
Fax: (573) 442-4352
E-mail: jmcquinn@coin.org
Web site: <www.anarchymag.org>

An international magazine for anarchist resistance. Neither left nor right, just uncompromisingly anti-authoritarian, radically cooperative and communitarian, ecological, and feminist.

ANIMAL PEOPLE
P.O. Box 960
C.linton, WA 98236-0960
Tel: (360) 579-2505
E-mail: anmlpepl@whidbey.com
Web site: <www.animalpeoplenews.org>

Animal People is the leading independent newspaper and electronic information service providing original investiation of animal protection worldwide.

THE ANIMALS' AGENDA
P.O. Box 25881
Baltimore, MD 21224
Tel: (410) 675-4566
Fax: (410) 675-0066
E-mail: office@animalsagenda.org
Web site: <www.animalsagenda.org>

The Animals' Agenda is a bimonthly news magazine dedicated to informing people about animal rights and cruelty-free living for the purpose of inspiring action for animals. The Animals' Agenda is committed to serving—and fostering cooperation among—a combined audience of animal advocates, interested individuals, and the entire animal rights movement.

ARAB AMERICAN
NEWS
5706 Chase Road
Dearborn, MI 48126
Tel: (313) 582-4888
Fax: (313) 582-7870
E-mail: osibilani@aol.com
Web site: <www.arabamericannews.com>

The *Arab American News* is a nationally circulated, bilingual weekly newspaper serving the nation's three million Arab Americans.

ARMS SALES MONITOR
Published by the Federation of American Scientists
1717 K Street, NW, Suite 209
Washington, DC 20036
Tel: (202) 546-3300 ext. 193
Fax: (202) 675-1010
E-mail: tamarg@fas.org
Web site: <www.fas.org/asmp/>

Highlights U.S. government policies on arms exports and conventional weapons proliferation.

ASHEVILLE GLOBAL REPORT
P.O. Box 1504
Asheville, NC 28802
Tel: (828) 236-3103
E-mail: editors@agrnews.org
Web site: <www.agrnews.org/issues/130/index.html>

We cover news under-reported by mainstream media, believing that a free exchange of information is necessary to organize for social change.

ASIANWEEK
809 Sacramento St.
San Francisco, CA 94108
Tel: (415) 397-0220
Fax: (415) 397-7258
E-mail: asianweek@asianweek.com
Web site: <www.asianweek.com>

A nationally circulated publication with a " community focus," covering news of Asian Americans.

THE BEAT WITHIN
Published by Pacific News Service
660 Market Street
San Francisco, CA 94104
Tel: (415) 438-4755
E-mail: pacificnews@pacificnews.org
Web site: <www.pacificnews.org/yo/beat/>

A weekly newsletter of writing and art by incarcerated youth.

BECAUSE PEOPLE MATTER
A Project of Sacramento Community for Peace and Justice
403 21st Street
Sacramento, CA 95814
Tel: (916) 444-3203
E-mail: JeKeltner@aol.com

Sacramento and the Foothill's progressive bimonthly newspaper.

THE BLACK WORLD TODAY
P.O. Box 328
Randallstown, MD 21133
Tel: (410) 521-4678
(410) 539-TBWT
Fax: (410) 521-9993
E-mail: editors@tbwt.net
Web site: <www.tbwt.com>

We are a collective of journalists, writers, artists, communicators, and entrepreneurs who have banded together to use the information revolution as one means towards the overall empowerment of black people in the United States and around the world.

BLK
P.O. Box 83912
Los Angeles, CA 90083-0912
Tel: (310) 410-0808
Fax: (310) 410-9250

E-mail: newsroom@blk.com
Web site: <www.blk.com>

News magazine for the black lesbian and gay community.

BRIARPATCH
Saskatchewan's Independent
News Magazine
2138 McIntyre Street
Regina, SK Canada
Tel: (306) 525-2949
Fax: (306) 565-3430
Web site: <www.briarpatchmagazine.com>

Alternative views on politics, labor, and international events.

BROKEN PENCIL
The Guide to Alternative
Culture in Canada
P.O. Box 203, Station P
Toronto, ON Canada
Tel: (416) 538-2813
E-mail: editor@brokenpencil.com
Web site:

Reviews the best zines, books, Web sites, videos, and artworks from the underground and reprints the best articles from the alternative press. Also, groundbreaking interviews, original fiction, and commentary on all aspects of the independent arts.

BULLETIN OF THE
ATOMIC SCIENTISTS
Education Foundation
for Nuclear Science
6042 South Kimbark Avenue
Chicago, IL 60637
Tel: (773) 702-2555
Fax: (773) 702-0725
E-mail: bulletin@thebulletin.org

Web site: <www.bullatomsci.org>

Since 1947, the Magazine of Global Security News and Analysis. Covers international security, military affairs, nuclear issues. Bimonthly.

CALIFORNIA PRISON FOCUS
2940 - 16th Street, #307
San Francisco, CA 94103
Tel: (415) 252-9211
Fax: (415) 252-9311
E-mail: info@prisons.org
Web site: <www.prisons.org>

A newsletter that provides information about control unit prisons, conditions in California, and provides a voice for the prisoners.

CANADIAN DIMENSION (CD)
For People Who Want to Change the World
2B-91 Albert Street
Winnipeg, MB Canada
Tel: (800) 737-7051
Fax: (204) 943-4617
E-mail:
info@canadiandimension.mb.ca
Web site:

For 35 years, *CD* has been a source of intormation and inspiration for activists and intellectuals on the left. Principled and independent hard news and analysis from a left-wing perspective. Multiple winner of Project Censored's Canada awards.

CAPITAL EYE
Center for Responsive Politics
1101 14th Street, NW, Suite 1030
Washington, DC 20005-5635
Tel: (202) 857-0044

Fax: (202) 857-7809
E-mail: info@crp.org
Web site: <www.crp.org>

Quarterly that aims to educate its
readers and to encourage them to
examine the role of money in the
U.S. political system. It includes
substantive, topical articles on issues
related to money and politics.

CENSORSHIP NEWS
Journal of the National Coalition
Against Censorship
275 7th Avenue, 20th Floor
New York, NY 10001
Tel: (212) 807-6222
Fax: (212) 807-6245
E-mail: ncac@ncac.org
Web site: <www.ncac.org>

Published quarterly, it contains
information and discussion about
freedom of expression issues,
including current school censorship
controversies and threats to the free
flow of information.

CENTER FOR RESEARCH
ON GLOBALIZATION
Tel: (888) 713-8500
E-mail: editor@globalresearch.ca
Web site: <www.globalresearch.ca>

An independent research and media
group committed to curbing the tide
of "globalization" and "disarming"
the New World Order. Based in
Montréal, CRG publishes news
articles, commentary, background
research and analysis on a broad
range of issues, focussing on the
interrelationship between social,
economic, strategic, geopolitical
and environmental processes.

THE CHRONICLE OF
HIGHER EDUCATION
1255 23rd Street, NW
Suite 700
Washington, DC 20037
Tel: (202) 466-1000
Fax: (202) 296-2691
E-mail: help@chronicle.com
Web site: <www.chronicle.com>

The number-one news source for
college and university faculty about
issues in higher education.

CIVIL LIBERTIES
Published by the American
Civil Liberties Union
125 Broad Street, 18th Floor
New York, NY 10004-2400
Tel: (212) 549-2500
Fax: (212) 549-2646
E-mail: nauer@citylimits.org
Web site: <www.aclu.org>

Issues of civil liberties including
online information on Internet free
speech issues.

COLORLINES MAGAZINE
(Formerly: *Third Force*)
Journal of the Applied Research
Center and Center for Third World
Organizing
PMB 319,
4096 Piedmont Avenue
Oakland, CA 94611
Tel: (510) 653-3415
Fax: (510) 653-3427
E-mail: colorlines@arc.org
Web site: <www.arc.org>

A quarterly magazine that focuses on
race, culture, and organizing within
communities of color.

CONGRESSIONAL QUARTERLY
WEEKLY REPORT
1414 22nd Street, NW
Washington, DC 20036
Tel: (202) 887-8500
Fax: (202) 728-1863
E-mail: customer service @cq.com
Web site: <www.cq.com>

A world-class provider of information
on government, politics, and public
policy.

CONNECTIONS
Published by Peace
and Justice Network
P. O. Box 4123
Stockton, CA 95204
Tel: (209) 467-4455
E-mail: dsteele@igc.apc.org
Web site: <www.sonnet.com/usr/pjc>

San Joaquin County's alternative
newspaper.

CONSUMER REPORTS
Published by Consumer's Union
101 Truman Avenue
Yonkers, NY 10703-1057
Tel: (914) 378-2000
Fax: (914) 378-2992
Web site: <www.consumerreports.org>

The oldest, most reliable and complete source for independent reviews
of products and services. Consumer's
Union is a non-profit organization that
has been testing products on behalf of
consumers for more than 60 years.

CORPORATE CRIME REPORTER
1209 National Press Building
Washington, DC 20045
Tel: (202) 737-1680
<russell@essential.org>

Legal weekly covering issues of
corporate and white-collar crime.

COUNTER MEDIA
1573 North Milwaukee Avenue
#517
Chicago, IL 60622
Tel: (312) 243-8342
E-mail: lquilter@igc.apa.org
Covers protests, actions, and issues
ignored by conventional media
sources.

COUNTERPOISE
Quarterly Journal of the American
Library Association's Social
Responsibilities Round Table
1716 SW Williston Road
Gainesville, FL 32608-4049
Tel: (352) 335-2200
Fax: Call first
E-mail: willet@liblib.com
Web site:
<www.civicmediacenter.org/counter
poise/>

Counterpoise is the only review
journal that makes alternative points
of view widely accessible to librarians,
scholars, and activists.

COUNTERPUNCH
3220 N. Street, NW
Suite 346
Washington, DC 20007
Tel: (800) 840-3683
E-mail: counterpunch@counterpunch.
org
Web site: <www.counterpunch.org>

Twice a month *Counterpunch* brings
its readers the stories that the
corporate press never prints. Theirs
is muckraking with a radical attitude.
COVERTACTION QUARTERLY

CovertAction
c/o Institute for Media Analysis, Inc.
143 West 4th Street
New York, NY 10012
Tel: (212) 477-2977
Fax: (212) 477-2977
E-mail: info@covertaction.org
Web site: <www.covertaction.org>
Investigative journalism exposing
malfeasance and covert activities in
government, corporations, and other
areas affecting the public.

THE CULTURAL
ENVIRONMENT MONITOR
Newsletter of the CEM
(Cultural Environment Movement)
P.O. Box 31847
Philadelphia, PA 19104
Tel: (888) 445-4526
Fax: (215) 204-5823
E-mail: cem@libertynet.org
Web site: <www.cemnet.org>

A publication that focuses on gender
equity and general diversity in mass
media employment, ownership, and
representation. Focuses primarily on
equality across all sectors.

CULTURAL SURVIVAL
QUARTERLY (CSQ)
215 Prospect Street
Cambridge, MA 02139
Tel: (617) 441-5400
Fax: (617) 441-5417
E-mail: csinc@cs.org
Web site: <www.cs.org>

The mission of this quarterly
magazine is based on the belief that
the survival of indigenous people
and ethnic minorities depends on
the preservation of their rights in
deciding how to adapt traditional

ways to a changing world.

CURVE MAGAZINE
1 Haight Street, Suite B
San Francisco, CA 94102
Tel: (415) 863-6538
Fax: (415) 863-1609
E-mail: shop@curvemag.com
Web site: <www.curvemag.com>

Curve, the nation's best-selling lesbian
magazine, spotlights all that is fresh,
funny, or controversial in lesbian community entertainment profiles issues
and investigative pieces.

DARK NIGHT FIELD NOTES
Published by: Dark Night Press
P.O. Box 3629
Chicago, IL 60690-3629
Tel: (207) 839-5794
Fax: (773) 373-7188
E-mail: darknight@igc.org
Web site: <www.darknightpress.org/>

A quarterly publication covering
issues related to the recognition and
liberation of indigenous peoples.

DEFENSE MONITOR
1779 Massachusetts Avenue, NW
6th Floor
Washington, DC 20036
Tel: (202) 332-0600
Fax: (202) 462-4559
E-mail: info@cdi.org
Web site: <www.cdi.org>

A journal that provides independent
research on the social, economic,
environmental, political, and military
components of global security.
DEMOCRATIC LEFT
Published by the Democratic
Socialists of America

180 Varick Street, 12th Floor
New York, NY 10014
Tel: (212) 727-8610
Fax: (212) 727-8616
E-mail: dsa@dsausa.org
Web site: <www.dsausa.org/dl/index.
html>

A quarterly review of socialist issues
and activities.

DESIGNER/BUILDER
A journal of the human environment
2405 Maclovia Lane
Santa Fe, NM 87505
Tel and fax: (505) 471-4549

Published 12 times a year
by Fine Additions, Inc.

DISSENT
310 Riverside Drive
Suite 1201
New York, NY 10025
Tel: (212) 316-3120
Fax: (212) 316-3145
E-mail: editors@dissentmagazine.org
Web site: <www.dissentmagazine.org>

A quarterly magazine of politics,
culture, and ideas. *Dissent* covers
national and international politics from
a progressive perspective with focus
on providing forums for debate, dis-
agreement, and discussion on the left.

DOLLARS AND SENSE:
WHAT'S LEFT IN ECONOMICS
Published by the The Economic
Affairs Bureau, Inc.
740 Cambridge Street
Cambridge, MA 02141-1401
Tel: (617) 876-2434
Fax: (617) 876-0008
E-mail: dollars@dollarsandsense.org

Web site:
Reports on issues of social justice and
economic policy. Prints articles by
journalists, activists, and scholars on
a broad range of topics with an
economic theme.

DOMES
P.O. Box 413
Milwaukee, WI 53211
Tel: (414) 229-4709
Fax: (414) 229-4848
E-mail: info@sois.uwm.edu
Web site:

Biannual provides for a balance
of views on the Middle East.

E: THE ENVIRONMENTAL
MAGAZINE
P.O. Box 5098
Westport, CT 06881
Tel: (203) 854-5559
Fax: (203) 866-0602
E-mail: info@emagazine.com
Web site: <emagazine.com>

E is an independent newsstand-
quality publication that focuses
on environmental issues. *E* strives
to educate, inspire, and empower
Americans to make a difference
for the environment.

EARTH FIRST! JOURNAL
P.O. Box 3023
Tucson, AZ 85702-6900
Tel: (520) 620-6900
Fax: (413) 254-0057
E-mail: collective@earthfirstjournal. org
Web site: <www.earthfirstjournal.org>
Earth First! Journal reports on the
radical environmental movement.
The journal publishes hard-to-find

information about strategies to stop
the destruction of the planet.

EARTH ISLAND JOURNAL
300 Broadway, Suite 28
San Francisco, CA 94133-3312
Tel: (415) 788-3666
Fax: (415) 788-7324
E-mail: journal@earthisland.org
Web site: <earthisland.org/>

International environmental news
magazine focusing on socioeconomic,
political issues affecting Earth's
ecosystems and on the work being
done to conserve, preserve, and
restore the earth.

EAT THE STATE!
P.O. Box 85541
Seattle, WA 98145
Tel: (206) 903-9461
E-mail: ets@scn.org
Web site: <EatTheState.org>

A forum for anti-authoritarian political
opinion, research, and humor.

THE ECOLOGIST
c/o MIT Press Journals
1920 Martin Luther King Jr. Blvd.
Berkeley, CA 94704
Tel: (510) 548-2032
Fax: (510) 548-4916
E-mail: theecologist@earthlink.net
Web site: <www.theecologist.org>

Produced monthly, *The Ecologist*
is the world's longest-running
environmental magazine. Thirty-third:
Campaigns on the environment and
social issues facing this planet.
ECONOMIC JUSTICE NEWS
3628 12th Street, NE
Washington, DC 20017

Tel: (202) 463-2265
Fax: (202) 879-3186
E-mail: 50years@50years.org
Web site: <www.50years.org>

Economic Justice News is the quarterly
newsletter produced by the 50 Years
Is Enough Network; a network of 200
social and economic justice organizations working to bring about radical
reform of the World Bank and the
International Monetary Fund.

ECONEWS
Published by the Northcoast
Environmental Center
879 9th Street
Arcata, CA 95521
Tel: (707) 822-6918
Fax: (707) 822-0827
E-mail: nec@igc.org
Web site: <www.necandeconews.to>

One of the world's oldest bioregional
newsletters, *ECONEWS* presents
action-oriented and timely articles
on forestry, wildlife, toxics, recycling,
energy, endangered species, and
air and water quality in northern
California, the Pacific Northwest,
and beyond. It's all done in
journalistic style, and leavened
with humor and humanity.

THE ELECTRONIC JOURNALIST (TEJ)
Published by the Society
of Professional Journalists
3909 North Meridian Street
Indianapolis, IN 46208
Tel: (317) 927-8000
Fax: (317) 920-4789
E-mail: spj@spj.org
Web site: <www.spj.org>

To ensure that the concept of self-government outlined by the U.S. Constitution remains a reality into future centuries, the American people must be well informed in order to make decisions regarding their lives, and their local and national communities. TEJ is a national magazine dedicated to improving and protecting journalism.

ESSENCE MAGAZINE
1500 Broadway
New York, NY 10036
Tel: (212) 642-0600
Fax: (212) 921-5173
Web site: <www.essence.com>

News and commentary for African-American women.

EVERYONE'S BACKYARD
Published by CHEJ
P.O. Box 6806
Falls Church, VA 22040-6806
Tel: (703) 237-2249
Fax: (703) 237-8389
E-mail: info@chej.org
Web site: <www.chej.org>

The journal of the Grassroots Movement for Environmental Justice.

EXTRA!
Published by Fairness and Accuracy in Reporting
112 West 27th Street
New York, NY 10001
Tel: (212) 633-6700
Fax: (212) 727-7668
E-mail: info@fair.org
Web site: <www.fair.org>
Provides media criticism featuring articles on biased reporting, censored news, media mergers, and more.

FACTSHEET 5
P.O. Box 170099
San Francisco, CA 94117-0099
Tel: (415) 668-1781
E-mail: seth@factsheet5.com
Web site: <www.factsheet5.com>

Guide to the 'zine revolution; resources and reviews of thousands of underground publications.

FELLOWSHIP MAGAZINE
Box 271
Nyack, NY 10960
Tel: (845) 358-4601
Fax: (845) 358-4924
E-mail: for@forusa.org
Web site: <www.forusa.org>

Seeks to replace violence, war, racism, and economic injustice with nonviolence, peace, and justice.

FILIPINAS MAGAZINE
1486 Hunington Avenue
Suite 300
South San Francisco, CA 94080
Tel: (800) 654-777
Fax: (650) 872-8651
E-mail: mail@filipinasmag.com
Web site: <www.filipinasmag,com>

A monthly that covers Filipino American interests and affairs, with both the immigrant and U.S.–born sectors of the more than two million Filipinos in this country as its target. The magazine features achievers, role models, politics, and issues both in the United States and the Philippines that are relevant to its readers.

FILIPINO REPORTER
350 5th Avenue, Suite 601
Empire State Building
New York, NY 10018-0110
Tel: (212) 967-5784
Fax: (212) 967-5848
E-mail: FilipinoReporter@worldnet.
att.net or BPelayo@aol.com
Web site: <www.filipinoreporter.com>

National English-language weekly
of particular interest to Asian/Pacific
Islanders.

THE FIRE INSIDE
Published by California Coalition
for Women Prisoners
100 McAllister St.
San Francisco, CA 94102
Tel: (415) 255-7036 ext. x4
Fax: (415) 552-3150
E-mail: ccwp@igc.org
Web site: <www.prisonactivist.org/
ccwp>

Quarterly newsletter covering issues
related to incarcerated women.

FOOD FIRST NEWS
Institute for Food and Development
Policy
398 60th Street
Oakland, CA 94618
Tel: (510) 654-4400
Fax: (510) 654-4400
E-mail: foodfirst@igc.apc.org
Web site: <www.foodfirst.org>

Information and reader action guide
for ending world hunger and poverty.

FOREST MAGAZINE
Conserving our national heritage
P.O. Box 11646
Eugene, OR 97440

Tel: (541) 484-2692
E-mail: info@forestmag.org
Web site: <www.forestmag.org>

The magazine for people who care
about forests.

FORWARD NEWSPAPER
45 East 33rd Street
New York, NY 10016
Tel: (212) 889-8200
Fax: (212) 447-6406
E-mail: acaroll@forward.com
Web site: <www.forward.com>

National/Weekly—the *Forward*
fought for social justice and helped
generations of immigrant Jews enter
American life - and still does.

FREE INQUIRY: THE
INTERNATIONAL SECULAR
HUMANIST MAGAZINE
Published by the Council
for Secular Humanism
P.O. Box 664
Amherst, NY 14226
Tel: (716) 636-7571
Fax: (716) 636-1733
Web site: <www.secularhumanism.
org>

A quarterly magazine that celebrates
reason and humanity.

FREEDOM SOCIALIST
NEWSPAPER
Published by Revolutionary
Feminist Internationalists
4710 University Way, NE, #100
Seattle, WA 981045
Tel: (206) 985-4621
Fax: (206) 985-8965
E-mail: fspnatl@igc.apc.org
Web site: <www.socialism.com>

An international socialist feminist quarterly providing news, analysis, reviews, and humor aimed at ridding the world of bigots, bosses, and patriarchs. Special attention to the issues and leadership of women, people of color, and sexual minorities.

FRONTIERS NEWS MAGAZINE
P.O. Box 46367
West Hollywood, CA 90046
Te;: (213) 848-2222
Fax: (213) 656-8784
E-mail: webmaster@frontiersweb.com
Web site: <www.frontiersweb.com>

A comprehensive magazine for and about lesbian/gay issues and rights.

FUSE MAGAZINE
401 Richmond Street West, Suite 454
Toronto, ON Canada
Tel: (416) 340-8026
Fax: (416) 340-0494
E-mail: fuse@interlog.com
Web site:

Blend of critical analysis of contemporary art, curatorship, and social/political events related to art practices in diverse cultural and racial communities. Special focus on cultural politics and explorations of the relationship between art and social changes.

GENEWATCH
Published by the Council for Responsible Genetics
5 Upland Road, Suite #3
Cambridge, MA 02140
Tel: (617) 868-0870
Fax: (617) 491-5344
E-mail: crg@gene-watch.org
Web site:

Publication which provides a forum for discussing, evaluating and distributing information and opinions about the social and environmental aspects of genetic engineering.

GEO NEWSLETTER
Grassroots Economic Organizing
177 Kiles Road
Stillwater, PA 17878
Tel: (570) 784-7384
E-mail: editors@geonewsletter.org
Web site: <www.geonewsletter.org>

GEO (Grassroots Economic Organizing) Newsletter is a bimonthly publication that reports on worker cooperatives and community-based economies in the U.S. and worldwide, and their development through local cooperative action. GEO also provides a global forum for the cooperative movement.

GLAADNOTES
150 West 26th Street, Suite 503
New York, NY 10001
Tel: (800) GAY-MEDIA
E-mail: glaad@glaad.org
Web site: <www.glaad.org>

Quarterly newsletter promoting fair, accurate, inclusive media representation of lesbian, gay, bisexual, and transgendered people.

GLOBAL INFORMATION NETWORK
146 West 29th Street, #7E
New York, NY 10001
Tel: (212) 244-3123
Fax: (212) 244-3522
E-mail: ipsgin@igc.org
Web site: <www.globalinfo.org>
Global Information Network, a not-

for-profit news and world media operation, is the largest distributor of Developing World news services, including the award-winning Inter Press Service, in the U.S.

GOVERNMENT INFORMATION INSIDER
Published by OMB Watch
1742 Connecticut Avenue, NW
Washington, DC 20009
Tel: (202) 234-8494
Fax: (202) 234-8584
Web site: <www.ombwatch.org>

A magazine that focuses on government secrecy and the public's right to know.

GUILD NOTES
Published by the National Lawyers Guild
126 University Place, 5th Floor
New York, NY 10003
Tel: (212) 627-2656
Fax: (212) 627-2404
E-mail: nlgno@nlg.org
Web site: <www.nlg.org>

Newsletter of the National Lawyer's Guild.

HAITI PROGRES
1398 Flatbush Avenue
Brooklyn, NY 11210
Tel: (718) 434-5551
E-mail: editor@haiti-progres.com
Web site: <www.haiti-progres.com>

English, French, and Creole Haitian weekly.

666 Broadway, 11th Floor
New York, NY 10012
Tel: (212) 420-5720
Fax: (212) 228-5889
E-mail: letters@harpers.org
Web site: <www.harpers.org>

Founded in 1850, Harper's aims to provide readers with a unique perspective on the world. In its acclaimed essays, fiction, and reporting, Harper's continues to explore the issues and ideas in politics, science, and the arts that drive our national conversation.

HIGH COUNTRY NEWS
P.O. Box 1090
Paonia, CO 81428
Tel: (800) 905-1155
E-mail: editor@hcn.org
Web site: <www.hcn.org>

A non-profit, biweekly newspaper that reports on public lands and rural communities in the western U.S. for its 21,000 subscribers. It is a respected independent source for environmental news, analysis, and commentary.

THE HIGHTOWER LOWDOWN
P.O. Box 20596
New York, NY 10011
Tel: (212) 741-2365
Fax: (212) 979-2055
E-mail: info@jimhightower.com
Web site: <www.Jimhightower.com>

A twice-monthly populist newsletter featuring Jim Hightower.

HARPER'S MAGAZINE

HUMAN RIGHTS TRIBUNE

Human Rights Internet
8 York Street, Suite 302
Ottawa, ON Canada
Tel: (613) 789-7407
Fax: (613) 789-7414
E-mail: hri@hri.ca
Web site: <www.hri.ca>

Quarterly publication. Web site also
has links to human rights Web sites
worldwide; job postings from human
rights organizations and databases.

THE HUMANIST
A Journal of the American Humanist
Association
1777 T Street, NW
Washington , DC 20009-9088
Tel: (202) 238-9088; (866) 486-2647
Fax: (202) 238-9003
E-mail: AHA@erols.com
Web site: <humanist.net/publications/
humanist.html>

A magazine of critical inquiry and
social concern.

HUMANIST IN CANADA
Published by Canadian
Humanist Publications, Inc.
P.O. Box 3769, Station C
Ottawa, ON Canada
Tel: (613) 749-8929
Fax: (613) 749-8929
E-mail: jepiercy@cyberus.ca
Web site: <www.humanists.net/hic>

For non-believers interested in
social issues, *Humanist in Canada*
explores contemporary issues from
a humanistic viewpoint committed
to free inquiry in a pluralistic,
democratic society.

IMAGES

Gay & Lesbian Alliance
Against Defamation
150 West 26th Street, Suite 503
New York, NY 10001
Tel: (800) GAY-MEDIA
Fax: (617)426-3594
E-mail: images@glaad.org
Web site: <www.glaad.org>

A biannual journal, *Images* brings
together the voices of academic
researchers, activists, artists, journalists, and other media professionals to
explore the ways media shape lesbian,
gay, bisexual, and transgender lives
from a variety of perspectives.

IMPACT PRESS
Covering Issues the Way
the Media Should
PMB 361
10151 University Boulevard
Orlando, FL 32817
Tel: (407) 263-5504
E-mail: editor@impactpress.com
Web site: <www.impactpress.com>

IMPACT Press is a non-profit,
bimonthly, sociopolitical magazine
that features aggressive journalism,
biting commentary, and a healthy dose
of satire.

IN THESE TIMES
2040 North Milwaukee Avenue
2nd Floor
Chicago, IL 60647-4002
Tel: (773) 772-0100
Fax: (773) 772-4180
E-mail: itt@inthesetimes.com
Web site: www.inthesetimes.com

Provides independent news and views
you won't find anywhere else.
THE INDEPENDENT REVIEW

Published by the Independent Institute
100 Swan Way
Oakland, CA 94621-1428
Tel: (800) 927-8733
Fax: (510) 568-6040
E-mail: info@independent.org
Web site: <www.independent.org>

A journal of political economy.

INDIAN COUNTRY TODAY
(LAKOTA TIMES)
P.O. Box 4250
Rapid City, SD 57709
Tel: (605) 341-0011
Fax: (605) 341-6940
E-mail: editor@indiancountry.com
Web site: <www.indiancountry.com>

Weekly, with subscriptions and store
sales in all 50 states and 15 foreign
countries, it is reportedly the most
influential and widely read Native
American newspaper in the United
States. (It also has a regional section
covering the Pine Ridge Reservation.)

INDUSTRIAL WORKER
Published by Industrial
Workers of the World
103 West Michigan Avenue
Ypsilanti, MI 48197-5438
Tel: (313) 483-3548
Fax: (313) 483-4050
E-mail: iw@iww.org
Web site: <www.iww.org>

The *Industrial Worker* is the monthly
newspaper of the industrial workers
of the world, or Wobblies. Every
issue contains news of the world-labor
struggles, and analysis of the labor
movement and economy from a
Wobbly perspective.

INFUSION: THE CENTER

FOR CAMPUS ORGANIZING
The National Magazine for
Progressive Campus Activists
165 Friend Street, #1
Boston, MA 02114
Tel: (617) 725-2886
Fax: (617) 725-2873
E-mail: cco@igc.org
Web site:
<www.ippn.org/ORCCO.htm>

Provides news, analysis, action
guides, and organizing tips and
resources for progressive campus
activists.

THE INSURGENT
Erb Memorial Unnion, Suite 1
Eugene, OR 97403-1228
Tel: (541) 346-3716
E-mail: collective@theinsurgent.org
Web site: <www.theinsurgent.org>

A newspaper that seeks to provide
a forum for those working towards
a society free from oppression.

INTELLIGENCE REPORT
Journal of the Southern
Poverty Law Center
400 Washington Avenue
Montgomery, AL 36104
Tel: (334) 264-0286
Fax: (334) 956-8485
Web site: <www.splcenter.org>

A quarterly journal that offers in-
depth analysis of political extremism
and bias crimes in the United States.
The *Intelligence Report* profiles
far-right leaders, monitors domestic
terrorism and reports on the activities
of extremist groups.

THE IRE JOURNAL

Published by IRE (Investigative
Reporters and Editors, Inc.)
Missouri School of Journalism
138 Neff Annex
Columbia, MO 65211
Tel: (573) 882-2042
Fax: (573) 882-5431
E-mail: info@ire.org
Web site: <www.ire.org>

The *IRE Journal* is published six
times a year and contains journalist
profiles, how-to stories, reviews,
investigative ideas, and backgrounding
tips. The *Journal* also provides
members with the latest news on
upcoming events, training, and
employment opportunities in the
field of journalism.

JOURNAL OF PRISONERS
ON PRISONS
P.O. Box 70068
Place Bell R.P.O.
Ottawa, ON Canada
Tel: (613) 562-5800 ext. 1796
E-mail: jpp@jpp.org
Web site:

An independent, academic journal
that publishes the analysis and
commentary of prisoners and former
prisoners on contemporary criminal
justice issues.

JOURNALISM AND MASS
COMMUNICATION QUARTERLY
Published by The Association
for Education in Journalism and
Mass Communication
National Center for Communication
Studies, George Washington University
Washington, DC 20052
Tel: (204) 994-6226
Fax: (204) 994-5806

E-mail: aejmc@sc.edu
Web site:
<commfaculty.fullerton.edu/lester/
otherwork/aejmc/pubs.html#jmcq>

A scientific research publication
about journalism and mass
communication.

THE KONFORMIST
P.O. Box 24825
Los Angeles, CA 90024-0825
Tel: (310) 737-1081
Fax: (310) 737-1081
E-mail: robalini@aol.com
Web site: <www.konformist.com>

Promotes media activism and has
an Internet magazine dedicated to
"rebellion, conspiracy and
subversion."

LABOR NEWS FOR
WORKING FAMILIES
2521 Channing Way, #5555
Berkeley, CA 94720
Tel: (510) 643-7088
Fax: (510) 642-6432
E-mail: lpws@home.iir.berkeley.edu
Web site: <laborproject.berkeley.edu>

Highlights union policies and benefits
including family leave, child care,
elder care, and flexible work.

LABOR NOTES
7435 Michigan Avenue
Detroit, MI 48210
Tel;: (313) 842-6262
Fax: (313) 842-0227
E-mail: labornotes@labornotes.org
Web site:

News and information for workplace
activists. Aimed at rebuilding the
lavor movement through democracy

and member activity.

LEFT BUSINESS OBSERVER
P.O. Box 953
New York , NY 10014-0704
Tel: (212) 874-4020
Fax: (212) 874-3137
E-mail: dhenwood@panix.com
Web site: <www.panix.com/~dhen-
wood/LBO_home.html>

A monthly newsletter on economics
and politics in the U.S. and the world
at large.

LEFT CURVE
P.O. Box 472
Oakland, CA 94604-0472
Tel: (510) 763-7193
E-mail: leftcurv@wco.com
Web site: <www.ncal.verio.com/~left-
curv>

Artist-produced magazine addressing
problems of cultural forms emerging
from problems of modernity,
recognizing the destructiveness
of commodity systems to all life.

LM MAGAZINE
P.O. Box 769
New York, NY 10156
E-mail:
webmaster@mailinforminc.co.uk
Web site: <www.informinc.co.uk>

A loud-mouthed free speech magazine
that dares to publish what others are
frightened to whisper.

LRA'S ECONOMIC NOTES
330 West 42nd Street, 13th floor
New York, NY 10001

Tel: (212) 714-1677
Fax: (212) 714-1674
E-mail: info@laborresearch.org
Web site:

Labor, economics, and politics for
labor policymakers.

MEDIA BYPASS
4900 Tippecanoe Drive
Evansville, IN 47715
Tel: (812) 477-8670
Fax: (812) 477-8677
E-mail: subscribe@4bypass.com
Web site: www.mediaBypass.com

A national magazine from alternative
sources, providing unsuppressed
national news for concerned
Americans.

THE MEDIA CONSORTIUM
1355 North Highway Drive
Fenton, St. Louis County, MO 63099
Tel: (800) 325-3338
Fax: (636) 827-6761
E-mail: postmaster@delve.com
Web site: <207.239.118.26/delve
main.asp>

An independent, investigative news
company with the goal of generating
original journalism through a variety
of media outlets.

MEDIA WATCH
P.O. Box 618
Santa Cruz, CA 95061-0618
Tel: (800) 631-6355
Fax: (408) 423-6355
E-mail: mwatch@cruzio.com
Web site: <ww.mediawatch.com>
Media Watch works to challenge
media bias through education and
action.

MEDIAFILE
Published by Media Alliance
814 Mission Street, Suite 205
San Fransico, CA 94103
Tel: (415) 546-6334
Fax: 415/546-6218
E-mail: ma@igc.org
Web site: <www.media-alliance.org>

Includes independent reviews of
Bay Area media issues including
publications, broadcast outlets, and
Internet publishing.

MIDDLE EAST REPORT
1500 Massachusetts Avenue, NW
Suite 119
Washington, DC 20005
Tel: (202) 223-3677
Fax: (202) 223-3604
E-mail: ctoensing@merip.org
Web site: <www.merip.org>

Offering an independent critical
voice on the Middle East. Welcomes
and will pay for current, related
photographs.

MILITARY AND THE
ENVIRONMENT
Published by Pacific
Studies Center
222-B View Street
Mountain View, CA 94041
Tel: (415) 904-7751
Fax: (415) 904-7765
E-mail: cpro@igc.apc.org
Web site: <www.igc.org>

A citizen's report newsletter aimed
at educating the public about current
issues and legislation related to the
military and its impact on the
environment.

MONTHLY REVIEW
122 West 27th Street
New York, NY 10001
Tel: (212) 691-2555
Fax: (212) 727-3676
E-mail: promo@monthlyreview.org
Web site: <www.monthlyreview.org/>

An independent socialist magazine.
A unique blend of scholarship
and activism, critical understanding,
and accessibility.

MOTHER JONES
731 Market Street
6th floor
San Francisco, CA 94103
Tel: (415) 665-6637; (800) 438-6656
Fax: (415) 665-6696
E-mail: subscribe@motherjones.com
Web site: <www.motherjones.com>

The magazine of investigative
journalism; now with the online sister
"mojowire."

MS.
20 Exchange Place
22nd floor
New York, NY 10005
Tel: (212) 509-2092
Fax: (212) 509-2407
E-mail: info@msmagazine.com
Web site: <www.msmagazine.com>

Founding magazine of the feminist
movement, ad-free, national and international focus on issues affecting
women.

MSRRT NEWSLETTER:
LIBRARY ALTERNATIVES
Published by the Minnesota Library

Association Social Responsibilities
Round Table.
4645 Columbus Avenue South
Minneapolis, MN 55407
Tel: (612) 694-8572
Fax: (612) 541-8600
E-mail: edmiston@cs.unca.edu
Web site: <www.cs.unca.edu/~edmis
ton/msrrt/>

News, commentary, and networking
info for activist librarians and cultural
workers, with reviews of alternative
press publications and alternative
media. Issued in print under the
auspices of the Minnesota Library
Association.

MULTINATIONAL MONITOR
P.O. Box 19405
Washington, DC 20036
Tel: (202) 387-8030
Fax: (202) 234-5176
E-mail: monitor@essential.org
Web site: <www.essential.org>

Tracks corporate activity,
especially in the Third World.

EL MUNDO
630 20th Street
Oakland, CA 94612
Tel: (510) 287-8223
Fax: (510) 763-9670
E-mail: malpave@aol.com or
vsw@citycom.com

A national Spanish-language
publication.

NABJ JOURNAL
Published 10 times a year
8701 Adelphi Road

Adelphi, MD 20783-1716
Tel: (301) 445-7100
Fax: (301) 445-7101
E-mail: nabj@nabj.org
Web site:

The *NABJ Journal* is the publication
of the National Association of Black
Journalist, the largest media organization of people of color in the world.

NACLA REPORT
ON THE AMERICAS
475 Riverside Drive, Suite 454
New York, NY 10115
Tel: (212) 870-3146
Fax: (212) 870-3305
E-mail: nacla@nacla.org
Web site: <www.nacla.org>

NACLA has, for 30 years, been the
best source for alternative information
and analysis on Latin America, the
Caribbean, and U.S. foreign policy in
the region. *NACLA* analyzes the major
political, social, and economic trends
in Latin America, in an accessible
format not seen anywhere else.

NAJA NEWS
3359 36th Avenue South
Minneapolis, MN 55406
Tel: (612) 729-9244
Fax: (612) 729-9373
E-mail: naja@naja.com
Web site: <www.naja.com>

Quarterly newsletter of the Native
American Journalists Association.

THE NATION
33 Irving Place, 8th fFoor
New York, NY 10003

Tel: (212) 209-5400
Fax: (212) 982-9000
E-mail: info@thenation.com
Web site: <www.thenation.com>

Investigative journalism, a leading forum for leftist debate; home of Radio Nation and The Nation Institute.

NATIONAL CATHOLIC REPORTER
115 East Armour Boulevard
Kansas City, MO 64111
Tel: (816) 531-0538l (800) 333-7373
Fax: (816) 968-2268
E-mail: ncr_editor@natcath.com
Web site: <www.natcath.com>

An independent, Catholic newsweekly covering events related to the church over the past 30 years; inspired by the second Vatican.

NATIONAL GREEN PAGES
A Publication of Coop America
1612 K Street, NW, Suite 600
Washington, DC 20006
Tel: (800) 58-GREENl
(202) 872-5307
Fax: (202) 331-8166
E-mail: info@coopamerica.org
Web site: <www.greenpages.org>

A directory of thousands of responsible businesses, products, and services —a wonderful resource—published yearly.

NEW DEMOCRACY
P.O. Box 427
Boston, MA 02130
Tel: (617) 323-7213
E-mail: newdem@aol.com
Web site:
<www.newdemocracyworld.org>

Founded to help people in their struggle against capitalism, to shape the world with anti-capitalist values of solidarity, equality, and democracy.

NEW INTERNATIONALIST
P.O. Box 1143
Lewiston, NY 14092
Tel: (906) 946-0407
Fax: (906) 946-0410
E-mail: magazines@indas.on.ca
Web site:

An international journal that exists to report on the issues of inequality and world poverty; to focus attention on the unjust reltionship between the powerful and the powerless in both rich and poor countries; and to debate the campaign for the radical changes necessary.

NEW PERSPECTIVES QUARTERLY
10951 West Pico Boulevard, 3rd Floor
Los Angeles, CA 90064
Tel: (310) 474-0011
E-mail: npq@pacificnet.net
Web site:

Offering economic and political thought, on a global scale, from different points of view in a thematic format.

NEW POLITICS
328 Clinton Street
Brooklyn, NY 11231
Tel: (718) 237-2048
Email: newpol@igc.org
Web site:
www.wpunj.edu/~newpol/default.htm
A journal of socialist thought, *New Politics* insists on the centrality of democracy to socialism and on the need to rely on mass movements from

below for progressive social transformation.

NEW SOCIALIST
P.O. Box 167
Toronto, ON
Canada
Tel: (416) 969-3209
E-mail: newsoc@web.net
Web site:

A journal that rejects bureaucratic and authoritarian visions of socialism and looks instead to the radical tradition of socialism from below. Hopes to contribute to the building of a wider socialist movement in Canada and internationally.

NEW UNIONIST
2309 Nicollette Avenue, Suite 102
Minneapolis, MN 55408
Tel: (651) 646-5546
E-mail: nup@minn.net
Web site: <www1.minn.net/~nup>

A monthly paper dedicated to building a rank-and-file working-class movement for fundamental social change; to replace the present competitive, class-divided system of capitalism with the cooperative industrial community we call economic democracy.

NEWS FROM INDIAN COUNTRY
(NFIC)
7831 North Grindstone Ave.
Hayward, WI 54843-2052
Tel: (715) 634-5226
Fax: (715) 634-3243
E-mail: newsfic.aol.com
Web site:
<ww.indiancountrynews.com>

NFIC provides national Native news and information, as well as cultural and powwow updates.

NEWS INDIA TIMES
244 5th Avenue, Suite 400
New York, NY 10001
Tel: (877) 481-0395
E-mail: subscription@news-india.com
Web site:

The weekly is roughly divided into two parts. The first half is hard news: political news from India and the U.S. that concerns the large community here. The other half consists of features, columns on interest to women and children, classifieds, and so on. It is the only four-color English-language weekly serving the million-strong Asian Indians settled in the United States.

NEWS MEDIA AND THE LAW
Journal of the Reporter's Committee for Freedom of the Press
1815 North Fort Meyer Drive
Suite 900
Arlington, VA 22209
Tel: (800) 336-4243
Fax: (703) 807-2109
E-mail: rcfp@rcfp.org
Web site: <www.rcfp.org>

A quarterly magazine which covers issues related to news reporting and the media, and the legal issues therein.

NEWS MEDIA UPDATE
Newsletter of the Reporter's Committee for Freedom of the Press
1815 North Fort Meyer Drive
Suite 900

Arlington, VA 22209
Tel: (800) 336-4243
Fax: (703) 807-2109
E-mail: rcfp@rcfp.org
Web site:

A twice-monthly newsletter regarding
current media issues.

NEWS ON EARTH
541 West 25th Street
PMB 2245
New York, NY 10011
Tel: (212) 741-2365
Fax: (212) 979-2055
E-mail: earthchanges@earthlink.net
Web site:

A politically independent newsletter
that reports on the vital issues of the
day and tells the real story about what
is going on in Washington.

NEWSLETTER ON
INTELLECTUAL FREEDOM
Published by the American
Library Association (ALA)
50 East Huron Street
Chicago, IL 60611
Tel: (800) 545-2433
Fax: (312) 280-4227
E-mail: jkrug@ala.org
Web site:
<www.ala.org/alaorg/oif/nif_inf.html>

Newsletter of the ALA's office of
intellectual freedom.

NEWSPRINTS
Essential Information
P.O. Box 19405
Washington, DC 20036
Tel: (202) 387-8030

Fax: (202) 234-5176
E-mail: newsprints@essential.org
Web site: <www.essential.org/
newsprints/newsprints.html>

Twice a month, *Newsprints* publish
es leads that the national dailies and
network news shows miss: hard-hitting
investigations and commentary by
regional writers examining crucial
concerns from more than 100 of the
nation's highest circulating daily
newspapers.

NEWSWATCH MONITOR
NewsWatch Canada
c/o School of Communication
Simon Fraser University
8888 University Drive
Burnaby, BC Canada
Tel: (604) 291-4905
Fax: (604) 291-3687
E-mail: newswatch@sfu.ca
Web site: <newswatch.cprost.sfu.ca>

A quarterly newsletter which reports
on Canada's media performance.

NEXUS
2940 East Colfax, #131
Denver, CO 80206
Tel: (303) 321-5006
Fax: (603) 754-4744
E-mail: nexususa@earthlink.net
Web site: <www.nexusmagazine.com>

Since Nexus recognizes that humanity
is undergoing a massive transformation, it seeks to provide "hard-to-get"
information so as to assist people
through these changes. It is not linked
to any religious, philosophical, or
political ideology or organization.

THE NONVIOLENT ACTIVIST

P.O. Box 30947
Philadelphia, PA 19104
Tel: (212) 228-0450
Fax: (212) 228-6193
E-mail: nvweb@nonviolence.org
Web site:

Political analysis from a pacifist perspective.

NORTH BAY PROGRESSIVE
All the News That Didn't Fit
P.O. Box 14384
Santa Rosa, CA 95402
Tel: (707) 525-1422
Fax: (707) 595-4700
Web site:
<www.northbayprogressive.org>

Regional biweekly covering local, national, and international news.

NORTH COAST XPRESS (NCX)
P.O.Box 1226
Occidental, CA 95465
Tel: (707) 874-3104
Fax: (707) 874-1453
E-mail: doretk@sonic.net
Web site: <www.north-coast-xpress.com/~doretk/>

NCX supports grassroots movements and under-represented minorities, and exposes threats to the environment, an unjust criminal justice system, and corporate control of politics and the economy.

NOW MAGAZINE
189 Church Street
Toronto, ON Canada
Tel: (416) 364-1300
Fax: (416) 364-1433

E-mail: letters@nowtoronto.com or news@toronto.com
Web site: <www.nowtoronto.com>

Toronto's independent weekly magazine.

THE NUCLEAR MONITOR
1424 16th St., NW, Suite 404
Washington, DC 20036
Tel: (202) 328-0002
Fax: (202) 462-2183
E-mail: hirsnet@hirs.org
Web site: <www.nirs.org>

Networking and advocacy center for citizens and groups concerned with nuclear power, radioactive waste, and sustainable energy. Dedicated to a sound nonnuclear energy policy.

NUKEWATCH
The Progressive Foundation
P.O. Box 649
Luck, WI 54853
Tel: (715) 472-4185
Fax: (715) 472-4184
E-mail: nukewtch@lakeland.ws
Web site:

Focuses on covering, investigating, and exposing the nuclear industry.

OMB WATCHER
A Publication of OMB Watch
1742 Connecticut Avenue, NW
Washington, DC 20009-1171
Tel: (202) 234-8494
Fax: (202) 234-8584
E-mail: ombwatch@ombwatch.org
Web site: <www.ombwatch.org>

Focuses on budget issues, regulatory policy, non-profit advocacy, access to government information, and activities at the Office of Management and

Budget (OMB) in Washington.

ON EARTH
(Formerly the *Amicus Journal*)
40 West 20th Street
New York, NY 10011
Tel: (212) 727-4412
Fax: (212) 727-1773
E-mail: OnEarth@nrdc.org
Web site: <www.nrdc.org/OnEarth>

The quarterly journal of thought
and opinion on environmental issues
published by the National Resources
Defense Council.

OUR TIMES
Canada's Independent
Labour Magazine
1209 King Street West, Suite 201-A
Toronto, ON Canada
Tel: (800) 648-6131
Fax: (416) 531-7641
E-mail: ourstory@web.net
Web site: <www.ourtimes.web.net>

Focuses on social change through
unionism and democratic socialism.

PATHFINDER
Published by Nukewatch and
The Progressive Foundation
P.O. Box 649
Luck, WI 54853
Tel: (715) 472-4185
Fax: (715) 472-4184
E-mail: nukewatch@lakeland.ws
Web site: <www.nukewatch.com>

Encourages a non-violent change
for an environment free of the nuclear
industry and weapons of mass
destruction.

PEACE MAGAZINE

P.O. Box 248 Stn. P
Toronto, ON
Canada
Tel: (416) 533-7581
Fax: (416) 531-6214
E-mail: mspencer@web.net
Web site: <www.peacemagazine.org>

Peace Magazine is a valuable resource
for anyone wishing to keep on top of
the issues and activities of movements
for peace and non-violence around the
world.

PEACEWORK
2161 Massachusetts Avenue
Cambridge, MA 02140
Tel: (617) 661-6130
E-mail: pwork@igc.org
Web site:
<www.afsc.org/peacewrk.htm>

A monthly journal published since
1972, *Peacework* covers the full range
of "Global Thought and Local Action
for Non-violent Social Change," with
a special focus on the northeastern
United States. It is meant to serve the
movement as a trade journal, with
minimal pretensions.

PEOPLE'S WEEKLY WORLD
3940 High Street, Suite B
Oakland, CA 94691
Tel: (510) 336-0617
Fax: (510) 336-0617
E-mail: ncalview@ipc.org
Web site: <www.pww.org>
THE PERMACULTURE
ACTIVIST (THE PA)
P.O. Box 1209
Black Mountain, NC 28711
Tel: (828) 669-6336
Fax: (828) 669-5068
E-mail: pcactiv@metalab.unc.edu

Web site: <www.permacultureactivist.net/>

The PA advocates and documents ecological design of housing, landscapes, and settlements as a tool supporting food and resource security, community empowerment, and local economic self-reliance.

THE PLANET DRUM PULSE
Published by Planet Drum Foundation
P.O. Box 31251
San Francisco, CA 94131
Tel: (415) 285-6556
Fax: (415) 285-6563
E-mail: planetdrum@igc.org
Web site: <www.planetdrum.org>

A biannual review on issues of estoration ecology and the greening of cities.

POCLAD—THE PROGRAM
ON CORPORATIONS, LAW
& DEMOCRACY
Published by Council on International and Public Affairs (CIPA)
P.O. Box 246
South Yarmouth, MA 02664-0246
Tel: (508) 398-1145
Fax: (508) 398-1552
E-mail: people@poclad.org
Web site: <www.poclad.org>

A quarterly publication that instigates democratic conversations and actions that contest the authority of corporations to govern.

POOR MAGAZINE
Published by Poor News Network
255 9th Street
San Francisco, CA 94103
Tel: (415) 541-5629
E-mail: tiny@poormagazine.org
Web site: <www.poormagazine.org>

POOR is the publication of a literary, visual arts based community organization that provides vocational training, creative arts, and literacy education to very low- and no-income adults and children in the San Francisco Bay Area, with the goal of deconstructing the margins of class and race oppression.

PR WATCH
Published by Center for Media and Democracy
520 University Avenue
Suite 310
Madison, WI 53703
Tel: (608) 260-9713
Fax: (608) 260-9714
E-mail: editor@prwatch.org
Web site: <www.prwatch.org>

Investigates corporate and government propoganda. The editors also wrote *Toxic Sludge is Good For You: Lies, Damn Lies and the Public Relations Industry.*

PREVAILING WINDS MAGAZINE
A Publication of the Center for the Preservation of Modern History
P.O. Box 23511
Santa Barbara, CA 93121
Tel: (805) 899-3433
Fax: (805) 899-4773
E-mail: patrick@silcom.com
Web site: <www.prevailingwinds.org>

Devoted to exposing assassination, political scandals, medical fraud, crime, media manipulation, corruption, mind control, and high strangeness.

PRINCETON PROGRESSIVE
REVIEW

Princeton University
315 West College
Princeton, NJ 08544
E-mail:
progrev@phoenix.princeton.edu
Web site: <www.princeton.edu/
~progrev>

A journal of news analysis and
occasional cultural critique, voicing
social justice. Subscriptions are
online.

PRISON LEGAL NEWS (PLN)
2400 NW 80th Street, PMB 148
Seattle, WA 98117
Tel: (206) 789-1022
Fax: (206) 505-9449
E-mail: pln@prisonlegalnews.org
Web site: <www.prisonlegalnews.org>

PLN reports court rulings involving
prisoner rights as well as providing
news and commentary on criminal justice issues.

PROBE
David Zimmerman's newsletter—
The Probe Newsletter, Inc.
P.O. Box 1321, Cathedral Station
New York, NY 10025
Tel: (212) 647-0200
Fax: (212) 463-8002
Web site: <probenewsletter.com>

Probe is an investigative and
interpretive newsletter on science,
media, policy, and health in the spirit
of I.-F. Stone. It promotes science
and rationality as key elements in a
democratic society.

THE PROGRESSIVE
409 East Main Street
Madison, WI 53703

Tel: (608) 257-4626
Fax: (608) 257-3373
E-mail: circ@progressive.org
Web site: <www.progressive.org>

The Progressive discusses peace, politics, social justice, and environmental
concerns from a liberal point of view.

PROGRESSIVE LIBRARIAN
P.O.Box 2203
Times Square Station
New York, NY 10108
Tel: (973) 623-7642
E-mail: web@libr.org
Web site: <www.libr.org>

A journal for critical studies and progressive politics, *Progressive Librarian*
brings to librarianship perspectives
that challenge prevailing assumptions
concerning information technology,
library management, censorship, and
other such issues.

THE PROGRESSIVE POPULIST
P.O. Box 150517
Austin, TX 78715-0517
Tel: (512) 447-0455
E-mail: populist@usa.net
Web site: <www.populist.com>

It provides monthly reports from the
Heartland on issues of interest to
workers, farmers, and small business.
It promotes the idea that people are
more important than corporations.

THE PROGRESSIVE REVIEW
1312 18th Street, NW, #502
Washington, DC 20036
Tel: (202) 835-0770
Fax: (202) 835-0779
E-mail: news@prorev.com
Web site:
<emporium.turnpike.net/P/ProRev>

This is Washington's most unofficial source. It provides Green, populist perspectives.

PUBLIC CITIZEN MAGAZINE
1600 20th Street, NW
Washington, DC 20009
Tel: (202) 588-1000
Fax: (202) 588-7799
E-mail: pcmail@citizen.org
Web site: <www.citizen.org>

Consumer rights, safety issues, corporate and business accountability, environmental issues, and citizen empowerment.

THE PUBLIC EYE
A Publication of the Political Research Associates
1310 Broadway, Suite #201
Somerville, MA 02144
Tel: (617) 666-5300
Fax: (617) 666-6622
E-mail: pra@igc.org
Web site: <www.publiceye.org/pra/>

The Public Eye is a quarterly news-letter featuring an in-depth analysis and critique of issues pertaining to the U.S. political right wing.

PULSE OF THE TWIN CITIES
3200 Chicago Ave.
Minneapolis, MN 55407
Tel: (612) 824-0000
Fax: (612) 822-0342
E-mail: editor@pulsetc.com
Web site: <www.pulsete.com>

The alternative weekly of Minneapolis/ St. Paul and the Twin Cities area.

QUILL
Publication of the Society of Professional Journalists
3909 North Meridian Street
Indianapolis, IN 46208
Tel: (317) 927-8000
Fax: (317) 920-4789
E-mail: spj@spj.org
Web site: <www.spj.org>

A national magazine that reports on journalism.

RACE, POVERTY &
THE ENVIRONMENT
Urban Habitat Program
San Francisco, CA 94129
Tel: (415) 561-3333
Fax: (415) 561-3334
E-mail: contact@urbanhabitatprogram. org
Web site: <www.urbanhabitatpro gram. org/publications.htm>

A national journal of the environmental justice movement, co-published with the Center for Race, Poverty, and the Environment.

RACHEL'S ENVIRONMENTAL &
HEALTH WEEKLY
Published by the Environmental Research Foundation
P.O. Box 5036
Annapolis, MD 21403-7063
Tel: (410) 263-1584
Fax: (410) 263-8944; (888) 272-2435
E-mail: erf@rachel.org
Web site: <www.rachel.org>

Rachel's provides timely information on toxic substances and other environmental hazards. It covers many technical issues, but is written in plain language that anyone can understand.

RETHINKING SCHOOLS
An Urban Educational Journal
1001 East Keefe Avenue
Milwaukee, WI 53212
Tel: (800) 669-4192; (414) 964-9646
Fax: (414) 964-7220
E-mail: RSBusiness@aol.com
Web site:
<www.rethinkingschools.org>

Provides an alternative to mainstream educational materials, committed to issues of equity and social justice.

REVOLUTIONARY WORKER
Box 3486 Merchandise Mart
Chicago, IL 60654
Tel: (773) 227-4066
Fax: (773) 227-4497
Web site: <www.rwor.org>

The weekly newspaper of the Revolutionary Communist Party, USA.

RIGHTS
Center for Constitutional Rights
666 Broadway, 7th Floor
New York, NY 10012
Tel: (212) 475-7206
Fax: (212) 614-6499
Web site: <www.ccr-ny.org>

Covers issues involving freedoms guaranteed by the Constitution and Bill of Rights.
ROLLING STONE
1290 Avenue of the Americas
2nd Floor
New York, NY 10104
Tel: (212) 484-1616
Fax: (212) 767-8203
Web site: <www.rollingstone.com>

Rock and politics at the cutting edge.

RYERSON REVIEW
OF JOURNALISM
350 Victoria Street
Toronto, ON
Canada
Tel: (416) 979-5319. ext. 7434
E-mail: 1cunning@ryerson.ca
Web site: <www.ryerson.ca/rrj>

A progressive journalistic review from Ryerson Polytechnic University in Canada.

S.O.A. WATCH
(WASHINGTON)
P.O. Box 4566
Washington, DC 20017
Tel: (202) 234-3440
Fax: (202) 636-4505
E-mail: info@soaw.org
Web site: <www.soaw.org>

Tracks and reports on activities at the School of the Americas.

SAN FRANCISCO
BAY GUARDIAN
520 Hampshire
San Francisco, CA 94110-1417
Tel: (415) 255-3100
Fax: (415) 255-8762
E-mail: sfguardian@aol.com
Web site: <www.sfbg.com>

The best of the Bay...every week!
SAN FRANCISCO BAY VIEW
National Black Newspaper
4908 Third Street
San Francisco, CA 94124
Tel: (415) 671-0449
Fax: (415) 822-8971
E-mail: editor@sfbayview.com
Web site: <www.sfbayview.com>

SECRECY & GOVERNMENT

BULLETIN
Project on Government Secrecy
Federation of American Scientists
1717 K Street, NW, Suite 209
Washington, DC 20036
Tel: (202) 454-4691
Fax: (202) 675-1010
E-mail: saftergood@fas.org
Web site: <www.fas.org/sgp/>

Reports on new developments
in government secrecy policies.

SEJOURNAL
Published by Society
of Environmental Journalists
P.O. Box 2492
Jenkintown, PA 19046
Tel: (215) 884-8174
Fax: (215) 884-8175
E-mail: sej@sej.org
Web site: <www.sej.org>

The quarterly *SEJournal* is a
publication written primarily by
journalists for journalists. Its purpose
is to provide information and guidance
on covering the environment beat.

SHELTERFORCE
National Housing Institute
439 Main Street, Suite 311
Orange, NJ 07050-1523
Tel: (973) 678-9060
Fax: (973) 678-8437
E-mail: yvonne@nhi.org
Web site: <www.nhi.org>

National cross-disciplinary trade
magazine for community builders,
mixing coverage of local stories
with policy and theory to make
useful links between community
revitalization issues.

SIERRA MAGAZINE
Published by the Sierra Club
85 - 2nd Street, 2nd Floor
San Francisco, CA 94105
Tel: (415) 977-5500
Fax: (415) 977-5799
E-mail: information@sierraclub.org
Web site: <www.sierraclub.org>

The Sierra Club's grassroots advocacy
has made it America's most influential
environmental organization. Founded
in 1892, we are now more than
700,000 members strong.

SKEPTICAL INQUIRER
P.O. Box 703
Amherst, NY 14226-0703
Tel: (716) 636-1425
Fax: (716) 636-1733
E-mail: info@csicop.org
Web site: <www.csicop.org/si/>

The magazine for science and reason.

SOCIAL ANARCHISM
A Publication of the Atlantic Center
for Research and Education
2743 Maryland Avenue
Baltimore, MD 21218
E-mail: spud@nothingness.org
Web site:
<www.nothingness.org/sociala/>

A biannual anarchist journal with an
intended bias towards the social over
the individual, although in actual
practice it tends towards eclecticism.

SOCIAL POLICY
25 West 43rd Street
Room 620
New York, NY 10036-7406
Tel: (212) 642-2929
Fax: (212) 642-1956

E-mail: socpol@igc.apc.org
Web site: <www.sclplcy@aol.com>

Social Policy is a magazine about
social movements. It breaks new
ground with its in-depth and
thoughtful analysis of public policy
in America.

SOCIALIST REVIEW
1095 Market Street, Suite 618
San Francisco, CA 94103
Tel: (415) 255-2296
E-mail: socialistreview@earthlink.net
Web site:

A forum for radical politics, cultural
dissent, and socialist critique.

SOJOURNERS
2401 15th Street, NW
Washington, DC 20009
Tel: (202) 328-8842
Fax: (202) 328-8757
E-mail: listserv@sojourners.com
Web site: <www.sojo.net>

A grassroots network for personal,
community, and political
transformation rooted in prophetic
biblical tradition.

SOLIDARITY
Journal of the United
Auto Workers Union
8000 East Jefferson
Detroit, MI 48214
Tel: (313) 926-5000
E-mail: uaw@uaw.org
Web site: <www.uaw.org>

Official magazine of the
United Auto Workers.

SOUTHERN EXPOSURE
P.O. Box 531
Durham, NC 27702-0531
Tel: (919) 419-8311 ext. 26
Fax: (919) 419-8315
E-mail: info@i4south.org
Web site:

Award-winning magazine focused
on fighting for a better South.
Heavily deals with the work force
in the South and corporations.

SPIN
205 Lexington Avenue
New York, NY 10016
Tel: (212) 231-7400
Fax: (212) 231-7300
E-mail: info@spinmag.com
Web site: <www.spin.com>

News, issues, and profiles in
alternative music.

SPIRIT OF CRAZY HORSE
Published by Leonard Peltier
Defense Committee
P.O. Box 583
Lawrence, KS 66044
Tel: (785) 842-5774
Fax: (785) 842-5796
E-mail: lpdc@idir.net

Web site: <www.freepeltier.org/news
paper.htm>

A bimonthly newspaper. Learn
what we can do to help free Leonard.
Statements from and updates on
Leonard Peltier's case—also focuses
on native sovereignty and some prison
issues.

ST. LOUIS JOURNALISM
REVIEW (SJR)

8380 Olive Boulevard
St. Louis, MO 63132
Tel: (314) 991-1699
Fax: (314) 997-1898
E-mail: review@webster.edu
Web site: <www.webster.edu/~
review/>

SJR—the only local journalism review
in the U.S.—primarily critiques what
is covered or ignored by the local
media. It also covers some national
and international news.

STEELABOR
Five Gateway Center
Pittsburgh, PA 15222
Tel: (412) 562-2442
Fax: (412) 562-2445
E-mail: webmaster@uswa.org
Web site: <www.uswa.org/steelabor/
JulAug00/jul_aug.htm>

News and commentary about members
of steelworkers unions, plus political,
economic, and social issues of concern to steelworkers.

STUDENT PRESS LAW
CENTER REPORT
1815 North Fort Meyer Drive
Suite 900
Arlington, VA 22209-1817
Tel: (703) 807-1904
Fax: (703) 807-2109
E-mail: splc@splc.org
Web site: <www.splc.org>

Reports on cases, controversies,
and legislation relating to free press
rights of student journalists. Advice
and legal assistance at no charge to
students and the educators who work
with them.

SUSTAINABLE TIMES
1657 Barrington Street
Suite 508
Halifax, NS Canada
Tel: (902) 423-6852
Fax: (902) 423-9736
E-mail: ip-cuso@chebucto.ns.ca
Web site: <reseau.chebucto.ns.ca/
CommunitySupport/CUSO/descrip.
html>

Providing solutions to employment,
environment, and global development
challenges.

SYNTHESIS/REGENERATION
A Magazine of Green Social Thought
P.O. Box 24115
St. Louis, MO 63130
Tel: (314) 727-8554
Fax: Call first
E-mail: fitzdon@aol.com
Web site: <www.greens.org/s-r/>

A triannual magazine focusing on the
social aspects of environmentalism.

TEAMSTER MAGAZINE
Published by the International Broth-
erhood of Teamsters
25 Louisiana Avenue, NW
Washington, DC 20001
Tel: (202) 624-6800
Fax: (202) 624-6918
E-mail: feedback@teamster.org
Web site: <www.teamster.org>

A magazine that focuses on fighting
for the future and the rights of working
families in North America dedicated
to the trade union movement.

TELEMEDIUM, THE JOURNAL
OF MEDIA LITERACY
Published by the National

Telemedia Council
1922 University Avenue
Madison, WI 53705-4013
Tel: (608) 257-7712
Fax: (608) 257-7714
E-mail: NTelemedia@aol.com
Web site: <ddanenet.wicip.org/ntc/
NTC.HTM>

Publication that promotes media
literacy education with a positive,
non-judgmental philosophy.
Published by the oldest national
media literacy organization in the
U.S., it is in its 45th year.

TEMP SLAVE
P.O. Box 8284
Madison, WI 53708-8284
E-mail: grvsmth@panix.com
Web site: <www.panix.com/~grvsmth/
redguide/slave.html>

A mischievous and wildly amusing
zine documenting the often unpleasant
and bitter experiences of temp workers
and the drudgery of the workplace.

TERRAIN
2530 San Pablo Avenue
Berkeley, CA 94702
Tel: (510) 548-2235
Fax: (510) 548-2240
E-mail: terrain@ecologycenter.org
Web site: <www.ecologycenter.org>

A quarterly magazine focusing on
environmental issues.

THE TEXAS OBSERVER
307 West Seventh Street
Austin, TX 78701
Tel: (800) 939-6620
Fax: (512) 477-0746
E-mail: business@texasobserver.org

Web site: <TexasObserver.org/>

The Texas Observer writes about
issues ignored or under-reported in
the mainstream press. Our goal is
to cover stories crucial to the public
interest and to provoke dialogue that
promotes democratic participation
and open government.

THE UNABASHED LIBRARIAN
P.O. Box 325
Mount Kisco, NY 10549
Fax: (914) 244-0941
E-mail:
editor@unabashedlibrarian.com
Web site:
<www.unabashedlibrarian.com>

The "how I run my library good"
newsletter, believing that "the Library
is more than information."

THE URBAN ECOLOGIST
QUARTERLY
414 13th Street Suite 500
Oakland, CA 94612
Tel: (510) 251-6330
Fax: (510) 251-2117
E-mail:
urbanecology@urbanecology.org
Web site: <www.urbanecology.org>

A magazine dedicated to creating
ecologically and socially healthy
communities—highlights examples
from throughout the world.

VILLAGE VOICE
36 Cooper Square
New York, NY 10003
Tel: (212) 475-475-3300
Fax: (212) 475-8944
E-mail: info@villagevoice.com
Web site: <www.villagevoice.com>

A weekly newspaper covering regional, national, and international affairs from a New York perspective.

THE WASHINGTON SPECTATOR
P.O. Box 20065
London Terrace Station
New York, NY 10011
Tel: (212) 741-2365
E-mail: spectator@newslet.com
Web site: <www.newslet.com/wash.specg>

A politically independent newsletter that reports on the vital issues of the day and tells the real story about what is going on in Washington.

THE WASHINGTONIAN
1828 L Street, NW, Suite 200
Washington, DC 20036
Tel: (202) 296-3600
E-mail: editorial@washingtonian.com
Web site: <www.washingtonian.com>

The magazine Washington lives by—Founded in 1965.

THIRD WORLD RESURGENCE
Journal of the Third World Network
228 Macalister Road
Penang, 10400 Malaysia
Tel: 604-2266 728 or 6 159
Fax: 604-2264 505
E-mail: twn@igc.apc.org
Web site: <www.twnside.org.sg>

An international network of groups and individuals involved in efforts to bring about a greater articulation of the needs and rights of people in the Third World; a fair distribution of world resources; and forms of development that are ecologically sustainable and fulfill human needs.

THIS MAGAZINE
Because Everything is Political
401 Richmond Street West, Suite 396
Toronto, ON Canada
Tel: (416) 979-9426
Fax: (416) 979-1143
E-mail: thismag@web.net
Web site: <www.thismag.org>

Thirty-five years and still going strong, *This Magazine* is one of Canada's longest-publishing alternative journals. This focuses on Canadian politics, literature and culture, but in keeping with its radical roots, never pulls punches. Subversive, edgy, and smart, *This* is the real alternative to that.

TIKKUN
2107 Van Ness Avenue, Suite 302
San Francisco, CA 94109
Tel: (415) 575-1200
Fax: (415) 575-1434
E-mail: webshammas@tikkun.com
Web site: <www.tikkun.com> or <www.tikkun.org>

A magazine that focuses on topics of particular interest to the Jewish community, including culture, politics, and philosophy.

TOMPAINE.COMMONSENSE
A Journal of Opinion
Web site: <www.tompaine.com>

TomPaine.com seeks to enrich the national debate on controversial public issues by featuring the ideas, opinions, and analyses too often overlooked by the mainstream media. We promote these in our weekly advertisement on the op-ed page of *The New York Times*.

TOWARD FREEDOM (TF)
The Independent Media
Convergence Project
Box 468
Burlington, VT 05402-0468
Tel: (802) 654-8024
Fax: (802) 658-3738
E-mail: info@towardfreedom.com
Web site: <www.towardfreedom.com>

A progressive international news, analysis, and advocacy journal that helps strengthen and extend human justice and liberties. *TF* opposes all forms of domination that repress human potential to reason, work creatively, and dream.

TRUE DEMOCRACY
Published by News Source, Inc.
P.O. Box 882
Lakebay, WA 98349-0882
Tel: (253) 884-0833
E-mail: ajohnsonpresnsi
@truedemocracy.net
Web site: <truedemocracy.net/
index. htm>

A publication that aims to restore true democracy to the United States and the world. Provides research on the Trilateral Commission.

TURNING THE TIDE
Journal of Anti-Racist Activism, Research, and Education
P.O. Box 1990
Burbank, CA 91507
Tel: (310) 288-5003
E-mail: mnovickttt@igc.ap.org
Web site: <www.prisonactivist.org/
pubs/ttt/>

A 10-year-old journal that exposes the strategies of organized white supremacists and their roots in U.S. political , social, and economic structures. It promotes anti-racist acitivism.

TYNDALL WEEKLY REPORT
135 Rivington Street
New York , NY 10002
Tel: (212) 674-8913
Fax: (212) 979-7304
E-mail: andrew@tyndallreport.com
Web site: <www.tyndallreport.com/
tw0029. html>

A weekly fax-sheet monitoring the television networks' nightly newscasts.

UPPNET NEWS
Labor Education Services
437 Management and Economy Bldg.
University of Minnesota
271 19th Avenue South
Minneapolis, MN 55455
Tel: (612) 624-4326
E-mail: uppnet@labornet.org
Web site: <www.mtn.org/jsee/uppnet.
html>

Official publication of the Union Producers and Programmers Network, promoting production and use of TV and radio shows pertinent to the cause of organized labor and working people.

URBAN ECOLOGY
414 13th Street, Suite 500
Oakland, CA 94612
Tel: (510) 251-6330
Fax: (510) 251-2117
E-mail: urbanecology@urbanecology.org
Web site:

Founded in 1975, we envision, design, and plan cities to support a healthy natural environment, a multicultural and thriving community, and an innovative and vigorous local economy. Through educational programs, tools for community planning, and advocacy, *Urban Ecology* assists diverse constituencies engaged in changing their land use and building patterns in the San Francisco Bay Area.

URGENT ACTION NEWSLETTER
P.O. Box 1270
Nederland, CO 80466-1270
Tel: (303) 258-1170; (303) 258-7886
Fax: (303) 258-7881
E-mail: sharris@igc.apc.org
Web site: <www.amnestyusa.org/urgent/>

The newsletter for Amnesty International out of the Urgent Action Program Office.

UTNE READER
1624 Harmon Place
Suite 330
Minneapolis, MN 55403
Tel: (612) 338-5040
Fax: (612) 338-6043
E-mail: info@utne.com
Web site: <www.utne.com>

A digest of alternative ideas and material reprinted from alternative and independent media sources.

VERDICT
Offical publication of the National Coalition of Concerned Legal Professionals
Woolworth Building
233 Broadway, Suite 830
New York, NY 10279
Tel: (212) 346-7777

Covering the legal consequences flowing from complex systemic problems in our communities, *Verdict*

is a forum promoting involvement by legal professionals and others active in or searching for legal and organizational solutions to the problems facing our low-income communities.

VIBE
215 Lexington Avenue
3rd Floor
New York, NY 10016
Tel: (212) 448-7300
Fax: (212) 448-7400
E-mail: info@vibe.com
Web site: <www.vibe.com>

Provides news and features about goings-on in urban culture.

VOICE
P.O. Box 541
Northampton, MA 01061

The Pioneer Valley's corporate-free press—published monthly

THE VOICE
448 Main St.
Winsted, CT 06098
Tel: (800) 738-4026
Fax: (860) 738-1380
E-mail: Voicewin@aol.com
Web site: <www.thevoicenews.com>
Weeky newspaper committed to presenting the full spectrum of local citizen opinion and does not favor one school of opinion over another. News and views expressed in *The Voice* do not necessarily reflect those of the publisher and/or staff of the newspaper.

WAR AND PEACE DIGEST
Journal of the War and Peace Foundation

United Nations Bureau
777 U.N. Plaza
New York, NY 10017
Tel: (212) 557-2501
Fax: (212) 577-2515
E-mail: warpeace@interport.net
Web site: <www.warpeace.org>

An anti-nuclear publication
promoting peace, social justice,
and media reform.

WASHINGTON FREE PRESS
PMB No. 178
1463 East Republican Street
Seattle, WA 98112
Tel: (206) 860-5290
E-mail: freepress@scn.org
Web site: <www.speakeasy.org/wfp>
WASHINGTON MONTHLY
Journal of Washington Monthly Co.
733 15th Street, NW, Suite 1000
Washington, DC 20005
Tel: (202) 393-5155
Fax: (202) 332-8413
E-mail:
letters@washingtonmonthly.com
Web site: <www.washingtonmonthly.
com>

National opinion magazine covering
politics, media, and government.
WASHINGTON REPORT
ON MIDDLE EAST AFFAIRS
P.O. Box 53062
Washington, DC 20009
Tel: (202) 939-6050
Fax: (202) 265-4574
E-mail: info@washington-report.org
Web site: <www.wrmea.com>

*The Washington Report on Middle
East Affairs* is a 140-page magazine
published 10 times per year in
Washington, DC, that focuses on

news and analysis from and about
the Middle East and U.S. policy in
that region.

WELFARE MOTHERS VOICE (WMV)
2711 West Michigan
Milwaukee, WI 53208
Tel: (414) 342-6662
Fax: (414) 342-6667
E-mail: wmvoice@execpc.com
Web site: <www.execpc.com/~wm
voice>

WMV provides a voice for mothers and
children in poverty who have joined
together to make our voices heard in all
policies affecting families in poverty,
the larger community, and the earth.
It also covers activist movements
related to poverty around the world.

WHOLE EARTH MAGAZINE
P.O. Box 3000
Denville, NJ 07834-9879
Tel: (888) 732-6739
E-mail: info@wholeearthmag.com
Web site:

Provides access to tools, ideas, and
practices; reviews books and products
to help people help themselves;
publishes a catalogue.
WHY MAGAZINE
505 Eighth Avenue, Suite 2100
New York, NY 10018-0582
Tel: (212) 629-8850
Fax: (212) 465-9274
E-mail: why@worldhungeryear.org
Web site: <www.worldhungeryear.org/
publications/why_mag.html>

A quarterly publication that challenges the existance of hunger and
poverty, presenting leading thinkers
and activists with information, insight,

and opportunities for involvement.

WILD MATTERS
Published by Food & Water, Inc.
PO Box 543
Montpelier, VT 05601
Tel: (802) 229-6222
Fax: (802) 229-6751
E-mail: info@foodandwater.org
Web site: <www.wildmatters.org>

Formerly Food & Water Journal,
Wild Matters is now published 10
times a year. A magazine that
advocates for safe food and water
and a clean environment by educating
the public on the health and
environmental dangers of food
irradiation, genetic engineering,
and toxic pesticides.

WOMEN'S HEALTH LETTER
P.O. Box 467939
Atlanta, GA 31146-7939
Tel: (770) 668-0432
E-mail: feedback@soundpub.com
Web site: <www.ok.org/homemaker/
pesach99/healthpage.html>

The thinking woman's guide to
wellness: offers sane and sound health
and healing insights that are often
startlingly contrary to what the
medical industry would have us
believe.

WORLD POLICY JOURNAL
New School University
66 Fifth Avenue, 9th Floor
New York, NY 10011
Tel: (212) 229-5808, ext. 105
Fax: (212) 229-5579
E-mail: levarts@newschool.edu
Web site: <worldpolicy.org>

A leading, quarterly magazine
covering international affairs in the
United States.

WORLD PRESS REVIEW
700 Broadway, 3rd Floor
New York, NY 10003
Tel: (212) 982-8880
E-mail: worldpress@worldpress.org
Web site: <www.worldpress.org>

A digest of the global press, a
sampling of newspapers from around
the world.

WORLD RIVERS REVIEW
Published by the International Rivers
Network
1847 Berkeley Way
Berkeley, CA 94703
Tel: (510) 848-1155
Fax: (510) 848-1008
E-mail: irn@irn.org
Web site: <www.irn.org>

Provides the latest news on the worldwide movement to stop destructive
dams, information about alternatives
to large hydro projects, action alerts,
book reviews, and profiles of key
individuals and groups related to this
issue.

WORLD SOCIALIST WEB SITE
E-mail: Editor@wsws.org
Web site: <www.wsws.org>

The World Socialist Web Site is the
Internet center of the International
Committee of the Fourth International
(ICFI). It provides analysis of major
world events, comments on political,
cultural, historical and philosophical
issues, and valuable documents and
studies from the heritage of the socialist movement.

WORLD VIEW MAGAZINE
1900 L. Street, NW, #205
Washington, DC 20036
Tel: (202) 293-7728x16
E-mail: pubs@rpcv.org
Web site: <www.worldviewmagazine.
com>

WORLD WATCH
P.O. Box 879
Oxon Hill , MD 20797
Tel: (888) 544-2303; (310) 567-9522
Fax: (301) 567-9522
E-mail: worlwatch@worldwatch.org
Web site: <www.worldwatch.org>

A b-monthly publication that informs
the general public about the damage
done by the world economy to its
environmental support system.

WORLDVIEWS
Journal of the WorldViews
Resource Center
1515 Webster Street, #305
Oakland, CA 94612
Tel: (510) 451-1742
Fax: (510) 835-3017
E-mail: worldviews@igc.org
Web site: <www.igc.org/worldviews>

A quarterly review of resources for
education and action.

YES! A JOURNAL
OF POSITIVE FUTURES
P.O. Box 10818
Bainbridge Island, WA 98110-0818
Tel: (206) 842-0216; (800) 937-4451
Fax: (206) 842-5208
E-mail: yes@futurenet.org
Web site: <www.futurenet.org>

A journal that helps shape and
support the evolution of sustainable
cultures and communities.
It highlights ways that people are
working for a just, sustainable,
and compassionate future.

YO! (YOUTH OUTLOOK)
660 Market Street, Rm. 210
San Francisco, CA 94104
Tel: (415) 438-4755
Fax: (415) 438-4935
E-mail: crew@youthoutlook.org
Web site:
A weekly newsletter of writing and art
by incarcerated youth.

Z MAGAZINE
18 Millfield Street
Woods Hole, MA 02543
Tel: (508) 548-9063
Fax: Call first
E-mail: lydia.sargent@lbbs.org or
sysop@zmag.org
Web site: <www.lbbs.org>

An independent political magazine of
critical thinking on political, cultural,
social, and economic life in the
United States.

THIS MODERN WORLD

by TOM TOMORROW

Resource Guide:
Media Activist Organizations

50 YEARS IS ENOUGH:
U.S. NETWORK FOR
GLOBAL ECONOMIC JUSTICE
3628 12th Street, NE
Washington, DC 20017
Tel: (202)463-2265
Fax: (202) 879-3186
E-mail: 50years@50years.org
Web site: <www.50years.org>

A network of 200 social and economic
justice organizations working to
bring about radical reform of the
World Bank and the International
Monetary Fund. 50 Years is working
with domestic groups to strengthen
public understanding of the domestic
impacts of global economic policy,
and to mobilize Americans around
these issues.

A-INFOS NEWS SERVICE
E-mail: a-infos-org@ainfos.ca
Web site: <www.ainfos.ca>

The A-Infos Project is coordinated by
an international collective of revolutionary anti-authoritarian, anti-capitalist activists, involved with class
struggle and who regard it as a total
social struggle.

THE ABORIGINAL
MULTI-MEDIA SOCIETY
(AMMSA)
15001-112 Avenue
Edmonton, AB Canada
Tel: (780) 455-2700
Fax: (780) 455-7639
E-mail: market@ammsa.com
Web site: <www.ammsa.com/ammsa.
html>

Provides a forum through print and electronic media for the exchange of information about issues in Native communities and cultural issues and events.

ADVOCATES FOR YOUTH
1025 Vermont Ave., NW, Suite 200
Washington, DC 20005
Tel: (202) 347-5700
Fax: (202) 347-2263
E-mail: info@advocatesforyouth.org
Web site: <www.advocatesforyouth.org>

Seeks to support and educate teens and adolescents regarding sexuality, reproduction, and sexually transmitted diseases.

ALLAFRICA GLOBAL MEDIA
920 M Street, SE
Washington, DC 27702
Tel: (202) 546-0777
Fax: (202) 546-0676.
E-mail: info@allafrica.com
Web site:

Disseminates stories from African news organizations.

ALLIANCE FOR COMMUNITY MEDIA
666 11th Street, NW, Suite 740
Washington, DC 20001-4542
Tel: (202) 393-2650 , ext. 1
E-mail: acm@alliencecm.org
Web site:

The Alliance for Community Media is committed to assuring everyone's access to electronic media through public education, a progressive legislative and regulatory agenda, coalition building, and grassroots organizing.

ALLIANCE FOR CULTURAL DEMOCRACY
P.O. Box 192244
San Francisco, CA 94119-2244
Tel: (415) 821-9652; (415) 437-2721
Fax: (718) 488-8296
E-mail: ACD@f8.com/ACD/
Web site: <www.f8.com/ACD/>

Alliance for Cultural Democracy is a 25-year-old international organization and network of community and cultural activists working in a wide range of community arts, education, and cultural activism.

ALTERNATIVE PRESS CENTER
P.O. Box 33109
Baltimore, MD 21218
Tel: (410) 243-2471
Fax: (410) 235-5325
E-mail: altpress@altpress.org
Web site:

Alternative Press Center publish es the *Alternative Press Index* and *Annotations*. A guide to independent critical press (with the IPA). Also maintains a library.

AMERICAN FRIENDS SERVICE COMMITTEE (AFSC)
1501 Cherry Street
Philadelphia, PA 19102
Tel: (215) 241-7000
Fax: (215) 241-7275
E-mail: afscinfo@afsc.org
Web site: <www.afsc.org>

Founded in 1917, AFSC is a national Quaker organization that includes people of various faiths who are dedicated to humanitarian service, reconciliation, peace, and social justice issues.

AMERICAN LIBRARY
ASSOCIATION OFFICE FOR
INTELLECTUAL FREEDOM
50 East Huron Street
Chicago, IL 60611
Tel: (312) 280-4223; (800) 545-2433
Fax: (312) 280-4227
E-mail: oif@ala.org
Web site: <www.ala.org/oif.html>

Organized to educate librarians and
the general public about the nature
and importance of intellectual freedom
in libraries.

AMERICAN SOCIETY OF
JOURNALISTS AND AUTHORS
1501 Broadway, Suite 302
New York, NY 10036
voice mail: (212) 997-0947
Fax: (212) 768-7414
E-mail: 102535.2427@compuserve.
com
Web site: <www.asja.org>

A membership directory of our
members. It includes a list of 1,000
nonfiction freelance writers, their
telephone and fax numbers, office,
and specialty of writing.

AMERICAN SOCIETY OF
NEWSPAPER EDITORS
(ASNE)
11690 B Sunrise Valley Dr.
Reston, VA 20191-1409
Tel: (703) 456-1122
Fax: (703) 453-1133
E-mail: asne@asne.org
Web site: <www.asne.org>

Discusses topics related to the current
state and future of newspapers and
jounalism in this country.

AMNESTY INTERNATIONAL
322 8th Avenue
New York, NY 10001
Tel: (212) 807-8400
Fax: (212) 463-9193; (212) 627-1451
E-mail: admin-us@aiusa.org (to
become a member:
aimember@aiusa.org)
Web site: <www.amnesty.org>

An international organization that
works to ensure human rights
throughout the world and opposes
human rights abuses.

ASIAN-AMERICAN JOURNALISTS
ASSOCIATION (AAJA)
1182 Market Street, Suite 320
San Francisco, CA 94102
Tel: (415) 346-2051
Fax: (415) 346-6343
E-mail: national@aaja.org
Web site: <www.aaja.org>

Committed to insuring diversity in
American journalism and expressing
the Asian-American perspective.

ASSOCIATION FOR EDUCATION
IN JOURNALISM AND MASS
COMMUNICATION (AEJMC)
The University of South Carolina
234 Outlet Pointe Boulevard
Columbia, SC 29210-5667
Tel: (803) 798-0271
Fax: (803) 772-3509
E-mail: aejmc@aejmc.org
Web site: <www.aejmc.org>

AEJMC is the oldest and largest
association of journalism and mass
communication educators and
administrators at the college level,
promoting the highest possible
standards for education in journalism

and mass communication, to encourage the widest range of communication research, to encourage the implementation of a multicultural society in the classroom and curriculum, and to defend and maintain freedom of expression in day-to-day living.

ASSOCIATION OF ALTERNATIVE NEWSWEEKLIES
1020 16th Street, NW, 4th Floor
Washington , DC 20036-5702
Tel: (202) 822-1955
Fax: (202) 822-0929
E-mail: ann@aan.org
Web site: <aan.org>

A coordinating and administrative organization for 113 alternative newsweeklies in the U.S. and Canada.

ASSOCIATION OF AMERICAN PUBLISHERS (AAP)
71 5th Avenue
New York, NY 10003-3004
Tel: (212) 255-0200
Fax: (212) 255-7007
E-mail: amyg@publishers.org
Web site:

The Association of American Publishers (AAP), with some 310 members located throughout the United States, is the principal trade association of the book publishing industry.

BEYOND MEDIA, INC.
6960 North Sheridan Road, Store B
Chicago, IL 60626
Tel: (773) 973-2280
Fax: (773) 973-3367
E-mail: beyond@beyondmedia.org
Web site: <www.beyondmedia.org>

A non-profit organization dedicated to creating alternative media for positive social change. Through production of videos and other media arts and outreach campaigns, and by centering the programs and stories of specific women and girls within the framework of transcultural issues, we construct bridges across which members of widely diverse communities can work together and educate one another.

BLACK PRESS INSTITUTE
2711 East 75th Place
Chicago, IL 60649
Tel: (312) 375-8200
Fax: (312) 375-8262
E-mail: info@blackpressusa.com
Web site:
<www.blackpressusa.com/aboutus/aboutus.asp>

The Institute is a partnership between the National Newspaper Publishers Association Foundation (NNPAF) and Howard University. The Institute provides an academic link for the Black Press that coordinates national internship, fellowship, and scholarship programs and creates innovative programs designed to help close the digital media divide.

CALIFORNIA FIRST AMENDMENT COALITION
2701 Cottage Way, Suite 12
Sacramento, CA 95825-1226
Tel: (916) 974-8888
Fax: (916) 974-8880
E-mail: cfac@cfac.org
Web site: <cfac.org>

CAMPUS ALTERNATIVE

JOURNALISM PROJECT (CAJP)
Center for Campus Organizing
P.O. Box 425748
Cambridge, MA 02142
Tel: (415) 643-4401
Fax: (617) 547-5067
E-mail: cajp@indypress.org
Web site: <www.indypress.org/
programs/cajp.html>

CAJP supports the work of campus
progressive activists who make their
own printed media. We provide
resource guides, trainings, and
consultation, and organize a 100+
network of publications.

CENTER FOR DEFENSE
INFORMATION (CDI)
1779 Massachusetts Avenue, NW
Washington, DC 20036
Tel: (202) 332-0600
Fax: (202) 462-4559
E-mail: info@cdi.org
Web site: <www.cdi.org>

CDI opposes excessive military
expenditures that increase the dangers
of war. CDI believes that social,
economic, political, and environmental factors contribute as much
to a nation's security as does a strong
military defense.

THE CENTER FOR DEMOCRACY
AND TECHNOLOGY (CDT)
1634 Eye Street, NW Suite 1100
Washington, DC 20006
Tel: (202) 637-9800
Fax: (202) 637-0968
E-mail: feedback@cdt.org
Web site: <www.cdt.org>

The Center for Democracy and
Technology works to promote freedom

of speech, democratic values,
and constitutional liberties in the
digital age. With expertise in law,
technology, and policy, CDT seeks
practical solutions to enhance free
expression and privacy in global
communications technologies.

THE CENTER FOR DEMOCRATIC
COMMUNICATIONS OF THE
NATIONAL LAWYERS GUILD
240 Stockton Street, 3rd Floor
San Francisco, CA 94108
Tel: (415) 522-9814
Fax: (415) 381-9963
E-mail: cdc@nlg.org
Web site: <www.nlgcdc.org>

Focuses on the right of all peoples to
have access to a worldwide system of
media and communications with the
principle of cultural and informational
self-determination. This committee
is an important force in microradio
advocacy and activism.

CENTER FOR
DEMOCRATIC VALUES
5700 Cass Avenue, Room 2426
Detroit, MI 48202
Tel: (313) 577-0828
Fax: (313) 577-8585
E-mail: Raronso@cll.wayne.edu
Web site: <www.igc.apc.org/cdv>

CENTER FOR INTERNATIONAL
POLICY (CIP)
1755 Massachusetts Avenue, NW
Suite 550
Washington, DC 20036
Tel: (202) 232-3317
Fax: (202) 232-3440
E-mail: cip@ciponline.org
Web site: <www.us.net/cip>

CIP promotes a U.S. foreign policy that reflects democratic values. Programs include the Demilitarization Program to reduce the size and role of the military in Central America and the Intelligence Reform Program to reexamine and reform the U.S. intelligence community.

CENTER FOR INVESTIGATIVE REPORTING
500 Howard Street, Suite 206
San Francisco, CA 94105-3000
Tel: (415) 543-1200
Fax: (415) 543-8311
E-mail: CIR@igc.org
Web site: <www.muckraker.org/pubs/papertrails/index.html>

CENTER FOR MEDIA
AND DEMOCRACY
Publication: *PR Watch*
520 University Avenue, Suite 310
Madison, WI 53703
Tel: (608) 260-9713
Fax: (608) 260-9714
E-mail: editor@prwatch.org
Web site: <www.prwatch.org>

The Center specializes in "blowing the lid off today's multi-billion dollar propoganda-for-hire industry." Editors John Stauber and Sheldon Rampton wrote *Toxic Sludge is Good for You: Lies, Damn Lies, and the Public Relations Industry.*

CENTER FOR MEDIA EDUCATION
Former publication: *InfoActive Kids*
2120 L Street, NW, Suite 200
Washington, DC 20037
Tel: (202) 331-7833
Fax: (202) 331-7841
E-mail: cme@cme.org

Web site: <www.cme.org>

Focuses on child advocacy, consumer, health, and educational communities and is a resource for journalists covering children and media topics.

CENTER FOR MEDIA LITERACY
4727 Wilshire Boulevard
Suite #403
Los Angeles, CA 90010
Tel: (213) 931-4177; (800) 226-9494
Fax: (213) 931-4474
E-mail: cml@medialit.org
Web site: <www.medialit.org>

CENTER FOR THIRD WORLD
ORGANIZING (CTWO)
1218 East 21st Street
Oakland , CA 94606
Tel: (510) 533-7583
Fax: (510) 533-0923
E-mail: ctwo@ctwo.org
Web site: <www.ctwo.org>

CTWO is a national racial justice movement hub that works with individuals and organizations to craft political analysis, organizing skills, and visions of a just society.

CENTER FOR WAR, PEACE
AND THE NEWS MEDIA
New York University
418 Lafayette Street, Suite 554
New York, NY 10003
Tel: (212) 998-7960
Fax: (212) 995-4143
E-mail: war.peace.news@nyu.edu
Web site: <www.nyu.edu/globalbeat>

CENTER FOR RESEARCH
ON GLOBALIZATION
Tel: (888) 713-8500
Web site: <www.globalresearch.ca>

CHICAGO MEDIA WATCH
P.O. Box 268737
Chicago, IL 60626
Tel: (773) 604-1910
E-mail: cmw@mediawatch.org
Web site: <www.mediawatch.org/
~cmw>

CITIZENS FOR INDEPENDENT
PUBLIC BROADCASTING
901 Old Hickory Road
Pittsburg, PA 15243
Tel: (412) 341-1967
Fax: (412) 341-6533
E-mail: jmstarr@cais.com
Web site: <www.cipbonline.org>

Coordinates a national education
campaign to reform public
broadcasting as a public trust,
independent of government and
corporate control, and to organize
community groups to democratize
their local public broadcasting
stations.

CITIZENS FOR MEDIA LITERACY
34 Wall Street, Suite 407
Asheville, NC 28801
Tel: (828) 255-0182
Fax: (828) 254-2286
E-mail: cml@main.nc.us
Web site: <www.main.nc.us/cml>

THE CIVIC MEDIA CENTER
& LIBRARY, INC.
1021 West University Avenue
Gainsville, FL 32601
Tel: (352) 373-0010
E-mail: coordinator@civicmediacenter.
org
Web site: <www.civicmediacenter. org>

A non-profit library and reading room

of alternative press publications.
Contains books, periodicals, reference
materials (including the *Alternative
Press Index*), E-zine library, and an
audio and video collection.

CO-OP AMERICA
Publications: *National Green Pages
& Coop America Quarterly*
1612 K Street, NW, Suite 600
Washington, DC 20006
Tel: (800) 58-GREEN;
(202) 872-5307
Fax: (202) 331-8166
E-mail: info@coopamerica.org
Web site: <www.coopamerica.org>

A national non-profit organization
founded in 1982—the leading force in
educating and empowering people and
businesses to make significant
improvements through the economic
system.

COMMITTEE TO PROTECT
JOURNALISTS
330 7th Avenue, 12th Floor
New York, NY 10001
Tel: (212) 465-1004
Fax: (212) 465-9568
E-mail: Info@cpj.org
Web site: <www.cpj.org>

The Committee to Protect Journalists
is dedicated to safeguarding
journalists and freedom of expression
worldwide is a non-profit, nonpartisan
organization that monitors abuses of
the press and promotes press freedom
internationally.
COMMON CAUSE
1250 Connecticut Ave, NW
#600
Washington, DC 20036
Tel: (202) 833-1200

Fax: (202) 659-3716
E-mail: grassroots@commoncouse.org
Web site: <www.commoncause.org>

Supports open, accountable
government and the right of all
American citizens to be involved in
helping to shape the nation's public
policies. Common Cause presses for
the enactment of campaign finance
reform.

COMMUNICATIONS
CONSORTIUM AND
MEDIA CENTER
1333 H Street, NW, Suite. 700
Washington, DC 20005
Tel: (202) 682-1270
Fax: (202) 682-2154
Web site: <www.womenofcolor.org>

COMMUNITY MEDIA
WORKSHOP
Columbia College
600 South Michigan Avenue
Chicago, IL 60605-1996
Tel: (312) 344-6400
Fax: (312) 344-6404
E-mail: Cmw@newstips.org
Web site: <www.newstips.org>

Trains community organizations
and civic groups to use media more
effectively and helps journalists learn
of their stories. Publishers of *Getting
on the Air & Into Print*, a 200-page
citizen's guide to media in the
Chicago area.

CONSUMER PROJECT
ON TECHNOLOGY
P.O. Box 19367
Washington, DC 20036
Tel: (202) 387-8030
Fax: (202) 234-5176

E-mail: love@cptech.org
Web site: <www.cptech.org>

CPT is active in a number of issue
areas, including intellectual property,
telecomunications, privacy, and
electronic commerce, plus a variety
of projects relating to antitrust
enforcement and policy.

COUNCIL FOR A
LIVABLE WORLD
110 Maryland Avenue, NE
Washington , DC 20002
Tel: (202) 543-4100
Fax: (202) 543-6297
E-mail: clw@clw.org
Web site: <www.clw.org>

Founded in 1962, the Council
supports political candidates who
support deep military reductions
and elimination of nuclear weapons.
Its mission is to eliminate all weapons
of mass destruction.

COUNCIL OF CANADIANS
502-151 Slater Street
Ottawa, ON Canada
Tel: (613) 233-2773
Fax: (613) 233-6776
Web site: <www.canadians.org/>

The council has Maude Below,
the "Ralph Nader of Canada."

CULTURAL ENVIRONMENT
MOVEMENT (CEM)
Publishes *The Cultural Environment
Monitor*
3508 Market Street, Suite 30-030
Phildelphia, PA 19104

Tel: (888) 445-4526
Fax: (215) 204-5823
E-mail: cem@libertynet.org
Web site: <www.cemnet.org>

A broad-based international coalition of citizens, scholars, activists, and media professionals who promote democratic principles in the cultural environment.

ECONOMIC POLICY INSTITUTE
1660 L Street, NW, Suite 1200
Washington, DC 20036
Tel: (202) 775-8810
Fax: (202) 775-0819
E-mail: epi@epinet.org
Web site: <epinet.org>

Its mission is to broaden public debate over economic policy to better serve the needs of America's working people. It also seeks to expose the myths behind the supposed success of the neoliberal economic paradigm.

ELECTRONIC FRONTIER FOUNDATION
454 Shotwell Street
San Francisco, CA 94110
Tel: (415) 436-9333
Fax: (415) 436-9993
E-mail: Eff@eff.org
Web site: <www.eff.org>

A leading civil liberites organization devoted to maintaining the Internet as a global vehicle for free speech.

ENVIRONMENTAL NEWS NETWORK INC. (ENN)
2020 Milvia, Suite 411
Berkeley, CA 94704
Tel: (510) 644-3661
Fax: (208) 475-7986

E-mail: mgt@enn.com
Web site: <www.enn.com>

ENN produces news seven days a week with continuous updates throughout each day and has a multifaceted Web site aimed at educating about environmental issues.

ESSENTIAL INFORMATION
P.O. Box 19405
Washington, DC 20036
Tel: (202) 387-8030
Fax: (202) 234-5176
Web site: <www.essential.org>

Founded in 1982 by Ralph Nader, Essential Information is a non-profit, tax-exempt organization; we provide provocative information to the public on important topics neglected by the mass media and policymakers.

FAIRNESS AND ACCURACY IN REPORTING (FAIR)
112 West 27th Street
New York, NY 10001
Tel: (212) 633-6700
Fax: (212) 727-7668
E-mail: Fair@fair.org
Web site: <www.fair.org>

A national media watchdog group that focuses public awareness on "the narrow corporate ownership of the press…," FAIR seeks to invigorate the First Amendment by advocating for greater media pluralism and the inclusion of public interest voices in national debate.

FEDERATION OF AMERICAN SCIENTISTS, ARMS SALES MONITORING PROJECT

Publishes the *Arms Sales Monitor*
1717 K Street, NW, Suite 209
Washington, DC 20036
Tel: (202) 546-3300, ext. 193
Fax: (202) 675-1010
E-mail: tamarg@fas.org
Web site: <www.fas.org/asmp/>

Organized to promote accountability,
transparency, and reduction in
tranfers of U.S. conventional arms.
Has recently published "The Arms
Trade Revealed: A Guide for
Investigators and Activists" by
Laura Lumpe.

FEMINISTS FOR FREE
EXPRESSION
2525 Times Square Station
New York, NY 10108-2525
Tel: (212) 702-6292
Fax: (212) 702-6277
E-mail: Freedom@well.com
Web site: <www.ffeusa.org>

A national not-for-profit organization
of feminist women and men who share
a commitment both to gender equality
and to preserving the individual's
right to read, view, rent, or purchace
media materials of their choice, free
from government intervention.

FOOD & WATER INC.
Publishes *Wild Matters*
389 Route 215
Walden, VT 05873
Tel: (802) 563-3300
Fax: (802) 563-3310
E-mail: info@foodandwater.org
Web site: <www.foodandwater.org>

An organization that advocates for
safe food and water, and a clean
environment by educating the public

on the health and environmental
dangers of food irradiation, genetic
engineering, and toxic pesticides.

FREEDOM FORUM WORLD
CENTER
1101 Wilson Blvd
Arlington, VA 22209
Tel: (703) 528-0800
Fax: (703) 284-3770
E-mail: News@freedomforumu.org
Web site: <www.freedomforum.org>

A nonpartisan, international
foundation dedicated to free press,
free speech, and free spirit for all
people.

FREEDOM OF INFORMATION
CLEARINGHOUSE
P.O. Box 558
Topeka, KS 66601
Tel: (785) 272-7348
E-mail: freedom@freedomclearing
house.org
Web site:
FREEDOM TO READ FOUNDATION
Judith Krug,
Executive Director and Secretary
50 East Huron Street
Chicago, IL 60611
Tel: (800) 545-2433, ext.4226
Fax: (312) 280-4227
E-mail: Ftrf@ala.org
Web site: <www.ftrf.org>
Promotes and protects freedom
of spech and freedom of the press;
protects the public's right to access to
libraries, supplies, and legal counsel,
and otherwise supports libraries and
librarians suffering injustices due to
their defense of freedom of speech

and of the press (run by ALA, but a separate organization does First Amendment litigation).

FRIENDS OF THE EARTH
1025 Vermont Avenue, NW
Washington, DC 20005
Tel: (202) 783-7400; (877) 843-8687
Fax: (202) 783-0444
E-mail: foe@foe.org
Web site: <www.foe.org>

Dedicated to protecting the planet from environmental degradation; preserving biological, cultural, and ethnic diversity; and empowering citizens to have an influential voice in decisions affecting the quality of their environment.

FUND FOR INVESTIGATIVE JOURNALISM
P.O. Box 60184
Washington, DC 20039-0184
Tel: (202) 362-0260
Fax: (301) 422-7449
E-mail: fundfij@aol.com
Web site: <www.fij.org>

THE FUND FOR INVESTIGATIVE REPORTING (FIRE)
2 Wall Street, Suite 203
Asheville, NC 28801-2710
Tel: (828) 259-9179
Fax: (828) 251-1311
E-mail: fire@ncpress.net
Web site: <www.ncpress.net>
GLOBAL EXCHANGE
An Active Participant in the "50 Years Is Enough" Campaign
2017 Mission Street, Suite 303
San Francisco, CA 94110
Tel: (415) 255-7296
Fax: (415) 255-7498

E-mail: info@globalexchange.org
Web site: <www.globalexchange.org>

Global Exchange publishes books and pamphlets on various social and economic topics; promotes alternative trade for the benefit of low-income producers; helps build public awareness about human rights abuses; and sponsors Reality Tours to foreign lands, giving participants a feel for people of a country.

GLOBALVISION
1600 Broadway, Suite 700
New York, NY 10019
Tel: (212) 246-0202
Fax: (212) 246-2677
E-mail: roc@globalvision.org
Web site: <www.igc.org/globalvision/>

An independent film and television production company. Specializing in an "inside-out" style of journalism, it has produced *Rights & Wrongs: Human Rights Television* and *South Africa Now*, along with other highly acclaimed investigative documentaries.

GOVERNMENT ACCOUNTABILITY PROJECT
Mercatus Center,
George Mason University
3301 North Fairfax Drive
Arlington, VA 22201-4433
Tel: (800) 815-5711; (703) 993-4930
Fax: (703) 993-4935
E-mail: mercatus@gmu.edu
Web site:

An education, research, and outreach organization that works with scholars, policy experts, and government officials to bridge academic theory and real-world practice.

THE GRASSROOTS MEDIA NETWORK

1602 Chatham
Austin, TX 78723
Tel: (512) 459-1619
E-mail: rootmedia@mail.com
Web site: <www.geocities.com/root media/links.html> or
<www.crosswinds.net/~rootmedia/>

Grassroots News Network, Queer News Network, Pueblos-Unidos. Grassroots film and video collective.

GREENPEACE USA

702 H Street, NW
Washington, DC 20001
Tel: (800) 326-0959
Fax: (202) 462-4507
Web site: <www.greenpeaceusa.org>

Its purpose is to create a green and peaceful world. Greenpeace embraces the principle of nonviolence, rejecting attacks on people and property. It allies itself with no political party and takes no political stance.

HISPANIC EDUCATION AND MEDIA GROUP, INC.

Laurn Ann Gee-Devitt
We Penguins
102 Crown Circle
South San Francisco, CA 94080
Tel: (415) 331-8560
Fax: (415) 331-2636
E-mail: margotsegura@aol.com
Web site: <www.we-penguins.com/HEMG_page_1.htm>

Dedicated to improving the quality of life in the Latino community with main focus on high school dropout prevention and health issues.

HUCK BOYD NATIONAL CENTER FOR COMMUNITY MEDIA (HBNC)

105 Kedzie Hall
Kansas State University
Manhattan, KS 66506-1501
Tel: (785) 532-3958; (785) 532-0721
Fax: (785) 532-5484
E-mail: Huckboyd@ksu.edu
Web site:

The mission of HBNC is to strenghten local media in order to help create better, stronger communites in America.

HUMAN RIGHTS WATCH (HRW)

Washington DC Office
1630 Connecticut Avenue, NW
Suite 500
Washington, DC 20009
Tel: (202) 612-4321
Fax: (202) 612-4333
E-mail: hrwdc@hrw.org
Web site: <www.hrw.org>

HRW exposes and works to stop human rights abuses in over 70 countries. It struggles against summary executions, torture, restrictions on the freedoms of expression, and so on.

THE HUMANIST MOVEMENT

197 Harbord Street
Toronto, ON Canada
Tel: (416) 535-2094
E-mail: roberto@ilap.com
Web site: <www.cynaptica.com/hm>

Produces a widerange of media

outlets at the grassroots level through neighborhood newspapers, neighborhood radio, and neighborhood TV stations all over the world. These are completely non-profit, volunteer projects that focus on raising (and organizing around) issues ignored by the forces of big media.

INDEPENDENT PRESS ASSOCIATION
2729 Mission Street, #201
San Francisco, CA 94110-3131
Tel: (415) 643-4401
Fax: (415) 643-4402
E-mail: indypress@indypress.org
Web site: <www.indypress.org>

A membership-based association providing nuts-and-bolts technical assistance, loans, and networking to over 175 independent, progressive magazines and newspapers. Formed during the first Media & Democracy Congress in San Francisco (1996), the IPA promotes a diversity of voices of the newsstand.

INDEPENDENT PROGRESSIVE POLITICS NETWORK (IPPN)
P.O. Box 1041
Bloomfield, NJ 07003
Tel: (973) 338-5398
Fax: (973) 338-2210
E-mail: indpol@igc.org
Web site: <www.ippn.org>

IPPN brings together organizations and individuals committed to building a united party, or alliance of parties, as a progressive alternative to the Democrats or Republicans.

INFACT-CAMPAIGN FOR CORPORATE

ACCOUNTABILITY
46 Plympton Street
Boston, MA 02118
Tel: (617) 695-2525
Fax: (617) 695-2626
E-mail: info@infact.org
Web site: <www.infact.org>

INSTITIUTE FOR PUBLIC ACCURACY
65 Ninth Street
Suite 3
San Francisco, CA 94103
Tel: (415) 552-5378
Fax: (415) 552-6787
E-mail: Institute@igc.org
Web site: <www.accuracy.org>

Serves as a nationwide consortium of progressive policy researchers, scholars, and activists providing the media with timley information and perspectives on a wide range of issues.

INSTITUTE FOR ALTERNATIVE JOURNALISM
77 Federal Street
2nd Floor
San Francisco, CA 94107
Tel: (415) 284-1420
Fax: (415) 284-1414
E-mail: info@alternet.org
Web site:

INSTITUTE FOR FOOD AND DEVELOPMENT POLICY
Publication: *Food First News*
398 60th St.
Oakland, CA 94618
Tel: (510) 654-4400
Fax: (510) 654-4551
E-mail: foodfirst@foodfirst.org

Web site: <www.foodfirst.org>

Works to mobilize and organize people around the world to support the struggles of the hungry for the right to feed themselves and to promote awareness of economic, social, and cultural human rights.

INSTITUTE FOR MEDIA ANALYSIS
41 West 36th Street, 4th floor
New York, NY 10018
Tel: (212) 560-9240
Fax: (212) 560-9230
E-mail: infosa@mediatenor.com
Web site:

INSTITUTE FOR MEDIA POLICY
AND CIVIL SOCIETY
207 W. Hastings Street, Suite 910
Vancouver, BC Canada
Tel: (604) 682-1953; (877) 232-0122
Fax: (604) 682-4353
E-mail: media@impacs.org
Web site: <www.impacs.bc.ca>

The society's mission is to build strong communites by training and educating Canadian civil society organizations.

INSTITUTE OF GLOBAL
COMMUNICATIONS
Formerly *Institute For Policy Studies*
P.O. Box 29904
San Francisco, CA 94129
Tel: (202) 234-9382
Fax: (202) 387-7915
E-mail: support@igc.apc.org
Web site:
<www.igc.org/igc/gateway/index.html>

Since 1963, IGC (formerly IPS) has been the nation's leading center of progressive research link to activism.

INTERACTION
1717 Massachusetts Avenue, NW
Suite 701
Washington, DC 20036
Tel: (202) 667-8227
Fax: (202) 667-8236
E-mail: ia@interaction.org
Web site: <www.interaction.org>

A coalition of over 150 U.S.–based non-profits working to promote human dignity and development in 165 countries. It is active in programs to ease human suffering and to strengthen people's ability to help themselves.

INTERHEMISPHERIC
RESOURCE CENTER (IRC)
P.O. Box 4506
Albuquerque, NM 87196-4506
Tel: (505) 842-8288
Fax: (505) 246-1601
E-mail: resourcectr@igc.apc.org
Web site:

IRC believes that U.S. foreign policy and international economic relations should be reshaped to support a global economy that fosters broad development for all nations, political systems that are more participatory, and environmentally sustainable economic growth.

INTERNATIONAL
ACTION CENTER (IAC)
39 West 14th Street, # 206
New York, NY 10011
Tel: (212)633-6646
Fax: (212) 633-2889
E-mail: iacenter@action-mail.org
Web site: <www.iacenter.org>

Initiated in 1992 by former Attorney General Ramsey Clark and other anti-war activists, IAC coordinates international meetings, teach-ins, massive demonstrations, publishes news releases, and produces video documentaries.

INTERNATIONAL CONSORTIUM OF INVESTIGATIVE JOURNALISTS (ICIJ)
Center for Public Integrity
910 17th Street, NW, 7th Floor
Washington, DC 20006
Tel: (202) 466-1300
Fax: (202) 466-1101
E-mail: info@icij.org
Web site: <www.icij.org>

ICIJ is a working consortium of leading investigative reporters from around the world that sponsors investigations into pressing issues that transcend national borders.

INTERNATIONAL FORUM ON GLOBALIZATION
The Thoreau Center for Sustainability
1009 General Kennedy Avenue, #2
San Francisco, CA 94129
Tel: (415) 561-7650
Fax: (415) 561-7651
E-mail: ifg@ifg.org
Web site:

An alliance of 60 leading activists, scholars, economists, researchers, and writers that provide analysis, joint activity, and public education in response to economic globalization.

INTERNATIONAL MEDIA PROJECT
National Radio Project
1714 Franklin, #311

Oakland, CA 94612
Tel: (510) 251-1332
Fax: (510) 251-1342
E-mail: laura@radioproject.org
Web site: <www.radioproject.org>

Produces a half-hour, weekly, public affairs radio program called *Making Contact*, which is heard on 150 stations nationally, in Canada and South Africa. Shows also heard on the Internet as Radio for Peace International. Their mission is to air the voices of those not often heard in mass media.

INVESTIGATIVE JOURNALISM PROJECT
Fund for Constitutional Government
122 Maryland Avenue, NE, Suite 300
Washington, DC 20002
Tel: (202) 546-3732
Fax: (202) 543-3156
Web site: <www.epic.org/fcg/pro-jects.html>

IRE (INVESTIGATIVE REPORTERS AND EDITORS, INC.)
Missouri School of Journalism
138 Neff Annex
Columbia, MO 65211
Tel: (573) 882-2042
Fax: (573) 882-5431
E-mail: info@ire.org
Web site: <www.ire.org>
Investigative Reporters and Editors, Inc. is a grassroots non-profit organization dedicated to improving the quality of investigative reporting within the field of journalism.

JUST THINK FOUNDATION
29 Mesa Street, Suite 106
Presidio Park

San Francisco, CA 94129
Tel: (415) 561-2900
Fax: (415) 561-2901
E-mail: think@justthink.org
Web site: <www.justthink.org>

KLANWATCH AND MILITIA
TASKFORCE
Southern Poverty Law Center
400 Washington Avenue
Montgomery, AL 36104
Tel: (334) 264-0286
Fax: (334) 264-8891
Web site: www.splcenter.org/splc.html

LIVELYHOOD
1611 Telegraph Avenue
Suite 1550
Oakland, CA 94612
Tel: (510) 268-9675
Fax: (510) 268-3606
E-mail: info@theworkinggroup.org
Web site: <www.pbs.org/livelyhood
or www.pbs.org/noit>

A non-profit media production
company focussed on ordinary,
hard-working Americans. The group
has produced the *We Do The Work*
series and the *Not In Our Town*
specials, which gained national
recognition for showcasing positive
community response and intolerance
of hate violence.

LOOMPANICS UNLIMITED (LU)
P.O. Box 1197
Port Townsend, WA 98368
Tel: (360) 385-2230
Fax: (360) 385-7785
E-mail: operations@loompanics.com
Web site: <www.loompanics.com>

Champions of the First Amenment,
LU publishes and sells publications

covering a variety of controversial
topics. Has an online catalogue.

MACROMEDIA
Corporate Headquarters
600 Townsend Street
San Francisco, CA 94103
Tel: (415) 252-2000
Fax: (415) 626-0554
Web site: <www.mosaictv.com>

Provides the global truth perspective
for black people, featuring video
lectures, research, and coverage of
news that is ignored or purposefully
hidden by mainstream media.

MEDIA ACCESS PROJECT
1625 K Street, NW
Suite 1118
Washington, DC 20006
Tel: (202) 232-4300
Fax: (202) 466-7656
E-mail: info@mediaaccess.org
Web site:

MEDIA ALLIANCE
Publication: *Mediafile*
814 Mission Street, Suite 205
San Francisco, CA 94103
Tel: (415) 546-6334
Fax: (415) 546-6218
E-mail: info@media-alliance.org
Web site: <www.media-alliance.org>

Review and analysis of San Francisco
Bay Area media isues.

MEDIA COALITION/AMERICANS
FOR CONSTITUTIONAL FREEDOM
139 Fulton Street, Suite 302
New York, NY 10038
Tel: (212) 587-4025
Fax: (212) 587-2436
E-mail: mediacoalition@media

coalition.org
Web site: <www.mediacoalition.org>

An organization that defends the American public's First Amendment right to have access to the broadest possible range of opinion and entertainment.

THE MEDIA EDUCATION
FOUNDATION (MEF)
26 Center Street
Northampton, MA 01060
Tel: (800) 897-0089; (413) 584-8500
Fax: (800) 659-6882; (413) 586-8398
E-mail: info@mediaed.org
Web site: <www.mediaed.org>

MEF provides media research and production fostering analytical media literacy. It has produced and distributed a number of educational videos including *The Myth of the Liberal Media* (with Noam Chomsky and Ed Herman), *Killing Us Softly III* (with Jean Kilbourne), and *Tough Guise: Violence, Media & the Crisis of Masculinity* (with Jackson Katz).

MEDIA ISLAND
INTERNATIONAL (MII)
P.O. Box 7204
Olympia, WA 98507
Tel: (360) 352-8526
Fax: (360) 352-8490
E-mail: mii@olywa.net
Web site: <www.mediaisland.org>

MII works to popularize social, political justice, and environmental frontline issues by helping coordinate issue-focused organizations with media organizations and mapping allies for change internationally.

MEDIA NETWORK
Alternative Media Information Center
2565 Broadway, #101
New York, NY 10025
Tel: (212) 501-3841

MEDIAVISION
P.O. Box 1045
Boston, MA 02130
Tel: (617) 522-2923
Fax: (617) 522-1872
E-mail: mediavi@aol.com

Working for wider exposure of progressive views through mass media, MediaVision provides strategic media consulting, training, and other services for organizations and individuals.

MEIKLEJOHN CIVIL
LIBERTIES INSTITUTE
P.O. Box 673
Berkeley, CA 94701-0763
Tel: (510) 848-0599
Fax: (510) 848-6008
E-mail: mcli@igc.org
Web site: <www.sfsu.edu/~mclicfc/>

MINUTEMAN MEDIA
32 Allen Road
Norwalk, CT 06851
Tel: (203) 846-1109
Fax: (203) 846-1109
E-mail: speed1212@aol.com
Web site: <www.tidescenter.org/project_detail.cfm?id=170.0>

Minuteman Media's goal is to present regular, free, high-quality competing newspaper columns to small newspapers throughout the country in an effort to counteract the onslaught of right-wing editorials and op-ed pieces.

NATIONAL ASIAN AMERICAN
TELECOMMUNICATIONS
ASSOCIATION
346 Ninth Street, 2nd floor
San Francisco, CA 94103
Tel: (415) 863-0814
Fax: (415) 863-7428
E-mail: naata@naatanet.org
Web site: <www.naatanet.org>

An organization seeking to increase
Asian and Pacific Islanders'
participation in the media and
the promotion of fair and accurate
coverage of these communities.

NATIONAL ASSOCIATION
OF BLACK JOURNALISTS
University of Maryland
8701A Adelphi Road
Adelphi, MD 20783-1716
Tel: (301) 445-7100
Fax: (301) 445-7101
E-mail: nabj@nabj.org
Web site: <www.nabj.org>

Its mission is to strengthen ties among
African-American journalists, promote
diversity in newsrooms, and expand
job opportunities and recruiting activities for established African-American
journalists and students.

NATIONAL ASSOCIATION
OF HISPANIC JOURNALISTS
1000 National Press Building
Washington, DC 20045-2001
Tel: (888) 346-NAHJ; (202) 662-7145
Fax: (202) 662-7144
E-mail: nahj@nahj.org
Web site: <www.nahj.org>

NAHJ is dedicated to the recognition
and professional advancement of
Hispanics in the news industry.

NATIONAL ASSOCIATION OF
MINORITY MEDIA EXECUTIVES
1921 Gallows Road, Suite 600
Vienna, VA 22182
Tel: (703) 893-2410; (888) 968-7658
Fax: (703) 893-2414
Web site: <www.namme.org/>

NATIONAL ASSOCIATION OF
RADIO TALK SHOW HOSTS
Trade Association for
Radio Talk Industry
2791 South Buffalo Drive
Las Vegas, NV 89117
Tel: (702) 248-4884
Fax: (702) 889-1474
E-mail: carolnashe@mindspring.com
or carol@talkshowhosts.com
Web site: <www.talkshowhosts.com>

Provides a resource guide to talk radio
worldwide.

NATIONAL CENTER ON
DISABILITY AND JOURNALISM
Contact: Suzanne Levine
944 Market Street, Suite 829
San Francisco, CA 94102
Tel: (415) 291-0868
Fax: (415) 291-0869
E-mail: ncdj@ncdj.org
Web site: <www.ncdj.org>

NCDJ is a new non-profit organization
whose mission is to improve the
fairness, accuracy, and diversity of
news reporting on disability. We
do this by developing tools to help
journalists and educators examine
the complexity of disability issues
from differing perspectives.

NATIONAL COALITION
AGAINST CENSORSHIP

275 7th Avenue
New York, NY 10001
Tel: (212) 807-6222
Fax: (212) 807-6245
E-mail: ncac@ncac.org
Web site: <www.ncac.org>

Founded in 1974, NCAC is an
alliance of over 50 national non-profit
organizations. It works to educate
members and the public at large about
the dangers of censorship and how to
oppose it.

NATIONAL COALITON TO
PROTECT POLITICAL FREEDOM
(NCPPF)
Interreligious Foundation for
Community Organization (IFCO)
3321-12th Street, NE
Washington, DC 20017
Tel: (202) 529-4225
Fax: (202) 526-4611
E-mail: ifco@igc.apc.org
Web site: <www.ifconews.org/ncppf.
html>

A national membership organization
dedicated to protecting the First
Amendment and due process rights
of all Americans. It defends the right
of people to give humanitarian and
political support to causes in the U.S.
and abroad. It connects individuals
under attack with lawyers working on
these issues and provides legal support and briefs to educate individuals
on strategic media communication.

NATIONAL CONFERENCE
OF EDITORIAL WRITERS
6223 Executive Blvd.
Rockville, MD 20852
Tel: (301) 984-3015
Fax: (301) 231-0026

E-mail: ncewhqs@erols.com
Web site: <www.ncew.org>

An organization dedicated to
stimulating the conscience and
quality of the editorial.

NATIONAL EDUCATIONAL
MEDIA NETWORK
4096 Piedmont Avenue
PMB 373
Oakland, CA 94611
E-mail: nemn@nemn.org
Web site: <www.nemn.org>

NATIONAL FORUM ON
INFORMATION LITERACY
American Library Association
50 East Huron Street
Chicago, IL 60611
Web site:
<www.ala.org/contact_ala.html> or

NATIONAL LABOR COMMITTEE
275 7th Avenue, 15th Floor
New York, NY 10001
Tel: (212) 242-3002
Fax: (212) 242-3821
E-mail: nlc@nlcnet.org
Web site: <www.nlcnet.org>
Working to educate and actively
engage the U.S. public and media on
human and labor rights abuses by
corporations. Through this education
and activism, our goal is to end labor
and human rights violations, ensure
a living wage, and help workers and
their families live and work with
dignity.

NATIONAL LESBIAN AND GAY
JOURNALISTS ASSOCIATION
(NLGJA)

1420 K Street, NW, Suite 910
Washington, DC 20005
Tel: (202) 588-9888
Fax: (202) 588-1818
E-mail: info@nlgja.org
Web site: <www.nlgja.org>

NLGJA works from within the news
industry to foster fair and accuate
coverage of lesbian and gay issues
and opposes newroom bias against
lesbians, gay men, and all other
minorities.

NATIONAL RADIO PROJECT
Producer of *Making Contact*
1916 Telegraph Avenue
Oakland, CA 94612
Tel: (510) 251-1332
Fax: (510) 251-1342
Web site: <www.radioproject.org>

NATIONAL TELEMEDIA
COUNCIL (NTC)
Publication: *Telemedium*, The Journal
of Media Literacy
120 East Wilson Street
Madison, WI 53703
Tel: (608) 257-7712
Fax: (608) 257-7714
E-mail: ntc@danenet.wicip.org
Web site: <danenet.wicip.org/ntc>

NTC is a national non-profit
educational organization that promotes
media literacy education with a
positive, non-judgmental philosophy.
The oldest national media literacy
organization in the U.S., it is in its
49th year. (1953)

NATIONAL WRITERS UNION
(EAST) (NWU)
National office East
113 University Place, 6th floor

New York, NY 10003
Tel: (212) 254-0279
Fax: (212) 254-0673
E-mail: nwu@nwu.org
Web site: <www.nwu.org>

NWU publishes a national quarterly,
American Writer.

NET ACTION
601 Van Ness Avenue, #631
San Francisco, CA 94102
Tel: (415) 775-8674
Fax: (415) 673-3813
E-mail: audrie@netaction.org
Web site: <www.netaction.org>

Educates the public, policymakers,
and media about technology policy
issues; trains Internet users to use
technology for organizing, outreach,
and advocacy; promotes universal
accessibility and affordability of
information technology.

NEW MEXICO MEDIA
LITERACY PROJECT
6400 Wyoming Boulevard, NE
Albuquerque, NM 87109
Tel: (505) 828-3129
Fax: (505) 828-3320
E-mail: mccannon@aa.edu or
scottd@aa.edu or Torres@aa.edu
Web site: <www.nmmlp.org>

An organization whose goal is to be
the most successful and the most
declicated media education
organization in the U.S.

NEW YORK FREE MEDIA
ALLIANCE
Rutgers University, NY
Tel: (212) 969-8636
E-mail: iannacone@rocketmail.com

Web site: <artcon.rutgers.edu/paper-tiger/nyfma>

A regional coalition working to increase democracy and public space in local and national media. We seek to encourage and nurture the development of mass and alternative media that give access to, are accountable to, and accurately reflect all of the people in our communities.

NEWSWATCH
Marnard Institute for
Journalism Education
409 13th Street, 9th Floor
Oakland, CA 94612
Tel: (510) 839-2807
Fax: (415) 338-2084
E-mail: newsproj@mindspring.com
Web site: <newswatch.sfsu.edu>

Media watch organization and freedom of information advocacy group.

NEWSWATCH CANADA
School of Communication
Simon Fraser University
8888 University Drive
Burnaby, BC Canada
Tel: (604) 291-4905
Fax: (604) 291-3687
E-mail: newswtch@sfu.ca
Web site:

Canadian media watch organization and freedom of information advocacy group.

NICAR: NATIONAL INSTITUTE
FOR COMPUTER-ASSISTED
REPORTING
Missouri School of Journalism
138 Neff Annex
Columbia, MO 65211

Tel: (573) 882-2042 or -3364
Fax: (573) 882-5431; (573) 884-5549
E-mail: info@ire.org
Web site: <www.nicar.org>

A program of Investigative Reporters and Editors, Inc. and the Missouri School of Journalism. Founded in 1989, NICAR has trained thousands of journalists in the practical skills of finding, prying loose, and analyzing electronic information.

OCTOBER 22 COALITION
TO STOP POLICE BRUTALITY
P.O. Box 2627
New York, NY 10009
Tel: (888) NoBrutality; (212)477-8062
Fax: (212) 477-8015
E-mail: office@october22.org
Web site:
<www.office@october22.org>

Works to build toward a national Day of Protest, on October 22, to Stop Police Brutality, Repression, and the Criminalization of a generation. Those most targeted stand together with clergy, lawyers, artists, prominent people, and others to shout in a unified voice, NO MORE POLICE BRUTALITY. It participates, along with the Anthony Baez Foundation and the National Lawyers Guild, in The Stolen Lives Project, which collects and documents the names of victims killed by law enforcement agencies since 1990.

OFFLINE
Offline West
P.O. Box 45517
Seattle, WA 98145-0517
Tel: (206) 789-3597
E-mail: info@offlinemetworks.org

Web site:

A national arts organization that screens cable television and distributes independently produced films and videos. Serves as a creative conduit for numerous national and international screenings, arts organizations, micro-cinemas, festivals, netcast providers, and artists.

PACIFIC NEWS SERVICE
Publications: *The Beat Within*, *Yo!*, and *New California*
660 Market Street, Room 210
San Francisco, CA 94104
Tel: (415) 438-4755
Fax: (415) 438-4935
E-mail: pacificnews@pacificnews.org
Web site: <www.pacificnews.org>

Produces an article per day for reprint in a variety of newspapers worldwide.

PAPER TIGER TELEVISION
339 Lafayette St.
New York, NY 10012
Tel: (212) 420-9045
Fax: (212) 420-8223
E-mail: info@papertiger.org
Web site: <www.papertiger.org>

A non-profit volunteer collective that has been pioneering media criticism through video since 1981, conducting workshops, creating installations and producing videotapes. Its programs address issues of democratic communication, media representation, and the economics of the information industry. Smashes the myths of the information industry.

PARADIGM NEW MEDIA GROUP
1307 Washington Avenue
Suite 400
St. Louis, MO 63103
Tel: (314) 436-4003
Fax: (314) 436-0224
E-mail: info@pnmg.com
Web site:

A private network promoting individual, community and/or planetary evolution via print, Internet, radio, TV, music, theater, and so on.

THE PAUL ROBESON FUND
FOR INDEPENDENT MEDIA
Publication: *Funding Exchange*
666 Broadway, Suite 500
New York, NY 10012
Tel: (212) 529-5300, ext. 307
Fax: (212) 982-9272
E-mail: trinh.duong@fex.org
Web site: <www.namac.org/Directory/org_data/prfd.html>

The Paul Robeson Fund supports media activism and grassroots organizing by local, state, national or international organizations and individual media producers by funding radio, film, and video productions.

PEACE ACTION
1819 H Street, NW
Suite 420 and 425
Washington, DC 20006
Tel: (202) 862-9740
Fax: (202) 862-9762
E-mail: slynch@peace-action.org
Web site: <www.webcom.com/peace act/>

The largest membership and activist network of any peace and justice organization in the country. Peace Action members work for policy changes in Congress, state capitals, city halls, and the United Nations.

PEW OCEANS COMMISSION
2101 Wilson Boulevard, Suite 550
Arlington, VA 22201
Tel: (703) 516-0624
Fax: (703) 516-9551
Web site: <www.pewoceans.org>

The Pew Oceans Commission is an independent group of American leaders conducting a national dialogue on the policies needed to restore and protect living marine resources in U.S. waters.

POLITICAL RESEARCH
ASSOCIATES
(PRA)
1310 Broadway, Suite 201
Somerville, MA 02144-1731
Tel: (617) 666-5300
Fax: (617) 666-6622
E-mail: pra@igc.org
Web site: <www.publiceye.org/>

An organization focusing on research and analysis of right-wing political groups and their influence over media and policy making.

PROGRESSIVE MEDIA PROJECT
409 East Main Street
Madison, WI 53703
Tel: (608) 257-4626
Fax: (608) 257-3373
E-mail: pmproj@progressive.org
Web site: <www.progressive.org>

It provides opinion pieces from a progressive perspective to daily and weekly newspapers all over the country.

PROJECT CENSORED
Sociology Department

Sonoma State University
1801 East Cotati Avenue
Rohnert Park, CA 94928-3609
Tel: (707) 664-2500
Fax: (707) 664-2108
E-mail: censored@sonoma.edu
Web site: <www.projectcensored.org>

A faculty/student media research project dedicated to building free democratic news systems. It produces an annual yearbook that discusses the year's top 25 most under-reported stories.

PROJECT ON GOVERNMENT
OVERSIGHT (POGO)
666 11th Street NW, Suite 500
Washington, DC 20001
Tel: (202) 347-1122
Fax: (202) 347-1116
E-mail: pogo@pogo.org or
defense@pogo.org
Web site: <www.pogo.org>

The goal of POGO is to investigate, expose, and remedy abuses of power, mismanagement, and subservience to special interests by the federal government.

PUBLIC CAMPAIGN
1320 19th Street, NW
Suite M-1
Washington, DC 20036
Tel: (202) 293-0222
Fax: (202) 293-0202
E-mail: info@publicampaign.org
Web site: <www.publicampaign.org>

A non-profit, nonpartisan organization dedicated to sweeping reform that aims to dramatically reduce the role of special interest money in America's elections and the influence of big contributors in American politics.

PUBLIC CITIZEN
Global Trade Watch
1600 20th Street, NW
Washington, DC 20009
Tel: (202) 588-1000
Web site: <www.citizen.org>

PUBLIC MEDIA CENTER
466 Green Street
San Francisco, CA 94133
Tel: (415) 434-1403
Fax: (415) 986-6779
E-mail: info@publicmediacenter.org
Web site: <www.publicmediac
enter.org>

A non-profit, public interest
advertising agency focused on social,
political and environmental issues.

REDEFINING PROGRESS
1904 Franklin Street
6th Floor
Oakland, CA 94612
Tel: (510) 444-3041
Fax: (510) 444-3191
E-mail: info@rprogress.org
Web site: <www.rprogress.org/>

Redifining Progress is a non-profit
public policy and research
organization that develops policies
and tools to reorient the economy so
it will value people and nature first.

REPORTER'S COMMITTEE
FOR FREEDOM OF THE PRESS
Publications: *News Media Update*
and *News Media and The Law*
1815 North Fort Myer Drive, Suite 900
Arlington, VA 22209
Tel: (800) 336-4243; (703) 807-2100
Fax: (703) 807-2109
E-mail: rcfp@rcfp.org

Web site: <www.rcfp.org>

Serves as a major national and international resource in free speech
issues, disseminating information in a
variety of forms, including a quarterly
legal review, a biweekly newsletter,
a 24-hour hotline, and various
handbooks on media law issues.

SOCIETY OF ENVIRONMENTAL
JOURNALISTS
Publication: *SEJournal*
P.O. Box 2492
Jenkintown, PA 19046
Tel: (215) 884-8174
Fax: (215) 884-8175
E-mail: sej@sej.org
Web site: <www.sej.org>

Dedicated to supporting
environmental journalists and
furthering environmental journalism.

SOCIETY OF PROFESSIONAL
JOURNALISTS (SPJ)
Improving & Protecting Journalism
3909 North Meridian Street
Indianapolis, IN 46208
Tel: (317) 927-8000
Fax: (317) 920-4789
E-mail: questions@spj.org
Web site: <www.spj.org>

SPJ is the nation's largest and most
broad-based journalism organization.
It is a not-for-profit organization made
up of 13,500 members dedicated to
encouraging the free practice of
journalism, stimulating high standards
of ethical behavior, and perpetuating
a free press.

THE TELEVISION PROJECT
2311 Kimball Place

Silver Springs, MD 20910
Tel: (301) 588-4001
Fax: (301) 588-4001
E-mail: info@tvp.org
Web site: <www.tvp.org>

An organization to help parents understand how television affects their families and community, and to propose alternatives that foster positive emotional, cognitive, and spiritual development within families and communities.

THIRD WORLD NETWORK
Publication: *Third World Resurgence*
228 Macalister Road, 10400
Penang Malaysia
Tel: 604-2266 728 or 159
Fax: 604-2264 505
E-mail: twn.features@conf.igc.apc
or twin.info@conf.igc.apc
Web site: <www.twnside.org.sg/>

An international network of groups and individuals involved in efforts to bring about a greater articulation of the needs and rights of people in the Third World; a fair distribution of world resources; and forms of development that are ecologically sustainable and fulfill human needs.

THIRD WORLD NEWSREEL
545 Eighth Avenue, 10th floor
New York, NY 10018
Tel: (212) 947-9277
Fax: (212) 594-6417
E-mail: twn@twn.org
Web site: <www.twn.org>

THE THOMAS JEFFERSON
CENTER FOR THE PROTECTION
OF FREE EXPRESSION
400 Peter Jefferson Place

Charlottesville, VA 22911-8691
Tel: (434) 295-4789
Fax: (434) 296-3621
E-mail: freespch@tjcenter.org
Web site: <www.tjcenter.org>

An organization devoted to the defense of free expression in all its forms.

UNITY
Strategics alliance with: <aaja.org>, <nabj.org>, <nahj.org>, and <naja.org>.
1601 North Kent Street, Suite 1003
Arlington, VA 22209
Tel: (703) 469-2100
Fax: (703) 469-2108
E-mail: info@unityjournalists.org
Web site: <www.unityjournalists.org>

UPPNET: UNION PRODUCERS
AND PROGRAMMERS NETWORK
c/o Labor Education Service Union
Producers and Programmers Network
437 Management
and Economics Building
271 19th Avenue South
University of Minnesota
Minneapolis, MN 55455
Tel: (612) 624-4326
E-mail: uppnet@labornet.org
Web site: <www.mtn.org/jsee/uppnet.
html>

Organized to promote production and use of TV and radio shows pertinent to the cause of organized labor and working people. Publishes *UPPNET News*.

VIDEAZIMUT
3680 Rue Jeanne-Mance
Bureau 430
Montreal, QC Canada
Tel: (514) 982-6660
Fax: (514) 982-6122
E-mail: videaz@web.net

Web site: <commposite.uqam.ca/
videaz/videazmut.html>

An international nongovernmental
coalition promoting audiovisual
communication for development and
democracy.

WE INTERRUPT
THIS MESSAGE
160 14th Street
San Francisco, CA 94103
Tel: (415) 621-3302
Fax: (415) 621-3319
E-mail: interrupt@igc.org
Web site: <www.interrupt.org/
witm.html>

Builds capacity in public-interest
groups to do traditional media and
publicity work, as well as to reframe
public debate and interrupt media
stereotypes.

WHISPERED MEDIA
P.O. Box 40130
San Francisco, CA 94140
Tel: (415) 789-8484
E-mail: info@videoactivism.org
Web site: <www.videoactivism.org>

Provides video witnessing, video
post-production, and media resources
for grassroots activist groups.
Facilitates Bay Area Video Activist
Network (VAN). Specializes in
direct-action campaigns.

WOMEN'S INSTITUTE
FOR FREEDOM OF THE PRESS
(WPFC)
1940 Calvert Street
Washington, DC 20009-1502
Tel: (202) 265-6707
Fax: (202) 986-6355

E-mail: allen@wifp.org
Web site: <www.wifp.org>

Explores ways to assure that everyone
has equal access to the public,
speaking for themselves, so everyone's
information can be taken into account
when making decisions.

WORLD PRESS FREEDOM
COMMITTEE
The Newspaper Center
11690-C Sunrise Valley Drive
Reston, VA 20191
Tel: (703) 715-9811
Fax: (703) 620-6790
E-mail: freepress@wpfc.org
Web site: <www.wpfc.org>

A coordination group of national
and international news media
organizations, WPFC is an umbrella
organization that includes 44
journalistic organizations united
in the defense and promotion of
freedom.

WORLDWATCH INSTITUTE
1776 Massachusetts Avenue, NW
Washington, DC 20036-1904
Tel: (202) 452-1999
Fax: (202) 296-7365
E-mail: worlwatch@worldwatch.org
Web site:

The Worldwatch Institute is
dedicated to fostering the evolution
of an environmentally sustainable
society. The Institute seeks to achieve
this goal through research and
investigative journalism. Includes
an online global environmental media
center.

YOUTH MEDIA COUNCIL
160 14th Street
San Francisco, CA 94103
Tel: (415) 621-3302
E-mail: mcyril@interrupt.org
Web site:
<www.interrupt.org/ymc.html>

Eight youth organizations in the
San Francisco Bay Area have
partnered with We Interrupt This
Message to launch a Youth Media
Council, an organizing youth
development, media strategy, and
media watchdog project.

About the Editor

Peter Phillips is a Professor/Department Chair of Sociology at Sonoma State University and Director of Project Censored. He teaches classes in Media Censorship, Power, Political Sociology, and Sociology of Media. He has published six editions of *Censored: The News that Didn't Make the News* from Seven Stories Press. Also from Seven Stories Press is Project Censored's *Progressive Guide to Alternative Media and Activism 2002*.

Phillips writes op-ed pieces in the alternative press and independent newspapers nationwide, and has also been published in *Z Magazine*, *Social Policy*, *Briarpatch*, and numerous independents. He frequently speaks on media censorship, and various sociopolitical issues on radio and TV talks shows including *Talk of the Nation*, *Public Interest*, *Talk America*, *World Radio Network*, *Democracy Now*, and the *Jim Hightower Show*. He is also the national and international news editor with the Santa Rosa, California, *North Bay Progressive* newspaper, a bi-weekly regional publication serving a five-county area north of San Francisco.

Phillips earned a B.A. in Social Science in 1970 from Santa Clara University and an M.A. in Social Science from California State University at Sacramento in 1974. He earned a second M.A. in Sociology in 1991 and a Ph.D. in Sociology in 1994. His doctoral dissertation was entitled *A Relative Advantage: Sociology of the San Francisco Bohemian Club*.

A fifth-generation Californian who grew up on a family-owned farm west of the Central Valley town of Lodi, Phillips lives today in rural Sonoma County with his wife Mary Lia-Phillips, and their three cats, Moon, Gray, and Gracie.

Index

welfare, 29, 39, 50, 56, 63-64, 73-75, 156, 175, 209, 306, 347
Welfare Mothers Voice, 347
Westinghouse, 174-176
White House, 82-84, 143, 158, 203, 240, 243-244, 252, 256, 258
Whitney, Margaret A., 304
Wiesel, Elie, 304
Wilkinson, Alec, 300
Witness for Peace, 44-45
women's health laws, 78-79, 348
Women's Institute for Freedom of the Press, 376
Working for Change, 118, 293
World Assembly of Muslim Youth, 47
World Association of Community Radio Broadcasters (AMARC), 210
World Bank, 62, 89-90, 164-166, 320, 351
World Economic Forum, 90
World Health Organization, 99, 181, 190
World Press Freedom Committee, 376

World Radio Network, 378
World Socialist Web site, 85, 141, 159, 174, 349
World Trade Center (WTC), 47-48, 67, 130, 141-142, 241, 245, 252, 274
World Trade Organization (WTO), 39-41, 89, 164, 166, 216
World War I, 24
World War II, 24, 188
Worldwatch Institute, 377
WTC, *see* World Trade Center.
WTO, *see* World Trade Organization.
Wyeth-Ayerst, 102-104
Yahoo, 58, 292
Yemen, 157
Youth Media Council, 377
Yucca Mountain, 146
Yugoslavia, 66, 247, 249, 285
Z Magazine, 349, 378
Z Net, 48
Zahn, Paula, 47
zinc, 94

How to Support Project Censored

NOMINATE A STORY

To nominate a *Censored* story, send us a copy of the article and include the name of the source publication, the date that the article appeared, and page number. For Internet published news stories of which we should be aware, please forward the URL to <Censored@sonoma.edu> or go to www. project censored.org. The final deadline period for nominating a most *Censored* story is March of each year.

CRITERIA FOR PROJECT CENSORED NEWS STORIES NOMINATIONS

1. A censored news story is one which contains information that the general United States population has a right and need to know, but to which it has had limited access.

2. The news story is timely, ongoing, and has implications for a significant number of residents in the United States.

3. The story has clearly defined concepts and is backed up with solid, verifiable documentation.

4. The news story has been publicly published, either electronically or in print, in a circulated newspaper, journal, magazine, newsletter, or similar publication from either a foreign or domestic source.

5. The news story has direct connections to and implications for people in the United States, which can include activities that U.S. citizens are engaged in abroad.

SUPPORT PROJECT CENSORED BY MAKING A FINANCIAL GIFT

Project Censored is a self-supported 501-C-3 non-profit organization. We depend on tax-deductible donations and foundation grants to continue our work. To support our efforts for freedom of information, send checks to the address below or call (707) 664-2500. Visa and Mastercard accepted. Donate on the Web at: <www.projectcensored.org/contacts/donor>.

Project Censored Nominations
Sonoma State University
1801 East Cotati Avenue
Rohnert Park, CA 94928